Northeastern South America

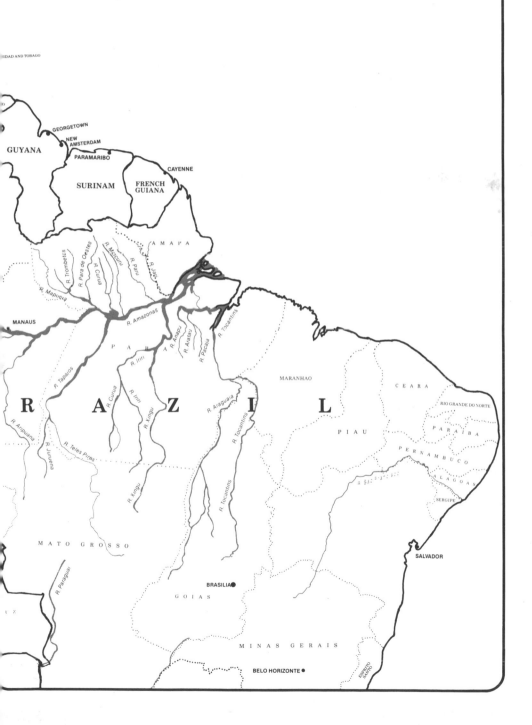

SOUTH AMERICAN
LAND BIRDS

SOUTH AMERICAN LAND BIRDS

A Photographic Aid to Identification

John S. Dunning

Research Associate
The Academy of Natural Sciences of
Philadelphia
Laboratory Associate
Cornell Laboratory of Ornithology

With the collaboration of

Robert S. Ridgely

Yale School of Forestry and
Environmental Studies

Sponsored by
The World Wildlife Fund

Harrowood Books ∎ Newtown Square ∎ Pennsylvania

Library of Congress Cataloging in Publication Data

Dunning, John S., 1906-
    South American Land Birds

    Sponsored by the World Wildlife Fund
    Bibliography: p.
    Includes index
    I. Birds — South America — Identification.
I. Ridgely, Robert S., 1946-   II. World
Wildlife Fund.   III. Title.
QL689.A1D86 1982   598.298   82-9351
ISBN 0-915180-21-9
ISBN 0-915180-22-7 (pbk.)

Harrowood Books
3943 N. Providence Rd.
Newtown Square, PA 19073

PRINTED IN THE UNITED STATES OF AMERICA

10 9 8 7 6 5 4 3 2 1
(last number denotes the printing)

Dedicated to my wife,
Harriet W. Dunning

Contents

Foreword

My acquaintance with John Dunning, and with South American birds, began, albeit independently but rather appropriately, about the same time in the mid-1960s. I was contacted by the secretary of the Yale Class of 1928, who knew of my interest in birds because of my father being a classmate, with the hope that I might join another of their classmates, a Mr. Dunning of Farmington, in a two generation presentation on birds to a gathering of the class.

Alas, I could not do it, but for the rather pleasant reason that I had plans to be in the Amazon at that time doing preliminary fieldwork for my Ph.D. thesis. So I did not meet Jack then, but I certainly was encouraged and excited to know that such an interesting man was among my father's classmates. I had met many and found them to be pleasant, nice people, but mostly being men of affairs, to my youthful stenoscopic view they *seemed* all a bit dull because, *after all*, nothing could matter more or be more interesting than natural history. And I like to think that Jack, for his part, was a bit intrigued by my reason for not being able to participate.

One of the great difficulties at that time in South America was the lack of field guides with ample illustration. One limped along as best one could with text decriptions or guides for adjacent areas. For my work at Belem in the Brasilian Amazon, I had even felt it necessary to prepare a field guide using photographs of museum specimens.

The situation is better now, with the advent of some new guides such as de Schauensee and Phelps' *A Guide to the Birds of Venezuela* and *A Guide to the Birds of Panama* by Bob Ridgely, who has also helped with this volume. Yet there are still many gaps and no guide with considerable illustrative material for the entirety of the "bird continent." Of course, even with John Dunning's considerable efforts, there still are many species for which adequate photographs do not exist, but what an advance this book is!

I know that Jack's interest in this book is not just to acquaint more people with the avian wonders of South America, but also by doing so, to alert them to what is happening to that continent's wild areas and their denizens. The sound of the axe and chainsaw, and the smell of smoke from burning woodland are evermore frequent, evermore present. The list of endangered bird species grows depressingly longer, and without major change and effort many species will only be removed from that list by transfer to the roster of extinct birds. Bound, too, with the fate of the birds is that of thousands upon thousands of other species.

Almost no part of South America is exempt from their discouraging trends; it is probably only a matter of time before some of the apparent exceptions succumb to the same pressures. The coastal forests of Brasil, with some 140 endemic species, are probably in the greatest peril of all: less than two percent of those forests remain.

The users of this book will undoubtedly encounter indications of this environmental destruction. Yet even they, except by noting the increasing difficulty of reaching untouched areas where many of these birds are to be found, may not preceive the incredible pace and scale at which this ecological juggernaut is advancing. While it might seem that this all is inevitably the result of population growth and national aspirations for economic development, it is a major irony that so often it is for little gain, even temporary, in human welfare. Indeed it is very much the reverse, for much of the destruction reduces the capacity of the land to support people: the poorer South America is in bird species, the poorer are its people.

There are, to be sure, bright spots in the gloomy picture: Surinam's park system, the major new increase in parks in Brasil, past gains in Argentina and Peru, Paraguay's nascent awareness. These initiatives are far from sufficient and the net picture is still "ecological red ink," but perhaps most importantly they show that things can be done to help the situation.

Today Jack and I are joined in an effort to stem that terrible tide in particular through the tropical forest program of World Wildlife Fund-U.S. which benefits from the sales of this book. We sincerely and fervently hope that in addition the book will stimulate new recruits to the tiny band of conservationists concerned with securing the future of the avifauna of the neotropical realm.

Thomas E. Lovejoy
Washington, D.C.
March, 1982

Introduction

This book is not for the scientist. It is designed to help the beginning bird-watcher identify the land birds of South America.

It is generally agreed that South American birds are the most difficult in the world to identify by field observation alone. South America has the largest number and variety of species found on any continent, thus the greatest number of possibilities to be eliminated, before one can be reasonably certain of the identity of a particular bird. This is an attempt to help solve that problem through photography.

All the birds in this book were wild and free just before being photographed. They were photographed by a method which my wife and I developed and have used for fifteen years. A portable enclosure about ten feet long is set up in the bird's own habitat with a natural perch mounted inside. An attempt is made to provide a perch similar to what we have seen the bird using in the wild. The bird is mistnetted, put in the enclosure, photographed and then released unharmed to resume its normal life in its own home area. I encourage others to use this method of showing people what wonderful creatures have resulted from evolution in tropical areas.

A Guide to the Birds of South America by Rodolphe Meyer de Schauensee has been my constant reference since it was published in 1970. Except for a number of accepted changes from studies since then, it is the basis of this book, which I regard as a first effort.

If this use of photography proves to be a valid approach to helping beginners (and I know it would have helped me a lot when I was a beginner) then a better book of this type should be brought out in the future. Despite my attempts to eliminate all mistakes, I know there still must be many, and I take full responsibility for them. If my readers will send a postcard to me at 2945 Estero Blvd., Fort Myers Beach, Fla. 33931, noting mistakes, I will make it available to whomever produces a future edition.

In a lifetime of enjoying the world of Nature, there has grown in me the strong feeling that by far the most important phase of conservation is habitat preservation. The world that I have known and loved is disappearing. The world we are creating in its place will be vastly different and there is considerable doubt about the future of the human race in that new world. Certainly many of the other forms of life on this planet are facing extinction. Hunters have often been denounced and I deplore the killing of any bird or animal except when needed for food or for scientific purposes. But if the habitat remains undestroyed and unpolluted, Nature can regenerate depleted populations. Actually the bull-dozer and the chain-saw kill much more wildlife than the hunter. Only in the case of a few large or vulnerable forms will hunters greatly affect the numbers of a species if its habitat remains.

What can be done? The only thing I can do is to try to interest more people in the battle to save habitat and that really is the basic reason for this book. If the thousands of bird-watchers can learn the names of the baffling Neotropical forest birds, they might become more interested in saving the habitat where those birds live.

Saving habitat in South America has been a difficult problem with a rapidly increasing human population. But it is there where our dollars and efforts can save the most species. The World Wildlife Fund has made a good start but more funding is needed. I am starting a Tropical Conservation Fund and directing the publishers of this book to send the first 10% of the sale price of each of these books to that fund. Also I encourage any readers who feel so inclined, to send additional contributions to the Tropical Conservation Fund, The World Wildlife Fund, 1601 Connecticut Ave., NW, Washington, D.C., 20009.

Acknowledgments

In addition to my own observations, which have been limited (since the photography demands almost my full attention in the field), the information in this book has come largely from three sources.

Robert S. Ridgely, collaborator on this book and author of *A Guide to the Birds of Panama,* has reviewed all the descriptions and suggested many changes, most of which were adopted. The range maps and habitat preferences, especially, are largely his work, based on his extensive work in most parts of South America over the last six years. He has my deepest gratitude for years of cooperation and deserves much of the credit for whatever help this book may be to birdwatchers.

A Guide to the Birds of South America (BSA) by Rodolphe Meyer de Schauensee has been my basic guide. The organization and English names used generally follow his book. I have a personal feeling of gratitude for his book as it was primarily responsible for steering my bird studies to South America.

A Guide to the Birds of Venezuela (BV) by Meyer de Schauensee and William H. Phelps, Jr., is a marvel of detail and accuracy. The superb plates and the facing page notes by Guy Tudor have been most helpful in solving many identification problems.

I am extremely grateful for time, suggestions and criticisms over the years by Dean Amadon, William Belton, Eugene Eisenmann and Sewall Pettingill.

The skin collection of The American Museum of Natural History has provided the ultimate solution of many problems of identification. For the use of it and for the help of its staff, I am grateful.

It would be impossible to thank all who have helped but in addition to those named above, the following have contributed in some important special way: Alexander Brash, Tom Butler, Roland Clement, Gary Clements, Elvina Crawley, Tina Garçon, Bob Godfrey, Paul Harris, Steve Hilty, Chris Hrdina, Margaret Hundley, Beryle Knowles, Doug Lancaster, Bud Lanyon, Philip Livingston, Horace Loftin, Tom Lovejoy, Russ Mason, Roger Morales, Manuel Parada, Roger Pasquier, Nera Poonai, George Powell, Hank Reichart, Augusto Ruschi, Joop Schulz, Les Short, Helmut Sick, Ram Singh, Alexander Skutch, Neal Smith, Kjell von Sneidern, Nina Steffee, Joe Tosi, Mike Tsalickis, Ed Tyson, Dora Weyer, Ed Willis.

I am very sad that Carlos Lehmann, Antonia Olivares, Paul Schwartz and Alexander Wetmore, who all helped greatly, could not live to see this long project completed.

The Precision Camera Repair Co., Chicopee, Mass. developed special equipment that made some of the photos possible.

Throughout the whole fifteen years, my wife, to whom this book is dedicated, has worked at my side — making and remaking the enclosure, bearing the discomforts of ants, chiggers, flies, mosquitoes and other bugs, living in the jungle without many of the comforts we had learned to take for granted — and helping with whatever needed to be done to try to get the best photographs possible. In addition she has kept records of the birds captured in each area and has spent untold hours typing, retyping and compiling the index. Her contribution has been incalculable.

How to Use This Book

All the regular South American land birds are briefly described in this book. Female descriptions are limited to those points which do not resemble the males. Sizes used are the estimated natural length of the bird which is shorter than the length of a stuffed bird used in some books. The words large, mid-size and small are used in a relative sense only in the bird's group or family.

The families generally follow the order in *A Guide to the Birds of South America* (BSA) by Rodolphe Meyer de Schauensee. Within each family the birds are usually grouped by size, the largest being first. This is varied when an obvious physical characteristic, or the several members of a genus, seem to make a different grouping more useful.

When an unknown bird is seen, the first problem is to decide in which family it belongs. By turning to the photos of the birds of the proper size in that family, some similar-looking pictures may be found. A quick check of the range maps will eliminate many possibilities. The descriptions then may solve the problem. If not, that bird may be described in the Non-Illustrated Section.

Whenever a genus represented in the Illustrated Section has species described on another page of the book, that page number is given in the sub-heading.

Abbreviations and terms used in the descriptions are explained on the following page.

Note: Words in italics indicate special distinguishing marks.
　　　Female like male except as noted.
　　　An asterisk after the scientific name denotes a migrant.

Altitudinal zone preferred.
L – *Low (Tropical)*
M – *Middle (Subtropical)*
H – *High (Temperata and Paramo)*

Foliage-type preferred:
F – *Forest. Thick forest with high trees, little underbrush.*
T – *Trees. Thin woodland, often with thick underbrush.*
S – *Scrub. Brush, thickets, shrubbery.*
O – *Open. Few if any trees.*
A – *Arid.*
W – *By water.*

Shading in this area indicates that bird appears in Panama.

Area where bird has been seen.

2. Tropical Screech-Owl LM-TSA
Otus choliba (*)　　　8" (21cm)
Small ear tufts. Above brown or rufous mottled buff and streaked black. *White stripe at each side of upper back.* Tail narrowly banded cinnamon buff. Legs feathered.

Estimated length in normal perching position.

Abbreviations and Definitions

" — inches

♀ — female   ♂ — male

* — (after scientific name) = migrant from North or Central America.

A — arid, desert

BSA — "A Guide to the Birds of South America" by Rodolphe Meyer de Schauensee

Bob — move tail up and down.

Buff — very light brownish yellow

BV — "Birds of Venezuela" by de Schauensee and Phelps.

Cere — lump at base of bill.

Chestnut — dark reddish brown.

Cinnamon — light yellowish brown with reddish tinge.

cm — centimeters.

Crissum — undertail coverts.

Curved — bill curved downward. If curved up, it is marked upturned.

e — east.

F — forest — thick forest with tall trees.

Genus — a closely related group denoted by the first word in the scientific name.

H — Highlands (Temperate and Puna Zones) over approx. 2500 meters elevation.

Imm — immature.

L — lowlands (Tropical Zone) up to approx. 1500 meters elevation.

Malar stripe — stripe above whisker.

M — Middle Altitude (Subtropical Zone) approx. 1500–2500 meters elevation.

Migrant — does not breed in South America.

n — north.

O — open country, grassland.

Ochraceous — brownish yellow.

Olive — dull green, usually tinged yellow, brown or gray.

Orbital — area around eye.

Rufous — reddish brown.

Rump — area at lower back including the uppertail coverts

s — south.

S — Scrub, brush, thickets, shrubbery.

Species — a kind of bird denoted by the second word in the scientific name.

T — trees, thin woodland, often with thick underbrush.

Tawny — light reddish brown.

Vermiculated — marked with fine, wavy lines.

w — west.

W — by water, marshes, swamps, river banks.

Wag — move tail side to side.

Wattle — lump hanging from throat

Wing-band — band on primaries, usually not visible when wing closed.

Wing-bar — bar (often two) on wing coverts, visible when wing closed.

Chart of a Bird

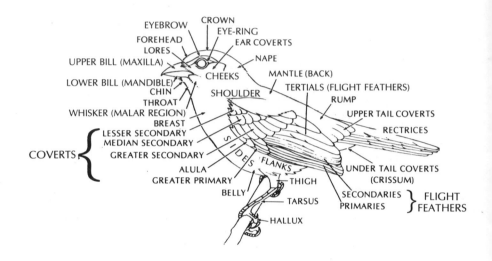

1. Greater Rhea   **L-0**
Rhea americana   48" (120cm)
Crown, back of neck, upper back and patch at base of neck black. Rest of plumage gray except underparts white. Legs yellow. Flightless.

2. Horned Screamer   **LM-0**
Anhima cornuta   32" (80cm)
Blackish. Shoulders, belly and some mottling on head and neck white. *Horn-like quill on top of head.* Legs thick. Feet very large.

3. Crested Guan   **L-F**
Penelope purpurascens
                34" (83cm)
The only large guan in its range. Quite *conspicuous bushy crest.* Head and neck dark brown. Above glossy olive brown, back more rufescent. Below brown, feathers of neck and breast prominently edged whitish. Throat and legs dark red.

4. Red-billed Curassow   **L-F**
Crax blumenbachii   31" (79cm)
Glossy black. Base of bill, *small knob and wattles red.* Belly white. Legs pink. ♀: Bill blackish. Wings with wavy rufous marking. Belly pale rufous.

5. Rufous-vented Chachalaca LM-FS
Ortalis ruficauda   21" (52cm)
Head and throat gray. Wattles red. Back bronzy olive. Below pale gray. Tail broad and long, dark bronzy, broadly tipped rufous or white. Legs gray.

6. Gray-winged Trumpeter   **L-F**
Psophia crepitans   21" (52cm)
Mostly black with metallic sheen, lower back and inner wing feathers gray. Bill short. Legs long, yellowish.

7. Black-legged Seriema   **L-SO**
Chunga burmeisteri   23" (57cm)
Mostly light brownish gray. *No crest.* Bill and legs black. Belly white. Tail gray, barred black. Similar: Red-legged Seriema (204-11) has conspicuous crest at base of bill.

8. Double-striped Thick-knee L-OA
Burhinus bistriatus   17" (43cm)
Bill black. Crown brown. Very broad eyebrow white bordered above by black line. Upperparts brown streaked buff. Throat white. Belly white. White patch on wing in flight. Legs olive.

1

2

RIDGELY

3

4

RIDGELY

6

8

RIDGELY

A FEW TERRESTRIAL WATER-TYPE BIRDS

Tinamous TINAMOUS - 193.
Crypturellus TINAMOUS - 193, 194, 195.
Nothura NOTHURAS - 195, 196.
Attagis SEEDSNIPES - 206.
Thinocorus SEEDSNIPES - 206.

1. White-throated Tinamou   L-F
Tinamus guttatus   12" (30cm)
Crown gray. Throat white. Back dark brown, more or less spotted white. Below light pinkish brown, darkest on breast.

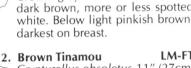

2. Brown Tinamou   LM-FT
Crypturellus obsoletus 11" (27cm)
Head gray. Back varies from dark brown to reddish brown. Below rufous. Legs gray.

3. Spotted Nothura   LM-SO
Nothura maculosa   9" (23cm)
Crown black streaked buff. Back brown streaked buff. Throat white. Below buff, streaked chestnut and black on breast. Flanks barred.

4. Rufous-bellied Seedsnipe   H-O
Attagis gayi   11" (27cm)
Bill ½x head. Breast cinnamon scalloped blackish. Belly cinnamon buff. Above dark brown barred or spotted cinnamon.

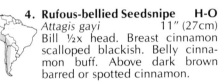

5. Gray-breasted Seedsnipe   H-O
Thinocorus orbignyianus
8" (20cm)
Bill ½x head. Forehead, neck and breast gray. Back mixed black, brown and buff. Throat white enclosed by narrow black line. Belly white separated from breast by narrow black bar.

6. Cattle Egret   L-O
Bubulcus ibis   15" (38cm)
Bill 1¼x head, *yellow.* White (head and breast tinged buff in breeding season). Legs and feet yellowish, or blackish. Often around cattle. Heron-like.

7. Southern Lapwing   MH-O
Vanellus chilensis   12" (30cm)
Bill ⅔x head. Above grayish. Forehead, *long thin crest,* throat and breast black. Rump and belly white. Tail black, tipped white. Similar; Andean Lapwing (not in book) is at very high altitudes. It has *pale gray breast.*

8. Common Snipe   LM-W
Gallinago gallinago   10" (26cm)
Bill 2x head. Crown and stripe through eye black. Back black mottled buff. Throat white. Breast brownish. Belly white. Tail white barred brown.

9. Spotted Rail   L-F
Rallus maculatus   9" (24cm)
Bill longer than head, yellowish, red at base. Back brown streaked white. Below black barred white.

10. Killdeer   LM-O
*Charadrius vociferus**   8" (20cm)
Bill ⅔x head. Above grayish brown. Forehead, stripe behind eye, throat and sides of neck white. Below white with *two black bands across breast.*

11. Spotted Sandpiper   LMH-W
*Actitis macularia**   7" (18cm)
Bill = head. Non-breeding plumage: Eyebrow white. Above brownish. Below white. A *gray smudge* at each side of breast. *Teeters constantly.*

Cathartes VULTURES - 196.
(Various) EAGLES - 198, 199, 200.
Buteo HAWKS - 198.
Leucopternis HAWKS - 198, 199.
Buteogallus HAWKS - 199.

1. **King Vulture**   **L-FTS**
Sarcoramphus papa   28" (70cm)
Head and neck bare, orange, red
and blue. Body creamy white.
Rump, wings and tail black. From
below the front part of the wing
(underwing coverts) is white and
the rear part of the wing (flight
feathers) is black.

2. **Turkey Vulture**   **LM-FTSO**
Cathartes aura   25" (65cm)
Blackish. Head bare, *red*. In flight
holds wings above horizontal. Gray
flight feathers contrast with black
underwing coverts. Tail much
longer than outstretched legs.

3. **Black Vulture**   **LM-TSO**
Coragyps atratus   22" (55cm)
Black. Head and neck bare, *black*.
In flight whitish areas show at end
of wings. Tail about same length
as outstretched legs.

4. **Solitary Eagle**   **LM-FTS**
Harpyhaliaetus solitarius
                        26" (63cm)
Dark bluish gray. Lores and legs
yellow. Tail black with broad white
band. In flight shows *no white in
wing*. Imm: Dark brown above.
Below buffy heavily blotched
blackish.

5. **White-tailed Hawk**   **LM-SO**
Buteo albicaudatus   23" (58cm)
Head blackish. Above light gray or
dark gray, shoulders rufous. Underparts white. *Tail white with single broad black bar near end.* Imm:
Heavily blotched below.

6. **Savanna Hawk**   **L-SO**
Heterospizias meridionalis
                        21" (53cm)
Mostly rufescent brown. Back
grayer. Rather short tail black with
one white band. Below rufous narrowly barred black. Imm: Blackish

brown above, mottled rufous on
shoulders. Below buffyish streaked
or mottled brown. Tail narrowly
barred. Often perches on or near
ground.

Puna (Variable) Hawk   **H-O**
Buteo poecilochrous   20" (52cm)
Variable. Usually gray above, white
below with rufous back. *Tail always white with broad black band
near end.*

7. **Immature:** Usually dark brown
above, whitish streaked brown
below and tail grayish barred
brown.

8. **White Hawk**   **L-FT**
Leucopternis albicollis 18"(47cm)
White. Lores and wings black.
Crown and back more or less
spotted black. Tail white with sin-
gle broad black band.

9. **Common Black Hawk**   **L-SOW**
Buteogallus anthracinus
                        17" (45cm)
Black. Facial skin and legs yellow.
Tail with one median band and
white tip. Imm: Blackish brown.
Tail black with four prominent
white bars and white tip.

10. **Black-collared Hawk**   **L-SWO**
Busarellus nigricollis 17" (45cm)
Head whitish. Black shield on
upper breast. Otherwise mostly
bright rufous chestnut. Tail barred
black and rufous (no white). Underwing coverts rufous chestnut.
Flight feathers mostly black.

11. **Roadside Hawk**   **LM-TSO**
Buteo magnirostris   14" (34cm)
Above varies from gray to brown
to almost black. *Rufous patch* in
primaries shows in flight in all
races. Tail brown with four or five
gray or buff bars. Wings short,
rounded. Imm: Above brown.
Below tawny, streaked brown on
throat and breast. Barred reddish
brown on belly.

1. Gray-headed Kite   L-F
Leptodon cayanensis   23" (57cm)
Head gray. Below white. Back and wings blackish. Tail black with two visible broad white bars. Imm: Light phase — head white, crown black. Dark phase — above brown, below heavily streaked.

2. Double-toothed Kite   L-FT
Harpagus bidentatus   13" (32cm)
Above slaty gray. Throat white, dark stripe down center. Below rufous barred with whitish or grayish (more uniform rufous in female). Tail blackish with three or four gray bars.

3. Immature: Brown above, streaked below, but still with distinctive *dark throat stripe.*

4. Sharp-shinned Hawk   LMH-FT
Accipiter striatus   10" (26cm)
Above dark gray. Below white (or cinnamon) narrowly barred brownish. Thighs rufous. Tail long, dark with three or four light bars. An all-dark phase occurs in the Andes. Imm: Browner above, pale below streaked dusky.

5. Crested Caracara   LMH-OW
Polyborus plancus   22" (54cm)
Crown black, slightly crested. Sides of head, neck and breast white. Breast and hindneck barred blackish. Above blackish, with prominent pale patch at base of primaries, conspicuous in flight. Rump and tail whitish, latter tipped black. Belly blackish. *Facial skin red,* long legs yellow. Imm: Browner and more streaked, but already with adult's basic pattern.

6. Mountain Caracara   H-O
Phalcoboenus megalopterus
                          19" (47cm)
Black. Bare facial skin reddish. Rump and belly white. Tail tipped white. Legs orange yellow. Imm:

Tawny brown with large buffy patch on rump.

7. Yellow-headed Caracara LM-TO
Milvago chimachima   16" (41cm)
Head and underparts buff. Black stripe behind eye. Back brown. Tail long, buffy, barred and tipped black. Striking pale patch near end of wings in flight. Imm: Head, neck and underparts streaked dusky.

8. Laughing Falcon   LM-FTS
Herpetotheres cachinnans
                          18" (47cm)
Crown, mantle and underparts buffy. Conspicuous broad black mask extends around back of head. Back and wings dark brown. Tail narrowly barred black and buff.

9. Barred Forest-Falcon   LM-F
Micrastur ruficollis   14" (35cm)
Upperparts, throat and breast gray or rufous. Belly evenly banded black and white. Tail long, black with 3 or 4 narrow white bands. Imm: Barred dusky below.

10. Spot-winged Falconet   L-S
Spiziapteryx circumcinctus
                          10" (26cm)
Above grayish brown, narrowly streaked black. Eyebrow and malar stripe white. Wings and sides of tail with small white spots. Rump white. Below whitish, lightly streaked dusky.

11. American Kestrel   LMH-TSO
Falco sparverius   9" (22cm)
Above rufous, crown and wings gray. Face white with two vertical black stripes. Below whitish. ♀: Wings rufous. *Upperparts and tail all barred black.*

12. Bat Falcon   LM-T
Falco rufigularis   10" (26cm)
Above black. Semi-collar and throat white. Breast black, narrowly barred white. Belly rufous. Tail black narrowly barred whitish.

WITH UNSPOTTED WINGS

Columba PIGEONS - 206, 207.
Geotrygon QUAIL-DOVES - 208.
Leptotila DOVES - 208.

1. **Band-tailed Pigeon** **LM-FT**
Columba fasciata 13″ (34cm)
Bill and legs yellow. Eye-ring red.
Head and underparts gray tinged
reddish. Band across hindneck
white. Back bronzy. Tail dark gray,
paler at end.

2. **Dusky Pigeon** **L-F**
Columba goodsoni 9″ (24cm)
Bill black. *Head and underparts
gray.* Nape gray, glossed purple.
Back, wings and tail bronzy gray
sometimes glossed purple.

3. **White-throated Quail-Dove**
LM-F
Geotrygon frenata 11″ (28cm)
Crown gray. *Narrow black line
through eye.* Above dark brown,
glossed purplish. Throat white.
Whiskers black. Underparts
brownish. Tail short.

4. **Lined Quail-Dove** **LM-F**
Geotrygon linearis 11″ (27cm)
Forecrown cinnamon buffy, becoming *brown on crown and gray
on nape.* Above rufous brown
glossed purple on upper back.
Sides of head and throat whitish
crossed by narrow black malar
stripe. Breast grayish buff, belly
buffy brown. Tail short.

5. **Sapphire Quail-Dove** **L-F**
Geotrygon saphirina 10″ (26cm)
Forehead white. Crown gray. *Broad
stripe below eye white,* bordered
below by dark violet stripe. Back
bronzy brown. Rump blue. Below
white. Tail black, tipped white or
gray on outer feathers. Tail short.

6. **Ruddy Quail-Dove** **LM-T**
Geotrygon montana 9″ (23cm)
Above rufous, back glossed purple. *Throat and stripe under eye
white.* White mark on shoulder
sometimes does not show. Below
buffy, tinged tawny on breast. Tail
short.

7. **Female:** Above olive brown. Breast
cinnamon.

8. **Olive-backed Quail-Dove** **L-F**
Geotrygon veraguensis 9″ (24cm)
*Forehead and broad stripe under
eye white.* Crown and nape light
gray. Upperparts and breast
brownish, belly lighter. Tail short.

9. **White-Tipped Dove** **LM-TSA**
Leptotila verreauxi 11″ (27cm)
Above grayish brown. *Skin around
eye blue.* Throat white. Rest of underparts pinkish. Tail wedge-
shaped with conspicuous white
tips on outer feathers showing in
flight.

10. **Gray-fronted Dove** **L-F**
Leptotila rufaxilla 10″ (26cm)
Crown blue gray, forehead
whitish. Skin around eye red. Back
and wings dark olive-brown. Underparts pale pinkish or buff. Tail
dark brown, outer feathers tipped
white.

11. **Gray-chested Dove** **L-F**
Leptotila cassinii 9″ (23cm)
Back olive brown. Lores red. *Breast
gray.* Belly whitish. Tail grayish,
very narrowly tipped white on
outer feathers.

12. **Gray-headed Dove** **L-TS**
Leptotila plumbeiceps 9″ (23cm)
Crown and *nape bluish gray.* Lores
red. Above chestnut-brown. Below
pinkish white. Tail dusky with outer
feathers tipped white.

WITH SPOTTED WINGS

Zenaida DOVES - 207.
Claravis GROUND-DOVES - 207.
Columbina GROUND-DOVES - 207.

1. **Eared Dove**   **LMH-OA**
   Zenaida auriculata   9" (22cm)
   Crown gray. Rest of head, breast
   and underparts pinkish. *Narrow
   black line back of eye.* Above olive
   brown. Tail pointed, outer feathers
   broadly tipped white.

2. **Scaled Dove**   **LM-S**
   Scardafella squammata 8" (20cm)
   Above brown, below whitish, *both
   scaled black. Tail long* and graduated. In flight wings show rufous,
   and outer tail feathers show mostly
   white.

3. **Blue Ground-Dove**   **L-TS**
   Claravis pretiosa   8" (20cm)
   Above blue gray, wing coverts
   spotted black. Throat whitish.
   Below pale gray. Outer tail feathers black.
4. **Female:** Above brown, *wings with
   large rufous spots.* Throat and belly
   whitish. Breast brown. Usually
   seen in pairs.

5. **Picui Ground-Dove**   **L-TO**
   Columbina picui   7" (18cm)
   Above light olive brown. Below
   whitish. In flight wings show black
   and white and *outer tail feathers
   mostly white.* Tail short.

6. **Ruddy Ground-Dove**   **L-SO**
   Columbina talpacoti 6½" (17cm)
   Head gray. Above cinnamon rufous, lighter below. Wing coverts
   spotted black. Throat whitish.
   Outer tail feathers black, tipped
   cinnamon. Tail short.
7. **Female:** Like ♂ but olive brown
   above and pale buffy brown below.

8. **Scaly (Common) Ground-Dove**
                           LM-OA
   Columbina passerina 5½" (14cm)
   Head scaly. Above grayish or olive
   brown, spotted black on wing
   coverts. Below pinkish, scaled
   dusky on throat and breast. *Tail
   without light tips.* Tail short.

9. **Plain-breasted Ground-Dove**
                           L-SO
   Columbina minuta   5" (13cm)
   Small. Head and nape tinged blue
   gray, *not scaly. Above pale grayish
   brown.* Wing coverts spotted
   blackish. Below light grayish.
   Outer tail feathers gray, blackish at
   end. *Chestnut primaries* prominent in flight. Tail short.
10. **Female:** Crown brownish. Throat
    and belly white.

Ara MACAWS - 209.
(Various) PARROTS - 210, 213, 214, 215.
Aratinga PARAKEETS - 209, 210.

1. Red-and-green Macaw   L-F
Ara chloroptera   34" (85cm)
Bare facial skin white with narrow lines of red feathers. Shoulder red. Wing coverts green *(no yellow on wings)*. Primaries blue. Tail long, pointed, red tipped blue.

2. Scarlet Macaw   L-FT
Ara macao   32" (80cm)
Scarlet. Bare facial skin all white. Broad patch of yellow on wing coverts. Primaries blue. Lower back and rump light blue. Tail long, pointed, red tipped blue.

3. Blue-and-yellow Macaw   L-FT
Ara ararauna   32" (80cm)
Above bright blue, forehead green. Below bright yellow, throat patch black. Tail long, pointed.

4. Red-fronted Macaw   M-F
Ara rubrogenys   22" (55cm)
Green. Crown, thighs and spot on ear coverts red. Primaries and tail bluish.

5. Red-shouldered Macaw   L-TO
Ara nobilis   13" (33cm)
A parakeet-sized macaw. Small bare facial area white. Mostly green, including primaries, bluer on crown. Shoulder red. Underside of primaries and tail olive yellowish.

6. Burrowing Parrot   LMH-O
Cyanoliseus patagonus
17" (43cm)
Above olive brown, lower back and rump yellow. Throat and breast grayish brown. Belly yellow, center of belly red. Tail short and square.

7. Turquoise-fronted Parrot   L-TS
Amazona aestiva   14" (35cm)
Mostly green, feathers edged black, especially on nape, neck and underparts. *Forehead blue.* Top of crown, facial area and throat yellow. Bend of wing and speculum red. Tail short and square.

8. Mitred Parakeet   LM-FT
Aratinga mitrata   14" (35cm)
Green. Forecrown, throat and feathers around eye red. Underwing coverts green. Tail long and pointed.

9. Sun Parakeet   L-FTO
Aratinga solstitialis   12" (29cm)
Mostly yellow, strongly tinged *orange on head and breast.* Wing coverts partly green, primaries blue. Tail olive tipped blue. Tail long and pointed.

10. Brown-throated Parakeet   L-SO
Aratinga pertinax   9" (23cm)
Variable. Mostly green, crown bluish in most races. Orange-yellow feathers around eye in most races. *Throat and breast* usually *contrastingly brown* to grayish brown (forehead, cheeks and throat yellow-orange in Guianas). Lower underparts paler green. Tail long and pointed.

11. Monk Parakeet   LM-TO
Myiopsitta monachus 10" (26cm)
Forehead gray. Above green. *Breast gray* (scaled white in some races). Belly yellowish, rest of underparts green. Tail long and pointed, green.

Pyrrhura PARAKEETS - 210, 211.
Brotogeris PARAKEETS - 212.
Touit PARROTLETS - 212, 213.
Forpus PARROTLETS - 212.

1. Green-cheeked Parakeet LM-FT
Pyrrhura molinae   10" (26cm)
Mostly green. Crown and nape dull brownish, ear coverts grayish brown. *Throat, sides of neck and breast brown, edged whitish or yellow giving scaly appearance.* Center of belly and tail reddish. Tail long, pointed. Includes Yellow-sided Parakeet, *Pyrrhura hypoxantha;* considered to be a separate species in BSA.

2. Maroon-tailed Parakeet LM-FT
Pyrrhura melanura   9" (23cm)
Mostly green, crown browner. Skin around eye white. Red and yellow patch on wings. Breast brown, feathers pale-edged producing scaled look. Tail maroon above, long, pointed. Includes Berlepsch's Parakeet, *Pyrrhura berlepschi;* considered a separate species in BSA.

3. Painted Parakeet   L-FT
Pyrrhura picta   9" (22cm)
Mostly green, rump red. Forehead varies from blue to red. Bare skin around eye gray or white. Shoulder red (or green in some races). *Below brownish, breast feathers pale-edged.* Center of belly red. Tail long, pointed.

4. Canary-winged Parakeet L-TS
Brotogeris versicolurus 8" (21cm)
Green. *Prominent patch on wing yellow.* Races in n and w part of range also have white on primaries which shows only in flight. Tail long, pointed.

5. Cobalt-winged Parakeet L-FT
Brotogeris cyanoptera
7½" (19cm)
Green. Forehead yellowish. Wings darker green, flight feathers violet-blue. Bend of wing shows yellow. *Small chin spot orange.* Tail much brighter green than back. Tail long, pointed.

6. Lilac-tailed Parrotlet   L-F
Touit batavica   5½" (14cm)
Head greenish yellow. *Back and wings black. Wing coverts prominent yellow.* Red at shoulder (sometimes not visible). Below bluish green. *Tail short, square, violet with black bar.*

7. Spectacled Parrotlet   L-TS
Forpus conspicillatus 4½" (12cm)
Above and below greenish. *Bright blue around eye* and on rump. Wing feathers blue. Tail short.

8. Female: Below yellowish green. Area around eye bluish green.

Dusky-billed Parrotlet   L-T
Forpus sclateri   4½" (12cm)
Green. Wings darker green, coverts blue, bend of wing yellow. Rump blue. *Most of upper bill dark.* Tail short.

9. Female: Extensive   yellowish around head. Rump green.

10. Pacific Parrotlet   L-TSA
Forpus coelestis   4½" (12cm)
Crown and cheeks light green. Spot behind eye, nape and shoulders blue. *Back and wings grayish green, rump deep purple.* Below light green. Tail bright light green, short.

11. Green-rumped Parrotlet LM-TSO
Forpus passerinus   4½" (12cm)
Bill horn-colored. Green, paler and brighter on face, underparts and rump. Primary coverts and underwing coverts blue (♀ green). Tail short.

RIDGELY

Piaya CUCKOOS - 216.
Coccyzus CUCKOOS - 215, 216.
Crotophaga ANIS - 216.

1. Squirrel Cuckoo   LM-T
Piaya cayana   17" (43cm)
Bill yellowish, curved. Eye-ring red or yellow. Above chestnut. Throat and breast light rufous, *contrasting with grayish belly. Tail very long, broadly tipped white.*

2. Little Cuckoo   L-SW
Piaya minuta   11" (27cm)
Like preceding but *much smaller.* Bill yellowish, curved. Eye-ring red. Above chestnut brown. Below rufous, tinged grayish on belly but showing little contrast. Tail long, tipped white.

3. Striped Cuckoo   LM-TS
Tapera naevia   10" (26cm)
Crown rufous, crested, streaked black. Back brown, streaked buff and black. Eyebrow whitish. Throat and belly white, narrow whisker black. Tail long, mostly brown.

4. Guira Cuckoo   LM-TS
Guira guira   15" (37cm)
Crown brown, crested. Above dark brown streaked white. Rump white. Below white, narrowly streaked black on breast. Tail long, dark, broadly tipped white.

5. Yellow-billed Cuckoo   LM-T
Coccyzus americanus*
          ·11" (27cm)
Bill dark above, yellow below. Above grayish brown. Tail long, feathers broadly tipped white from below. In flight shows rufous in wings.

6. Black-billed Cuckoo   L-TS
Coccyzus erythropthalmus
          11" (27cm)
Bill all black. Above brown. Eye-ring red. Below white. Tail long, feathers narrowly tipped white.

7. Dark-billed Cuckoo   L-S
Coccyzus melacoryphus
          9" (22cm)
Bill all black. Crown and nape dark gray, ear coverts blackish. Back brown. Below mostly buff, sides of breast gray. Tail long, feathers broadly tipped white.

8. Smooth-billed Ani   LM-SO
Crotophaga ani   13" (33cm)
All black. High smooth *thin ridge on bill* producing "humped" look. Tail long, often ragged looking.

9. Groove-billed Ani   L-SOA
Crotophaga sulcirostris
          12" (31cm)
All black. Bill with longitudinal groove marks (hard to see in field), lacks "hump" on ridge, is smoothly curved on top. Tail long, often ragged looking.

1

2

3

5

4

6

7

8

9

1. Spectacled Owl　　　　**L-TS**
Pulsatrix perspicillata　17″ (43cm)
No ear tufts. Eye yellow. Upperparts brown. Eyebrows and spectacles white. Underparts whitish with broad brown band across breast. Wings and tail barred dark grayish.

2. Tropical Screech-Owl　**LM-TSA**
Otus choliba　　　　8″ (21cm)
Small ear tufts. Above brown or rufous mottled buff and streaked black. *White stripe at each side of upper back.* Tail narrowly banded cinnamon buff. Legs feathered.

3. Ferruginous Pygmy-Owl　**LM-TS**
Glaucidium brasilianum
　　　　　　　　　6″ (16cm)
No ear tufts. Above brown or rufous, *crown streaked (not spotted)* buff. Two black eye-like spots on back of head. Short eyebrow white. Below white, broadly streaked brown or rufous. Tail with five or six dusky bars. Flies day or night.

4. Andean Pygmy-Owl　　**MH-FT**
Glaucidium jardinii　5½″ (14cm)
No ear tufts. Brown or rufous, *crown spotted (not streaked)* buff. Back spotted buff. Two black eye-like spots on back of head. Short eyebrow white. Below more or less streaked white. Tail with four dusky bars. Flies day or night.

5. Burrowing Owl　　　**LMH-OA**
Athene (Speotyto) cunicularia
　　　　　　　　　8″ (20cm)
No ear tufts. Above brown spotted whitish. Forehead and eyebrow white. Below white barred brown. *Legs long. Terrestrial.* Flies in daytime.

6. Common Potoo　　　　**L-FT**
Nyctibius griseus　　14″ (34cm)
Perches motionless on vertical stub

by day. Two color phases, brown or gray, both mottled to resemble bark. Tail long.

7. Oilbird　　　　　　**LM-FT**
Steatornis caripensis　17″ (42cm)
Stays in caves in day-time. Above and below brown spotted white, more pinkish below. Tail long, brown, lightly barred black.

8. Ladder-tailed Nightjar　**L-TSW**
Hydropsalis climacocerca
　　　　　　　　　10″ (26cm)
Throat and belly white. Four outer primaries with white bar. Tail long, two outer feathers with wide diagonal white patch. ♀: Has cinnamon in place of white.

9. Pauraque　　　　　**LM-TS**
Nyctidromus albicollis
　　　　　　　　　10″ (25cm)
Grayish brown or reddish brown with large velvety black spots margined buff. Sides of head rusty brown. Underparts buff lightly barred black. Tail rounded, black. In flight shows much white in tail.

10. Female: Outer tail feathers barred rufous.

White-tailed Nightjar　　**LM-O**
Caprimulgus cayennensis
　　　　　　　　　8″ (21cm)
Above mottled brown and gray. Cinnamon collar on back. Throat white. Below buffy. Broad white bar in wing and much white in tail show in flight. Usually on ground.

11. Female: No white. Tail barred black and rufous.

12. Little Nightjar　　　**L-TSO**
Caprimulgus parvulus　7″ (18cm)
Above grayish brown streaked black. Rufous collar on hindneck. Large white throat patch. Breast sooty brown spotted white. Belly buff narrowly barred dusky. White band across primaries. Tail tipped white. ♀: Throat buff, no white in wings or tail.

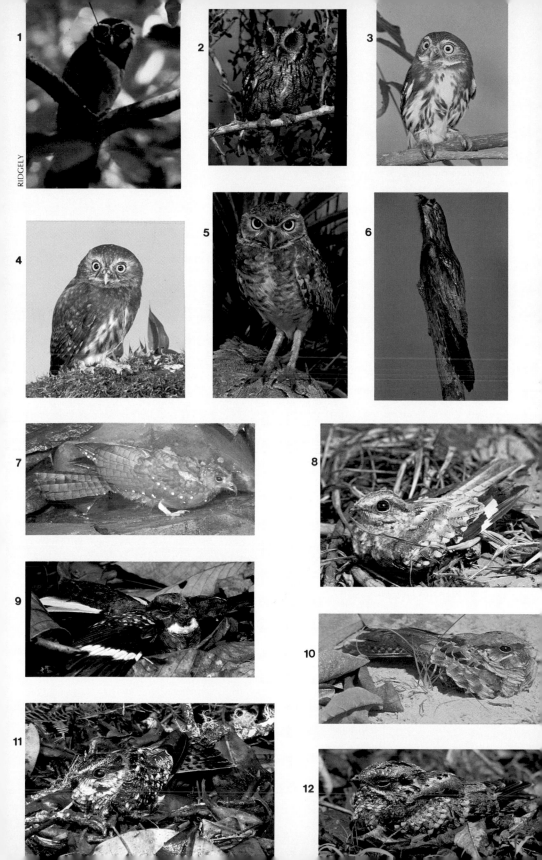

With the Hummingbirds, bill length is compared to head length. Bill is straight and black unless noted.

*Phaethornis*HERMITS - 223, 224.

1. Long-tailed Hermit　　　**LM-FT**
Phaethornis superciliosus
6" (15cm)
Bill 2x head, curved. Above bronzy, buffy on rump. Below grayish buff. Tail dark, central feathers very long, white.

2. Tawny-bellied Hermit　　**LM-FT**
Phaethornis syrmatophorus
5½" (14cm)
Bill 2x head, curved, lower red at base. Above bronzy. Rump cinnamon. Below light rufous. Side feathers of tail broadly tipped cinnamon.

3. Scale-throated Hermit　　**LM-FT**
Phaethornis eurynome 6" (15cm)
Bill 2x head, curved. Crown blackish. Back olive. *Throat feathers black edged buff giving scaled appearance.* Sides of throat white. *Below light gray,* tinged pinkish on belly.

4. Pale-bellied Hermit　　　**L-T**
Phaethornis anthophilus
5½" (14cm)
Bill 1¾x head, slightly curved. Above bronzy olive. Conspicuous black patch back of eye. Below whitish, streaked black on throat.

5. Planalto Hermit　　　　**MH-T**
Phaethornis pretrei 5½" (14cm)
Bill 1¾x head, curved. Above bronzy green, *rump rufous. Below pinkish buff.* Tail graduated, side feathers tipped white.

6. Straight-billed Hermit　　**L-TS**
Phaethornis bourcieri 5½" (14cm)
Bill 1¾x head, *only slightly curved.* Above bronzy. Throat whitish. Below grayish. Central tail feathers elongated, white.

7. Sooty-capped Hermit　　**L-FT**
Phaethornis augusti 5½" (14cm)
Bill 1¾x head, curved. Above bronzy green. *Distinct eyebrow*

and whisker *white.* Below gray. Tail graduated with much white at sides.

8. White-bearded Hermit　　**L-FT**
Phaethornis hispidus 5½" (14cm)
Bill 1¾x head, curved. Back grayish olive. Rump gray. Throat and breast gray with prominent *white streak down center of throat.*

9. Green Hermit　　　　**LM-FT**
Phaethornis guy 5½" (14cm)
Bill 2x head, curved, lower red. A dark species. Above green. Eyebrow and whisker buff. Throat tawny or gray. Breast greenish (♀ gray). Belly gray. A *buffy line down center of throat* and breast. Central tail feathers broadly tipped white; rest black, narrowly tipped white.

10. White-whiskered Hermit　　**L-FT**
Phaethornis yaruqui 5½" (14cm)
Bill 2x head, curved, lower red at base. Above and below dark green with buffy line down center of throat. *Prominent whisker white.* Central tail feathers tipped white, *rest with no white.* ♀: Line down center of throat and breast white. Belly gray.

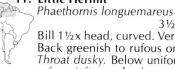

11. Little Hermit　　　　**L-TS**
Phaethornis longuemareus
3½" (9cm)
Bill 1½x head, curved. Very small. Back greenish to rufous on rump. *Throat dusky.* Below uniform light rufous (often paler in center). *No black breast band.* Central tail feathers somewhat longer, white at end.

12. Reddish Hermit　　　　**L-TS**
Phaethornis ruber 3" (8cm)
Tiny. Bill 1½x head, curved. Throat not dusky. Above greenish olive, rump rufous. Narrow *black band across breast,* sometimes not visible. (♀ sometimes lacking). Tail copper color, central feathers tipped white but *not much elongated.*

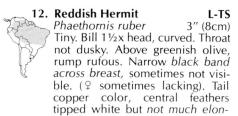

LOWLAND HUMMINGBIRDS WITH LONG BILL. HERMITS WITHOUT ELONGATED CENTRAL TAIL FEATHERS.

1. White-tipped Sicklebill **L-F**
Eutoxeres aquila 5" (13cm)
Bill (chord) 1¼x head, very strongly curved, heavy. Crown dark brown. Back dark green. Underparts streaked buff and black. Tail *greenish tipped white.* Similar: Buff-tailed Sicklebill (224-4) has outer tail feathers buff, not greenish.

2. Gray-breasted Sabrewing **LM-FTS**
Campylopterus largipennis 5" (13cm)
Bill 1¼x head. Above green. *Below uniform gray.* Central tail feathers green, outers black with white or gray tips.

3. Black-throated Mango **L-SO**
Anthracothorax nigricollis 4½" (11cm)
Bill 1½x head, curved. Above green. *Throat, center of breast and belly black,* bordered on each side with glittering blue. Tail purple.

4. Female: Below white with black stripe from chin to belly. Tail purple with small white tips.

Green-throated Mango **L-SO**
Anthracothorax viridigula 4½" (12cm)
Bill 1½x head, curved. Above shining bronzy green becoming bronzy gold on rump. *Throat glittering emerald green.* Center of breast and belly black. Tail shining purple.

5. Female: Center of underparts black and green. Tail tipped white.

6. Long-billed Starthroat **L-TSO**
Heliomaster longirostris 5" (13cm)
Bill 2x head. Crown glittering bluish green. Small white spot back of eye. Back coppery green. Throat

glittering red with prominent white stripe at each side. Breast and belly gray with white line down center. Tail dark, outer feathers tipped white. ♀: Lacks glittering crown patch.

7. Violet-chested Hummingbird **LM-F**
Sternoclyta cyanopectus 5" (13cm)
Bill 1½x head, curved. Above shining green. Throat glittering green. *Breast glittering violet.* Belly gray. Tail bronzy with white tips.

8. Female: Throat and breast green with white spots. *Belly rufous.*

9. Pale-tailed Barbthroat **L-F**
Threnetes leucurus 4½" (12cm)
Bill 2x head, curved. Above green. Chin blackish with white lines at sides. *Throat orangy buff.* Breast dark green. Belly gray. Tail looks *mostly white* (from below) except two central feathers green.

10. Band-tailed Barbthroat **L-F**
Threnetes ruckeri 4½" (12cm)
Bill 2x head, curved. Very like preceding except tail white at base and tips, with *broad black band.*

11. Rufous-breasted Hermit **L-FT**
Glaucis hirsuta 4¼" (11cm)
Bill 2x head, curved. Above bronzy green. *Below dull rufous.* Outer *tail feathers reddish,* central ones green, all ending in black, tipped white.

12. Bronzy Hermit **L-F**
Glaucis aenea 4" (10cm)
Bill 2x head, curved. *Above coppery bronze.* Below uniform cinnamon. Outer tail feathers reddish, central ones bronzy, all ending in black, tipped white.

LOWLAND HUMMINGBIRDS WITH MID-LENGTH BILL - 1

Amazilia EMERALDS - 30, 227, 228.

1. Gilded Sapphire (Hummingbird)
L-SO
Hylocharis chrysura   4" (10cm)
Bill 1¼x head, red with black tip.
Above and below *shining golden
green*. Chin pale rufous. Tail glit-
tering copper color.

2. Blue-headed Sapphire   **L-TS**
Hylocharis grayi   4" (10cm)
Bill 1¼x head, *red, tipped black*.
Entire head glittering blue. Back
shining bronze-green. Below glit-
tering green. Tail steel blue. ♀:
Below white, spotted green. Tail
pale-tipped.

3. White-chinned Sapphire   **L-TS**
Hylocharis cyanus   3½" (9cm)
Bill 1¼x head, red, tipped black.
Head purple. Back greenish be-
coming bronzy purple on rump.
Small white chin-spot usually not
visible in the field. Throat and
breast violet. Belly dark green.
Thighs white. *Tail black*.

4. Rufous-throated Sapphire   **L-FT**
Hylocharis sapphirina   3½" (9cm)
Bill 1¼x head, red, tipped black.
Above dark green. Breast glittering
violet. Belly grayish. *Tail rufous*.

5. Female: Lower bill red at base.
Above coppery green. Below
whitish speckled on breast. Tail
rufous, outer feathers tipped white.

**6. Rufous-tailed Emerald (Hum-
mingbird)**   **LM-TS**
Amazilia tzacatl   4" (10cm)
Bill 1¼x head, red, tipped black
(sometimes mostly black). Above
bronzy green. Throat and breast
glittering green. Belly gray. *Tail rufous edged bronze*.

**7. Copper-rumped Emerald (Hum-
mingbird)**   **LM-TSO**
Amazilia tobaci   4" (10cm)
Bill 1¼x head, lower red, tipped
black. Crown and upper back

bronzy green. Lower back coppery, contrasting with steel blue
tail. Below glittering green. Thighs
white.

8. Plain-bellied Emerald   **L-S**
Amazilia leucogaster   4" (10cm)
Bill 1¼x head, lower red, tipped
black. Crown glittering green.
Sides of head, neck, throat and
breast glittering golden green,
center of underparts white.

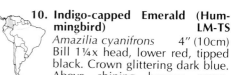

9. Glittering-throated Emerald L-TS
Amazilia fimbriata   4" (10cm)
Bill 1¼x head, lower red, tipped
black. Above shining green, coppery on rump. Throat and breast
glittering green. Belly green or dark
gray with *white line down center*.
Undertail coverts whitish. Tail central feathers green, rest black.

**10. Indigo-capped Emerald (Hum-
mingbird)**   **LM-TS**
Amazilia cyanifrons   4" (10cm)
Bill 1¼x head, lower red, tipped
black. Crown glittering dark blue.
Above shining bronzy green,
bronzier on rump. Underparts glittering emerald green. Tail steel
blue.

**11. Steely-vented Emerald (Hum-
mingbird)**   **LM-TS**
Amazilia saucerottei   3½" (9cm)
Bill 1¼x head, lower red, tipped
black. Above shining green. Below
glittering green. Thighs white. Tail
steel blue, *strongly contrasting with
green back*.

**12. Purple-chested Emerald (Hum-
mingbird)**   **L-S**
Amazilia rosenbergi   3½" (9cm)
Bill 1¼x head, lower red, tipped
black. Above green. Throat glittering green. *Breast purple*. Belly gray
with green disks. Vent white. ♀:
Throat and breast white speckled
green.

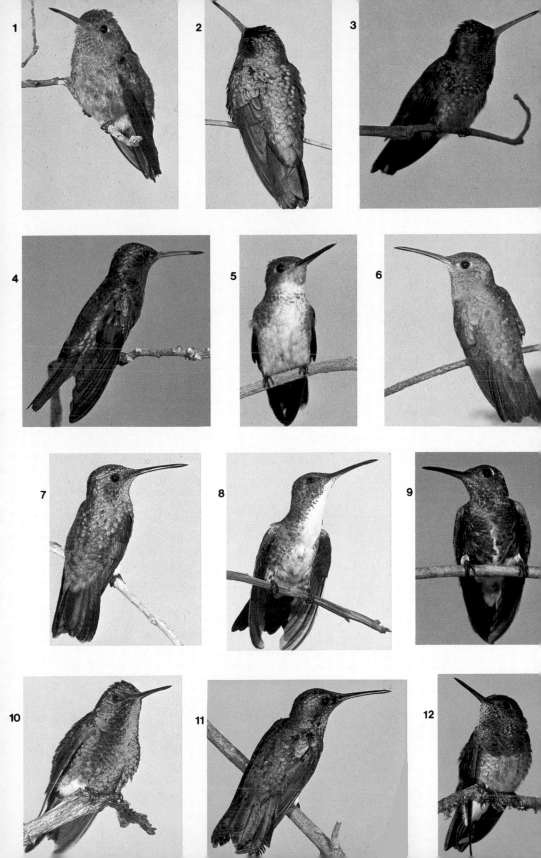

LOWLAND HUMMINGBIRDS WITH MID-LENGTH BILL - 2

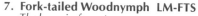

Chalybura PLUMELETEER - 228.
Thalurania WOODNYMPHS - 226.
Polytmus GOLDENTHROATS - 227.

1. **White-vented Plumeleteer   L-TS**
Chalybura buffonii   4½" (12cm)
Bill 1¼x head, slightly curved, rather heavy. Above shining green. Below green, *prominent, long undertail coverts white.* Tail blackish.

2. **Female:** Below all gray, undertail coverts like male. Tail with large white tips.

3. **White-necked Jacobin   L-FT**
Florisuga mellivora   4½" (11cm)
Bill = head, slightly curved. Head, throat and breast all blue. *White crescent on upper back.* Back dark green. Belly white. Tail mostly white, tipped black.

4. **Female:** Above green. Below white, *prominently scaled blackish on throat and breast,* green on sides. Tail green, outer feathers tipped white.

5. **Gould's Jewelfront   L-F**
Polyplancta aurescens
4½" (12cm)
Bill = head, slightly curved. Back shining green. Small chin spot black. Throat glittering green. *Broad band across breast rufous.* Below green. Tail central feathers bronze-green, rest chestnut.

6. **White-throated Hummingbird**
LM-TS
Leucochloris albicollis
4½" (11cm)
Bill = head. Above green. *Throat white.* Breast shining green. *Belly and long undertail coverts white.* Outer tail feathers dark blue with large white tips.

7. **Fork-tailed Woodnymph LM-FTS**
Thalurania furcata
4¼" (11cm) ♀: 4" (10cm)
Bill = head, curved. Crown dark green or glittering purple. Above dark green, *shoulders purple.* Throat glittering green, below glittering purple (below all green in w Ecuador). Vent white. Tail forked, blue-black.

8. **Female:** Back shining green. Below light gray, darker on belly. Vent white. Tail slightly forked, outer feathers tipped whitish.

9. **Violet-capped Woodnymph**
LM-TS
Thalurania glaucopis
4¼" (11cm)
Bill = head, crown glittering violet. Back shining green. Underparts glittering golden green. Tail forked, steel blue. ♀: Very like ♀ Fork-tailed Woodnymph (preceding) but tail more forked.

10. **Brazilian Ruby   LM-TS**
Clytolaema rubricauda
4¼" (11cm)
Bill = head. Crown glittering green. Above bronzy. *Throat glittering red.* Breast shining green. Belly grayish. *Tail bright rufous,* tipped dusky. ♀: Green above, *cinnamon below.*

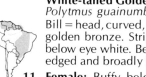

White-tailed Goldenthroat L-SO
Polytmus guainumbi 4¼" (11cm)
Bill = head, curved, reddish. Above golden bronze. Stripe behind and below eye white. Below green. Tail edged and broadly tipped white.

11. **Female:** Buffy below with green disks on throat and breast.

12. **Green-tailed Goldenthroat L-SO**
Polytmus theresiae   4" (10cm)
Bill = head, curved. Above and below glittering green. *Partial eyering white.* Lower bill red at base. *Tail shining green above and below.* ♀: Similar but smaller. Below mostly green speckled white.

LOWLAND HUMMINGBIRDS WITH MID-LENGTH BILL - 3, OR SHORT BILL.

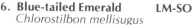

Amazilia EMERALDS - 26, 227, 228.
Lepidopyga HUMMINGBIRDS - 226, 227.
Chlorostilbon EMERALDS - 226.
Heliothryx FAIRY - 233.
Lophornis COQUETTES - 225, 226.

1. Versicolored Emerald   **L-TS**
Amazilia versicolor   3½" (9cm)
Bill = head, lower red tipped black. Above green (sometimes with blue cap) becoming more bronzy on rump. Below white (with green disks on throat and breast s of the Amazon). Tail olive.

2. White-chested Emerald   **L-TS**
Amazilia chionopectus
                3½" (9cm)
Bill = head, all black. Head shining green. Back bronzy green. Below white with green disks on sides. Tail bronzy with *dusky bar near end.*

3. Shining-green Hummingbird
                 L-TS
Lepidopyga goudoti   3½" (9cm)
Bill = head, lower red, tipped black. Above shining green. Below glittering green, undertail coverts white. *Tail* steel blue, *forked.*

4. Glittering-bellied Emerald
                LM-SO
Chlorostilbon aureoventris
              3" (8cm)
Bill = head, pink, tipped dusky. Very small. Crown and belly glittering bronzy green. Throat and breast glittering blue-green. Tail steel blue, slightly forked.

5. Red-billed Emerald   **LM-S**
Chlorostilbon gibsoni   3" (8cm)
Bill = head, lower red, tipped black. Very small. Above green. Below glittering green. Tail steel blue, quite forked, longer than in next species. ♀: *Eyebrow whitish.* Tail broadly tipped white. Underparts whitish.

6. Blue-tailed Emerald   **LM-SO**
Chlorostilbon mellisugus
              3" (8cm)
Bill ¾x head, *all black.* Very small. Above and below glittering green. Tail steel blue, slightly forked.

7. Female: Eyebrow white. *Black mask through eye.* Below light gray. Tail blue.

8. Violet-bellied Hummingbird L-TS
Damophila julie   3" (8cm)
Bill = head, lower flesh color. Above shining green. Throat glittering green. *Below glittering violet.* Tail steel blue, graduated, not forked. ♀: Above shining green. Below pale gray, speckled green at sides of breast. Tail steel blue, outer feather pale-tipped.

9. Blue-chinned Sapphire   **L-TS**
Chlorestes notatus   3½" (9cm)
Bill = head, lower reddish, tipped dusky. Above green. Below glittering green. Thighs white. Tail steel blue.

10. Female: Underparts whitish, speckled green, center of belly white. Tail *not tipped.*

11. Purple-crowned Fairy   **L-FT**
Heliothryx barroti   4" (10cm)
Bill ⅔x head. Crown glittering purple. Above shining green. *Area below eye black. Underparts pure white.* Tail deeply forked, outer feathers white, central ones dark blue. ♀: Lacks purple crown.

Tufted Coquette [1]   **L-TS**
Lophornis ornata   2¾" (7cm)
Bill ⅔x head, flesh colored, tipped dusky. Very small. Crown, crest and plumes at sides of head rufous. Back green with *white band across rump.* Underparts shining green.

12. Female: Lacks crest and plumes. Green above with *buff band across rump.* Below rufous. Tail coppery.

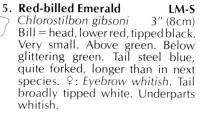

HIGHLAND HUMMINGBIRDS WITH LONG BILL.

Doryfera LANCEBILL - 223.
Coeligena STARFRONTLETS *and INCAS* - 230.

1. Sword-billed Hummingbird
MH-FT
Ensifera ensifera   8″ (20cm)
Bill 3x head. Amazingly long bill unmistakable. Above greenish. Throat blackish. Breast glittering green. Belly grayish. Usually perches with bill pointed nearly straight up.

2. Tooth-billed Hummingbird LM-F
Androdon aequatorialis 5″ (13cm)
Bill 2x head, *slightly upcurved.* Above bronze green. *Prominent white band* across rump. Below whitish strongly streaked dusky on throat and breast. Tail blackish, tipped white.

3. Green-fronted Lancebill   MH-F
Doryfera ludoviciae   5″ (13cm)
Bill 2x head, *thin.* Above bronzy green with strikingly *long straight bill.* Forehead glittering green. Below uniform greenish brown. Tail black, outer feathers tipped gray.

4. Buff-winged Starfrontlet   H-FT
Coeligena lutetiae   5½″ (14cm)
Bill 1½x head. Forehead glittering green. Above black with blue rump. *Buff patch on wing,* conspicuous when perched and in flight. *Throat spot glittering violet.* Below glittering green. Tail dark green.

5. White-tailed Starfrontlet MH-FT
Coeligena phalerata   5″ (13cm)
Bill 1¼x head. Crown glittering blue. Back dark green. Throat glittering purple. *Tail pure white.*

Female: Green above. Below uniform cinnamon rufous. Tail bronzy, outer feathers tipped buff.

7. Brown Inca   LM-FT
Coeligena wilsoni   4¼″ (11cm)
Bill 1½x head. Above reddish brown tinged green. Underparts dark grayish brown, conspicuous *white spot at each side of breast.* Throat glittering violet. Tail bronze.

8. Bronzy Inca   LM-FT
Coeligena coeligena   5″ (13cm)
Bill 1½x head. Above shining reddish brown tinged green. *Throat whitish speckled brown.* Below brown. Tail dusky.

9. Collared Inca   MH-FTS
Coeligena torquata   5″ (13cm)
Bill 1½x head. Above and below blackish (or shining green in some races). *Large breast patch white* (cinnamon in some races). All but central tail feathers white, broadly green at ends. ♀: Green above. Throat white with green disks. Breast white. Belly gray.

10. White-tailed Hillstar   M-FT
Urochroa bougueri   5″ (13cm)
Bill 1½x head. *Rufous line at base of bill* (not present e of the Andes). Back purplish or greenish. Throat and breast glittering blue. Belly dark gray with shining green disks. Tail mostly white, central and outer pairs black.

11. Mountain Velvetbreast   MH-TS
Lafresnaya lafresnayi 4¼″ (11cm)
Bill 1¼x head, thin, curved. Above shining green. Throat and breast shining green. Belly velvety black. All but central tail feathers white or buffy, broadly tipped black.

12. Female: Below white, speckled green.

HIGHLAND HUMMINGBIRDS WITH MID-LENGTH BILL - 1.

Colibri VIOLETEARS - 225.
Heliodoxa BRILLIANTS - 229.
Aglaeactis SUNBEAMS - 230.
Campylopterus SABREWINGS - 24, 224.

Great Sapphirewing   **H-TS**
Pterophanes cyanopterus
7½" (19cm)

Bill = head. Large. Has slow wing-beat when flying. Dark green. Wings dark blue. Tail black, forked.

1. **Female:** Head brown. Back shining green. Below cinnamon with green disks on sides.

2. **Sparkling Violetear**   **MH-SO**
Colibri coruscans   5½" (14cm)
Bill = head. Above and below shining green. *Chin, ear coverts and patch on belly purple.* Undertail coverts green. Tail shining green with *dusky bar near end.*

3. **White-vented Violetear LMH-SO**
Colibri serrirostris   5" (13cm)

Bill = head. Above and below shining green. Ear coverts purple. *Glittering violet mark below cheek. Undertail coverts white.* Tail shining green with *dusky bar near end.*

4. **Empress Brilliant**   **M-F**
Heliodoxa imperatrix 5½" (14cm)
Bill = head. Above dark green. Spot on throat glittering violet. Breast and belly glittering green. *Tail dark bronzy, long, deeply forked,* extends about 2 cm beyond folded wings.

5. **Green-crowned Brilliant**   **LM-FT**
Heliodoxa jacula   4½" (12cm)

Bill = head. Crown glittering green. Back green. *Glittering purple spot on throat.* Tail steel blue, forked, extends about 1 cm beyond folded wings.

6. **Female:** Above coppery green. Prominent white line below eye. Below white *densely spotted green.* Tail steel blue, tipped white, forked.

Black-throated Brilliant   **LM-TS**
Heliodoxa schreibersii
5½" (14cm)
Bill = head. Above shining green. Underparts black, patch on lower throat glittering purple. Tail steel blue, well-forked.

7. **Female:** Like ♂ but has long white (sometimes rufous) line under eye.

8. **Fawn-breasted Brilliant**   **M-FT**
Heliodoxa rubinoides
4¼" (11cm)
Bill = head. Above green. Below brownish with green disks at sides and small glittering violet spot on throat.

9. **Shining Sunbeam**   **H-SO**
Aglaeactis cupripennis
4½" (12cm)
Bill = head. Above buffy brown, rump glittering green. Underparts and sides of head rufous, sometimes with dusky marks on throat. Tail bronzy.

10. **Lazuline Sabrewing**   **MH-TS**
Campylopterus falcatus
4½" (12cm)
Bill = head, curved. Above glittering green. Throat and breast glittering blue. Belly green. *Tail chestnut.*

11. **Female:** Above glittering green (white line under eye in some races). Throat green. Below gray.

12. **Whitetip**   **M-FTS**
Urosticte benjamini   3½" (9cm)
Bill = head. Above shining green. Spot behind eye white. Throat glittering green or purple. Breast whitish, belly gray, *all thickly spotted green.* Tail dusky, *central feathers tipped white.* ♀: Below white, spotted green. Outer tail feather tipped white.

HIGHLAND HUMMINGBIRDS WITH MID-LENGTH BILL - 2, OR SHORT BILL.

Eriocnemis PUFFLEGS - 231.
Haplophaedia PUFFLEGS - 231.
Boissonneaua CORONETS - 230.

1. **Long-tailed   (Sapphire-vented)
   Puffleg   MH-TS**
   Eriocnemis luciani   4½" (12cm)
   Bill = head. Above shining green.
   Below glittering green. Undertail
   coverts glittering purple. Tail long,
   black, *deeply forked*. Leg puffs
   white.

2. **Glowing Puffleg   H-TS**
   Eriocnemis vestitus   4" (10cm)
   Bill = head. Dark green. Rump glittering golden green. Throat glittering purple. Below glittering green,
   vent glittering purple. Leg puffs
   white. Tail forked.

3. **Female:** Breast buff with green
   disks. Belly whitish with glittering
   green disks.

4. **Golden-breasted Puffleg   H-S**
   Eriocnemis mosquera   5" (13cm)
   Bill = head. Above green. Below
   glittering coppery green, tinged
   golden on breast. Throat glittering
   green. Tail long, forked, blackish.
   Large leg puffs white.

5. **Coppery-bellied Puffleg MH-TS**
   Eriocnemis cupreoventris
                          3½" (9cm)
   Bill = head. Above green. Breast
   glittering green. *Belly golden copper*. Undertail coverts purple. Tail
   black. Leg puffs white.

   Greenish Puffleg   M-FT
   Haplophaedia aureliae 4" (10cm)
   Bill = head. Above shining coppery
   green, crown and face tinged more
   coppery. Below green. Prominent
   leg puffs white. Tail blue-black.

6. **Female:** Belly grayish with green
   disks mostly on sides.

7. **Colorful Puffleg   MH-TS**
   Eriocnemis mirabilis   3½" (9cm)
   Bill = head. Above shining green.
   Forehead glittering emerald green.
   Throat and breast blue-green. Belly
   glittering blue. Vent glittering red.
   Large leg puffs white tipped cin-
   namon. Tail bronzy.

8. **Female:** Below white, throat and
   breast with greenish disks.

9. **Buff-tailed Coronet   MH-FT**
   Boissonneaua flavescens
                          4¼" (11cm)
   Bill ⅔x head. Crown glittering
   green. Small white spot behind
   eye. Back green. Throat and breast
   glittering green. Belly buff with
   green disks. Thighs white. *Tail buff
   tipped dusky*, central feathers
   bronze.

10. **Female:** Throat and breast mostly
    green, some buff showing through.
    Belly whitish in center with green
    disks on sides.

11. **Wedge-billed Hummingbird
                           MH-FT**
    Schistes geoffroyi   3½" (9cm)
    Bill ⅔x head. Above bronzy green,
    white streak behind eye. Throat
    glittering green. Belly gray with
    green disks. Patches at sides of
    breast white. Tail bronzy with blue
    band near end. ♀: Like ♂ (or with
    throat white w of Andes).

12. **Speckled Hummingbird   M-FT**
    Adelomyia melanogenys
                           3½" (9cm)
    Bill ¾x head. Above shining green.
    *Prominent whitish streak behind
    eye*. Cheeks dusky. Below whitish,
    speckled dusky on throat and
    upper breast. Tail blackish, tipped
    white or buff.

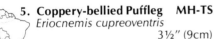

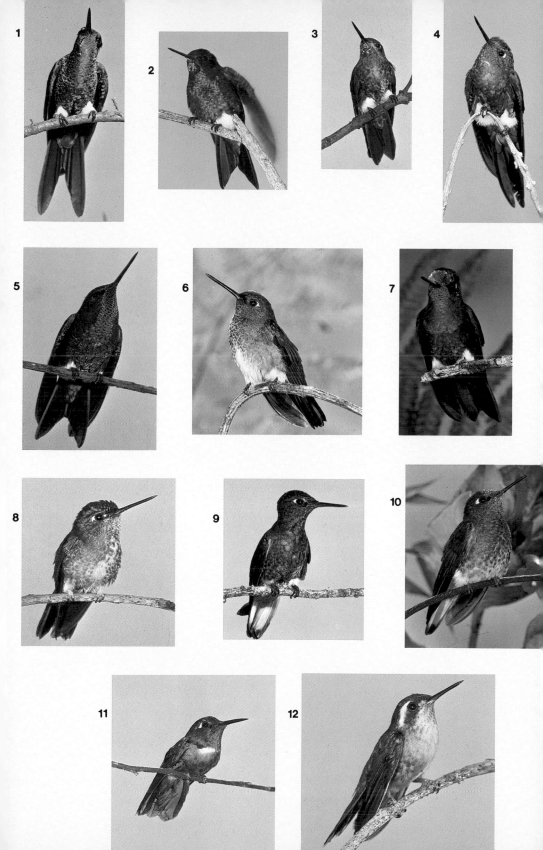

HIGHLAND HUMMINGBIRDS WITH VERY SHORT BILL.

Lesbia TRAINBEARERS - 232.
Heliangelus SUNANGELS - 231.
Metallura METALTAILS - 232.
Ramphomicron THORNBILLS (see also *Chalcostigma*) 232, 233.

1. **Long-tailed Sylph**   **LM-FT**
Aglaiocercus kingi
     up to 7" (18 cm); ♀ 4" (10 cm)
Bill ⅔x head. *Crown glittering green.* Back dark green. Below bronzy green with small glittering blue spot on throat. *Tail very long, deeply forked, shining blue or green above, underside blackish.*

2. **Female:** *Below cinnamon.* Throat white, spotted green. Tail normal length, forked, outer feathers broadly tipped white.

Violet-tailed Sylph   **L-TS**
Aglaiocercus coelestis
          7" (18cm); ♀ 4" (10 cm)
Bill ⅔x head. Above dark green, bluish on lower back. Below bronzy green with large glittering blue spot on throat. *Tail very long, deeply forked, violet.*

3. **Female:** Crown glittering blue. Throat white, speckled green. *Breast white.* Below rufous. Tail normal length.

4. **Green-tailed Trainbearer**
          MH-FTS
Lesbia nuna
          6½" (16 cm); ♀: 5" (13cm)
Bill ½x head. Above shining green, no glittering crown or throat. Below green. White leg puffs. Tail about as long as body, black with green tips. ♀: Below white, thickly spotted green. Tail like male but much shorter.

5. **Booted Racket-Tail**   **MH-FT**
Ocreatus underwoodii
          4½" (12 cm); ♀: 3½" (9cm)
Bill ½x head. Above shining green. Throat and breast glittering green. Leg puffs white. Tail long, forked, ending in *blackish rackets.*

6. **Female:** *Below white* lightly spotted green. Tail normal length, forked, outer feathers black, tipped white.

7. **Amethyst-throated Sunangel**
          MH-FT
Heliangelus amethysticollis
          4" (10cm)
Bill ½x head. Forehead glittering green. Above shining green. Throat purple. *Band across breast white,* bordered below by glittering green band. Below buff. Outer tail feathers blue black. ♀: Throat black.

8. **Tourmaline Sunangel**   **MH-F**
Heliangelus exortis   4¼" (11cm)
Bill ½x head. Above dark green. *Throat glittering purple.* Breast glittering green. Belly dusky with green disks. Undertail coverts white. *Tail rather long, forked.* ♀: *Throat white* speckled dusky (occasionally all white). Belly dark gray.

9. **Tyrian Metaltail**   **MH-TS**
Metallura tyrianthina   3½" (9cm)
Bill ½x head. Above shining green. White spot behind eye. Throat glittering green. Below green with gray base of feathers showing through. *Tail shining coppery purple.*

10. **Female:** Above shining green. Throat and breast rufous with small black dots on throat. Belly white spotted black and rufous. Tail shining purple.

11. **Purple-backed Thornbill** **MH-FT**
Ramphomicron microrhynchum
          3½" (9cm)
Bill ⅓x head. *Above shining purple.* Throat glittering green. Below bronzy green. Tail rather long, blackish, forked.

12. **Female:** Above green. Underparts white with green disks. Tail black, slightly forked, outer feathers broadly tipped white.

Surucua Trogon   LM-FT
Trogon surrucura   10" (26cm)
Bill greenish. *Head and breast blue*. Back coppery green, wing coverts freckled black and white. Belly red. Central tail feathers blue, outers mostly white.

1. **Female:** Slaty gray, wing coverts black finely barred white. Belly red. Tail white on outer web of outer feathers.

Masked Trogon   MH-FT
Trogon personatus   10" (26cm)
Bill greenish yellow. *No noticeable eye-ring*. Face and throat black. Upperparts and breast golden green with narrow white band across breast. Belly red. Tail finely barred white.

2. **Female:** *Bill all yellow.* Upperparts and breast brown. *Face and throat black* with conspicuous small white spot behind eye. Belly pink.

3. **Collared Trogon   LM-FT**
Trogn collaris   9" (24cm)
Very like ♂ Masked Trogon (preceding) but tail bars broader. ♀: Very like ♀ Masked Trogon but face is only blackish instead of deep black and upper bill is dusky, not all yellow.

4. **Black-throated Trogon   L-FT**
Trogon rufus   10" (26cm)
Bill greenish. Above coppery green. Wings black with fine wavy white lines. *Eye-ring light blue*. Throat black. Breast greenish. Belly yellow.

5. **Female:** Upperparts, throat and breast brown. Belly yellow. Outer tail feathers barred black and white. *It is the only brown trogon with yellow belly.*

6. **White-tailed Trogon   LM-TS**
Trogon viridis   10" (26cm)
Head and breast violet, cheeks and throat black. *Eye-ring blue*. Back green. Rump blue. Belly yellow. Tail shows much white below.

7. **Female:** Gray with yellow belly. Wings narrowly barred white.

8. **Violaceous Trogon   L-FT**
Trogon violaceus   9" (22cm)
Head and throat purple-blue bordered below by narrow white band on breast. *Eye-ring bright yellow.* Back metallic greenish. Belly yellow. Tail with narrow white bars. ♀: Has conspicuous ring of white feathers around eye.

9. **Blue-crowned Motmot   L-TS**
Momotus momota   16" (40cm)
Crown and sides of head black, surrounded by shining blue. Above green to olive brown. Below olive green to cinnamon rufous. Small black spot on breast. Tail long, blue above, dusky below, *ending in rackets.*

10. **Rufous Motmot   L-FT**
Baryphthengus ruficapillus
                      16" (40cm)
Bill serrated, not flat. Back green. Head rufous with black mask. *Underparts rufous* except small black spot on breast (or underparts olive with broad rufous band across belly in se part of range). Vent greenish. Tail long, greenish, with rackets in nw (without rackets in se).

11. **Broad-billed Motmot   L-FT**
Electron platyrhynchum
                      14" (35cm)
Bill flat, broad, not serrated. Back green. Head rufous with black mask. Throat and breast rufous. *Belly greenish.* Tail long, greenish; has rackets only w of Andes.

12. **Tody Motmot   L-F**
Hylomanes momotula
                      6½" (17cm)
Bill very heavy for such a small bird. Crown and nape chestnut. *Eyebrow blue.* Ear coverts black *bordered below by white stripe.* Back dull green. Below brownish. Throat and center of belly whitish. Tail short, greenish; *no* rackets.

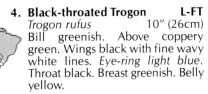

RIDGELY

Kingfishers have long sharp bills. Jacamars have long thin bills.

(Various) KINGFISHERS - 236.
(Various) JACAMARS - 236.

1. Ringed Kingfisher   LMH-W
Ceryle torquata   15" (38cm)
Large size, crested. *Above blue-gray.* Spot before eye, throat and collar white. Below all chestnut. Tail blackish, spotted or banded white. ♀: Has blue-gray band across breast. Belly chestnut.

Amazon Kingfisher   L-W
Chloroceryle amazona
                         10" (26cm)
Above dark green with few or no white spots on wings. Throat and collar white. Below white with broad chestnut band across breast. Similar to male Green Kingfisher but larger and with less white on wings and tail.

2. Female: Chestnut band replaced by green spots or broken green band.

3. Green Kingfisher   LM-W
Chloroceryle americana
                         7½" (19cm)
Above dark green with *many small white spots on wings.* Breast chestnut. Belly spotted green. Tail with much white on sides which flashes conspicuously in flight.

4. Female: Lacks chestnut band, has instead two narrow green bands across breast.

5. Green-and-rufous Kingfisher
                         L-WFT
Chloroceryle inda   8" (20cm)
Above dark green with small white spots on wings. Collar orange buff. Below all orange rufous. Tail with sparse white barring. ♀: Like male but has green and white breast band.

6. Pygmy Kingfisher   L-WFT
Chloroceryle aenea   4½" (12cm)
Sparrow size. Above dark green. Below rich rufous, center of belly white.

7. Female: Has green breast band.

8. Paradise Jacamar   L-FT
Galbula dea   12½" (31cm)
Very dark looking. Crown brown. Above shining greenish black. Throat white. Breast and belly black. *Tail very long, pointed,* blackish.

9. Rufous-tailed Jacamar   L-TS
Galbula ruficauda   9" (23cm)
Crown, back and breast shining green. Chin white (black w of Andes). Throat white. Below rufous. Tail green above, *rufous below.* ♀: Throat buffy.

10. White-chinned Jacamar   L-F
Galbula tombacea   8" (20cm)
Crown brown. Above green. *Only chin white.* Throat and breast green. Central tail feathers green, outers rufous, tipped bronze.

Yellow-billed Jacamar   L-FT
Galbula albirostris   7" (18cm)
Bill yellow with more or less black on ridge of upper bill. Crown blue or purple. Back, wings and central tail feathers metallic golden green. Throat white, below rufous or chestnut.

11. Female: Lacks white on throat.

1. White-fronted Nunbird   LM-F
Monasa morphoeus   11" (28cm)
Dark slaty gray, head and neck
blacker. *Bill bright red,* slender,
curved. *Forehead and chin white*
(only forehead white in nw Colombia). Tail black.

2. Black-fronted Nunbird   L-F
Monasa nigrifrons   11" (27cm)
All blackish gray, blacker on fore-
head. Bill red, slender, curved.

3. Yellow-billed Nunbird   LM-F
Monasa flaviorostris 10" (25cm)
All black except more or less white
on wing coverts. Bill slender, yellow, curved.

4. Moustached Puffbird   LM-F
Malacoptila mystacalis 8" (20cm)
Upper bill black, lower greenish.
Eye red. *Prominent white forehead
and whiskers.* Above brown with
buff spots on back and wings.
Below rufous, unstreaked, becom-
ing duller on belly.

5. Crescent-chested Puffbird LM-F
Malacoptila striata   8" (20 cm)
Bill black. Crown and back brown,
streaked buff. Lores and eyebrow
buff. Below brown becoming paler
on belly. Two narrow bands on
breast—white above, black below.

6. White-whiskered Puffbird   L-FT
Malacoptila panamensis
                        7½" (19cm)
Upper bill black, lower part of
lower bill yellowish. Above rufous
brown, lightly spotted buffy. Throat

and breast cinnamon. White whiskers not very prominent. Belly
whitish streaked brown.

7. Spot-backed Puffbird   LM-TSO
Nystalus maculatus   7½" (19cm)
Above dark brown spotted buff.
Throat white. Lower throat or-
ange. Rest of underparts white
spotted black.

8. White-eared Puffbird   LM-TSO
Nystalus chacuru   7½" (19cm)
Bill red. Above brownish, collar
white. Ear coverts and lores white,
surrounded by black. Underparts
whitish.

9. Sooty-capped Puffbird   L-FT
Bucco noanamae   7" (18cm)
Bill heavy, hooked. Above dark
brown, feathers fringed buff. Forehead and eyebrow grayish. Throat
white. Breast blackish brown. Belly
white spotted blackish.

10. Spotted Puffbird   L-FT
Bucco tamatia   6½" (17cm)
Bill heavy, hooked. Above brown,
spotted fulvous on back. Narrow
collar white. Throat orange. Below
white, heavily spotted black.

11. Chestnut-capped Puffbird   L-FT
Bucco macrodactylus 5½" (14cm)
Bill heavy, hooked. Crown chestnut. Collar rufous. Back brown
spotted whitish. Throat and breast
white with black band across lower
throat. Belly buffy, lightly barred
dusky. Tail brown.

12. Gray-cheeked Nunlet   L-FT
Nonnula ruficapilla   5½" (14cm)
Bill relatively heavy, curved, gray,
tipped black. Crown reddish
brown. *Narrow eye-ring red.* Back
brown. Cheeks gray. Underparts
cinnamon, center of belly white.

Capito BARBETS - 238.
Eubucco BARBETS - 238, 239.

1. **Swallow-Wing**   **LM-TSO**
Chelidoptera tenebrosa
5½" (14cm)
Bill slender, curved, black. Back blackish, *rump white.* Breast blackish. Belly cinnamon.

2. **Spot-crowned Barbet**   **L-F**
Capito maculicoronatus
6½" (16cm)
Forehead, face, nape, back and wings black. *Crown brown spotted white.* Below white with yellow band across breast, *flanks spotted black and red.*

3. **Female:** Like male but throat and breast also black.

4. **Black-spotted Barbet**   **L-FT**
Capito niger   6½" (16cm)
Crown yellow or orange or red. Eyebrow yellow. *Back black streaked yellow.* Face black. Throat orange (scarlet in some races). Underparts creamy yellow, lightly spotted black on flanks.

5. **Female:** *Above yellow spotted black.* Cheeks streaked black and white. Throat orange. Below yellow, *heavily spotted black on breast and sides,* belly paler yellow.

6. **Scarlet-crowned Barbet**   **L-F**
Capito aurovirens   6½" (16cm)
Crown and nape red. Back olive. Chin white. Throat and breast orange. Belly olive.

7. **Female:** *Crown and nape whitish* instead of red. Breast yellow.

Lemon-throated Barbet   **L-F**
Eubucco richardsoni   6" (15cm)
Top, sides of head and chin red (or black in Colombia and Peru n of the Marañon River). Nape blue (or yellowish green in Brazil and s Peru). Back green. *Throat yellow. Breast orange.*

8. **Female:** Above greenish olive. Sides of face black. Throat gray, breast orange yellow. Belly grayish olive.

9. **Red-headed Barbet**   **LM-FT**
Eubucco bourcierii   5½" (14cm)
Bill yellow. *Whole head, throat and upper breast red,* bordered on back by narrow bluish white collar. Back and tail green. Lower breast orange. Belly yellowish.

10. **Female:** Has no red. Forehead black. Crown yellow shading to green on back. *Cheeks blue.* Throat gray. Breast yellow. Belly whitish, streaked green.

ALL HAVE VERY LARGE BILLS

Ramphastos TOUCANS - 241.
Pteroglossus ARAÇARIS - 239, 240.
Aulacorhynchus TOUCANETS - 239.

1. Toco Toucan   **L-T**
Ramphastos toco   21" (53cm)
Mainly black. *Bill orange* with large black oval spot near tip. Crown brownish. Throat, upper breast and rump white. Vent red.

2. Keel-billed Toucan   **LM-FT**
Ramphastos sulfuratus
         20" (50cm)
Mainly black. Upper bill green, tipped red. Lower bill light blue, green at base. Crown and upper back brownish. Rump white. Throat and breast deep yellow, bordered below by narrow red band. Undertail coverts red.

3. Citron-throated Toucan   **LM-F**
Ramphastos citreolaemus
         21" (52cm)
Mainly black. Bill black, ridge and base yellow or light blue. Rump yellow. Throat and upper breast pale yellow, bordered below by narrow red band. Belly black. Undertail coverts red.

4. Channel-billed Toucan   **L-F**
Ramphastos vitellinus 18" (45cm)
Mostly black. *Bill all black* except blue at base. Bare skin around eye red or blue. Throat white or yellow. *Rump and vent both red.* Breast orange-yellow, bordered below by red band. Belly black.

5. Many-banded Araçari   **L-FT**
Pteroglossus pluricinctus
         17" (43cm)
Upper bill white with black on ridge. Lower bill black. Above black. Rump crimson. Area around eye blue. Throat black. Lower underparts yellow crossed by *two* mostly black bands.

6. Ivory-billed Araçari   **L-FT**
Pteroglossus flavirostris
         17" (43cm)
Bill ivory white with black "teeth" along upper cutting edge and brownish mark on lower bill. Head and throat dark brown. Back and tail dull green. *Breast red, lower breast black.* Belly yellow.

7. Collared Araçari   **L-FT**
Pteroglossus torquatus 17" (43cm)
Upper bill ivory white, ridge black. Lower bill black. Bill outlined with white at base. Area around eye red. Above black with chestnut collar and red rump. Throat black. Below yellow with *black spot on breast.* Band across belly black in middle, red at sides.

8. Pale-mandibled Araçari   **L-FT**
Pteroglossus erythropygius
         18" (45cm)
Very like Collared Araçari (above) but upper bill has black stripe on lower (cutting) edge and lower bill is blackish only at end.

9. Stripe-billed Araçari   **L-FT**
Pteroglossus sanguineus
         15" (38cm)
Very like Collared Araçari (above) but has *black stripe on middle of upper bill.* Lacks chestnut collar.

10. Crimson-rumped Toucanet   **LM-FT**
Aulacorhynchus haematopygus
         17" (42cm)
Green. *Bill dark red* with some black marks. Rump crimson. Undertail coverts chestnut. Central tail feathers tipped chestnut.

11. Emerald Toucanet   **LMH-FT**
Aulacorhynchus prasinus
         14" (35cm)
Green. Bill mostly black, yellow on top, lined white at base. Throat white, gray, blue or black, in different races. Undertail coverts and tips of all tail feathers chestnut.

1

2

3

4

5

6

7

8

9

10

11

Melanerpes woodpeckers do not have whiskers.

1. **Lineated Woodpecker   LM-TS**
Dryocopus lineatus   14" (34cm)
Above black. Crown, crest and whisker crimson. Line through eye black. White lines from bill *do not meet* on back. *Throat streaked.* Underparts barred or spotted dusky and whitish. ♀: No red except on nape.

Crimson-crested Woodpecker
Campephilus melanoleucos **LM-FT**
14" (34cm)

Crown, crest and sides of head crimson. Spot on cheek black and white. *Area at base of bill white.* White stripes down sides of neck join in a "V" on back. Back, wings, throat, breast and tail black. Belly barred black and whitish.

2. **Female:** Broad white stripe below eye.

3. **Chestnut Woodpecker   L-FT**
Celeus elegans   10" (26cm)
Long crest chestnut. Back chestnut without obvious barring. Rump yellow. Whisker and area under eye red. Underparts lighter chestnut. Vent yellowish. Tail black. ♀: No whisker.

4. **Blond-crested Woodpecker L-FT**
Celeus flavescens   8" (21cm)
Head and long bushy crest yellowish buff. Whisker red (♀ lacking). Back buff, barred or spotted blackish. Rump yellowish buff. Below blackish or brown.

5. **Cinnamon Woodpecker   L-F**
Celeus loricatus   8" (21cm)
Head and short bushy crest cinnamon or chestnut. Back and wings cinnamon heavily or lightly barred black. Throat and whiskers red. Below heavily barred white and black or cinnamon lightly spotted black. Tail black barred white or yellowish.

6. **Female:** Lacks red throat and whiskers.

Andean Flicker   MH-O
Colaptes rupicola   13" (32cm)
Crown gray. Back barred black and buff. Rump white. Below white, spotted black on breast. Tail black, barred on edges.

7. **Female:** Whisker all gray.

Field Flicker   L-TO
Colaptes campestroides
12" (30cm)

Above black, barred white on back and wings. Throat white. Whisker red. Cheeks and breast yellow. Belly white barred black.

8. **Female:** Whisker dusky.

9. **White Woodpecker   LM-TO**
Leuconerpes candidus 9" (24cm)
Head, rump and underparts white. Line across nape, spot on breast and center of belly yellow. Back, line through eye, wings and tail blackish.

10. **Crimson-mantled Woodpecker**
MH-FT
Piculus rivolii   10" (26cm)
Above crimson. Cheeks yellowish white. Whisker red (♀ lacking). Throat black. Breast barred black and whitish. Belly yellow.

11. **Yellow-tufted Woodpecker L-TS**
Melanerpes cruentatus
7½" (19cm)
Black. Forecrown red (♂ only). Eye-brow white. Band across nape yellow. Rump white. Belly red, sides barred black and white.

12. **Red-crowned Woodpecker**
LM-TS
Melanerpes rubricapillus
6½" (17cm)
Crown (♂ only) and nape red. Forehead yellow. Back barred black and white. Rump white. Cheeks and underparts pale grayish, darker on belly.

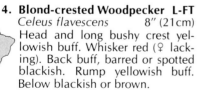

Veniliornis woodpeckers do not have whiskers.

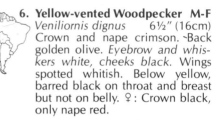

Green-barred Woodpecker
LM-TSO

Chrysoptilus melanochloros
                    10" (25cm)

Forecrown black. Hindcrown, nape and whisker red. Sides of head white. Back barred black and yellowish green, rump brighter and yellower. Throat yellowish finely streaked black. Below greenish spotted black. Tail black barred yellowish.

1. **Female:** Whisker black dotted white.

2. **Spot-breasted Woodpecker L-TS**
Chrysoptilus punctigula
                    8" (20cm)
Forecrown black. Hindcrown, nape and whiskers red. Back olive-yellow, spotted black. *Sides of head white.* Breast olive or reddish. *Below yellow spotted black.* Tail blackish, outer feathers brownish, barred black. ♀: Only nape red.

3. **Golden-olive Woodpecker**
LM-FTS

Piculus rubiginosus   8" (20cm)
Forecrown dark gray, hindcrown and nape red (or whole crown and nape red in some races). Whiskers red. Back olive. *Sides of head white.* Throat blackish. Below olive, barred yellowish. Tail black, outer feathers brownish, pale-barred.

4. **Female:** Lacks red whiskers.

5. **Red-stained Woodpecker   L-TS**
Veniliornis affinis   6½" (17cm)
Crown red. Nape or collar shows more or less yellow. Above golden olive, red on wing coverts not obvious. Below all barred dark olive and whitish. Tail barred black and

olive. ♀: Crown brown. Yellow on nape more pronounced.

6. **Yellow-vented Woodpecker M-F**
Veniliornis dignus   6½" (16cm)
Crown and nape crimson. Back golden olive. *Eyebrow and whiskers white, cheeks black.* Wings spotted whitish. Below yellow, barred black on throat and breast but not on belly. ♀: Crown black, only nape red.

7. **Red-rumped Woodpecker L-FTS**
Veniliornis kirkii   6½" (16cm)
Crown red. Nape yellow. Upperparts golden olive. *Rump red.* Below barred dark olive and whitish. Tail blackish.

8. **Female:** Lacks red on crown but has extensive red rump.

9. **Smoky-brown Woodpecker**
MH-FT
Veniliornis fumigatus   6" (15cm)
Uniform brown. Crown red. Area around eye whitish. Tail black. ♀: Crown dark brown instead of red.

10. **Little Woodpecker   L-TS**
Veniliornis passerinus   6" (15cm)
Forecrown gray. Hindcrown red. No yellow on nape. Back olive-yellow. Wing coverts spotted yellow. Whiskers white. Below olive barred whitish. Tail black, outer feathers sometimes barred olive. ♀: Crown olive, dotted whitish.

11. **Scarlet-backed Woodpecker**
L-TSA
Veniliornis callonotus   5" (13cm)
Crown and *back scarlet.* Cheeks gray. Below whitish, finely (and sometimes faintly) barred on breast. Tail black, outer feathers whitish barred dusky. ♀: Crown black surrounded at back by white.

Picumnus PICULETS - 241, 242. *Campylorhamphus* SCYTHEBILLS - 247.

1. **Mottled Piculet**   **LM-T**
Picumnus nebulosus   4" (10cm)
Forecrown crimson, hindcrown black dotted white. Back brown. Throat whitish. *Breast brown,* rest of underparts buff, *streaked black.*
♀ : Crown all brown dotted white.

2. **Rufous-breasted Piculet**   **L-FT**
Picumnus rufiventris   3½" (9cm)
Crown black dotted red. Back dark olive with rufous collar. Wings olive. *Below rufous.*

3. **Chestnut Piculet**   **L-SA**
Picumnus cinnamomeus 3" (8cm)
Forehead broadly white. Hindcrown black, spotted yellow. *Back and underparts all chestnut.* ♀ : Hindcrown spotted white.

4. **White-barred Piculet**   **L-T**
Picumnus cirrhatus   3" (8cm)
Crown red. Back brown (grayish brown in e Brazil). Underparts white *barred black.*

5. **Olivaceous Piculet**   **LM-TS**
Picumnus olivaceus   3" (8cm)
Forecrown black dotted orange (♀ white). *Back olive.* Throat whitish. Breast light brown. *Belly yellowish olive lightly streaked dusky.*

6. **Plain-breasted Piculet**   **L-T**
Picumnus castelnau   3" (8cm)
Crown black dotted red (♀ white). Back obscurely barred but appears plain dusky olive at a distance. Underparts plain pale yellow.

7. **Arrowhead Piculet**   **L-TS**
Picumnus minutissimus 3" (8cm)
Crown dotted red. Above grayish brown, *mantle with a few white spots.* Underparts whitish, feathers margined black, giving *scaled appearance.*

8. **Female:** Like ♂ but crown dotted white instead of red.

9. **Scaled Piculet**   **LM-FT**
Picumnus squamulatus 3" (8cm)
Crown dotted red. Above olive brown, feathers of back and wing coverts edged black producing scaled effect. Below whitish, feathers margined with black, giving scaled appearance. Very like Arrowhead Piculet. Separate by range.

10. **Greater Scythebill**   **M-F**
Campylorhamphus pucheranii
             9" (22cm)
Bill 1½x head, curved, brownish. Back brown. *Prominent white line under eye.* Rump, wings and tail rufous. Below brown, *not streaked.*

11. **Black-billed Scythebill**   **LM-F**
Campylorhamphus falcularius
             8" (21cm)
Bill 2x head, *much curved, blackish.* Crown black, streaked whitish. Wings and tail rufous. Throat white. Breast brown streaked buff.

12. **Red-billed Scythebill**   **LM-T**
Campylorhamphus trochilirostris
           7½" (19cm)
Bill 2x head, *much curved, reddish.* Crown and back brownish narrowly streaked buff. Wings and tail rufous. Throat whitish. Below brown, streaked whitish on breast. Race w of Andes is much smaller, otherwise the same.

STRONGLY STREAKED OR SPOTTED ON TOP OR SIDES OF HEAD
(Woodcreepers climb trees and are brown with rufous wings and tail unless noted.
Tails are stiffened and used in climbing).

Xiphocolaptes WOODCREEPERS - 246.
Dendrocolaptes WOODCREEPERS - 58, 246, 247.
Xiphorhynchus WOODCREEPERS - 58, 247.
Lepidocolaptes WOODCREEPERS - 58, 247.

1. White-throated Woodcreeper
                   LM-F
Xiphocolaptes albicollis
                   11″ (27cm)
Bill = head, heavy, jet black. *Eyebrow and throat white.* Buff streaks on top and sides of head sometimes to upper mantle. *Back unstreaked.* Breast streaked white. Belly barred black and white.

2. Black-banded Woodcreeper
                   LM-F
Dendrocolaptes picumnus
                   9″ (24cm)
Bill = head, pale bluish. Head, throat, breast and mantle streaked buff. *Belly barred black* (unbarred in s part of range).

3. Ocellated Woodcreeper   **L-F**
Xiphorhynchus ocellatus
                   7½″ (19cm)
Bill = head. Crown with small drop-shaped spots. Little or no streaking on back. Throat buffy. Below brown with distinct large buff spots, becoming narrow streaks on belly.

4. Buff-throated Woodcreeper L-FT
Xiphorhynchus guttatus 9″ (23cm)
Bill = head, horn color to black. Head streaked. Little or no streaking on back. Throat buffy. Upper breast streaked buff. Belly faintly streaked.

5. Chestnut-rumped Woodcreeper
Xiphorhynchus pardalotus **LM-FT**
                   9″ (22cm)
Bill = head. Crown blackish, spotted buff. Mantle reddish brown with long prominent drop-shaped marks. *Throat cinnamon-buff.* Rump, wings and tail chestnut. Breast brown streaked buff. Belly dull cinnamon-buff.

6. Spix's Woodcreeper   **LM-FT**
Xiphorhynchus spixii   8″ (20cm)
Brown. Bill ¾x head, lower pale. Crown and nape spotted buff. Upper back with buff, black-edged

streaks. Throat buff. Below with broad, black-edged streaks (or round, dark-edged spots in some races).

7. Straight-billed Woodcreeper
                   LM-FT
Xiphorphynchus picus   8″ (20cm)
Bill ¾x head, all *whitish,* cutting edge *very straight.* Crown brown spotted buff. Back not streaked. Throat white. Breast brown with broad, oval, white, black-bordered streaks. Belly brown.

8. Zimmer's Woodcreeper   **L-TS**
Xiphorhynchus necopinus
                   8″ (20cm)
Bill ¾x head, base dusky, rest whitish, nearly straight. Streaks go part way down back. Throat whitish. Breast streaks linear, not oval as in Straight-billed Woodcreeper.

9. Striped Woodcreeper   **L-FT**
Xiphorhynchus obsoletus
                   7″ (18cm)
Bill ½x head, dusky yellow. Head and back streaked. Throat whitish. Below all streaked whitish, broadest on breast.

10. Streak-headed Woodcreeper
                   LM-TS
Lepidocolaptes souleyetii
                   7″ (18cm)
Bill ¾x head, thin, *curved.* Crown and nape conspicuously streaked. Back brown, not streaked. Rump rufous. Throat buff. Below all streaked with broad, black-edged buffy streaks.

11. Scaled Woodcreeper   **L-F**
Lepidocolaptes squamatus
                   7″ (18cm)
Bill ¾x head, slender, curved, pale. Crown and nape dusky streaked buff (in Brazil crown is brown, spotted buff). Back brown, unstreaked. *Throat white.* Below olive brown with *broad black-edged white streaks.*

CROWN AND SIDES OF HEAD NOT STRONGLY STREAKED OR SPOTTED.

Dendrocolaptes WOODCREEPERS - 56, 246, 247.
Xiphorhynchus WOODCREEPERS - 56, 247.
Lepidocolaptes WOODCREEPERS - 56, 247.

1. Barred Woodcreeper **LM-F**
Dendrocolaptes certhia
10" (26cm)
Bill = head, heavy, slightly curved.
Mostly brown. Head, back and *all underparts barred dusky.* Rump rufous.

2. Tyrannine Woodcreeper **MH-F**
Dendrocincla tyrannina 9" (23cm)
Bill ¾x head. Brown. Throat and area around eye lighter brown. Unstreaked above and below except for faint buffy streaks on breast. Like much commoner and smaller Plain-brown Woodcreeper but occurs higher.

3. Plain-brown Woodcreeper **L-FT**
Dendrocincla fuliginosa
7" (18cm)
Bill ¾x head. Above and below plain brown (or with back olivaceous). *Gray patch* in front of eye usually extending behind eye, bordered below by dusky whisker.

4. Ruddy Woodcreeper **LM-FT**
Dendrocincla homochroa
7" (17cm)
Bill ¾x head. Uniform reddish brown. Crown dark chestnut. Throat noticeably paler. Frequently flicks its wings.

5. White-chinned Woodcreeper **L-F**
Dendrocincla merula 7" (17cm)
Bill ¾x head. Dark brown. Eye bluish gray. *Throat white.* Wings, rump and tail chestnut.

6. Spotted Woodcreeper **LM-F**
Xiphorhynchus erythropygius
8" (20cm)
Bill = head. Eye-ring prominent. Crown dark brown. Throat buff with small brownish spots. Below olive brown spotted buff.

7. Olive-backed Woodcreeper
LM-F
Xiphorhynchus triangularis
8" (20cm)
Bill = head. Above brownish olive lightly spotted buff on head and

upper back. Throat buff scaled black. Below olivaceous spotted buff.

8. Narrow-billed Woodcreeper
LM-TSO
Lepidocolaptes angustirostris
7" (18cm)
Bill ¾x head, slender, curved, pale. Crown and nape dusky, obscurely streaked whitish. Back brown. *Broad eyebrow white, cheeks black.* Below whitish, more or less streaked dusky on breast and belly.

9. Spot-crowned Woodcreeper
MH-FT
Lepidocolaptes affinis 7" (18cm)
Bill = head, thin, curved, pale. Crown and nape *finely dotted buff.* Throat white. *Below profusely striped* with black-edged white stripes (or drop-shaped marks in w Colombia).

10. Lesser Woodcreeper **LM-F**
Lepidocolaptes fuscus
6½" (17cm)
Bill ¾x head, slender, curved, upper dusky, lower pale. Back olive brown. *Dusky patch behind eye.* Throat and breast buffy whitish. Belly buffy with blurry dusky streaks.

11. Olivaceous Woodcreeper **LM-FT**
Sittasomus griseicapillus
6" (15cm)
Bill ½x head. Head, neck, mantle, wing coverts and underparts *olivaceous gray.* Flight feathers, rump and tail rufous. Buff wing band shows in flight.

12. Wedge-billed Woodcreeper
LM-FT
Glyphorynchus spirurus
5" (13cm)
Bill very short, lower mandible upturned. Above brown, faintly spotted buff on crown. Eyebrow and throat buff. Below brown streaked buff. Cinnamon wing band shows in flight.

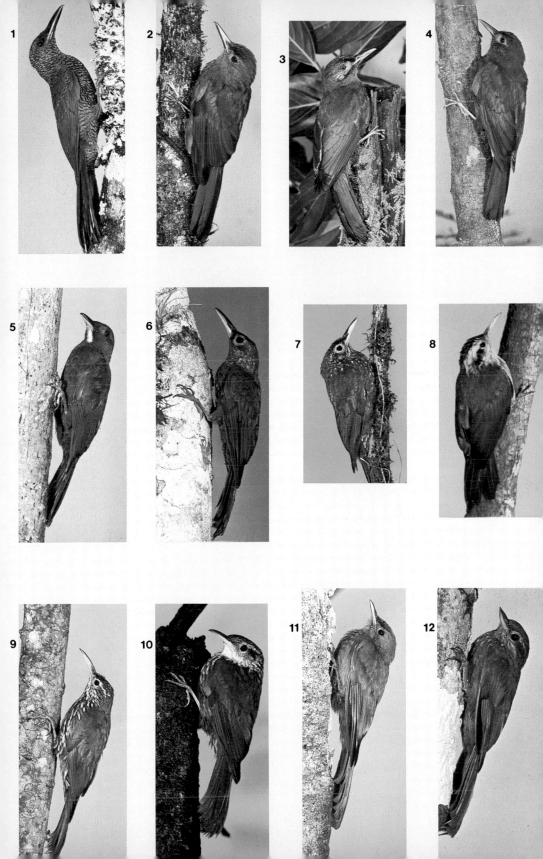

Furnariids have soft tails not used in climbing.

1. Scale-throated Earthcreeper
H-SO
Upucerthia dumetaria
8½" (21cm)
Bill 1¼x head, curved. Above brown. Wings with dull rufous band in flight. Below light brown, throat and breast feathers edged blackish giving distinct scaly look. Tail mostly blackish, edged buffy.

2. Streak-capped Treehunter   LM-F
Thripadectes virgaticeps
8" (20cm)
Bill ½x head, heavy. Crown and nape streaked whitish. Back brown, not streaked. Wings more rufescent. Rump and tail rufous. Underparts cinnamon, streaked dusky on throat and breast.

3. Striped Treehunter   LM-F
Thripadectes holostictus
7" (18cm)
Bill ½x head, heavy. Head, back and underparts brown prominently streaked buff. Wings rufous brown. Rump and tail rufous.

4. Uniform Treehunter   LM-F
Thripadectes ignobilis 6½" (17cm)
Bill ½x head, thick. Uniform dark brown, somewhat paler below. Throat and breast obscurely spotted buff.

5. Firewood-Gatherer   L-SO
Anumbius annumbi 7½" (19cm)
Bill ¾x head. Above light brown, vaguely streaked dusky, forehead tinged rufous. Eyebrow white. *Throat white surrounded with black spots.* Below buffy. Tail black, tipped white. Builds large stick nest.

6. Wing-banded Hornero   L-SOW
Furnarius figulus   7" (18cm)
Bill ¾x head. Above all bright cinnamon rufous (crown browner in Amazon valley). Eyebrow whitish. Throat white. Breast buff. Belly whitish. In flight shows two *buff bands on wings.* Legs dull grayish.

7. Rufous Hornero   L-SO
Furnarius rufus   7" (18cm)
Bill ¾x head. Above uniform light rufous brown. Eyebrow faint or lacking. Below light brown, throat and center of belly white. Wings with buffy patch in flight. Legs dusky.

8. Pale-legged Hornero   L-SO
Furnarius leucopus   6½" (16cm)
Bill = head, slender. Crown and nape gray or brown. Long eyebrow white. Above bright cinnamon rufous. Below buffy, throat and center of belly white. Legs pale. Includes *F. torridus,* considered a separate species in BSA.

9. Striated Softtail   LM-F
Thripophaga macroura
6½" (17cm)
Bill ¾x head. Crown chestnut and back reddish brown, both with pale shaft streaks. Eye-ring and line back of eye whitish. Throat rusty buff. Below brown with broad pale streaks. Long tail bright cinnamon.

10. Guttulated Foliage-gleaner M-F
Syndactyla guttulata 6½" (17 cm)
Bill ½x head, lower upturned. Eyebrow buff. Crown brown, unstreaked. *Mantle streaked white.* Throat buff. Below brown broadly streaked white. Rump and tail rufous.

11. Lineated Foliage-gleaner   M-F
Syndactyla subalaris 6½" (17cm)
Bill ½x head. Narrow streaks on crown and nape. Back plain brown. Narrow eyebrow white. Throat buff. Below brown all streaked buffy white. Rump and tail rufous.

12. Buff-browed Foliage-gleaner
M-FT
Syndactyla rufosuperciliata
6½" (17cm)
Bill ⅓x head. Above brown to olive. Eyebrow buff. Throat buffy white. Below all streaked olive and buffy white. Tail rufous.

1. **Streaked Tuftedcheek   MH-F**
Pseudocolaptes boissonneautii
                    8" (20cm)
Above brown, streaked buff. Underparts paler. Eyebrow, semi-collar and throat white.

2. **White-winged Cinclodes H-OW**
Cinclodes atacamensis 7" (18cm)
Bill ¾x head, curved. Above dark rufescent brown. *Long eyebrow white.* Underparts whitish stained brown, throat and breast spotted dusky. Tail like back, outer feathers tipped pure white.

3. **Buff-throated Foliage-gleaner**
Automolus ochrolaemus   **L-F**
                    7" (18cm)
Above olive brown, *rump* and *tail rufous.* Prominent eye-ring and narrow eyebrow buff. *Throat buff* (whitish w of Andes). Below dull ochraceous.

4. **Chestnut-crowned Foliage-gleaner   L-F**
Automolus rufipileatus 7" (18cm)
Iris yellow-orange. Mostly chestnut, slightly paler below. Rump and tail rufous.

5. **Ruddy Foliage-gleaner   LM-F**
Automolus rubiginosus 6¼" (16cm)
Very dark and unpatterned. Front half of eye-ring white. Above dark reddish brown. *Throat and breast cinnamon-rufous,* contrasting with buffy brown underparts. Birds w of Andes even darker, with black tail.

6. **Olive-backed Foliage-gleaner   L-F**
Automolus infuscatus
                    6½" (17cm)
Above olive brown. Inconspicuous buff eye-ring. *No eyebrow or streak behind eye.* Rump and tail rufous. Throat white. Below dull grayish, flanks and vent browner.

7. **White-eyed Foliage-gleaner   LM-FT**
Automolus leucophthalmus
                    7" (18cm)
Eye obviously white. Above reddish brown. Throat and upper breast white. Below pale ochraceous, browner on flanks and belly. Rump and tail rufous.

8. **White-collared Foliage-gleaner   LM-F**
Anabazenops fuscus   7" (18cm)
Bill ½x head, slightly upcurved. brown. Throat, collar and long eyebrow white. Below paler brown. Tail rufous.

9. **Buff-fronted Foliage-gleaner   LM-F**
Philydor rufus   6½" (17cm)
Bill ½x head. Forehead and eyebrow buff. Crown gray. Line back of eye dusky. Back olive brown. Wings and tail rufous. Below buffy ochraceous.

10. **Cinnamon-rumped Foliage-gleaner   L-F**
Philydor pyrrhodes   6" (15cm)
Bill ½x head. Crown and back rufescent olive (rufous brown w of Andes). *Wings contrastingly blackish.* Eyebrow, rump, tail and underparts bright cinnamon.

11. **Black-capped Foliage-gleaner   LM-F**
Philydor atricapillus   6" (15cm)
Bill ½x head. *Crown, stripe behind eye and whisker black.* Prominent eye-ring whitish. Above cinnamon brown. *Below bright ochraceous.* Tail rufous.

12. **Montane Foliage-gleaner   M-F**
Anabacerthia striaticollis
                    6" (15cm)
Bill ½x head. Crown dusky olive, back brown. *Prominent eye-ring and narrow line back of eye buffy.* Throat whitish, below pale brownish, *faintly streaked.* Rump and tail rufous.

1. Chotoy Spinetail   L-SO
Schoeniophylax phryganophila
                              8" (20cm)
Crown rufous streaked black.
Prominent white eyebrow. Above
brown, broadly streaked black.
Wing coverts rufous. Upper throat
yellowish, *patch on lower throat
black.* Below buffy whitish. *Tail
extremely long.*

2. White-chinned Thistletail   H-SO
Schizoeaca fuliginosa
                              6½" (17cm)
Above brown. *Eyebrow gray, eye-
ring and throat white.* Below gray
to brownish gray. Tail very long,
narrow, feathers ragged.

3. Plain-mantled Tit-Spinetail LM-S
Leptasthenura aegithaloides
                              5½" (14cm)
Crown and nape blackish boldly
streaked cinnamon. Lores and
short eyebrow white. *Back mostly
pale grayish brown,* some white
streaking on upper back. Throat
and breast white lightly streaked
dusky. Below pale buffy.

4. Rufous Spinetail   MH-FT
Synallaxis unirufa   6¼" (16cm)
Uniform rufous. Lores black. Some
races in Venezuela have blackish
spot on throat. Tail quite long.
Rather similar to Rufous Wren
(130-3) and Sepia-brown Wren
(130-4) but separated by complete
lack of barring.

5. Ruddy Spinetail   L-FT
Synallaxis rutilans   5½" (14cm)
Mostly rufous. Throat black. In ne
Brazil (s of Amazon) head grayish,
back dark olivaceous, below dark
olivaceous gray (washed rufous on
breast). Some races have browner
back. Rump gray, tail black.

6. Azara's Spinetail   MH-TS
Synallaxis azarae   6¼" (16cm)
Forecrown olive brownish. Crown,
nape and wing coverts bright

chestnut. Above olivaceous brown.
Throat speckled black and white.
Below pale grayish (darker gray in
most of Peru and Bolivia). Tail long,
chestnut.

7. Rusty-headed Spinetail   M-FT
Synallaxis fuscorufa   6¼" (16cm)
Mostly rufous. Back and rump
contrasting grayish. Throat buffy.
Below lighter rufous.

8. Slaty Spinetail   L-TS
Synallaxis brachyura   6" (15cm)
*Forecrown, sides of head, back and
underparts dark gray.* Crown and
most of wings rufous. Tail grayish
brown. (In Brazil blacker, with quite
short blackish tail.)

9. Dark-breasted Spinetail   L-TS
Synallaxis albigularis   6" (15cm)
Forecrown gray. Crown and most
of wings rufous. Upperparts grayish brown, *tail olive-brown.* Below
gray, some white showing on
throat.

10. Chicli Spinetail   LM-TS
Synallaxis spixi   6" (15cm)
Forehead, crown and wing coverts
rufous. Eyebrow and sides of head
grayish. Back and tail light olive-
brown. Throat gray but black bases
of feathers sometimes show. Breast
light gray. Belly white in center.

11. Pale-breasted Spinetail   LM-SO
Synallaxis albescens   6" (15cm)
Forehead dark gray. Crown and
wing coverts rufous. Back and tail
grayish brown. Lores and throat
whitish. Below whitish to pale gray
in center, darker gray on sides.
In some races the breast is also
darker gray.

12. Cabanis' Spinetail   LM-T
Synallaxis cabanisi   6" (15cm)
Crown, forehead, nape and wings
dark rufous. Cheeks and back
brownish gray. Underparts olive-
gray, speckled whitish on throat.
Tail rufous.

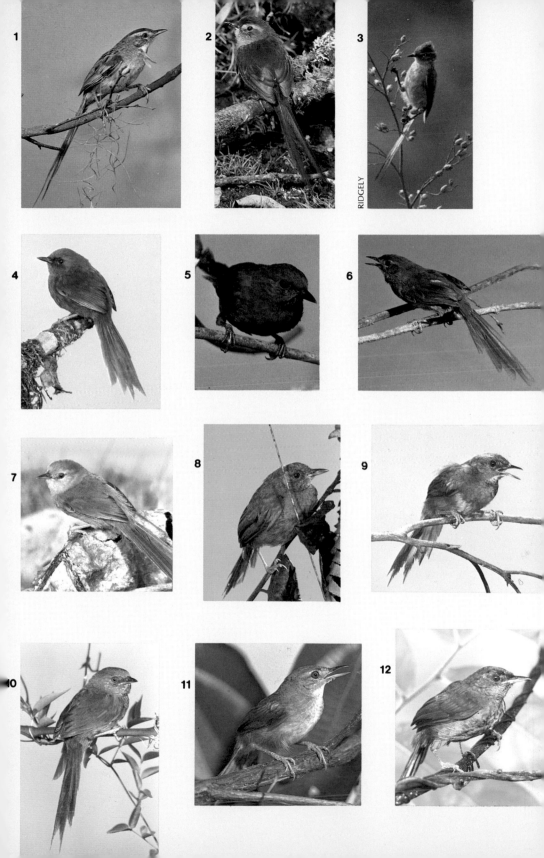

Synallaxis SPINETAILS - 64, 251, 252.
Poecilurus SPINETAILS - 252.
Cranioleuca SPINETAILS - 252, 253.

1. Sooty-fronted Spinetail   LM-S
Synallaxis frontalis   6" (15cm)
Forecrown olive. Crown, nape, wings and tail bright chestnut. Eyebrow, lores and partial eye-ring whitish. Back olive brown. Throat speckled black and white. Below grayish.

2. Rufous-capped Spinetail   LM-FT
Synallaxis ruficapilla   6" (15cm)
Crown and nape bright orange rufous. Prominent buff stripe behind eye. Above reddish brown, wing coverts chestnut. Throat gray, below dull buffy. Tail rather short, rufous.

3. Plain-crowned Spinetail   L-TS
Synallaxis gujanensis   6" (15cm)
Head all grayish, *no rufous on crown*. Back olive brown. Wings and tail bright rufous. Below white, clouded grayish brown on breast and flanks.

4. White-whiskered Spinetail
                          L-SO
Poecilurus candei   5½" (14cm)
Crown and nape gray. Back, wings, breast and thin line back of eye rufous. Cheeks and throat black. *Chin, whisker and center of belly white.* Tail rufous, blackish at end.

5. Yellow-chinned (-throated) Spinetail   L-SW
Certhiaxis cinnamomea
                        5½" (14cm)
Above all rufous. Indefinite eyebrow whitish. *Distinctive black line from lores through eye.* Chin pale yellow. Below white. Tail rufous, *spines conspicuously protruding.*

6. Red-and-white Spinetail   L-SW
Certhiaxis mustelina   5" (13cm)
Bill noticeably long and slender. Above all rufous red. Black line in front of eye. Below all pure white.

Very like Yellow-chinned Spinetail (preceding) but bill longer and chin not yellowish.

7. Red-faced Spinetail   LM-FTS
Cranioleuca erythrops
                        5½" (14cm)
Crown and *sides of head rufous.* Back olive-brown tinged rufous. Wings and tail bright rufous. Underparts whitish, grayer on throat.

8. Rusty-backed Spinetail   L-SW
Cranioleuca vulpina   5" (13cm)
Forehead grayish. Upperparts, wings and tail bright rufous. Lores and narrow eyebrow whitish. Below dingy brownish gray, whiter on throat.

9. Streak-capped Spinetail   MH-F
Cranioleuca hellmayri
                        5½" (14cm)
Crown chestnut, streaked black. Eyebrow and throat whitish. Back olive brown. Wings and tail rufous. Below light grayish brown. Only in Santa Marta Mountains.

10. Olive Spinetail   LM-F
Cranioleuca obsoleta 4½" (12cm)
Above olive-brown. Eyebrow whitish. Wing coverts and tail rufous. Underparts grayish buff.

11. Stripe-crowned Spinetail   LMH-S
Cranioleuca pyrrhophia 5" (13cm)
Crown strikingly streaked buff and black. Conspicuous eyebrow white. Back brown. Throat white, below brownish. Wing coverts and tail rufous.

12. White-browed Spinetail   MH-F
Synallaxis gularis   4½" (12cm)
Short eyebrow white. Above uniform reddish brown. Throat white, below cinnamon brown to brownish gray. *Tail short with protruding spines.* Looks and acts more like a wren than a spinetail.

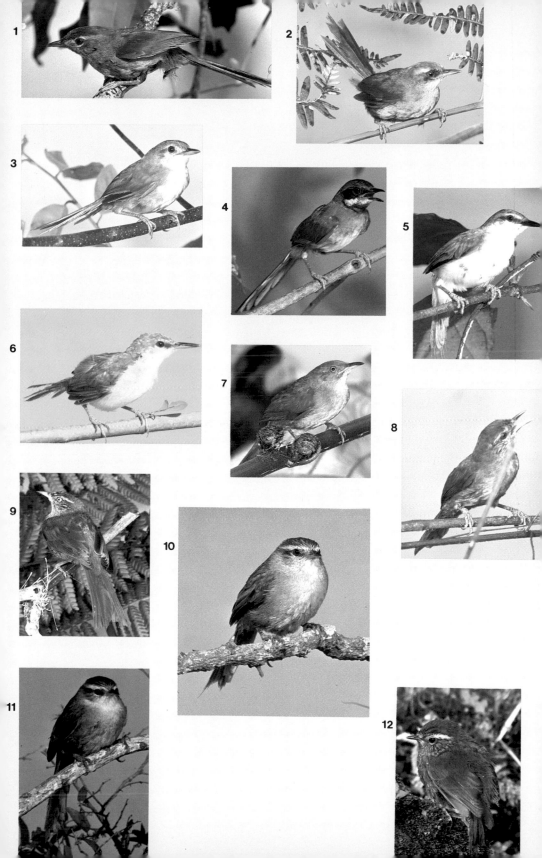

Sclerurus LEAFTOSSERS - 259, 260.
(Various) BARBTAILS - 257.
Xenops XENOPS - 259.

1. Curve-billed Reedhaunter L-OW
Limnornis curvirostris 6½" (17cm)
Bill pale, curved. Above light brown. Eyebrow and throat white. Below whitish. Tail rufous.

2. Straight-billed Reedhaunter
L-OW
Limnoctites rectirostris
6¼" (16cm)
Bill blackish, straight. Above light brown, crown grayer. Narrow eyebrow white. Below white, sides light brown. Wings and tail cinnamon, central tail feathers pointed.

3. Tawny-throated Leaftosser
(Leafscraper) LM-F
Sclerurus mexicanus 5½" (14cm)
Bill thin, nearly as long as head. Above dark brown. Rump and *throat rufous.* Breast dark rufous. Belly dark brown. Tail black.

4. Scaly-throated Leaftosser
(Leafscraper) L-F
Sclerurus guatemalensis
5½" (14cm)

Bill thin, about ¾x head. Above dark rich brown, *no rufous rump.* Throat white, scaled blackish. Below brown lightly spotted rufous on breast. Tail blackish.

5. Sharp-tailed Streamcreeper
LM-FW
Lochmias nematura 5½" (14cm)
Bill ¾x head, thin, slightly curved. Dark brown, *profusely spotted white* below. Eyebrow white in se. Tail black.

6. Wren-like Rushbird LMH-OW
Phleocryptes melanops
5¼" (13cm)
Crown dark brown streaked pale. *Broad eyebrow whitish.* Back streaked black and grayish. Rump brown. Wings blackish with two buff bands. Black stripe behind eye. Underparts mostly white. Tail mostly black, outers pale tipped.

7. Fulvous-dotted Treerunner M-F
Margarornis stellatus 5½" (14cm)
Above chestnut. *Throat white, bordered below by necklace of white spots edged with black.* Below rufous-chestnut. Tail chestnut, spines protruding.

8. Pearled Treerunner MH-F
Margarornis squamiger
5½" (14cm)
Above bright rufous-chestnut (crown browner). *Eyebrow and throat creamy white.* Below brown, *thickly spotted white.* Tail chestnut, spines protruding.

9. Spotted Barbtail M-F
Premnoplex brunnescens
5½" (14cm)
Above dark brown, with short buffy eyebrow. Throat ochraceous. Below brown, *thickly spotted ochraceous.* Tail dark brown, spines protruding.

10. Streaked Xenops LM-FT
Xenops rutilans 4½" (12cm)
Lower bill sharply upturned. Above rufous brown, crown and *mantle streaked buffy.* Rump rufous. Eyebrow and cheek-stripe white (usually more prominent than in this photo). Wing band cinnamon. Tail rufous with little or no black.

11. Plain Xenops L-FT
Xenops minutus 4¼" (11cm)
Lower bill upturned. Very like Streaked Xenops (preceding) but above plain brown, unstreaked.

12. Sharp-billed (Treehunter) Xenops
LM-FT
Heliobletus contaminatus
4¼" (11cm)
Above brown, narrowly streaked buff on crown, broadly streaked white on back. Long eyebrow and partial collar buff. Blackish patch behind eye. Throat whitish. Below pale brown broadly streaked white. Tail rufous. Bill very small.

ANTPITTA-LIKE ANTBIRDS WITH STOCKY, SHORT TAIL, LONG LEGS, USUALLY TERRESTRIAL.

Grallaria ANTPITTAS - 269, 270. *Chamaeza* ANTTHRUSHES - 268.
Formicarius ANTTHRUSHES - 268. *Pittasoma* ANTPITTA - 268.
Hylopezus ANTPITTAS - 270. *Grallaricula* ANTPITTAS - 271.

1. Chestnut-crowned Antpitta M-TS
Grallaria ruficapilla 7" (18cm)
Head all rufous. Back, wings and tail olive brown. Throat white. Below white streaked dusky. Legs gray.

2. Short-tailed Antthrush LM-F
Chamaeza campanisona
7½" (19cm)
Bill small. Above uniform brown. *Streak back of eye white.* Below whitish, streaked dusky. Tail short, brown, blackish bar near end and pale-tipped.

3. Barred Antthrush MH-F
Chamaeza mollissima 7" (18cm)
Bill small. Above uniform brown. Lines back of eye and below ear barred black and white. *Below narrowly barred black and whitish.*

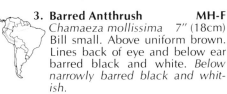

4. Rufous-capped Antthrush L-F
Formicarius colma 6¼" (16cm)
Crown and nape bright rufous (forehead black in upper Amazon). Back and wings olive. Bend of wing usually shows light rufous. Face, throat and breast black. Belly grayish. Tail blackish. ♀: Lores and throat white spotted black.

5. Black-faced Antthrush L-FT
Formicarius analis 6¼" (17cm)
Above brownish, tinged rufous on rump. Throat black. Below light to dark gray. Tail blackish, usually held erect. Vent chestnut.

6. Black-headed Antthrush LM-FTS
Formicarius nigricapillus
6" (15cm)
Entire head and neck dull black. Back and wings dark olive brown, tinged chestnut on rump. Throat and breast dull black. Flanks and belly dark olive. Vent chestnut.

7. Rufous-crowned Antpitta L-F
Pittasoma rufopileatum 6" (15cm)
Crown rufous, semi-collar lighter rufous. Long broad eyebrow black. Above brown streaked black. Below buffy (barred black in some races). Tail brown, very short.

8. Rufous Antpitta MH-FT
Grallaria rufula 5½" (14cm)
Uniform rufous brown to olive brown above. Below lighter rufous, more or less buffy on center of belly.

9. Streak-chested Antpitta L-F
Hylopezus perspicillatus
5" (13cm)
Crown gray. *Conspicuous eye-ring buff.* Above olive, streaked buff. Wing coverts tipped buff. Below white, *black streaks* on breast and sides.

10. Speckle-breasted Antpitta LM-FT
Hylopezus ochroleucus
4½" (12cm)
Above plain olive. Below whitish, spotted black on breast (or only on sides). Center of belly whitish without spots.

11. Rusty-breasted Antpitta M-F
Grallaricula ferrugineipectus
4¼" (11cm)
Above uniform olive brown. Prominent eye-ring buff. Below light rufous, usually with white crescent across throat. Belly white, sides rufous. *Legs pale pink.*

12. Slate-crowned Antpitta MH-F
Grallaricula nana 4" (10cm)
Above brownish. *Crown dark gray.* Eye-ring buff. *Below deep rufous* (white crescent across throat in some races). Belly white. *Legs light gray.*

LARGER ANTSHRIKES, MOSTLY WITH HEAVY HOOKED BILL.

Mackenziaena ANTSHRIKE - 260.
Thamnophilus ANTSHRIKES - 74, 76, 260, 261.
Sakesphorus ANTSHRIKES - 260.

Giant Antshrike   **LM-FT**
Batara cinerea   12" (31cm)
Crown black. Above black finely barred white. Below uniform gray.

1. Female: Crown chestnut. Above black barred rufous. Throat whitish. Below grayish brown.

Large-tailed Antshrike   **LM-FTS**
Mackenziaena leachii   9" (24cm)
Bill very small for size of bird. All black, thickly spotted white except on throat, breast and tail.

2. Female: Crown and nape chestnut, spotted tawny. Back and wings black, spotted buff. Below black thickly spotted whitish. *Tail long,* mostly black, lightly spotted buff.

3. Great Antshrike   **L-TS**
Taraba major   7½" (19cm)
Bill thick, hooked. *Eye red.* Above black, wings barred white. Below white. Tail black, outer feathers white. Usually near ground. Both male and female often raise crest.

4. Female: Above brown. Below whitish.

5. Fasciated Antshrike   **L-FT**
Cymbilaimus lineatus
     6½" (17cm)

Bill very heavy, hooked. Crown black. Eye red. Above and below *finely* barred black and white. Tail black with about eight fine white bars showing.

6. Female: Bill extremely heavy, hooked. Eye red. Crown rufous. Back, wings and tail dark brown *finely* barred buff. Below buff *finely* (sometimes faintly) barred dusky.

Castelnau's Antshrike   **L-T**
Thamnophilus cryptoleucus
     6¼" (16cm)
Bill small for size of bird. Black except wing coverts and wing feathers edged white.

7. Female: All black except underwing coverts white (not visible when perched).

Rufous-capped Antshrike   **LM-TS**
Thamnophilus ruficapillus
     6¼" (16cm)
Above reddish brown, rufous on crown. Below whitish lightly barred blackish on breast.

8. Female: Back olive brown. Bars on breast very faint or missing entirely.

9. Glossy Antshrike   **L-TSW**
Sakesphorus luctuosus
     6½" (17cm)
All black except small white patch on wing coverts and tips of tail white. Crest prominent.

10. Female: Long crest *chestnut.* Above black. Patch on wings and tips of tail white. Below dark grayish. Both male and female *often raise crest.*

11. Black-crested Antshrike   **L-SO**
Sakesphorus canadensis
     5½" (14cm)
Prominent crest black. *Head and broad band down center of breast black.* Collar and rest of underparts white. Back brown. Wings blackish, two wing-bars white. Tail black, edged and tipped white.

12. Female: *Crest rufous.* Sides of head speckled dusky and white. Back rufous brown. Below light brown or whitish, lightly *streaked dusky on breast.*

MID-SIZE ANTSHRIKES

Thamnophilus ANTSHRIKES - 72, 76, 260, 261.

1. Barred Antshrike   L-TSO
Thamnophilus doliatus
5½" (14cm)

Crown black (white bases of feathers often show through). Eye yellow. Throat and sides of head streaked black and white. Above and below banded black and white.

2. Female: Above rufous, *sides of head streaked black and white.* Below buffy, throat usually paler.

3. Lined Antshrike   L-TS
Thamnophilus palliatus
5½" (14cm)
Male very like ♂ Barred Antshrike (above) but white lines narrow giving a much blacker look. (In e Brazil back, wings and tail are chestnut as shown in photo). ♀: Very like ♀ Bar-crested Antshrike (below) but black lines wider producing *more blackish look.*

4. Bar-crested Antshrike   LM-TS
Thamnophilus multistriatus
5½" (14cm)
Male (at right) very like ♂ Barred Antstrike (74-1) but *crown barred or spotted instead of all black.* Female (at left): Crown, back and tail rufous chestnut. Below evenly barred black and white (not more heavily barred black as in Lined Antshrike (preceding).

5. Uniform Antshrike   M-F
Thamnophilus unicolor
5½" (14cm)

Slaty gray all over. *Eye pale grayish.*

6. Female: Above reddish brown. Throat and *sides of head gray.* Below light brown. Tail brownish.

7. Slaty Antshrike   LMH-TSO
Thamnophilus punctatus
5½" (14cm)

Forehead and face speckled gray. Upper bill black, lower grayish. Crown black. Back gray or blackish. Wings and coverts black, feathers edged white. Below gray or light gray. Tail black, tipped white.

8. Female: Crown rufous. Above reddish brown. Cheeks and lores whitish, speckled or streaked dusky. Throat grayish. Below pale brownish.

Amazonian Antshrike   LM-FT
Thamnophilus amazonicus
5½" (14cm)
Male almost exactly like ♂ Slaty Antshrike (above).

9. Female: *Head rufous.* Back gray. Wings and tail black edged and tipped white. *Underparts rufous* (belly white in some races).

10. Variable Antshrike   LM-TS
Thamnophilus caerulescens
5½" (14cm)

Crown black. Back gray spotted black. Wing-bars white. Underparts vary greatly from whitish to cinnamon to black (barred black and white in some races). Tail black, tipped white.

11. Female: Crown gray (sometimes tinged rufous). Wing coverts like male (or sometimes unmarked). Throat and breast grayish, *belly cinnamon buff.*

MID-SIZE AND SMALLER ANTSHRIKES

Thamnomanes ANTSHRIKES - 261, 262.
Thamnophilus ANTSHRIKES - 72, 74, 260, 261.

1. Russet Antshrike   **LM-FT**
Thamnistes anabatinus
                        5½" (14cm)
Bill heavy. Crown, wings and tail reddish brown. Back brown. *Eyebrow,* throat and breast *buffy.* Belly gray.

2. Cinereous Antshrike   **L-FT**
Thamnomanes caesius
                        5½" (14cm)
Uniform dark gray. No white on wing or tail. (Throat mottled white s of the Amazon). *Eye dark.*

3. Female: Above brownish. Throat whitish. Breast olive. Belly rufous.

4. Dusky-throated Antshrike   **L-F**
Thamnomanes ardesiacus
                        4½" (12cm)
Uniform gray, usually with *black throat patch.* No spots on wings. Tail narrowly fringed white.

5. Female: Above olive brown slightly grayer on crown and rufous on rump. Below ochraceous, paler on throat and tinged grayish on breast.

6. Black-capped Antshrike   **L-FT**
Thamnophilus schistaceus
                        5" (13cm)
Eye reddish. Uniform gray (with black crown e Colombia, ne Peru and Amazonian Brazil). Males without black crown very like ♂ Cinereous Antshrike (76-2) but have heavier bill and more reddish eye.

7. Female: *Crown rufous.* Back olive brown. Below ochraceous.

8. Mouse-colored Antshrike   **L-TS**
Thamnophilus murinus
                        4½" (12cm)
Light gray. Bill quite "plump". Wings brownish with *small buffy tips* to wing coverts. Tail blackish tipped white.

9. Female: Crown rufous. Back reddish brown. *Small buffy tips to wing coverts.* Throat and belly white. Breast and sides of body olive brown.

10. Black Antshrike   **L-TS**
Thamnophilus nigriceps
                        5½" (14cm)
All black. Eye light brown.

11. Female: (narrow streaked form). There are two forms both with back, wings and tail rufous. More common, apparently, is the narrow streaked form shown here.

12. Female: (broad streaked form) is similar but has broad, buffy, black-edged streaks on head and underparts.

LARGE ANTBIRDS.

Pyriglena FIRE-EYES - 266.
Cercomacra ANTBIRDS - 80, 265.
Phlegopsis BARE-EYES - 268.
Myrmeciza ANTBIRDS - 82, 266, 267.

1. White-backed Fire-eye   LM-FT
Pyriglena leuconota 6½" (17cm)
Bill less than half head length. Eye red. Glossy black with white patch on upper back often visible.

2. Female: Above brown, small white patch on back usually visible. Some races have black head and some have white eyebrow. Below grayish olive or brownish or black. Tail black.

3. White-shouldered Fire-eye   L-FT
Pyriglena leucoptera 6¼" (16cm)
Bill less than half head length. Eye red. Glossy black with *narrow white bars on wings.*

4. Female: Like ♀ White-backed Fire-eye (above) but has *no white patch on back.*

5. Mato Grosso Antbird   L-TS
Cercomacra melanaria
           6½" (17cm)
Black. Shoulders white. Wing coverts tipped white. Tail black, much graduated, all but central feathers tipped white.

6. Female: Ashy gray above, paler gray below, whitish on throat and belly.

7. Ocellated Antbird   L-F
Phaenostictus mcleannani
           7" (18cm)
Crown grayish brown. Collar rufous. Back feathers blackish, fringed buff, giving *scalloped look. Bare skin around eye bright blue.* Throat black. Below rufous, *spotted black.*

8. Black-spotted Bare-Eye   L-FT
Phlegopsis nigromaculata
           6¼" (16cm)
Head, neck and breast black. *Bare skin around eye red. Back and wings brown with large black spots.* Belly brown. Primaries and tail rufous.

9. Immaculate Antbird   LM-F
Myrmeciza immaculata
           6½" (17cm)
Black. Skin around eye blue. Small amount of white at bend of wing (usually not visible). Tail extends about 5 cm beyond wings.

10. Female: Brown. Bare skin around eye as in male. Sides of head and upper throat blackish. Tail black.

11. Plumbeous Antbird   L-F
Myrmeciza hyperythra
           6¼" (16cm)
Male (left) uniform dark leaden gray. Wings black with conspicuous small white spots. Bare skin around eye whitish or bluish. Female (right) below all uniform bright rufous.

MID-SIZE ANTBIRDS

Cercomacra ANTBIRDS - 78, 265.
Rhegmatorhina ANTBIRDS - 267, 268.

1. Bare-crowned Antbird　　　L-FT
Gymnocichla nudiceps
　　　　　　　　　6" (15cm)
Top and sides *of head bare, bright blue.* Above and below blackish. Wings with three whitish wing-bars.

2. Female: Above brown. Bare skin around eye blue. *Three obscure* rufous *wing-bars.* Below rufous. Top of head feathered.

3. Black Bushbird　　　　　L-F
Neoctantes niger　　6" (15cm)
All deep black. Bill narrow, *lower bill much upturned.*

4. Female: All black but *breast chestnut.* Bill like male.

5. Blackish Antbird　　　　L-FT
Cercomacra nigrescens
　　　　　　　　　5½" (14cm)
Blackish. Bend of wing whitish (sometimes does not show). Wing coverts very narrowly edged white.

6. Female: Forecrown rufous. Above olive brown. Below rufous. Tail olive brown.

7. Dusky Antbird　　　　　LM-FT
Cercomacra tyrannina
　　　　　　　　　5½" (14cm)
Uniform gray. Wing coverts black edged white. Usually a hint of rufous on edges of primaries. Tail blackish with very narrow white tips (sometimes worn away).

8. Female: Above olive brown. Below uniform bright ochraceous, becoming grayish at rear.

9. Jet Antbird　　　　　　L-T
Cercomacra nigricans
　　　　　　　　　5½" (14cm)
Slender. Black. White patch on shoulders sometimes visible. Wing coverts tipped white. Tail graduated, *broadly tipped white.*

10. Female: Above like male but dark gray instead of black. *Throat streaked white.* Breast more or less streaked white. Belly gray.

Chestnut-crested Antbird　　L-F
Rhegmatorhina cristata
　　　　　　　　　6" (15cm)
Crown, nape and back chestnut. Wings and tail brown. Large patch of bare skin around eye light blue or whitish. Face and throat black. Below rufous chestnut.

11. Female: Has a few black spots on mantle.

12. Silvered Antbird　　　　L-FTW
Sclateria naevia　　5½" (14cm)
Bill long and slender. Above leaden gray to slaty black. Wing coverts with *small round white dots.* Throat white. Below whitish (scalloped or streaked gray in some races). Legs pinkish. ♀: Brown instead of gray. Rufous eyebrow. Below white. Sides rufous.

MID-SIZE AND SMALL ANTBIRDS

Myrmeciza ANTBIRDS - 78, 266, 267.
Gymnopithys ANTBIRDS - 267.
Drymophila ANTBIRDS - 88, 265.

1. Squamate Antbird   **L-F**
Myremeciza squamosa
5½" (14cm)
Above brown, speckled black on back. Wing coverts black. Wing-bars and eyebrow white. Throat black. Below whitish, *scalloped black.*

2. Female: Lacks black throat. Underparts faintly spotted dusky.

3. White-bibbed Antbird   **M-F**
Myremeciza loricata 5½" (14cm)
Above brown mottled black on crown and back. *Broad white eyebrow.* Throat black, upper breast and belly white. *Broad band of black and white feathers across lower breast.* ♀: Eyebrow and throat buff.

Ferruginous-backed Antbird **L-F**
Myrmeciza ferruginea
5½" (14cm)
Bare skin around eye blue. White stripe behind eye. Back, wings and tail reddish brown. Wing coverts black, barred white. Sides of head, throat and upper breast black. Lower breast scalloped black and white. Belly brownish.

4. Female: Like male but throat white.

5. White-bellied Antbird   **L-TS**
Myrmeciza longipes   5" (13cm)
Above rufous. Broad eyebrow gray. Throat and breast black. Belly white. ♀: Like male except black replaced by cinnamon. Distinctive *dusky area on cheek.*

6. Chestnut-backed Antbird   **L-FT**
Myrmeciza exsul   5" (13cm)
Crown, nape and throat blackish. Skin around eye blue. Back, wings and tail brown, wing coverts with small white spots (no white spots in some races). Breast and belly dark gray.

7. Female: Breast and belly rufous.

8. Bicolored Antbird   **L-FT**
Gymnopithys leucaspis 5" (13cm)
Above reddish brown or dark brown. *Broad gray area back of eye.* (Skin around eye blue in some races.) *Black cheek patch.* Below white, sides black or brown (or spotted in some races).

9. Rufous-throated Antbird   **L-FT**
Gymnopithys rufigula   5" (13cm)
Above brown. Bare skin around eye bluish. *Throat rufous.* Breast buff darkening to olive brown on sides and belly. ♀: Has pinkish patch which shows on center of back.

10. Long-tailed Antbird   **M-FT**
Drymophila caudata 5½" (14cm)
Above black streaked white. *Rump rufous.* Breast buffy streaked black. Belly rufous. Tail long, dusky, tipped white.

11. Ferruginous Antbird   **LM-FT**
Drymophila ferruginea 5" (13cm)
Crown and sides of head black. Long eyebrow, lores and lower cheeks white. Back brown. *Rump chestnut.* Wing-bars white. Below rufous. Tail gray, tipped white.

12. Dusky-tailed Antbird   **LM-FT**
Drymophila malura   5" (13cm)
Crown, nape, *throat and breast streaked black and whitish.* Back and belly gray (♀ brownish). Tail long, dusky, faintly pale-tipped.

SMALL ANTBIRDS

1. Esmeraldas Antbird **LM-F**
Sipia rosenbergi 4½″ (12cm)
Dark gray. Rump brown. Eye red.
Wing coverts black, *tipped white.*
♀: Head and underparts dark gray.
Throat spotted white. Above dark
brown, coverts spotted white and
buff.

2. Black-headed Antbird **L-TS**
Percnostola rufifrons 5″ (13cm)
Leaden gray. *Eye red.* Crown and
throat black. Wing coverts black,
three wing-bars white. Tail blackish *without white tips.*

3. Female: Back brownish gray. *Three
prominent wing-bars* buff. Breast
and belly rufous.

4. Ash-breasted Antbird **L-F**
Myrmoborus lugubris 5″ (13cm)
Forehead pale gray. Above gray.
No wing-bars. Face, throat and
upper breast black. Below whitish.

5. Female: Above all reddish brown
(face black in some races). Obscure wing-bars buffy. Throat and
underparts white.

6. White-browed Antbird **L-FT**
Myrmoborus leucophrys
4½″ (12cm)
Gray. *Forehead and long broad
eyebrow white.* Cheeks, throat and
upper breast black.

7. Female: Crown rufous. Back,
wings and tail brown with small
buffy tips forming wing-bars. Broad
black line under eye. Below white.

8. Black-faced Antbird **L-F**
Myrmoborus myotherinus
4½″ (12cm)
Above gray, forehead whitish.
Wings with *three white bars. Face,
throat and upper breast black.*
Below pale gray.

9. Female: Above brown with buffy
wing-bars. Mask black. Throat
white. Below buffy-cinnamon with
few black spots on upper breast
(or breast all spotted in some
races).

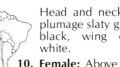

Black-tailed Antbird **L-F**
Myrmoborus melanurus
4¼″ (11cm)
Head and neck blackish, rest of
plumage slaty gray. Wings and tail
black, wing coverts margined
white.

10. Female: Above brown, face olive
brown. Wing coverts black margined white. Below white, tinged
brown on breast.

11. Large-billed Antwren **L-S**
Herpsilochmus longirostris
5″ (13cm)
Crown black. Long eyebrow white.
Short black line back of eye. Back
gray. Wings black, spotted white.
Underparts whitish with pale gray
spots on breast. Tail black broadly
tipped white.

12. Female: Head and neck rufous.
Back gray. Wings black, coverts
broadly tipped white. Underparts
cinnamon, paler on belly. Tail
blackish, broadly tipped white.

SMALL ANTBIRDS

Black-bellied Antwren　　　**L-S**
Formicivora melanogaster
　　　　　　　　　5" (13cm)

Above dark brown. Long eyebrow white. Underparts black, *flank feathers long, gray.*

1. Female: Like male but throat white, breast and belly buffy.

2. White-fringed Antwren　　**L-TS**
Formicivora grisea　　4½" (12cm)
Above grayish brown or reddish brown. Long eyebrow white. Below black surrounded by white fringe. Flank feathers long, white (often not visible). Tail black, edged and tipped white.

3. Female: Below varies greatly from buff to cinnamon with or without small black spots on breast.

4. Spot-breasted Antvireo　　**LM-F**
Dysithamnus stictothorax
　　　　　　　　　4¼" (11cm)
Crown gray. Back grayish olive. Wing coverts black, tipped white. Face gray with small white spots except on ear coverts. Below whitish, *spotted gray on breast.* Tail grayish olive.

5. Female: *Crown bright rufous.*

6. Spot-crowned Antvireo　　**L-F**
Dysithamnus puncticeps
　　　　　　　　　4¼" (11cm)

Crown black spotted gray. Back, wings and tail gray. Wing coverts spotted white. Below white, lightly streaked gray on throat and breast.

7. Female: Crown black, spotted rufous. Above brown. Below buff, lightly streaked dusky on throat and breast.

8. Plain Antvireo　　　**LM-FT**
Dysithamnus mentalis
　　　　　　　　　4¼" (11cm)
Above all gray, wing coverts tipped white. Distinctive *blackish smudge on cheek.* Throat white or grayish. Belly usually yellowish.

9. Female: *Crown rufous.* Eye-ring white. Back, wings and tail dull olive to olive-brown. Belly yellowish to whitish.

10. Rufous Gnateater　　　**LM-FT**
Conopophaga lineata 4¼" (11cm)
Above uniform brown. Eyebrow grayish. White tuft back of eye. Throat and breast rufous (usually with white crescent). Belly white.

11. Black-cheeked Gnateater　**LM-F**
Conopophaga melanops
　　　　　　　　　4¼" (11cm)
Crown bright orange-rufous. Sides of head black. Above grayish brown. Wing coverts tinged rufous. White tuft back of eye (sometimes not present). Throat and belly white, sides gray. Breast gray.

12. Female: Above brownish. Throat and breast rufous. Center of belly white.

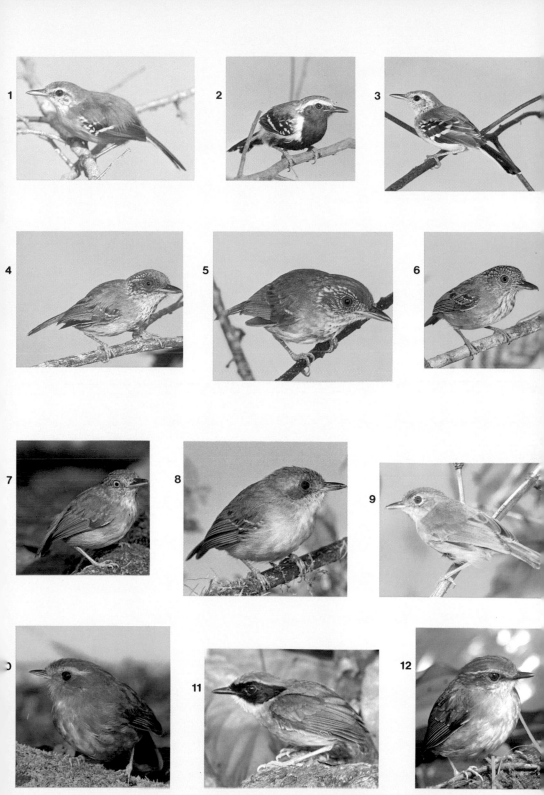

SMALL ANTBIRDS

Drymophila ANTBIRDS - 82, 265. *Pithys* ANTBIRD - 267.

1. Scaled Antbird   **L-F**
Drymophila squamata
                    4¼" (11cm)
Upperparts black *spotted white*
(crown and nape unspotted in
some races). Long eyebrow of
many short white streaks. Black
line through eye. Below white
spotted black. Tail black barred
white. ♀: Above brown with large
rufous spots on lower back. Below
white, streaked black. Tail barred
buff.

2. Scale-backed Antbird   **L-FT**
Hylophylax poecilonota
                    4½" (12cm)
Gray (throat black in some races).
Back and wings black, feathers
ending in *white tips producing
scaled effect*. Tail black with white
spots and tips.

3. Female: Head rufous. Back brown
scaled white. Below light gray (or
rufous in some races).

Dot-backed Antbird   **L-F**
Hylophylax punctulata 4" (10cm)
Above blackish, spotted *white on
back and rump. Lores and cheeks
whitish*. Throat black. Below white,
spotted black on breast. Tail short,
brown, tipped white.

4. Female: Browner above. Throat
white, broad *whiskers black.*

5. Spot-backed Antbird   **L-F**
Hylophylax naevia   4" (10cm)
Top and sides of head gray. Back
dark brown *spotted buff*. Rump
olive brown, *not spotted*. Wing
coverts black, tipped white. Throat
black. Below white, *breast spotted
black*. Tail short, brown, tipped
white.

6. Female: Throat white. Breast and
belly light rufous, spotted as in
male.

7. Spotted Antbird   **L-F**
Hylophylax naevioides 4" (10cm)
Head dark gray. Back chestnut.
Wing coverts black with *chestnut
wing-bars*. Throat black. Below
white with band of *black spots
across breast*. Tail short, blackish,
tipped buff.

8. Female: Throat and underparts
whitish with band of dusky spots
across breast.

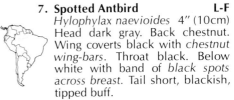

9. Black-and-white Antbird   **L-TS**
Myrmochanes hemileucus
                    4¼" (11cm)
Above black, white of dorsal patch
shows through. Rump gray. Wing
coverts and tail tipped black. *This
is probably an immature male.* ♀:
Like male but lores white and
lower bill pale.

10. White-plumed Antbird   **L-F**
Pithys albifrons   4½" (12cm)
White plumes around face. Head
black (narrow eyebrow white in
some races). Back and wings gray.
Collar, all underparts, rump and
tail chestnut.

11. Dot-winged Antwren   **L-FT**
Microrhopias quixensis
                    4¼" (11cm)
Black. *Wing coverts conspicuously
spotted* and tipped white. Tail
broadly tipped white.

12. Female: Above gray. *Below chestnut* (with black on throat and/or
belly in some races).

SMALL ANTBIRDS

Terenura ANTWRENS - 265.
Hypocnemis ANTBIRDS - 266.
Myrmotherula ANTWRENS - 262, 263, 264.

1. Banded Antbird   **L-F**
Dichrozona cincta   4¼" (11cm)
Bill long and slender. Crown and mantle brown. *Lower back black, crossed by white (♀ buff) band.* Rump black-gray. Wings barred buff. Below white, breast spotted black. Tail short, black, edged white.

2. Rufous-rumped Antwren   **M-F**
Terenura callinota   4" (10cm)
Crown black. Broad eyebrow white. Back olive, *rump rufous.* Shoulders bright yellow. Wing coverts black, wing-bars pale yellow. Cheeks, throat and breast pale gray. *Belly yellow.* Tail dark gray. ♀: Crown brown. Back olive.

3. Warbling Antbird   **L-FT**
Hypocnemis cantator   4" (10cm)
Crown black with central line of white spots. *Above streaked black and white.* White spots on wings. Long eyebrow white. *Below white or yellow, more or less streaked black. Sides rufous.* ♀: Back browner.

4. Streaked Antwren   **L-TW**
Myrmotherula surinamensis
          3½" (9cm)
Above and below *streaked black and white* (underparts not streaked w of Andes). Tail black narrowly tipped white.

5. Female: Head and breast rufous. Throat and belly whitish (unstreaked w of Andes, streaked black e of Andes).

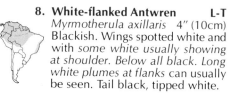

6. Checker-throated Antwren   **L-FT**
Myrmotherula fulviventris
          4" (10cm)
Above grayish brown. *Eye pale.* Wings brown, coverts blackish, wing-bars buff. *Throat white more or less checkered black.* Tail brown.

7. Female: Throat buffy brown. *Eye pale.* Below brownish.

8. White-flanked Antwren   **L-T**
Myrmotherula axillaris   4" (10cm)
Blackish. Wings spotted white and with *some white usually showing* at shoulder. Below all black. Long *white plumes at flanks* can usually be seen. Tail black, tipped white.

9. Female: Above gray to reddish brown, *wing coverts edged rufous. Eye dark.* Throat white. Below buff. Tail brown. White flank feathers often not visible.

10. Slaty Antwren   **LM-FT**
Myrmotherula schisticolor
          3½" (9cm)
Dark gray with *black throat and breast in contrast.* Wings spotted white. Tail tipped white.

11. Female: *Eye dark:* Above brownish gray. *No wing-bars.* Throat and breast buffy.

Ornate Antwren   **L-F**
Myrmotherula ornata   3½" (9cm)
Above gray, rump chestnut (upperparts all gray in central and s Peru and Bolivia). Wing coverts black dotted white. Throat black. Below gray, flanks browner.

12. Female: Above like male. Throat white checkered black (no black in Brazil). Below reddish brown.

Rupicola COCK-OF-THE-ROCK - 278. Lipaugus PIHAS - 276, 277.
Cotinga COTINGAS - 274. Tityra TITYRAS - 277.
Pipreola FRUITEATERS - 275, 276. Platypsaris BECARDS - 94.
Pachyramphus BECARDS - 94, 277.

1. Andean Cock-of-the-Rock
                                    LM-FW
Rupicola peruviana   10" (26cm)
Bright orange-red. Wings black,
inner feathers pearl gray. Crest
covers most of bill. Tail black. ♀:
Dark brown. Crest smaller.

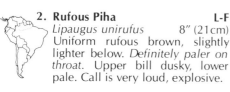

2. Rufous Piha   **L-F**
Lipaugus unirufus   8" (21cm)
Uniform rufous brown, slightly
lighter below. *Definitely paler on
throat.* Upper bill dusky, lower
pale. Call is very loud, explosive.

Plum-throated Cotinga   **L-F**
Cotinga maynana   7½" (19cm)
Shining blue. Throat purple. Wings
and tail black.

3. Female: Above brown, feathers
edged buff. Below buff spotted
brown. Tail brown.

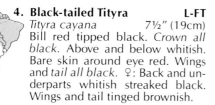

4. Black-tailed Tityra   **L-FT**
Tityra cayana   7½" (19cm)
Bill red tipped black. *Crown all
black.* Above and below whitish.
Bare skin around eye red. Wings
and *tail all black.* ♀: Back and un-
derparts whitish streaked black.
Wings and tail tinged brownish.

5. Barred Fruiteater   **MH-FT**
Pipreola arcuata   8" (20cm)
Bill and legs reddish. Head and
throat black. Eye orange. Above
olive green with single whitish
wing-bar, inner wing feathers
tipped white. Breast and belly
barred yellow and black. Tail
blackish, pale-tipped.

6. Female: Crown and sides of head
green like back. Throat barred like
rest of underparts.

7. Green-and-black Fruiteater
                                    MH-F
Pipreola riefferii   7" (18cm)
Bill and legs red. Head and throat
blackish. *Narrow semi-collar yellow.* Back, wings and tail green,
inner wing feathers prominently
tipped whitish. Belly yellow mottled green.

8. Female: Head and breast green
like back. Eye-ring yellow.

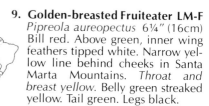

9. Golden-breasted Fruiteater LM-F
Pipreola aureopectus 6¼" (16cm)
Bill red. Above green, inner wing
feathers tipped white. Narrow yellow line behind cheeks in Santa
Marta Mountains. *Throat and
breast yellow.* Belly green streaked
yellow. Tail green. Legs black.

10. Female: *Below green streaked
yellow.*

Crested Becard   **L-FTS**
Platypsaris rufus   6½" (17cm)
Head with flat, black crest. Crown
glossy black. Back, wings and tail
grayish black. Below all brownish
(or gray in se Peru).

11. Female: Crown dark gray. Back,
wings and tail rufous. Underparts
all buff.

Green-backed Becard   **L-FTS**
Pachyramphus viridis 5" (13cm)
Crown black. Lores and forehead
white. Above uniform olive green.
Collar gray (lacking in n part of
range). Below white, broad breast
band yellowish.

12. Female: Crown gray. *Wing coverts
chestnut.*

Platypsaris BECARDS - 92. *Pachyramphus* BECARDS - 92, 277.

1. Pink-throated Becard   **L-FT**
Platypsaris minor   6" (15cm)
Male: (right). Above black. *Pink patch on throat.* Below gray. Tail black. Female: (left). *Head gray.* Broad semi-collar rufous. Back rufous tinged gray. Rump, wings and tail rufous. Below buff.

2. One-colored Becard   **L-FTS**
Platypsaris homochrous
         5½" (14cm)
Crown dark gray. Back gray. Wings black with white at bend of wing usually showing. Below light gray. Tail black.

3. Female: Very like the Cinnamon Becard (94-8) but has little or no white line above lores. Crown rufous.

4. White-winged Becard   **LM-TS**
Pachyramphus polychopterus
         5½" (14cm)
In e part of range: all black except more or less white on wings. Tail broadly tipped white.

5. In w part of range: Crown and mantle black. *Collar,* rump and underparts gray. Wing coverts and edges of primaries white. Tail black broadly tipped white.

6. Female: Olive above, browner on crown. Partial eye-ring and lores white. *Wing-bars, tips and sides of tail buff. Below pale yellowish.*

7. Chestnut-crowned Becard
                      LM-FT
Pachyramphus castaneus
         5" (13cm)
Crown dark chestnut. *Broad eyebrow gray joining at back of head.* Back, wing coverts and tail rufous. Below light rufous, whitish in center.

8. Cinnamon Becard   **L-TS**
Pachyramphus cinnamomeus
         5" (13cm)
Rufous brown above. Lores dusky. *Line above lores buffy.* Below pale cinnamon. Tail like back. Sexes alike. Similars: ♀ One-colored Becard (94-2) has no stripe above lores. ♀ Cinereous Becard (following) has less prominent line above lores.

9. Cinereous Becard   **L-TS**
Pachyramphus rufus   5" (13cm)
Forehead and lores white. Crown and nape black. Back light gray. Wings and tail dark gray, feathers edged white. Below white, tinged gray on breast and sides. ♀: Very like ♀ Cinnamon Becard (preceding) but white line above lores less prominent.

Black-and-white Becard   **LM-FT**
Pachyramphus albogriseus
         5" (13cm)
Very like grayish form of White-winged Becard (above at 94-5) but *back plain gray* instead of black.

10. Female: Cap chestnut, *margined at sides and back with black.* Forehead and eyebrow white. Cheeks gray. Back olivaceous. Wings and tail blackish, feathers edged and tipped cinnamon. Underparts yellowish, tinged olive on breast.

11. Barred Becard   **M-FT**
Pachyramphus versicolor
         4½" (12cm)
Crown and back glossy black. Rump and tail gray. Wings black, coverts profusely tipped white forming white patch. *Sides of head and throat greenish yellow. Below dull white finely barred dusky.*

12. Female: *Crown dark gray.* Back olive green. Wings blackish with *prominent rufous patch.* Eye-ring white. Lores whitish. Underparts yellowish faintly barred dusky.

WITH RED ON MORE THAN JUST TOP OF HEAD OR WITH PROMINENT
YELLOW.

1. Helmeted Manakin   L-FT
Antilophia galeata   5½" (14cm)
Black. *Projecting frontal crest,*
crown, nape and mantle red. ♀ at
100-8.

2. Pin-tailed Manakin   LM-FT
Ilicura militaris   4¾" (11cm)
Forecrown and *rump red.* Back
black. Eye bright yellowish. Sides
of head, throat and underparts
whitish. Tail black, *central feathers
long,* pointed. ♀: Eye yellow.
Above bright olive green. Sides of
head gray. Below whitish. *Tail like
♂.*

3. Crimson-hooded Manakin   L-FT
Pipra aureola   4" (10cm)
*Crown, nape, breast and center of
belly red.* Forehead and throat yellow. Back, wings and tail black.
♀ at 102-8.

4. Red-capped Manakin   L-FT
Pipra mentalis   3½" (9cm)
All glossy black except head and
nape red. Thighs yellow. Eye white.
♀ at 102-5.

5. Red-headed Manakin   L-T
Pipra rubrocapilla   4" (10cm)
Black. Head red. *Thighs red* with
small amount of white at knees.
Immature at 100-11. ♀: Above
dark olive-green. Underparts dull
gray, tinged olive on breast.

6. Striped Manakin   L-F
Machaeropterus regulus 3" (8cm)
Crown and nape red. Entire back
and sides of head greenish olive
or brownish olive. Throat grayish.
Below red striped white. Tail short,
brownish. ♀ at 100-10.

7. Wire-tailed Manakin   L-TS
Teleonema filicauda
      4" (10 cm plus tail filaments)
Crown and nape red. Back black.
Forehead and underparts yellow.
Tail black, ending in *long hair-like
filaments.* ♀: Above olive. Below
yellowish. *Tail like ♂ but shorter.*

8. Yellow-headed Manakin   M-F
Chloropipo flavicapilla
                           4¼" (11cm)
Crest and nape yellow. Eye bright
light orange. Back olive yellow.
Breast brownish. Belly pale yellow. ♀: Crown olive yellow like
back.

9. Golden-collared Manakin   L-T
Manacus vitellinus   4" (10cm)
Crown, upper back, wings and tail
black. Rump olive. *Collar, throat
and breast bright yellow.* Belly yellowish olive. Legs orange. ♀ at
102-2.

10. Golden-headed Manakin   L-FT
Pipra erythrocephala   3½" (9cm)
All black except *head yellow.*
Thighs red. Legs flesh color. ♀ at
102-3. Immature at 100-12.

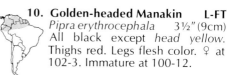

11. Golden-winged Manakin   LM-FT
Masius chrysopterus   4" (10cm)
Black. *Crest yellow, curving forward.* Hindcrown orange. Spot on
breast *yellow* (or throat and upper
breast yellow). Legs reddish. *Wings
and tail show much yellow in
flight.* ♀ at 100-9.

12. White-fronted Manakin   L-T
Pipra serena   3½" (9cm)
Black. *Forehead white. Rump
bright blue.* Throat and breast
black. Patch in center of breast orange or yellow. Below yellow. ♀ at
102-12.

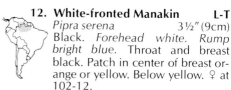

MOSTLY BLACK AND WHITE, OR BLUE, OR WITH RED ONLY ON TOP OF HEAD.

Chiroxiphia MANAKINS - 102.
Pipra MANAKINS - 96, 100, 102, 278, 279.
Manacus MANAKINS - 96, 102.
Corapipo MANAKINS - 102, 279.

1. **Blue (Swallow-tailed) Manakin**   **LM-FT**
Chiroxiphia caudata   5½" (14cm)
Crown red. Back blue. Nape, face, wings and throat black. *Below all blue.* Tail black, central feathers blue, lengthened. Legs dark flesh color. ♀: Olive green, paler below. *Tail like ♂.*

2. **Immature male:** Olive green with *prominent red forecrown.*

3. **Lance-tailed Manakin**   **L-TS**
Chiroxiphia lanceolata
                         4½" (12cm)
Black. Crown red. *Upper back blue.* Central *tail feathers lengthened, pointed.* ♀: Olive green, paler below. *Tail like ♂.* Legs orange.

4. **Blue-backed Manakin**   **LM-FT**
Chiroxiphia pareola   4¼" (11cm)
Black. Crown red. *Upper back blue.* Tail black, *normal shape.* ♀ at 102-4.

5. **Club-winged Manakin**   **L-FT**
Allocotopterus deliciosus
                         3½" (9cm)
Crown red. Nape, back, throat and breast brown. Wings black, *some white usually showing.* Bend of wing yellow. Belly blackish. ♀ at 102-7.

6. **Blue-crowned Manakin**   **L-F**
Pipra coronata   3" (8cm)
All black except crown blue. Belly sometimes grayish. Some races have mostly olive and green underparts, others have green back and breast with pale yellow belly. Legs black. ♀ at 102-10.

7. **Black Manakin**   **L-FT**
Xenopipo atronitens   5" (13cm)
Black. Wings and *fairly long tail* brownish black. ♀: Above dark green. Below paler green.

8. **White-bearded Manakin**   **L-T**
Manacus manacus   3½" (9cm)
Crown, back, wings and tail black. *Collar, throat and breast white.* Belly light gray. Rump gray. *Legs orange.* ♀ at 102-1.

9. **Immature male:** Olive. Throat grayish or varying amount of white. Belly whitish in center.

10. **White-ruffed Manakin**   **LM-F**
Corapipo leucorrhoa   3½" (9cm)
All glossy black except *throat and sides of neck white.* Vent whitish. ♀ at 102-9.

11. **White-crowned Manakin**   **LM-FT**
Pipra pipra   3½" (9cm)
All glossy black except *crown and nape white.* Eye orange-red. Legs black. ♀ at 102-11.

WITHOUT BRIGHT COLORS. SOME FEMALES AND SOME CONFUSING
IMMATURES IN CHANGING PLUMAGE.

Chloropipo MANAKINS - 96, 98, 279.
Piprites MANAKINS - 280.
Neopelma TYRANT-MANAKINS - 280.
Machaeropterus MANAKINS - 96, 279.
Pipra MANAKINS - 96, 98, 102, 278, 279.

Thrush-like Manakin **LM-F**
Schiffornis turdinus 6" (15 cm)
Variable. Uniform olive brown to
reddish brown, without distinctive
marks. Sometimes whitish around
eye. Wings and tail often more rufous than back.
1. **Brownish form.**
2. **Olivaceous form.**

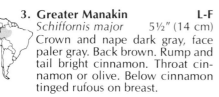

3. **Greater Manakin** **L-F**
Schiffornis major 5½" (14 cm)
Crown and nape dark gray, face
paler gray. Back brown. Rump and
tail bright cinnamon. Throat cinnamon or olive. Below cinnamon
tinged rufous on breast.

4. **Greenish Manakin** **LM-F**
Schiffornis virescens 5½" (14 cm)
Dull olive, paler below. *Wings and
tail reddish brown.* Very like dull
olive races of Thrush-like Manakin, above.

5. **Green Manakin** **L-F**
Chloropipo holochlora
4¼" (11 cm)
Above green. Throat and breast
green, tinged grayish on throat.
Belly yellowish. ♂ and ♀ alike.

6. **Wing-barred Manakin** **LM-F**
Piprites chloris 4¼" (11 cm)
Above olive green, nape gray.
Wing-bars yellowish white. Prominent *eye-ring* whitish. Lores and
throat yellow. Breast yellowish
olive or gray. Belly bright yellow
or gray.

7. **Wied's Tyrant-Manakin** **LM-F**
Neopelma aurifrons 4½" (12 cm)
Very plain. Semi-concealed crown
streak yellow to orange. Above
olive green. Below grayish, whiter
on throat, more olive on breast
and sides. Belly yellow. ♀: Like ♂
but crown streak smaller.

Helmeted Manakin **L-FT**
Antilophia galeata 5½" (14 cm)
♂ at 96-1.
8. **Female:** Olive green, paler below.
Frontal crest smaller than ♂ but
still evident.

Golden-winged Manakin **LM-FT**
Masius chrysopterus 4" (10 cm)
♂ at 96-11.
9. **Female:** Olive green. Throat, upper
breast and center of belly tinged
yellowish.

Striped Manakin **L-F**
Machaeropterus regulus 3" (8 cm)
♂ at 96-6.
10. **Female:** Above olive green. Below
whitish with distinct but dull
brownish streaking.

Red-headed Manakin **L-T**
Pipra rubrocapilla 4" (10 cm)
♂ at 96-5.
11. **Immature male:** Above dark olive.
Below dull gray. Varying amounts
of red on head.

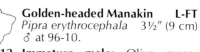

Golden-headed Manakin **L-FT**
Pipra erythrocephala 3½" (9 cm)
♂ at 96-10.
12. **Immature male:** Olive green.
Head shows varying amount of
yellow. Above and below show
varying amounts of black.

Female Manakins arranged here from orange legs through flesh or horn color legs to black legs. The following four female Manakins are not shown as they are easily recognized by tails with protruding feathers similar to males.

Swallow-tailed Manakin
Wire-tailed Manakin
Lance-tailed Manakin
Pin-tailed Manakin

White-bearded Manakin   L-T
Manacus manacus   3½" (9 cm)
♂ at 98-8.

1. **Female:** Above olive-green. Throat and breast grayish. Belly light yellowish. *Legs orange.*

Golden-collared Manakin   L-T
Manacus vitellinus   4" (10 cm)
♂ at 96-9.

2. **Female:** Above olive-green. Throat lighter olive shading to yellow on belly. *Legs orange.*

Golden-headed Manakin   L-FT
Pipra erythrocephala   3½" (9 cm)
♂ at 96-10.

3. **Female:** Varies from olive-green to brownish. Bill varies from yellowish to brown. *Eye-ring whitish.* Belly yellowish, whitish in center. *Legs pinkish.*

Blue-backed Manakin   L-T
Chiroxiphia pareola   4¼" (11 cm)
♂ at 98-4.

4. **Female:** Above olive-green. Breast paler olive. Belly yellowish. Legs light flesh color.

Red-capped Manakin   L-FT
Pipra mentalis   3½" (9 cm)
♂ at 96-4.

5. **Female:** Olive-green. Underwing coverts and belly yellowish. Legs brownish.

Band-tailed Manakin   L-FT
Pipra fasciicauda   4" (10 cm)
Male: Crown and nape red. Back and wings black. (Wings show white band in flight) Throat and belly yellow. Breast red or orange. Tail black with *whitish median band. Eye white.*

6. **Female:** Olive-green, paler and yellower below. Legs dark flesh color.

Club-winged Manakin   L-FT
Allocotopterus deliciosus
                              3½" (9 cm)
♂ at 98-5.

7. **Female:** Above olive-green. Throat white bordered at sides by cinnamon. Breast and sides olive. Center of belly and bend of wing yellow. Legs gray.

Crimson-hooded Manakin   L-FT
Pipra aureola   4" (10 cm)
♂ at 96-3.

8. **Female:** Olive-green, paler and yellower below. Legs blackish.

White-ruffed Manakin   LM-F
Corapipo leucorrhoa   3½" (9 cm)
♂ at 98-10.

9. **Female:** Olive-green. Throat and sides of head gray. Belly and undertail coverts yellowish. Legs black.

Blue-crowned Manakin   L-F
Pipra coronata   3" (8 cm)
♂ at 98-6.

10. **Female:** *Above bluish-green.* Throat grayish. Breast green. Belly yellow (gray in some races). Legs black.

White-crowned Manakin LM-FT
Pipra pipra   3½" (9 cm)
♂ at 98-11.

11. **Female:** *Eye bright orange. Head gray.* Back olive. Below grayish or yellowish. Legs black.

White-fronted Manakin   L-T
Pipra serena   3½" (9 cm)
♂ at 96-12.

12. **Female:** Above green (not olive), turning bluish green on rump. Throat whitish. Breast yellow with *green band* across lower breast. Belly yellow. Legs black.

LARGE FLYCATCHERS 1, WITH BRIGHT YELLOW UNDERPARTS.

Myiodynastes FLYCATCHERS - 108, 285.
Tyrannus FLYCATCHERS - 284.
Tyrannopsis FLYCATCHERS - 284.
Myiozetetes FLYCATCHERS - 285.

1. Boat-billed Flycatcher   LM-FT
Megarhynchus pitangua
8½" (21 cm)
Bill ¾x head, *broad, flat, heavy.*
Concealed crest yellowish. Face
black, eyebrow white. Above olive
brown. Throat white. Below bright
yellow.

2. Great Kiskadee   L-TSO
Pitangus sulphuratus   8" (20 cm)
Bill ¾x head, *high, ridged.* Semi-
concealed crest lemon yellow. Face
black, eyebrow white. Above
brown, wings and tail mostly rufous. Throat white. Below bright
yellow.

3. Lesser Kiskadee   L-SOW
Pitangus lictor   6½" (17 cm)
Very like Great Kiskadee (preceding) but smaller and *bill more
slender.*

**4. Golden-crowned Flycatcher
MH-FT**
Myiodynastes chrysocephalus
8" (20 cm)
Bill ½x head. Semi-concealed crest
yellow. Face dusky. Eyebrow and
whisker white. Back olive. Throat
white. Below yellow, tinged gray
on breast.

5. Tropical Kingbird   LMH-TSO
Tyrannus melancholicus
8" (20 cm)
Bill ⅔ x head. *Head and nape
gray.* Back grayish olive. Wings
dusky with *no rufous.* Cheeks
dusky. Throat whitish. Breast olive.
Belly yellow. Tail blackish, slightly
forked. Perches conspicuously.

6. White-throated Kingbird   L-TO
Tyrannus albogularis   7" (18 cm)
Very like Tropical Kingbird (preceding) but *back light gray* (not
grayish olive). Throat pure white
and rest of underparts bright yellow.

7. Cattle Tyrant   L-SO
Machetornis rixosus   7" (18 cm)
Bill ½x head. Crown and nape light
gray. Back light brown. Throat
white (or yellow in Colombia and
Venezuela). Below yellow. Legs
long. *Usually on ground.*

8. Sulphury Flycatcher   L-FTS
Tyrannopsis sulphurea
6½" (17 cm)
Bill ½x head. Narrow whitish line
over eye usually indistinct. Head
and back brownish gray. Wings
brown, thin edges of flight feathers
rufous. Sides of face dusky. Throat
white, below yellow vaguely
streaked olive on breast. Tail
brown, square.

**9. Rusty-margined Flycatcher
LM-TSW**
Myiozetetes cayanensis
6¼" (16 cm)
Bill very short, less than half head
length. Crown blackish with
usually *concealed yellow crest.*
Long eyebrow white. Broad line
through eye blackish. Back brown.
Primaries with rufous edges.
Throat white. Below all yellow.
Usual call is a high pitched
long-drawn "peeeeeer".

**10. Social (Vermilion-crowned)
Flycatcher   L-TSO**
Myiozetetes similis   6" (15 cm)
Bill short. Crown grayish with usually *concealed red crest.* Long eyebrow white. Very like Rusty-margined Flycatcher (preceding) but
broad line through eye not as deep
black and edges of primaries not
rufous (immatures sometimes have
some rufous). Throat white. Below
yellow. Noisy. Most common call
"kree-yoo".

11. Yellow-browed Tyrant   LM-TO
Satrapa icterophrys   6" (15 cm)
Bill ½ x head. Above olive, wings
blackish with gray wing-bars. *Long
broad eyebrow bright yellow.*
Cheeks blackish. Underparts bright
yellow. Tail black.

LARGE FLYCATCHERS 2, WITHOUT BRIGHT YELLOW UNDERPARTS.

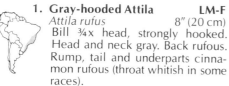

1. Gray-hooded Attila   LM-F
Attila rufus   8″ (20 cm)
Bill ¾x head, strongly hooked.
Head and neck gray. Back rufous.
Rump, tail and underparts cinna-
mon rufous (throat whitish in some
races).

2. Bright-rumped Attila   LM-FT
Attila spadiceus   7″ (18 cm)
Bill nearly as long as head, strongly
hooked. Eye red or orange. Upperparts vary from olive to brown
to rufous, but in all races can be
recognized by *bright yellow rump*.
Throat and breast olive to brown,
streaked dusky. Belly whitish.

3. Cinnamon Attila   L-TS
Attila cinnamomeus   7″ (18 cm)
Bill black. Above rufous, paler on
rump. Wing coverts blackish, margined rufous. Primaries dusky
brown. Throat and breast brownish, belly lighter.

4. Rufous Mourner   LM-FT
Rhytipterna holerythra· 7″ (18 cm)
Uniform plain rufous brown, paler
below. Upper bill dusky, lower bill
pale, usually tipped black. No eye-
ring.

5. Cinereous Mourner   L-FT
*Laniocera hypopyrrha*7½″ (19 cm)
bove gray, wings brownish gray
with *two rows of cinnamon spots.*
Underparts gray. Vent blackish or
cinnamon. Tail gray, tipped cinnamon.

6. Speckled Mourner   L-FT
Laniocera rufescens   7″ (18 cm)
Mostly rufous brown. *Well-formed
eye-ring* light rufous. Wing coverts
dusky with cinnamon tips. Below
somewhat lighter rufous brown,
breast faintly scalloped or spotted
dusky.

7. Smoky Bush-Tyrant   H-FT
Myiotheretes fumigatus
                        7½″ (19 cm)
*Above and below dark smoky
brown.* Faint wing-bars clay color.
Prominent rufous patch shows on
open wing. Thin eyebrow and line
below eye whitish. Line through
eye dark brown. Throat streaked
white.

8. Crested (Black-Tyrant) Tyrant
                               L-SO
Knipolegus lophotes   7″ (18 cm)
All glossy blue black. *Conspicu-
ously crested. Bill black.* Promi-
nent white band in wings in flight.
♀: Like ♂ but smaller.

9. Swainson's Flycatcher   L-TS
Myiarchus swainsoni   7″ (18 cm)
Bill black or lower bill brownish.
Dark olive brown above. No ru-
fous in wings or tail. Throat and
breast pale gray. Belly pale yellow.
Outer tail feather narrowly edged
pale.

10. Brown-crested Flycatcher   L-S
Myiarchus tyrannulus   7″ (18 cm)
Crown and back brownish. Wings
with white bars and thin rufous
edging to primaries. Throat paler
gray than breast. Belly light yellow. *Much rufous shows in tail.*

11. Short-crested Flycatcher   L-TS
Myiarchus ferox   6½″ (17 cm)
Bill black. Above dull dark olive.
Wing-bars not prominent. *No rufous in wings or tail of adult.* Throat
and breast pale grayish. Belly light
yellow.

12. Dusky-capped Flycatcher LM-FT
Myiarchus tuberculifer
                        6¼″ (16 cm)
Crown blackish. Back olive. Wing
feathers edged rufous. Throat and
breast pale gray. Belly pale yellow.
Tail without rufous in most races
but does have some rufous in w
Colombia.

LARGE FLYCATCHERS 3, AND MID-SIZE FLYCATCHERS 1, WITHOUT BRIGHT YELLOW UNDERPARTS.

Myiodynastes FLYCATCHERS - 104, 285.
Xolmis MONJITAS - 281.
Contopus PEWEES - 116, 286.

1. Streaked Flycatcher   LM-TS
Myiodynastes maculatus
7" (18 cm)
Upper bill black, *lower light colored at base.* Above dark brown *streaked buff.* Below whitish, *streaked black* except on center of belly. Tail rufous. Very like Sulphur-bellied Flycatcher (285-5) but underparts whitish instead of yellowish.

Black-and-white Monjita   L-SW
Xolmis dominicana   7" (18 cm)
All white except tail and folded wings black. Black primaries show white tips in flight.
2. Female: Crown, nape and back brownish.

3. White Monjita   L-SO
Xolmis irupero   6½" (17 cm)
All white except primaries and broad tips of tail black.

4. Greater Pewee   MH-F
Contopus fumigatus   6½" (17 cm)
Crested. Upper bill dusky, lower yellowish. *Lower bill yellowish.* Above dark gray. Below lighter gray (throat and/or center of belly whitish in some races). Tail dark gray (outer feather edged whitish in some races).

5. Black Phoebe   LMH-W
Sayornis nigricans   6½" (17 cm)
Black. Some white shows on edges of wing feathers and edges of tail. *Belly white.* Usually found around rocky streams. Bobs tail.

6. Sirystes   L-FT
Sirystes sibilator   6½" (17 cm)
Crown and nape black. Back grayish. Much white edging shows on wing feathers. *Rump white* in some races. Throat and breast light gray becoming white on belly. Tail black (with white tip w of Andes).

7. Sharpbill   LM-F
Oxyruncus cristatus   6¼" (16 cm)
Bill short, sharply pointed. Back olive green. Below pale yellow or white, *profusely spotted black.* Wings and tail blackish. Is in a separate family.

8. Royal Flycatcher   L-FT

Onychorhynchus coronatus
6¼" (16 cm)
Large crest red tipped blue but practically never seen in the wild. Folded crest gives head a *hammerhead look.* Above brown, wing coverts spotted buff. Throat whitish. Below brownish. *Rump and tail cinnamon.*

9. Brownish Flycatcher   L-FT
Cnipodectes subbrunneus
6¼" (16 cm)
Eye light orange. Above brown. Throat grayish. Breast brown. Belly whitish. Rump and tail brown tinged rufous.

10. Fulvous-breasted Flatbill   LM-F
Rhynchocyclus fulvipectus
6" (15 cm)
Bill very broad and flat. Eye-ring not prominent. Above olive. *Throat tawny.* Breast streaked dusky. Belly yellow. Tail olive.

11. Olivaceous Flatbill   L-FT

Rhynchocyclus olivaceus
5½" (14 cm)
Bill very broad and flat. *Eye-ring whitish.* Above olive green. Throat and breast light grayish olive, streaked yellow. Belly pale yellow. Tail greenish.

12. Eye-ringed Flatbill   L-F

Rhynchocyclus brevirostris
5½" (14 cm)
Bill very broad and flat. *Prominent eye-ring whitish.* Above dark olive green. Below yellowish streaked olive on breast.

MID-SIZE FLYCATCHERS 2

Elaenia ELAENIAS -293.
Knipolegus TYRANTS - 106, 283, 284.

1. Highland Elaenia   LM-FT
Elaenia obscura   6½" (17 cm)
Large size. Above uniform dark dull olive to olive brown. *No crown patch.* Two conspicuous broad white wing-bars. *Below uniform greenish yellow,* center of belly slightly paler.

2. White-crested Elaenia   MH-S
Elaenia albiceps   5½" (14 cm)
Above dark olive. Wing-bars whitish. Eye-ring white, prominent. Throat and breast grayish. Belly white.

3. Yellow-bellied Elaenia   LM-TSO
Elaenia flavogaster   6" (15 cm)
Bill quite short. Above grayish olive, wing-bars whitish. Throat white. Below pale yellow, tinged olive on breast. *Crest frequently raised showing white in center.*

4. Small-billed Elaenia   LM-TS
Elaenia parvirostris   5½" (14 cm)
Bill short. *Eye-ring white, well marked.* Above olive tinged greenish. Wing-bars prominent. Throat and breast pale gray. Belly pale yellow.

5. Rufous-crowned Elaenia   LM-F
Elaenia ruficeps   5½" (14 cm)
Crown patch rufous, usually visible. Above dark brown. Throat whitish. Below pale yellow with blurry gray streaking on throat and breast. Wing-bars conspicuous, pale gray.

6. Plain-crested Elaenia   L-SO
Elaenia cristata   5" (13 cm)
No crown patch. Above brownish *gray, with little olive.* Conspicuous white wing-bars. Throat whitish. Breast pale gray. Belly pale yellow.

**7. Blue-billed (Black-Tyrant) Tyrant
LMH-TS**
Knipolegus cyanirostris
5½" (14 cm)
All black. *Bill blue.* Eye red.

8. Female: Crown dull rufous. Back dark brown. Rump rufous. Below whitish *heavily streaked black.*

9. Riverside Tyrant   L-W
Knipolegus orenocensis
5½" (14 cm)
Dark slaty gray. Crown, lores and wings blackish. Bill pale blue. Eye reddish brown. ♀: Like ♂ but more brownish gray (or below buffy in e Brazil), (or above brown buffy streaked gray in Peru and w Brazil).

10. Rufous-tailed Tyrant   MH-TS
Knipolegus poecilurus   5" (13 cm)
Eye red. Above grayish. Wings black, *broad wing-bars buffy.* Throat buffy. Breast obscurely streaked gray. Belly pale brown. Tail inner webs rufous (tail all dark gray in some races).

11. Piratic Flycatcher   L-T
Legatus leucophaius 5½" (14 cm)
Bill less than ½ head length. Crown brownish. Eyebrow whitish. Ear coverts dusky. Back brown. *No rufous in wings or tail.* Throat white. Narrow whisker dusky. Breast whitish streaked dusky. Belly yellow.

Spectacled Tyrant   LM-W
Hymenops perspicillata 5" (13 cm)
Black. Bill and *skin around eye yellow.* Primaries white, tipped black.

12. Female: Above brownish, streaked black. Eye-ring yellow. Primaries rufous, tipped black. Wing coverts tipped buff. Below buffy, streaked dusky on breast.

MID-SIZE FLYCATCHERS 3, AND SMALL FLYCATCHERS 1.

1. Yellow-olive Flycatcher   LM-TS
Tolmomyias sulphurescens
5½" (14cm)
Bill wide, upper dark, lower pale. Eye usually pale. Crown and nape gray or olive. *Lores white.* Back olive. Below olive yellow, yellow on center of belly.

2. Gray-crowned Flycatcher   L-TS
Tolmomyias poliocephalus
4½" (12cm)
Bill wide, dark except base of lower. Crown and nape dark gray. Lores whitish. Back olive. Underparts olive yellow.

3. Yellow-breasted Flycatcher   L-S
Tolmomyias flaviventris
4½" (12cm)
Bill wide. Crown olive with no grayish tinge. *Lores yellow. Below yellow* (breast sometimes washed with olive). Wing-bars sometimes not well-defined.

4. Dusky-tailed Flatbill   L-F
Ramphotrigon fuscicauda
5" (13cm)
Bill very wide and flat. Above dull olive. Wings blackish with two cinnamon bars. Throat yellowish streaked dusky. *Breast olive.* Belly dull yellow, streaked dusky. Tail blackish.

5. Large-headed Flatbill   L-F
Ramphotrigon megacephala
5" (13cm)
Bill very wide and flat. *Crown dark brown.* Above olive. Eye-ring and narrow eyebrow yellowish. Wings with two broad cinnamon bars. Below dull pale yellow, streaked olive on breast.

6. Slaty-capped Flycatcher   LM-F
Leptopogon superciliaris 5" (13cm)
Crown dark gray. Narrow eyebrow and lores whitish. Ear spot black. Cheeks marbled black and white. Back olive green. Wings blackish with two bars. Throat grayish. Breast light olive. Belly pale yellow.

7. Sepia-capped Flycatcher   L-FT
Leptopogon amaurocephalus
4½" (12cm)
Crown dark brown. Back olive green. *Wings brownish with two buff bars.* Lores whitish. *Spot on ear coverts dusky.* Throat grayish. Breast light olive. Belly pale yellow.

8. Brown-backed Chat-Tyrant   H-S
Ochthoeca fumicolor 5" (13cm)
Above grayish brown. *Broad eyebrow buffy white* (rufous in Venezuela). *Rufous wing-bars conspicuous.* Throat grayish. Below rufous brown. Tail dusky.

9. Slaty-backed Chat-Tyrant   MH-F
Ochthoeca cinnamomeiventris
4½" (12cm)
Upperparts and throat dark slaty gray with *prominent, but short, white eyebrow.* Underparts dark chestnut (or belly gray, or all underparts gray, in different races).

**10. Rufous-breasted Chat-Tyrant
MH-T**
Ochthoeca rufipectoralis
4½" (12cm)
Above dark brown. Wings with well-marked rufous bars (no wing-bars in Bolivia). *Prominent white eyebrow very long.* Throat grayish. *Breast rufous.* Belly white. Tail blackish, outer feathers white.

11. Crowned Chat-Tyrant   H-S
Ochthoeca frontalis 4½" (12cm)
Above dark brown. *Forehead and eyebrow yellow becoming white back of eye.* Wings dark brown, no wing-bars (with rufous bars in s). *Underparts gray.*

**12. Yellow-bellied Chat-Tyrant
MH-F**
Ochthoeca diadema 4¼" (11cm)
Crown blackish. *Forehead and long eyebrow yellow.* Back brownish. Wings usually with two rufous bars. Throat and breast yellowish olive, belly bright yellow. Tail dark brown, edged olive.

MID-SIZE FLYCATCHERS 4, AND SMALL FLYCATCHERS 2.

Myiopagis ELAENIAS — 293,294.
Phylloscartes TYRANNULETS — 290.
Mecocerculus TYRANNULETS — 292, 293.
Stigmatura WAGTAIL-TYRANT — 292.
Corythopis ANTPIPIT — 295.

1. Greenish Elaenia   **L-TS**
Myiopagis viridicata   5½"(14cm)
Above olive with *semi-concealed*
(but often visible) *yellow crown*
patch. Wings edged yellow, but
with *no* (or very indistinct) bars.
Throat whitish. Breast grayish
olive. Belly pale yellow.

2. Gray Elaenia   **L-FT**
Myiopagis caniceps   4½"(12cm)
Above all gray (or back olive
green). *Large crown patch yellow.*
Wings black with *two bold white
bars and edging.* Below whitish,
tinged gray on breast.
3. Female: Above olive-green. Throat
gray. *Below yellow.*

4. Forest Elaenia   **L-FT**
Myiopagis gaimardii   4½"(12cm)
*Crown gray. Semi-concealed crown
stripe yellowish white.* Lores and
eye-ring white. Above greenish
olive. Wings with two whitish bars.
Throat whitish. Below pale yellow,
tinged gray on breast.

5. Mottle-cheeked Tyrannulet M-FT
Phylloscartes ventralis 4½"(12cm)
Above olive. Lores dusky. *Bold
double wing-bars pale yellow.*
Throat grayish yellow. Below dull
yellow, flecked with olive on
breast. *Long tail often "half-
cocked".*

6. Serra do Mar Tyrannulet   LM-FT
Phylloscartes difficilis 4½"(12cm)
Above olive green, wing and tail
feathers edged yellowish. No wing-
bars. *Prominent eye-ring white.*
Throat and breast gray mottled
white. Belly white.

7. White-throated Tyrannulet
      MH-TS
Mecocerculus leucophrys
            5"(13cm)
Above brown or olive brown or
dark reddish brown. Short eyebrow white. Wings dusky with two
prominent whitish or rufous bars.
Throat contrastingly white. Breast
grayish. Belly yellowish. Tail rather
long, brown.

8. Fuscous Flycatcher   **L-TSO**
Cnemotriccus fuscatus   5"(13cm)
Above grayish brown to reddish
brown. *Long eyebrow buffy. Wing-
bars cinnamon to buffy.* Throat
white. Breast grayish. Belly white
or pale yellow. Tail brown without
white tip. Bill all black.

9. Cinnamon Flycatcher   **M-FT**
Pyrrhomyias cinnamomea
            4½"(12cm)
Above brownish olive with indefinite collar, rump and *prominent
wing patch cinnamon. Underparts
cinnamon* becoming lighter on
belly.

10. Form in Venezuela and ne Colombia is all cinnamon.

11. Lesser Wagtail-Tyrant   **L-S**
Stigmatura napensis   5"(13cm)
Above brownish olive. *Single broad
wing-bar white.* Eyebrow and underparts pale yellow. Tail long, with
median white band and broad
white tip (no tip on central feathers).

12. Ringed Antpipit   **L-F**
Corythopis torquata   5"(13cm)
Above reddish brown. Sides of
head gray in some races. Throat
white. Below white with *black
band across breast,* becoming
black streaks below. Terrestrial.
Walks, wagging tail.

MID-SIZE FLYCATCHERS 5, AND SMALL FLYCATCHERS 3.

Contopus PEWEES - 108, 286.
Empidonax FLYCATCHERS - 287.

1. Fork-tailed Flycatcher   L-SO

Muscivora tyrannus   5" (13 cm)
(up to 28 cm with elongated tail)
Above gray, rump black. Head
black. Below white. Tail black. *Two
outer tail feathers very long,* sometimes edged white.

2. Long-tailed Tyrant   L-T

Colonia colonus   4½" (12 cm)
(up to 20 cm with elongated tail)
Black except head grayish white
and rump white (center of back
also white w of Andes). *Two central tail feathers greatly elongated,
very narrow.*

3. Masked Water-Tyrant   L-W

Fluvicola nengeta   5" (13 cm)
Head, rump and underparts white.
Long black stripe through eye.
Back pale brown. Wings black.
Tail black tipped white.

4. Pied Water-Tyrant   L-W

Fluvicola pica   4½" (12 cm)
White with wings, nape, mantle
and tail black (♀ dark brown).
Southern races have lower back
also black.

5. Wood Pewee   LMH-FT

*Contopus virens**   5" (13 cm)
Upper bill black, lower light.
Above gray. Eye-ring faint (or absent). *Lores gray.* Throat white.
Breast gray. Belly whitish. Wings
relatively long, reaching more than
halfway down tail when perching.
Typical call: "pee-wee" or "pee-a-
wee."

6. Tropical Pewee   LM-TS

Contopus cinereus   4½" (12 cm)
Crown dark grayish. Back brownish gray. Lores and throat whitish.
Breast grayish. Belly white (sometimes tinged yellow). Wings relatively short, reaching less than
halfway down tail when perching.
Typical call: an upward-inflected
"seerip."

7. Traill's Flycatcher   L-TS

*Empidonax traillii**   5" (13 cm)
Eye-ring buffy. Above brownish
olive. Wing-bars and throat white.
Breast grayish. Belly pale yellow.
Usual non-breeding call short, one
syllable.

8. Acadian Flycatcher   LM-T

*Empidonax virescens**   5" (13 cm)
Eye-ring buffy. Above olive green.
Wing-bars and throat white. Breast
grayish. Belly pale yellow. Usual
non-breeding call: two syllables,
rising, "peet-suh".

9. Euler's Flycatcher   L-FT

Empidonax euleri   4½" (12 cm)
Above brownish. *Wing-bars buff
or cinnamon.* Eye-ring and lores
whitish. No eyebrow. Throat whitish. Breast grayish brown. Belly
pale yellow. Upper bill black,
lower pale.

10. Gray-hooded Flycatcher   LM-TS

Pipromorpha rufiventris 5" (13 cm)
Entire head and throat gray contrasting with olive back and ochraceous breast and belly. Wings and
tail brownish.

11. Ochre-bellied Flycatcher   L-TS

Pipromorpha oleaginea
4½" (12 cm)
Bill rather long and slender. Base
of lower bill light colored. *Above
olive green. Wing-bars buffy, not
obvious.   Below   ochraceous,*
strongly tinged olive on throat.

12. McConnell's Flycatcher   LM-F

Pipromorpha macconnelli
4½" (12 cm)
Very like Ochre-bellied Flycatcher
(preceding) but *wings without bars.*
Mouth-lining dark (flesh in Ochre-
bellied).

MID-SIZE FLYCATCHERS 6, AND SMALL FLYCATCHERS 4.

Uromyias FLYCATCHERS - 292.
Myiophobus FLYCATCHERS - 122, 287.

1. Streak-necked Flycatcher   M-FT
Mionectes striaticollis   5" (13 cm)
Head all gray, sides sometimes finely streaked white. Back olive green. Wings and tail brown. Usually no wing-bars. *Throat* and breast gray, *streaked white.* Belly yellow, usually not streaked in center of belly.

2. Olive-striped Flycatcher   L-FT
Mionectes olivaceus   5" (13 cm)
Very like preceding but at lower elevations. Head not so solid gray. White spot back of eye more prominent. Streaking on breast wider and usually has some streaks in center of belly. Some races have wing-bars.

3. Agile Tit-Tyrant   MH-F
Uromyias agilis   4½" (12 cm)
Long crest black bordered by thin whitish line on each side. Back brown streaked dusky. Below light yellow *strongly streaked* dark brown on throat and breast. Tail long, dark brown.

4. Vermilion Flycatcher   LMH-SO
Pyrocephalus rubinus 4½" (12 cm)
Resident and migrant. Back and tail dark brownish. Head and underparts red (in w Peru an all-black phase occurs).

5. Female: Above dark grayish brown. Eyebrow whitish (lacking in some races). Below whitish, streaked dusky on breast. Belly usually with some pink or yellow.

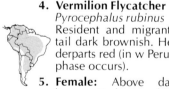

6. Black-tailed Flycatcher   L-T
Myiobius atricaudus 4½" (12 cm)
Semi-concealed crown patch yellow. Above brownish olive. *Large rump patch yellow. Breast light brownish.* Belly yellow. Tail long, black, rounded. Much like next species.

7. Sulphur-rumped Flycatcher   L-F
Myiobius barbatus   5" (13 cm)
Semi-concealed crown patch yellow. Above olive green. *Rump pale yellow, conspicuous.* Throat whitish. *Breast olive* (brighter ochraceous w of Andes). Belly yellow. Tail black. Much like preceding species.

8. Tawny-breasted Flycatcher   M-F
Myiobius villosus   5" (13 cm)
Semi-concealed crown patch yellow. Above dark olive. *Rump pale yellow,* Throat whitish, *below reddish brown.* Center of belly yellow.

9. Orange-crested Flycatcher   L-F
Myiophobus phoenicomitra
4½" (12 cm)
Like Flavescent Flycatcher (following) but darker olive above. Semi-concealed crown patch cinnamon rufous. Below light yellow with contrasting breast band and sides olive green.

10. Flavescent Flycatcher   M-T
Myiophobus flavicans
4½" (12 cm)
Semi-concealed crown patch yellow. Incomplete eye-ring yellowish. Above olive brown or olive green. Wings with *two* ochraceous bars. Below yellow usually shaded olive on breast. Tail grayish brown.

Bran-colored Flycatcher LM-TSO
Myiophobus fasciatus 4¼" (11 cm)
Varies from grayish brown to reddish brown which look quite different in the field. Semi-concealed crown patch yellow to orange. Throat white. *Breast conspicuously streaked.* (Underparts all plain cinnamon along Pacific coast).

11. Reddish brown race in w part of range.

12. Grayish brown race in rest of range.

SMALL FLYCATCHERS 5.

1. Tufted Flycatcher   LM-T
Mitrephanes phaeocercus
4½" (12 cm)
Crest brownish. Above dull olive. *Throat and breast buffy.* Below pale yellow. Grayish wing-bars very indistinct in Columbia and Ecuador; more prominent to s.

2. Pale-tipped Tyrannulet   L-S
Inezia subflava   4¼" (11 cm)
Above olive or brownish. Wings brown, wing-bars whitish. Eyebrow and eye-ring white. *Eye pale.* Below dull yellow, more or less clouded olive on breast. Tail tipped white or ochraceous, and with *outer web white.*

3. Ornate Flycatcher   LM-T
Myiotriccus ornatus   4¼" (11 cm)
Crown black. Prominent *white spot in front of eye.* Back olive, *rump yellow.* Throat gray. Below yellow, tinged olive on breast. Tail blackish or cinnamon.

4. Bronze-olive Pygmy-Tyrant   M-F
Pseudotriccus pelzelni
4¼" (11 cm)
Above uniform greenish olive. Below yellowish *tinged brownish on breast and sides.* West of Andes crown is slaty, throat and belly are light yellowish.

5. Rufous-headed Pygmy-Tyrant
MH-F
Pseudotriccus ruficeps
4¼" (11 cm)
Head and throat rufous. Back dark olive. Below olive, yellow in center of belly. Wings, rump and tail chestnut.

6. Sharp-tailed Tyrant   L-S
Culicivora caudacuta 4¼" (11 cm)
Above brown streaked black. Crown and sides of head blackish, lores and eyebrow white. Below pale brownish. *Tail narrow and pointed.*

7. White-headed Marsh-Tyrant L-W
Arundinicola leucocephala
4¼" (11 cm)
All black except *head and throat white.* Bill black, lower yellow at base.

8. Female: Above gray. Forecrown and underparts white. Tail black.

9. Torrent Tyrannulet   M-W
Serpophaga cinerea   4¼" (11 cm)
Head, wings and tail black. Some races have definite wing-bars. *Back light gray.* Below whitish. Usually by rocky streams. Bobs tail.

10. River Tyrannulet   L-OW
Serpophaga hypoleuca 4" (10 cm)
Above grayish brown. No wing-bars. *Crest blackish.* Below white, washed gray on breast. Tail dark brown, outer feathers edged whitish.

11. White-crested Tyrannulet LM-TS
Serpophaga subcristata 4" (10 cm)
Bill all black. Crown gray with semi-concealed white crest. Back greenish gray. Wings dusky, wing-bars yellowish white. Throat white. Breast gray. Belly pale yellow.

2

3

5

6

8

9

10

11

SMALL FLYCATCHERS 6.

1. Variegated Bristle-Tyrant   M-F
Pogonotriccus poecilotis
                    4¼" (11 cm)
Crown gray. Back olive. Lores and
eye-ring white. *Two very broad
ochraceous wing-bars.* Below yellowish. Note white mark back of
black ear patch.

2. Marbled-faced Bristle-Tyrant M-F

Pogonotriccus ophthalmicus
                    4¼" (11 cm)
Crown gray. Face speckled white.
Back olive green. Two narrow
olive-yellow wing-bars. Breast
olive, belly yellow or whitish.
White mark back of black ear patch.

3. Ashy-headed Tyrannulet   M-F
Tyranniscus cinereiceps 4" (10 cm)
Crown blue gray. Forehead and
face grizzled white. Back greenish
olive. Black spot on ear coverts.
Wings black, bars buffy. Throat
and breast greenish yellow. Belly
bright yellow.

4. Paltry Tyrannulet   LM-T
Tyranniscus vilissimus
                    4¼" (11 cm)
Crown slaty. Eyebrow whitish.
Below pale grayish, lighter throat
and becoming yellowish on belly.
Back olive. *Wing feathers conspic-
uously edged yellow,* without bars.

5. Golden-faced Tyrannulet LM-FT
Tyranniscus viridiflavus 4" (10 cm)
Forehead and lores yellow. Crown
and back grayish olive. No wing-
bars but each wing feather sharply
edged yellow. Chin yellowish.
Below light gray or yellowish.

6. Black-capped Tyrannulet MH-FT
Tyranniscus nigrocapillus
                    4¼" (11 cm)
Crown black (or dark brown). Back
olive green. Wings blackish. Eyebrow, wing-bars and throat whitish. Below yellow. Breast olive in
some races.

7. Tawny-rumped Tyrannulet MH-F
Tyranniscus uropygialis
                    4¼" (11 cm)
Crown dark brown. Eyebrow white.
Back brown, rump tawny. Wings
black with two buffy bars. Throat
and breast pale grayish, below pale
yellowish.

8. Ruddy-tailed Flycatcher   L-FT
Terenotriccus erythrurus
                    4" (10 cm)
Bill less than half head length.
Crown and nape grayish. Back gray
becoming cinnamon on rump.
Throat buffy to cinnamon, rest of
*underparts bright cinnamon. Tail
bright rufous.*

9. Brown-breasted Pygmy-Tyrant
                    M-F
Hemitriccus obsoletus

                    4½" (11 cm)
Above brown. Large buffy spot in
front of eye. Breast brown, sometimes lightly flecked whitish. Belly
yellowish.

10. Handsome Flycatcher   M-F
Myiophobus pulcher   4" (10 cm)
Crown gray or olive. Back olive or
brownish. Wings black, bars buffy
or cinnamon. Throat and breast
yellow, more or less tinged orange. Belly light yellow. Tail
brownish.

11. Mouse-colored Tyrannulet L-SO
Phaeomyias murina   4" (10 cm)
Above dull brown. White eyebrow
and lores poorly marked. Wings
darker brown with two buffy bars.
Throat whitish. Breast pale gray.
Belly whitish. Tail brown.

12. Many-colored Rush-Tyrant
                    LMH-W
Tachuris rubrigastra   4" (10 cm)
Crown black, central stripe red.
Long eyebrow whitish or yellowish. Back greenish. *Single wing-
bar white. Black mark at sides of
breast.* Below either yellow or
white. Tail black, outer feathers
white.

SMALL FLYCATCHERS 7.

1. Russet-winged Spadebill   LM-F
Platyrinchus leucoryphus
                        4¼"(11cm)
*Bill very broad and flat. Eye-ring
and spot in front of eye white.*
Above dull olive, *wings rufous.*
Below white, brownish at sides of
breast. Tail short.

2. White-throated Spadebill   LM-F
Platyrinchus mystaceus 3½"(9cm)
Bill very broad and flat. Semi-concealed crown patch yellow. Eye-
ring white. Above brown. Throat
white. Breast brownish. Belly buff
to white. Tail short. ♀: Lacks crown
patch.

3. Cinnamon-crested Spadebill   L-F
Platyrinchus saturatus   3½"(9cm)
Bill very broad and flat. Crown orange. Above dark olive brown.
Throat and belly whitish. Breast
whitish, olive brown on sides. Tail
short.

4. Golden-crowned Spadebill   L-F
Platyrinchus coronatus 3½"(9cm)
Bill very broad and flat. Crown rufous bordered by chestnut. Above
greenish olive. *Broad eyebrow
black.* Below light yellow. Tail
short. ♀: Eyebrow buffy white.

5. Scale-crested Pygmy-Tyrant LM-F
Lophotriccus pileatus   4"(10cm)
Bill less than half head length.
*Head crested, feathers edged ru-
fous.* Eye pale. Back olive, wing-
bars inconspicuous. Throat and
breast whitish streaked gray. Belly
pale yellow.

**6. Double-banded Pygmy-Tyrant
                        L-FT**
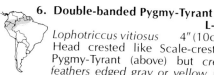
Lophotriccus vitiosus   4"(10cm)
Head crested like Scale-crested
Pygmy-Tyrant (above) but *crest
feathers edged gray or yellow* in-
stead of rufous. Back olive green.
Wing bars obvious. Below yellow-
ish, streaked gray.

7. Helmeted Pygmy-Tyrant   L-FT
Colopteryx galeatus   4"(10cm)
*Head crested, feathers black edged
olive.* Above olive. Below whitish
with more or less gray streaking
on breast.

**8. Southern Beardless Tyrannulet
                        LM-SO**
Camptostoma obsoletum
                        3½"(9cm)
Crown brownish, usually crested.
Above olive or grayish. Narrow
eyebrow, eye-ring and lores white.
Wing-bars whitish or yellowish (or
buff to cinnamon w of Andes).
Below yellowish (whitish in some
races). Often cocks tail.

**9. Rufous-crowned Tody-Tyrant
                        M-F**
Poecilotriccus ruficeps 3½"(9cm)
Crown bright rufous bordered be-
hind by thin black line. Nape gray.
Back olive green. Wing coverts
black, wing-bars yellowish or buffy.
Throat white (rufous in some
races). Below bright yellow.

10. Stripe-necked Tody-Tyrant   L-FT
Idioptilon striaticolle   4"(10cm)
Above olive green or grayish. Eye-
ring and lores white. Throat and
breast whitish, *boldly streaked
black.* Sides of breast olive. Belly
bright yellow.

**11. Black-throated Tody-Tyrant
                        MH-FT**
Idioptilon granadense   4"(10cm)
*Prominent white patch in front of
eye.* Above olive green. Bend of
wing yellow. *Throat black.* Breast
gray. Belly white.

12. Eye-ringed Tody-Tyrant   LM-F
Idioptilon orbitatum   4"(10cm)
Eye-ring white. Above olive. Inner
wing feathers edged *white show-
ing as a stripe.* Throat whitish.
Breast brownish. Belly yellow.

SMALL FLYCATCHERS 8.

Todirostrum TODY-FLYCATCHERS — 288

1. Southern Bentbill **L-FT**
Oncostoma olivaceum 3½" (9cm)
Upper bill much decurved, appears too heavy for such a small bird. Above uniform olive. Below yellow with grayish wash on throat and breast.

2. Yellow-crowned Tyrannulet L-TS
Tyrannulus elatus 3½" (9cm)
Bill less than half head length. *Yellow crest usually shows*. Sides of crown blackish. Back light grayish olive. Wings and tail dark brown. Wing-bars whitish, usually quite obvious. Throat grayish. Below pale yellow.

3. Slate-headed Tody-Flycatcher L-S
Todirostrum sylvia 3½" (9cm)
Bill flat, nearly as long as head. *Crown and nape gray. Lores white.* Back olive. Wings black. *Bend of wing* and *two wing-bars yellow.* Throat whitish. Breast pale gray. Belly yellow.

4. Ochre-faced Tody-Flycatcher
LM-TS
Todirostrum plumbeiceps
3½" (9cm)
Bill flat, ¾x head. Crown dark gray. Back olive. *Face and throat cinnamon with dusky spot below eye.* Patch on upper breast white. Below whitish gray on sides.

5. Spotted Tody-Flycatcher **L-TS**
Todirostrum maculatum
3½" (9cm)
Bill flat nearly as long as head. Eye pale. Crown grayish (or blackish). Back olive green. Throat white. Below yellow, *spotted black* except on belly.

6. Rusty-fronted Tody-Flycatcher
L-S
Todirostrum latirostre 3½" (9cm)
Bill flat. Above olive, darker on crown. *Lores and around eye ochraceous.* Two usually well marked wing-bars. Throat whitish. Belly white. Tail black, edged olive.

7. Common Tody-Flycatcher L-TSO
Todirostrum cinereum 3½" (9cm)
Bill flat, nearly as long as head. Eye pale. *Crown blackish.* Back gray or olive. Throat yellow (white in some races).*Below bright yellow.* Tail rather long. tipped white.

8. Smoky-fronted Tody-Flycatcher
L-SO
Todirostrum fumifrons 3" (8cm)
Bill flat. Forehead grayish. *Around eye buffy white.* Crown and back olive green. Wings blackish with two prominent yellowish white bars. Throat white. *Below pale yellow,* brighter on belly. Tail blackish edged yellow.

9. Pale-eyed Pygmy-Tyrant **L-S**
Atalotriccus pilaris 3" (8cm)
Above olive green. *Eye pale.* Wings dusky with two whitish or yellowish bars. Below whitish, obscurely streaked dusky. Tail feathers dusky, edged olive yellow.

10. Eared Pygmy-Tyrant **L-T**
Myiornis auricularis 3" (8cm)
Bill about half head length. Above olive green, tinged brown on crown. *Conspicuous ear patch black* (or gray in Peru and Bolivia). Double wing-bars yellowish. Throat white streaked black. Below yellow streaked dusky on breast.

11. Short-tailed Pygmy-Tyrant **L-FT**
Myiornis ecaudatus 2¾" (7cm)
Extremely small. Lores black. *Conspicuous white line above lores and eye-ring white. Crown gray* (or black w of Andes). Back bright olive green. Below white (shaded dusky on breast in some races). *Tail very short.*

2

3

5

6

8

9

10

11

1. Brown-chested Martin   L-TO
Progne (Phaeoprogne) tapera
            6¼"(16cm)
Above smoky brown, wings and
tail darker. Below white with
brownish breast band. Tail forked.

2. Rough-winged Swallow   LM-TSO
Stelgidopteryx ruficollis
            4½"(12cm)
Above glossy brown, darker on
crown, *distinctly paler on rump.*
Wings and slightly forked tail
blackish. *Throat cinnamon.* Breast
and sides grayish brown. Belly pale
yellowish.

Tree Swallow   L-O
Tachycineta bicolor*   4½"(12cm)
*Above shining blue-green. Below
immaculate white.* Wings and
slightly forked tail black.

3. Immature: Above   brownish,
sometimes with brownish breast
band.

4. White-rumped Swallow   LM-O
Tachycineta leucorrhoa 5"(13cm)
Above shiny bluish green. *Rump
and narrow line on forehead white.*
Underparts white.

5. Blue-and-white Swallow
                 LMH-SO
Notiochelidon cyanoleuca
            4¼"(11cm)
Above all *glossy steel blue.* Throat,
breast and belly white, often with
a few small blackish spots on
breast. *Vent black. Tail forked.*

6. Brown-bellied Swallow   MH-O
Notiochelidon murina 4½"(12cm)
Above steely blue or green. Wings
and *rather deeply forked tail*
blackish brown. *Below uniform
grayish brown.*

7. White-thighed Swallow   L-FT
Neochelidon tibialis   4½"(12cm)
Above dark brown with slight
greenish gloss. Rump lighter brown
than back (same as back in some
races). Underparts grayish brown.
Thighs white. Vent blackish. Tail
notched.

8. Long-billed Gnatwren   L-TS
Ramphocaenus melanurus
            4½"(12cm)
Bill slender, straight, very long.
Above grayish brown, sides of head
and neck cinnamon. Below buffy
to light cinnamon. *Tail* rather *long,*
narrow, usually held upright.

9. Tawny-faced (Half-collared)
   Gnatwren   L-F
Microbates cinereiventris
            4"(10cm)
Bill slender, straight, long. Above
reddish brown to olive brown. *Face
tawny rufous* (with dusky line back
of eye w of Andes). Throat whitish,
whiskers black. Below gray,
streaked black on upper breast.
Tail short, usually held upright.

10. Tropical Gnatcatcher   L-FTS
Polioptila plumbea   4"(10cm)
Crown black (eyebrow white in
some races). Back gray. Below
white. Tail long, often held upright, black, outer feathers white.
♀: Lacks black on head.

11. Masked Gnatcatcher   L-S
Polioptila dumicola   4¼"(11cm)
Above blue gray. *Mask black.*
Throat white or gray. Below pale
blue gray (belly white in some
races). Tail rather long, often held
upright, black, edged white.

12. Yellowish Pipit   L-O
Anthus lutescens   4½"(12cm)
Bill thin. Above brownish, streaked
buff. Below yellowish white
streaked dusky. Tail blackish, outer
feathers show white in flight. Terrestrial. Walks.

1. Bicolored Wren　　　　　L-SO
Campylorhynchus griseus
　　　　　　　　　　　7"(18cm)
Crown and streak through eye
blackish. *Long, broad eyebrow and
entire underparts white.* Back rufous brown or blackish. Wings not
barred. Tail blackish with some
white at end.

2. Band-backed Wren　　　L-FT
Campylorhynchus zonatus
　　　　　　　　　　　6¼"(16cm)
Crown gray streaked whitish. Narrow eyebrow white. Back and
wings *black barred whitish.* Throat
and breast white *spotted* black.
Belly rufous, barred black on sides.
Tail barred black and whitish.

3. Rufous Wren　　　　　MH-F
Cinnycerthia unirufa　6¼"(16cm)
Uniform rufous chestnut or chestnut brown with wings and tail
faintly barred black but appearing
uniform in the field. Lores black.
Immatures have forecrown and
cheeks whitish.

4. Sepia-brown Wren　　　MH-FT
Cinnycerthia peruana　6"(15cm)
All brown with white on forehead
and/or eyebrow in some races.
Wings and tail narrowly barred
black.

5. Moustached Wren　　　LM-T
Thryothorus genibarbis　6"(15cm)
Crown and nape gray or brownish
gray. Eyebrow whitish. Cheeks
striped. Back brown. *Wings not
barred.* Throat white with *prominent black whisker.* Breast grayish.
Belly buffy. Tail barred black (all
rufous in one race in Venezuela).

6. Rufous-and-white Wren　　LM-S
Thryothorus rufalbus　5½"(14cm)
Above rufous, wings and tail barred
black. Prominent eyebrow white.
Cheeks streaked black and white.
Below white. Sides rufous.

7. Black-bellied Wren　　　L-T
Thryothorus fasciatoventris
　　　　　　　　　　　5½"(14cm)
Above rufous. Eyebrow, throat and
breast white. Wings faintly barred
blackish. *Belly black narrowly
barred white.* Tail rufous barred
black.

8. Bay Wren　　　　　　L-TS
Thryothorus nigricapillus
　　　　　　　　　　　5"(13cm)
Crown black. Back bright chestnut. Wings and tail barred. *White
spot on ear coverts.* Cheeks striped.
Throat white. *Breast barred black
and white* (mostly white in Ecuador). Belly brownish, barred black.

9. Coraya Wren　　　　　LM-TO
Thryothorus coraya　5"(13cm)
Above brownish rufous. *Wings not
barred. Cheeks nearly solid black.*
Throat white. Below dingy grayish. Tail barred (unbarred in central Brazil).

10. Buff-breasted Wren　　　L-TS
Thryothorus leucotis　5"(13cm)
Above brown becoming rufous on
rump. Wings and tail barred black.
Eyebrow and *throat white.* Cheeks
streaked. *Breast buff.* Belly rufous.

11. Rufous-breasted Wren　　LM-T
Thryothorus rutilus　5"(13cm)
Above brown. Wings not barred.
Throat and sides of head checkered black and white. Breast rufous (spotted black in ne Colombia). Belly white in center, brown
on sides.

12. Spot-breasted Wren　　　M-T
Thryothorus maculipectus
　　　　　　　　　　　5"(13cm)
Above reddish brown to olive
brown. Wings not barred. Eyebrow and eye-ring white. *Sides of
head, throat and breast white spotted black (little spotting in
Ecuador).* Belly dull rufous, lightly
barred dusky.

Thryothorus WRENS - 130, 299
Troglodytes WRENS - 299
Cistothorus WRENS - 299
Microcerculus WRENS - 299, 300
Scytalopus TAPACULOS - 273
Cinclus DIPPERS - 298

1. Chestnut-breasted Wren   M-F
Cyphorhinus thoracicus
5½"(14cm)
Above dark brown. *Wings not barred. Throat, breast and sides of head chestnut rufous.* Belly dark brown. Tail black, not barred.

2. Musician Wren   L-FT
Cyphorhinus arada   4¼"(11cm)
Head and throat rufous. *Collar of white and black stripes (lacking in some races).* Back brown, wings and tail barred black. Breast rufous. Belly whitish.

3. Song Wren   L-FT
Cyphorhinus phaeocephalus
4¼"(11cm)
Bare blue skin around eye. Back and belly dark brown. Wings and tail barred black. *Throat and breast rufous.* Considered a race of *Cyphorhinus arada* (preceding) in BSA.

4. Stripe-throated Wren   L-F
Thryothorus thoracicus
4¼"(11cm)
Above brown. Eyebrow white. Wings and tail barred black. *Sides of head and throat streaked black and white.* Below rufous or brownish.

5. House Wren   LMH-SO
Troglodytes aedon   4"(10cm)
Above reddish brown to grayish brown. Lores whitish. Below whitish or light cinnamon. Wings and tail lightly barred blackish.

6. Grass Wren   LMH-O
Cistothorus platensis   4"(10cm)
Crown brown (streaked black in some races). Narrow eyebrow buffy. *Back black streaked buffy white.* Underparts buff, center of belly white. Wings and short tail rufous, barred black.

7. Gray-breasted Wood-Wren
MH-FT
Henicorhina leucophrys 4"(10cm)
Above rufous brown faintly barred black on wings and tail. Long eyebrow whitish or grayish. Cheeks strongly streaked black and white. Throat grayish. *Below gray to dark gray.* Tail short.

8. White-breasted Wood-Wren
LM-FT
Henicorhina leucosticta
3½" (9cm)
Very like Gray-breasted Woodwren (preceding) but *crown and nape black. Throat and breast white.* Tail short.

9. Nightingale Wren   LM-F
Microcerculus marginatus
4"(10cm)
Bill rather long. Above deep reddish brown. Wings and tail not barred. *Tail very short.* Below white.

10. Immature: Young birds have more or less dark brown below.

11. Pale-throated Tapaculo   LMH-F
Scytalopus panamensis
4¼"(11cm)
Above blackish becoming dark brown on lower back. Eyebrow grayish on male in some races. Throat and breast gray. Flanks and belly chestnut brown, barred black. Usually on ground and hard to see.

12. White-capped Dipper   MH-W
Cinclus leucocephalus 5"(13cm)
Brown or gray with crown, throat and most of underparts white. *Patch on center of back white.* Around rocky streams.

Cyanocorax JAYS - 297, 298
Mimus MOCKINGBIRDS - 300
Turdus THRUSHES - 136, 300, 301

1. **Green Jay** **LM-T**
Cyanocorax yncas 10½" (26cm)
Frontal crest and face blue. Crown
and nape blue or yellow. Back and
wings green. Throat and breast
black. *Belly yellow.* Tail green,
outer feathers yellow.

2. **Chalk-browed Mockingbird**
LM-SO
Mimus saturninus 9" (23cm)
Above dark brown. *Broad eyebrow white.* Stripe through eye
black. Below whitish. Tail long,
blackish, edged and tipped white.

3. **Tropical Mockingbird** **LM-SOA**
Mimus gilvus 9" (23cm)
Above pale gray. Dusky patch
through eye. Below whitish. Tail
long, blackish with *broad white
tips* which show prominently in
flight.

4. **Black-capped Mocking-Thrush**
L-SW
Donacobius atricapillus 8" (20cm)
Orange or yellow eye. Above black
or blackish. *Below light cinnamon,* more or less barred black on
sides. Tail black, broadly tipped
white.

5. **Great Thrush** **MH-TS**
Turdus fuscater 12" (30cm)
Color varies from blackish to light
brown, underparts paler. Eye-ring,
bill and legs yellow orange. Identify by *large size.*

6. **Glossy-black Thrush** **MH-F**
Turdus serranus 9" (23cm)
Uniform *glossy black.* Eye-ring, bill
and legs yellow-orange.

7. **Female:** Uniform brown. Bill and
legs yellowish.

8. **Rufous-bellied Thrush** **LM-TSO**
Turdus rufiventris 9" (23cm)
Above olive brown. Throat white,
streaked brown. Breast light brown.
Rest of underparts rufous. ♀: Paler
below than male.

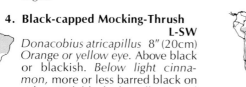

9. **Pale-breasted Thrush** **LM-TSO**
Turdus leucomelas 9" (22cm)
Head gray. Back brownish. *Ear
coverts streaked white.* Throat
white streaked brown. Below pale
grayish or pale brownish. Center
of belly white.

10. **Creamy-bellied Thrush** **LM-TS**
Turdus amaurochalinus 9" (22cm)
Bill yellow (♀ blackish). Above
dark olive brown. *Lores blackish.*
Throat white, streaked blackish.
Patch at base of throat white. *Breast
pale smoky gray.* Belly and vent
white.

11. **Immature:** Bill dusky. Above
brown spotted buff. Below whitish, spotted dark brown.

12. **Clay-colored Thrush** **L-TS**
Turdus grayi 9" (22cm)
Bill greenish yellow. Above dark
brown. Below uniform pale brown.
Throat whitish, inconspicuously
streaked dusky.

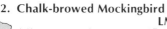
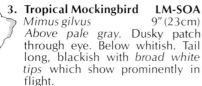

1. **Cocoa Thrush**   **L-FT**
   Turdus fumigatus   8½" (21cm)
   Bill brown. Above *reddish* brown,
   paler below. Throat whitish
   streaked brown. Center of belly
   white.

2. **Black-billed Thrush**   **LM-TSO**
   Turdus ignobilis   8½" (21cm)
   Bill black. Above grayish brown.
   Throat lightly streaked white.
   (Lower throat pure white in some
   races). *Breast grayish brown.* Belly
   whitish.

   Pale-vented Thrush   **LM-F**
   Turdus obsoletus   8½" (21cm)
   Adult like Pale-breasted Thrush
   (134-9) but back darker and only
   undertail coverts pure white.

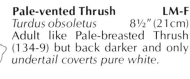

3. **Immature:** Above more or less
   spotted buff. Below whitish spotted brown. Vent white.

4. **Black-hooded Thrush**   **LM-FT**
   Turdus olivater   8½" (21cm)
   Bill and eye-ring yellow. *Entire
   head, throat and upper breast black*
   (throat grayish streaked black in
   some races). Back olive brown.
   Underparts light brown. Tail
   blackish. Legs yellowish.

5. **Female:** Like ♂ but black replaced
   by olive-brown.

6. **Bare-eyed Thrush**   **LM-TO**
   Turdus nudigenis   8½" (21cm)
   Bill olive yellow. Above olive
   brown. *Large eye-ring yellow.*
   Throat streaked. Below light
   brown, center of belly white. Vent
   white.

7. **White-necked Thrush**   **LM-FT**
   Turdus albicollis   7½" (19cm)
   Above rich, dark brown. *Throat
   white conspicuously streaked dark
   brown. Lower throat pure white.*
   Breast may vary from grayish to
   dark brown. Center of belly white.

8. **Slaty Thrush**   **M-F**
   Turdus nigriceps   8½" (21cm)
   Mostly slaty gray or blackish.
   Throat white sharply streaked
   black. *Center of belly white.* Bill
   and legs yellow. ♀: Gray and black
   replaced by brown.

9. **Yellow-legged Thrush**   **LM-FT**
   Platycichla flavipes   8" (20cm)
   Head, throat, breast, wings and
   tail black. *Bill, eye-ring and legs
   yellow.* Back gray (black in some
   races).

10. **Female:** Upperparts, wings and tail
    brown. Bill blackish with *yellow
    ridge.* Narrow eye-ring and legs
    yellow. *Below pale brown,* streaked
    dusky on throat.

11. **Pale-eyed Thrush**   **M-F**
    Platycichla leucops   8" (20cm)
    Glossy black. Eye white. Bill and
    legs orange yellow.

12. **Female:** Bill all blackish. Above
    dark brown. Eye brown, eye-ring
    yellow. Throat and breast brown.
    Belly pale grayish. Legs yellowish.

1. Black Solitaire   **LM-F**
Entomodestes coracinus
            8¼"(21cm)
Black except *cheek patch,* shoulders and part of outer tail feathers white.

2. Rufous-brown Solitaire   **M-F**
Myadestes leucogenys 7½"(19cm)
Upperparts, wings and tail reddish brown. Throat and breast more rufous. Belly pale grayish.

3. Andean Solitaire   **M-FT**
Myadestes ralloides   6¼"(16cm)
Bill short and wide. Back rufous brown. *Head and underparts all leaden gray.* (Nape like back in some races.) Tail dark brown, white on inner web of outer feathers.

4. Veery   **LM-T**
Catharus fuscescens*   6¼"(16cm)
Upperparts, wings and tail *uniform reddish brown.* Throat whitish. Breast buffy, lightly spotted dusky.

5. Swainson's Thrush   **LM-T**
Catharus ustulatus*   6¼"(16cm)
Above brown. *Prominent eye-ring and sides of head buffy.* Throat and breast whitish *spotted dusky.* Belly white.

6. Gray-cheeked Thrush   **LM-FT**
Catharus minimus*   6"(15cm)
Upperparts, wings and tail olive brown. *Sides of head grayish.* Eye-ring not prominent. Throat white. Breast rather *boldly spotted blackish.* Belly white in center, gray on sides.

7. Slaty-backed Nightingale-Thrush   **M-F**
Catharus fuscater   6¼"(16cm)
Eye white, eye-ring orange. Above dark gray. Below paler gray, center of belly white. Bill and legs orange.

8. Spotted Nightingale-Thrush   **LM-F**
Catharus dryas   6¼"(16cm)
Bill reddish. Head black. Back, wings and tail dark gray. Eye-ring and legs orange. *Below yellow, heavily spotted dusky* on throat and breast.

9. Orange-billed Nightingale-Thrush   **LM-TS**

Catharus aurantiirostris   6"(15cm)
Above brown (crown grayish in some races). Eye-ring, *bill and legs orange.* Throat and center of belly white. Sides and breast gray.

10. Immature: Bill black. Underparts all brown, spotted white.

11. Rufous-browed Peppershrike   **LM-TS**
Cyclarhis gujanensis 5½"(14cm)
Bill heavy, strongly hooked. Variable, but all races have *broad rufous eyebrow.* Crown gray or chestnut or olive. Back greenish or yellowish olive. Below white, gray or yellow.

12. Black-billed Peppershrike   **M-TS**
Cyclarhis nigrirostris 5½"(14cm)
Bill heavy, strongly hooked, black. Crown and back olive green. *Narrow eyebrow* and forehead *deep chestnut.* Throat gray. Upper breast olive yellow. Below gray, whitish in center.

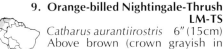

Smaragdolanius SHRIKE-VIREOS - 302.
Hylophilus GREENLETS - 302.

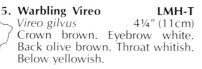

1. Slaty-capped Shrike-Vireo   LM-F
Smaragdolanius leucotis
5½"(14cm)
Bill quite heavy, strongly hooked. Back, wings and tail olive green. Crown dark gray. *Long broad eyebrow and spot below eye yellow.* (Birds n of the Amazon and e of the Andes have white streak back of yellow spot). Underparts bright yellow.

2. Yellow-throated Vireo   LM-FT
Vireo flavifrons*   5"(13cm)
Above olive. Eye-ring and lores bright yellow. Wings blackish. Two prominent wing-bars white. Throat and breast yellow. Belly white. This is the only Vireo with wing-bars in South America.

3. Black-whiskered Vireo LM-TSO
Vireo altiloquus*   5"(13cm)
Bill 3/4 head length. Above dull olive green, sometimes tinged grayish on crown. Bill larger than Red-eyed Vireo (following). Eyebrow white. Below white with *narrow black whiskers.*

4. Red-eyed Vireo   LMH-TS
Vireo olivaceus   4½"(12cm)
Bill about half head length. Crown and nape gray. Eyebrow whitish bordered above with *thin black line.* Back dull olive green. Wings and tail dusky, feathers edged olive. Below white (yellowish in some races).

5. Warbling Vireo   LMH-T
Vireo gilvus   4¼" (11cm)
Crown brown. Eyebrow white. Back olive brown. Throat whitish. Below yellowish.

6. Rufous-naped Greenlet   M-F
Hylophilus semibrunneus
4½"(12cm)
Crown and nape rufous. Eye dark. Lores and around eye whitish. Back olive green. Throat grayish white. Breast buffy, tinged rufous at sides. Belly white.

7. Rufous-crowned Greenlet   LM-F
Hylophilus poicilotis 4½"(12cm)
Crown rufous. Eye dark. *Cheeks dusky.* Above yellowish olive green. Throat and breast light gray. Belly yellow, white in center.

8. Lemon-chested Greenlet   L-TS
Hylophilus thoracicus 4¼"(11cm)
Crown and nape gray. *Eye pale.* Back, wings and tail yellowish olive. Throat grayish. *Breast lemon yellow.* Belly grayish.

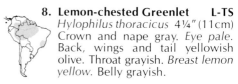

9. Ashy-headed Greenlet   L-TS
Hylophilus pectoralis   4"(10cm)
Eye dark. Crown, nape and sides of head gray. Back and wings yellowish olive green. Throat and belly white. Broad breast band lemon yellow.

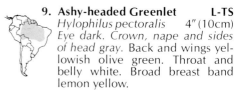

10. Golden-fronted Greenlet   L-TS
Hylophilus aurantiifrons 4"(10cm)
Forehead dull yellow. Crown brown. Above olive. Throat whitish. Below buffy yellowish.

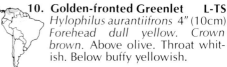

11. Gray-chested Greenlet   L-F
Hylophilus semicinereus
4"(10cm)
Eye pale. Forecrown, back, wings and tail olive green. Nape and underparts gray, tinged yellowish on sides of breast.

12. Tawny-crowned Greenlet   L-F
Hylophilus ochraceiceps
4"(10cm)
Forecrown rufous. Eye pale. Above greenish olive. *Throat pale gray.* Breast yellowish. Belly gray.

OROPENDOLAS AND CACIQUES HAVE CHARACTERISTIC LONG POINTED CONICAL BILL

Psarocolius OROPENDOLAS - 303.
Cacicus CACIQUES - 303.
Pseudoleistes MARSHBIRDS - 305.
Molothrus COWBIRDS - 302.

1. Russet-backed Oropendola   **LM-FT**
Psarocolius angustifrons
     ♂17"(43cm); ♀14"(35cm)
Bill gray or blackish. *Head and throat olive.* Back olive becoming brownish on rump. Underparts olivaceous brown, vent rufous chestnut. Tail above dusky in center, bright yellow on edges. Tail below mostly yellow.

2. Crested Oropendola   **LM-FT**
Psarocolius decumanus
     ♂15"(38cm); ♀12"(30cm)
Black. *Bill white.* Eye blue. Rump chestnut. Tail mostly yellow.

3. Yellow-rumped Cacique   **L-FTS**
Cacicus cela
     ♂10"(25cm); ♀8"(20cm)
Bill yellowish green (or dusky green w of Andes). *Eye blue.* All glossy black except wing coverts, lower back, *rump and basal half of tail yellow.*

4. Yellow-billed Cacique   **LMH-TS**
Cacicus holosericeus
     ♂9"(23cm); ♀7½"(19cm)
All dull black. *Eye pale yellow.* Bill yellowish white.

5. Scarlet-rumped Cacique   **LM-F**
Cacicus uropygialis   10"(25 cm)
Black. *Rump red.* Bill yellow at base, rest greenish yellow. Eye blue. Race w of Andes is smaller.

6. Red-rumped Cacique   **L-FT**
Cacicus haemorrhous
     ♂10"(25cm); ♀8"(20cm)
Glossy black. *Lower back and rump red.* Eye brown or blue. Bill yellowish white.

7. Solitary (Black) Cacique   **L-TS**
Cacicus solitarius
     ♂10½"(26cm); ♀9"(23cm)
All black except bill yellowish white. *Eye brown.*

8. Brown-and-yellow Marshbird   **L-TWO**
Pseudoleistes virescens
     8½"(21cm)
Head, throat and breast dark brown. Back brown, feathers edged olivaceous. Wing coverts and belly bright yellow. Tail dark brown.

9. Velvet-fronted Grackle   **L-SW**
Lampropsar tanagrinus
     7½"(19cm)
Silky black. Eye brown. Bill rather short, pointed. *Forehead feathers dense, plush-like.* Tail rounded.

10 Shiny Cowbird   **LM-SO**
Molothrus bonariensis   8"(20cm)
All black with shining purplish gloss. Bill short, conical, black.
11. Female: Grayish brown above, lighter grayish brown below with faint dusky streaks on breast.

12. Bay-winged Cowbird   **L-SO**
Molothrus badius   7½"(19cm)
Bill short, conical, black. *Upperparts grayish brown. Wings rufous.* Below gray. Tail blackish.

ORIOLES, BLACKBIRDS

Icterus ORIOLES - 305.
Agelaius BLACKBIRDS - 304.

1. Oriole Blackbird   L-SO
Gymnomystax mexicanus
                    10½"(26cm)
Golden yellow. Back, wings and
tail black. *Skin around eye and
short "whisker" bare, black.*

2. Troupial   L-TSW
Icterus icterus   8½"(21cm)
Bare skin around eye blue. Head,
throat and breast black (crown orange in some races). Above orange with variable amount of black
on back. Wings black, *coverts
showing white.* Belly orange. Tail
black.

3. Yellow-tailed Oriole   L-TSW
Icterus mesomelas   8½"(21cm)
Mostly bright yellow with black
back, throat and breast. Wings
black with *yellow wing coverts.*
Belly yellow. Tail *yellow, central
feathers black.*

4. Yellow-backed Oriole   LMH-TS
Icterus chrysater   8"(20cm)
Orange yellow, *including back. No
yellow on wing coverts.* Forehead,
sides of head, wings, throat, breast
and tail black.

5. Moriche Oriole   L-FT
Icterus chrysocephalus
                    7½"(19cm)
Mostly black. Back of crown,
shoulders and thighs yellow.

6. Yellow Oriole   L-SO
Icterus nigrogularis   7"(18cm)
Lemon yellow. Throat, wings, tail
and skin around eye black. Some
white shows on wing coverts.

7. Northern (Baltimore) Oriole
                              LMH-T
Icterus galbula*   6½"(17cm)
Male (above): *Whole head,* back
and throat black. Wings black,
coverts orange, inner feathers
edged white. Central tail feathers
black, outers mostly yellow. Rest
of plumage *orange.* **Female**
(below): Crown and back grayish
olive, tinged yellow. Below dull
orange. Tail brownish.

8. Saffron-cowled Blackbird   L-W
Xanthopsar flavus   7½"(19cm)
Male (left): Head, shoulders, rump
and entire underparts *bright golden
yellow.* Lores, back, wings and tail
glossy black. Female (right): Above
brown. Shoulders, eyebrow, rump
and underparts *dull yellow.*

9. Yellow-hooded Blackbird
                              LM-OW
Agelaius icterocephalus
                    6½"(17cm)
Black, except *head, neck and
breast bright yellow.* Eye dark. ♀:
Head olive yellow. Back olive
brown streaked black. *Eyebrow
and throat bright yellow.* Below
olive yellow, more grayish on belly.

10. Yellow-winged Blackbird
                              LMH-OW
Agelaius thilius   6½"(17cm)
All black or brownish except
shoulders yellow.

11. Female: Above and below blackish, streaked brown. Eyebrow
whitish. Small shoulder spot yellow.

12. Chestnut-capped Blackbird L-OW
Agelaius ruficapillus 6¼" (16cm)
All glossy black except *crown,
throat and breast chestnut.* ♀:
Brownish, throat olive.

MOST SHOWN IN NON-BREEDING PLUMAGE.

Seiurus WATERTHRUSHES 306.
Myioborus WHITESTARTS - 306.
Oporornis WARBLERS - 306.

1. Northern Waterthrush   LM-TSW
Seiurus noveboracensis *
                    5" (13cm)
Above dark ashy brown. Long eyebrow whitish. *Throat whitish, finely
streaked black. Breast* yellowish
white, heavily *streaked black.*
Usually on ground. Teeters.

2. Ovenbird   LM-T
Seiurus aurocapillus *   5" (13cm)
Crown stripe rufous bordered at
each side by conspicuous black
line. Above olive brown. Eye-ring
white. *No eyebrow.* Below white,
whisker and *spots on breast and
sides* black.

**3. Yellow-crowned Whitestart
(Redstart)   MH-FT**
Myioborus flavivertex   5" (13cm)
*Center of crown, lores and under-
parts* yellow. Back olive. Front of
crown, sides of head and wings
black. Tail black, outer feathers
white.

**4. Golden-fronted Whitestart
(Redstart)   MH-FT**
Myioborus ornatus   5" (13cm)
Forecrown, face and underparts
yellow (chin and sides of head
white in some races). Back and
wings dark gray. Tail blackish,
outer feathers white.

**5. Slate-throated Whitestart
(Redstart)   LM-FT**
Myioborus miniatus   5" (13cm)
Crown chestnut. Upperparts and
throat blackish. Breast and belly
bright yellow. Undertail coverts
white. Tail black, outer feathers
white. Often spreads tail.

6. Masked Yellowthroat   L-SW
Geothlypis aequinoctialis
                    5" (13cm)
*Crown gray. Broad mask through
eye and forehead black.* Back,
wings and tail olive green. Entire
underparts bright yellow.

7. Female: Crown olive or grayish.
Black replaced by olive.

**8. Olive-crowned Yellowthroat
                             L-SW**
Geothlypis semiflava   5" (13cm)
Large black patch on forecrown
and sides of head. Above olive
green. Below bright yellow.

9. Female: Black replaced by olive.

10. Kentucky Warbler   LM-FT
Oporornis formosus *   4½" (12cm)
Back, wings and tail olive. *Black
stripe from eye down sides of neck.*
Eyebrow and underparts bright
yellow.

11. Mourning Warbler   LM-TS
Oporornis philadelphia *
                    4½" (12cm)
Head and *throat gray. No eye-ring
in breeding plumage.* Back, wings
and tail olive. Breast band black.
Belly yellow.

12. Female: Head, throat and breast
light gray. Partial white eye-ring.
Belly bright yellow.

MOST SHOWN IN NON-BREEDING PLUMAGE.

Dendroica WARBLERS - 306.

1. Prothonotary Warbler   L-TSW
Protonotaria citrea*   4½" (12cm)
Head all yellow. Back olive yellow. Below all yellow. Wings and tail blue gray with white on outer tail feathers.

2. Canada Warbler   LM-FT
Wilsonia canadensis* 4½" (12cm)
Above gray. Eye-ring white. Below yellow with *band of dusky spots across breast.* Undertail coverts white. ♀ and ♂ alike in winter.

3. Yellow Warbler   LM-TSW
Dendroica petechia   4½" (12cm)
Appears yellow all over. (Head more or less chestnut in some races near salt water). Back yellowish olive. Below yellow, streaked chestnut on breast. Tail dusky yellow edged bright yellow. ♀: Has little or no chestnut.

4. Bay-breasted Warbler   LM-FT
Dendroica castanea* 4½" (12cm)
Back olive, streaked black. Prominent wing-bars white. *Faint chestnut tinge on flanks.* White patch on outer tail feathers. *Legs dark,* not pale as in Blackpoll Warbler (306-2).

5. Blackburnian Warbler   LMH-FT
Dendroica fusca*   4½" (12cm)
Long orange eyebrow surrounding black ear and cheek. Back black with white stripes. *Throat and breast intense orange.* (Yellow-orange in non-breeding plumage.) Below white, streaked black on sides. ♀: Back brown. Facial pattern and orange areas much paler.

6. Black-and-white Warbler LM-FT
Mniotilta varia*   4¼" (11cm)
Crown black with central white stripe (not solid black as in Blackpoll Warbler (306-2). Above streaked black and white, eye-

brow white. Cheeks and throat black. Below white, streaked black on breast and sides. ♀ and non-breeding ♂ have white cheeks and throat and less black streaking below.

7. American Redstart   LM-TS
Setophaga ruticilla*   4¼" (11cm)
Black. *Shoulders, patch on wings and patches at sides of tail orange.* Belly white.

8. Female: Above grayish or olive brown. Eye-ring prominent. Orange patches of ♂ replaced by yellow. Throat, belly and center of breast white.

9. Cerulean Warbler   LM-T
Dendroica cerulea*   4" (10cm)
Above grayish blue streaked black. Wing-bars white. *Breast crossed by narrow black band.* Below white, streaked black on sides. ♀: Olive green above with narrow eye-stripe and two whitish wing-bars. Whitish below usually tinged yellowish on breast.

10. Golden-winged Warbler LM-FT
Vermivora chrysoptera* 4" (10cm)
Blue gray. Crown and *wing coverts yellow. Stripe through eye black.* Throat black. Belly white in center. ♀: Black is replaced by grayish.

11. Tennessee Warbler   LM-TS
Vermivora peregrina*   4" (10cm)
Crown gray. Lores and *eyebrow white.* Upperparts olive green. *Single faint wing-bar.* Below dingy yellowish. Undertail coverts white. A very plain-looking warbler.

12. Tropical Parula   LM-FTS
Parula pitiayumi   4" (10cm)
Above bluish with yellowish patch in center of back. Wing-bars white. Black stripe through eye. Breast yellow (tinged orange in some races). Tail gray, patch on outer feathers white.

150 WARBLERS — III

1. Flavescent Warbler **L-TS**
Basileuterus flaveolus 5"(13cm)
Lores yellow. Above bright yellow-ish green. Below bright yellow, tinged olive on breast. *Legs light yellowish.* Fans tail.

2. Citrine Warbler **MH-FT**
Basileuterus luteoviridis 5"(13cm)
Upperparts, wings and tail olive. *Eyebrow yellow.* Underparts *dull yellow.* In s part of range has black forehead and bright yellow under-parts. Legs dark.

3. Black-crested Warbler **H-T**
Basileuterus nigrocristatus
5"(13cm)
Center of crown black. Prominent black spot in front of eye. Back and tail olive. Below bright yellow.

4. Golden-crowned Warbler
LM-FTO
Basileuterus culicivorus
4½"(12cm)
Center of crown yellow or orange. *Eyebrow whitish.* Back olive (gray in n). Below dull yellow (some-times bright yellow).

5. Golden-bellied Warbler **L-TS**
Basileuterus chrysogaster
4½"(12cm)
Crown stripe orange bordered by broad black lines. Back, wings and tail olive. *Eyebrow olive.* Under-parts yellow, shaded olive.

6. Russet-crowned Warbler MH-FT
Basileuterus coronatus 5"(13cm)
Crown patch rufous. Broad eye-brow, throat and sides of head gray (throat lighter gray in some races.) Stripe through eye black. Back and tail olive. Below yellow (or whitish in s part of range).

7. White-bellied Warbler **LM-TS**
Basileuterus hypoleucus
4½"(12cm)
Crown rufous, two broad black stripes at sides of crown. *Lores and long eyebrow white.* Back, wings and tail olive gray. *Underparts white clouded gray.*

8. White-browed Warbler **LM-FT**
Basileuterus leucoblepharus
5"(13cm)
Crown striped gray in center, bor-dered by black. *Narrow eye-ring and lores white.* Back olive. Below whitish, grayish on sides. Under-tail coverts yellowish.

9. Rufous-capped Warbler **L-TS**
Basileuterus rufifrons 4¼"(11cm)
Crown and ear coverts chestnut. Eyebrow white. Back, wings and tail olive green. Underparts bright yellow.

10. Three-striped Warbler **LM-FT**
Basileuterus tristriatus 4½"(12cm)
Back, wings and tail dull olive. *Crown stripe and broad eyebrow buffy olive* with broad black stripe above eyebrow. Prominent white spot below eye in most races. Below yellowish or whitish.

11. River Warbler **L-FTW**
*Phaeothlypis (Basileuterus)
rivularis* 4¼"(11cm)
Above olive, grayish on crown. *Eyebrow and cheeks buff.* Under-parts vary from whitish to solid cinnamon buff. Rump and tail olive (buff in w part of range).

Cyanerpes HONEYCREEPERS - 308
Dacnis DACNIS - 308, 309

1. **Green Honeycreeper**   **LM-FT**
   Chlorophanes spiza   5"(13cm)
   Bill nearly straight, upper black,
   lower yellow. All shining green except head and sides of neck black.

2. **Female:** Above grass green, no
   black. Below green marked with
   more or less yellow on throat and
   belly.

3. **Red-legged Honeycreeper L-FTS**
   Cyanerpes cyaneus   4½"(12cm)
   Bill curved. *Crown shining light
   blue.* Stripe through eye, upper
   back, wings and tail black. Rest of
   body plumage purple blue. *Legs
   red.* ♀: Above dark green. Eyebrow and throat whitish. Below
   pale green streaked yellowish.
   Belly yellow.

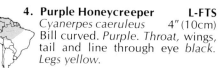

4. **Purple Honeycreeper**   **L-FTS**
   Cyanerpes caeruleus   4"(10cm)
   Bill curved. *Purple. Throat,* wings,
   tail and line through eye *black.
   Legs yellow.*

5. **Female:** *Sides of head tawny.* Back
   and tail grass green. Throat buff,
   bordered by blue whisker. *Breast
   green streaked yellowish.* Belly and
   undertail coverts white.

6. **Bananaquit**   **LMH-TSO**
   Coereba flaveola   4"(10cm)
   Bill distinctive, *short, curved.*
   Above black or dark gray. Rump
   yellow. *Long eyebrow,* speculum
   and undertail coverts white. *Throat
   gray.* Breast and belly yellow.

7. **Black-faced Dacnis**   **L-FTS**
   Dacnis lineata   4½"(12cm)
   Conspicuous yellow eye. Forehead, sides of head, back, wings
   and tail black. *Crown, rump, throat
   and breast light blue. Belly white*
   (yellow w of Andes). ♀: Above
   dull green. Wings and tail brown.
   Below pale greenish.

8. **Scarlet-thighed Dacnis**   **L-FT**
   Dacnis venusta   4¼"(11cm)
   Crown, back, sides of head and
   mark on shoulder blue. Forehead,
   area around eye, throat, sides of
   back and underparts black. *Thighs
   red.*

9. **Female:** Above greenish blue.
   Below, including thighs, *buffy.* Tail
   mostly black.

10. **Blue Dacnis**   **L-FTS**
    Dacnis cayana   4¼"(11cm)
    Blue. Forehead, lores, throat,
    wings, tail and center of back
    black. Small red spot at base of
    lower bill. *Legs reddish.*

11. **Female:** Green. *Head blue.* Throat
    grayish. Wings and tail blackish,
    feathers edged green.

12. **Yellow-bellied Dacnis**   **L-F**
    Dacnis flaviventer   4¼"(11cm)
    Crown bluish green. Forehead,
    sides of head, back, wings, tail
    and throat black. *Eye red.* Whis-
    ker, shoulder, rump and *under-
    parts golden yellow.* ♀: Above dull
    green. Below buffy.

CONEBILLS, FLOWER-PIERCERS
Flower-piercers have a distinctive upcurved bill, strongly hooked at tip

Conirostrum CONEBILLS - 307, 308.
Diglossa FLOWER-PIERCERS - 308.

1. Blue-backed Conebill   MH-TS
Conirostrum sitticolor 4½" (12cm)
Head, throat, upper breast, wings
and tail black. (Eyebrow blue in
some races.) *Back bright blue.*
Lower breast and belly cinnamon.

2. Rufous-browed Conebill   H-TS
Conirostrum rufum   4½" (12cm)
Above dark gray. Wings and tail
slaty black, inner wing feathers
lined whitish. *Forehead, eyebrow*
and all underparts rufous.

3. Bicolored Conebill   L-TSW
Conirostrum bicolor   4¼" (11cm)
Eye pale reddish. *Above blue gray.*
Below, grayish buff, becoming
whitish on center of belly. *Legs*
gray. Almost always in or near
mangroves or large body of water.

4. Masked Flower-piercer   MH-FT
Diglossa cyanea   5" (13cm)
Dark purplish blue with *black*
forehead and mask. Eye red.

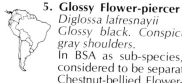

5. Glossy Flower-piercer   MH-TS
Diglossa lafresnayii   5" (13cm)
Glossy black. Conspicuous blue
gray shoulders.
In BSA as sub-species, but now
considered to be separate species:
Chestnut-bellied Flower-piercer D.
gloriosissima. Rump slaty. Throat
slaty, *below chestnut.* Moustached
Flower-piercer,   D.   mysticalis.
Conspicuous whisker and white
breast band. Belly and vent chestnut. Whisker cinnamon and no
breast band in s.

6. Black Flower-piercer   MH-TS
Diglossa humeralis   4½" (12cm)
All glossy black. In w Venezuela
and ne Colombia has small gray
area on shoulders. In Santa Marta
has rump slaty. Considered a sub-
species of *Diglossa carbonaria* in
BSA.

7. White-sided Flower-piercer
                           MH-TS
Diglossa albilatera   4½" (12cm)
Above slaty gray. Below lighter
slaty gray. *White patch on sides,*
not always visible.

8. Female: Brown, belly buff. *White*
patch on sides like ♂.

9. Rusty (Slaty) Flower-piercer
                            M-TS
Diglossa sittoides   4¼" (11cm)
Above bluish gray (forehead and
sides of head blackish in Colombia and Venezuela). *Below all cin-*
namon. ♀: Above brown. Below
buffy, *streaked dusky on breast.*
Considered a subspecies of D.
baritula in BSA.

10. Bluish Flower-piercer   MH-F
Diglossa caerulescens 4½" (12cm)
Bill slightly upturned and hooked.
Above bluish or bluish gray. Below
paler. Bill and legs blackish.

11. Indigo Flower-piercer   LM-F
Diglossa indigotica   4¼" (11cm)
Lores black. Edges of flight feathers and tail feathers bright greenish blue.

LARGE TANAGERS 1.

1. Magpie Tanager   LM-FTS
Cissopis leveriana   10¼" (26cm)
Eye yellow. Head, mantle, throat
and breast black. Back and belly
white. Wings black, coverts tipped
white. *Tail long, black, feathers
edged white.* Shows much white
when flying.

2. Grass-green Tanager   MH-F
Chlorornis riefferii   8" (20cm)
Bright *grass green*. Face and center
of belly and undertail coverts
chestnut red. Bill and legs red.

3. Hooded Mountain-Tanager MH-F
Buthraupis montana   8" (20cm)
Eye red. Head and throat black.
Back shining purplish blue. Wings
and tail black, feathers edged purplish blue. Underparts golden yellow with blue band at vent. Thighs
black.

**4. Rosy (Rose-breasted) Thrush-Tan-
ager   L-TS**
Rhodinocichla rosea   7½" (19cm)
Upperparts all blackish. *Eyebrow
rosy* in front of eye, *whitish* behind
eye. Shoulder and *underparts
bright rosy.* Usually on ground.
♀: Rosy replaced by cinnamon.

**5. Scarlet-bellied Mountain-Tanager
                            H-TS**
Anisognathus igniventris 7" (18cm)
Above, head and throat black.
Patch on ear coverts red. Wing
coverts and rump shining blue.
Lower breast and belly red (belly
black in Peru and Bolivia). Tail
black.

**6. Black-cheeked Mountain-Tanager
                            MH-F**
Anisognathus melanogenys
                            7" (18cm)
Crown and nape bright blue. Sides
of head black. Back, wings and
tail dull bluish. *Small spot below*

eye and underparts golden yellow.
Only found in Santa Marta Mountains.

**7. Blue-winged Mountain-Tanager
                            M-FT**
Anisognathus flavinucha
                            6½" (17cm)
Above black (or back olive and
rump blue in s part of range).
Crown and entire underparts *yellow.* Wing coverts blue. Primaries
and tail feathers edged blue.

**8. Lacrimose Mountain-Tanager
                            MH-FT**
Anisognathus lacrymosus
                            6½" (17cm)
Crown and back blackish, bluish
on rump. Sides of head black with
two yellow spots. Wings and tail
blackish, feathers edged blue.
Wing coverts bright purplish blue.
Below dull yellow to orange.

**9. Buff-breasted Mountain-Tanager
                            MH-FTS**
Dubusia taeniata   7" (18cm)
Crown and sides of head black.
Forecrown and *long eyebrow
spangled blue.* Wings and tail
black, feathers edged blue. Throat
black. Breast buffy. Below golden
yellow.

10. Diademed Tanager   LM-FTS
Stephanophorus diadematus
                            7" (18cm)
Above shining blue. Small *crest
white with red patch* in center. Fo-
recrown, lores and throat black.
Below shining dark purple.

11. Yellow-rumped Tanager LM-TS
Ramphocelus icteronotus
                            7" (18cm)
Black. Bill light blue. *Lower back
and rump bright yellow.* Tail
blackish.

12. Female: Crown and back brownish, *rump yellow.* Underparts yellow.

LARGE TANAGERS 2.

Ramphocelus TANAGERS - 156, 312.
Piranga TANAGERS - 312.
Habia ANT-TANAGERS - 313.

1. Flame-rumped Tanager   LM-TS
Ramphocelus flammigerus
7"(18cm)
Black. Bill light blue. *Lower back and rump bright red.*

2. Female: Above dark brown. *Breast and rump orange.* Belly yellow.

3. Masked Crimson Tanager L-FTW
Ramphocelus nigrogularis
6½"(17cm)
Upper bill blackish, *lower silvery.* All crimson except upper back, wings, tail, *mask* and center of belly black.

4. Brazilian Tanager   L-TS
Ramphocelus bresilius
6½"(17cm)
Scarlet, somewhat darker on mantle. Base of lower bill silvery. Wings and tail black.

5. Female: *Whole head and neck brown.* Back reddish brown. Wings and tail brownish black. Rump and vent dull crimson. Breast and *belly reddish brown.*

6. Crimson-backed Tanager   L-TS
Ramphocelus dimidiatus
6¼"(16cm)
Upper bill dusky, lower white at base. Head, mantle, throat and breast blackish red. Wings and tail black. *Rump* and vent *bright crimson.* Belly crimson with black patch in center (lacking in some races). ♀: Head and throat dusky brown.

7. Silver-beaked Tanager   L-TSO
Ramphocelus carbo 6¼"(16cm)
Base of lower bill *silvery white.* Above blackish red to velvety black. Throat and breast deep crimson. Belly black or dark crimson. Wings and tail black. Similar: Crimson-backed Tanager (preceding) has bright crimson rump.

8. Female: Brownish with rufous tinge. Paler below.

9. Hepatic Tanager   LM-TSO
Piranga flava   6½"(17cm)
Above dark red to light orange red, depending on race. Lighter below. *Bill dusky* with *conspicuous notch* on upper bill. ♀: Olive above, bright yellow below.

10. Summer Tanager   LMH-T
*Piranga rubra**   6¼"(16cm)
Rosy red. Bill yellowish and *without notch.* ♀: Above olive. Below yellow. Bill like ♂.

11. Red-crowned Ant-Tanager L-FT
Habia rubica   6¼"(16cm)
Bill blackish. *Brownish red,* brightest on throat and breast. *Crown stripe scarlet,* bordered by narrow black lines.

12. Female: Concealed crown stripe yellowish. Above olive brown. Throat yellowish. Below yellowish brown to olive brown.

LARGE TANAGERS 3, MID-SIZE TANAGERS 1.

Thraupis TANAGERS - 312.
Mitrospingus TANAGERS - 313.
Chlorothraupis TANAGERS - 313.

1. Azure-shouldered Tanager
                    LM-FT
Thraupis cyanoptera   7"(18cm)
Head blue, back lighter blue. Wing coverts shiny dark violet blue. Below gray in center, tinged greenish on sides. Similar: Blue-gray Tanager (below) has head lighter, more grayish than back.

2. Palm Tanager   **LM-TSO**
Thraupis palmarum   6½"(17cm)
Grayish olive, sometimes glossed blue or violet, especially underparts. *Wings bicolored,* grayish olive with black primaries. Whitish speculum sometimes shows.

3. Sayaca Tanager   **LM-TSA**
Thraupis sayaca   6¼"(16cm)
Like duller races of Blue-gray Tanager (following) with blue shoulders but still duller and grayer. *Wing feathers edged greenish blue* (not purplish blue). Northern form has grayer head, whiter belly.

4. Blue-gray Tanager   **LM-TO**
Thraupis episcopus   6¼"(16cm)
Body all pale blue or bluish gray, paler on head and somewhat darker on back. Wings and tail dark blue. Shoulder blue (or *white e of Andes*).

5. Blue-and-yellow Tanager
                    MH-TSO
Thraupis bonariensis   6½"(17cm)
Male (left): Upper bill dusky, lower pale. Head and throat blue, lores black. Back black. *Rump* and underparts *orange yellow.* Wings and tail black, feathers heavily margined blue. Female (right): Back olive. Underparts olive to buff.

6. Blue-capped Tanager   **MH-FTS**
Thraupis cyanocephala
                    6½"(17cm)
Crown and nape bright blue. Lores black. Back, wings and tail yellowish olive. Underparts gray (or blue in n Venezuela). *Thighs bright yellow.*

7. Dusky-faced Tanager   **L-FT**
Mitrospingus cassinii 6½"(17cm)
Forehead, face, back and tail blackish. Crown and nape olive yellow. Throat gray. Below olive yellow.

8. Ochre-breasted Tanager   **L-FT**
Chlorothraupis stolzmanni
                    6¼"(16cm)
Head and nape olive or grayish olive. Back, wings and tail brownish olive. Throat grayish buffy. Center of breast and belly ochraceous buff.

9. Lemon-browed Tanager   **L-F**
Chlorothraupis olivacea 6"(15cm)
Dark olive. *Prominent yellow lores and eye-ring.* Throat and center of belly yellowish.

10. Black-backed Bush-Tanager   **H-T**
Urothraupis stolzmanni
                    6¼"(16cm)
Above black. Throat white. Below gray mottled white on center of breast and belly. Sides and undertail coverts ashy gray.

11. Gray-headed Tanager   **L-TS**
Eucometis penicillata 6¼"(16cm)
Head gray. *Throat whitish.* Back, wings and tail bright olive yellow. Breast and belly *bright yellow.*

12. Gray-hooded Bush-Tanager   **H-F**
Cnemoscopus rubrirostris
                    6¼"(16cm)
Eye pinkish. *Bill pink* (black in Peru). *Head, nape, throat and breast gray.* Back, wings and tail olive. Belly bright yellow.

LARGE TANAGERS 4, MID-SIZE TANAGERS 2.

Tachyphonus TANAGERS - 166, 313.

1. **Ruby-crowned Tanager** **LM-T**
   Tachyphonus coronatus
   6¼"(16cm)
   Glossy blue black. Stripe on crown red, usually concealed. White on wing shows only in flight.

2. **Female:** Eye-ring and lores whitish. Crown and sides of head grayish contrasting with reddish brown back, wings and tail. Throat whitish. Below ochraceous streaked grayish on breast.

3. **White-lined Tanager** **L-TS**
   Tachyphonus rufus 6¼"(16cm)
   Normally appears all black with *small white line* showing *at shoulder.* Sometimes no white shows at rest but white shoulders prominent in flight.

4. **Female:** Upperparts, wings and tail uniform rufous brown. Below slightly lighter rufous brown.

5. **Red-shouldered Tanager** **L-SO**
   Tachyphonus phoenicius
   6"(15cm)
   Glossy black. Small shoulder spot red, usually not visible in field. Wing coverts may show a little white.

6. **Female:** Above brownish gray, blackish around and below eye. Below whitish tinged grayish on breast. Tail blackish.

7. **Flame-crested Tanager** **L-FT**
   Tachyphonus cristatus 6"(15cm)
   Black. *Crest red.* Rump and *throat buff.* White patch sometimes shows at shoulder.

8. **Female:** Above all brownish. Narrow eye-ring buffy. Throat whitish. Below ochraceous.

9. **Fulvous-crested Tanager** **L-FT**
   Tachyphonus surinamus 6"(15cm)
   Glossy blue black. Small white patch on shoulder. *Crest* and rump *ochraceous* (or chestnut in Peru and w Brazil). Flanks chestnut.

10. **Female:** *Top and sides of head gray, tinged yellowish around eye.* Back, wings and tail olive. Below cinnamon buff.

11. **Tawny-crested Tanager** **L-F**
    Tachyphonus delatrii 5½"(14cm)
    All black except prominent *orange yellow crest* and nape.

12. **Female:** Above dark olive brown, wings darker. Below uniform brown. Tail blackish.

LARGE TANAGERS 5, MID-SIZE TANAGERS 3.

1. **Golden-crowned Tanager   H-FT**
Iridosornis rufivertex   6¼" (16cm)
Bill small. Head black, *crown rich yellow.* Above and below *shining purple blue.* Belly chestnut in some races. Undertail coverts chestnut (or blue in central Colombia).

2. **Purplish-mantled Tanager   M-F**
Iridosornis porphyrocephala
6"(15cm)
Purplish blue. Wings and tail black broadly edged blue. *Throat bright yellow.* Center of belly buff.

3. **Moss-backed Tanager   LM-FT**
Bangsia edwardsi   6¼"(16cm)
Above mostly moss green. Crown, around eye and throat black. *Sides of head blue.* Wings edged grayish blue, coverts bluer. Below mostly yellowish green, with *bright yellow-orange patch on center of breast.*

4. **Golden-chested Tanager   L-F**
Bangsia rothschildi   6¼"(16cm)
Mainly glossy blue black, blacker on throat and sides of head. *Band across breast orange.* Vent yellow.

5. **Black-faced Tanager   L-TSO**
Schistochlamys melanopis
6¼"(16cm)
Bill short and stubby. *Head, throat and breast black.* Body gray, paler below. Tail gray.

6. **Cinnamon Tanager   LM-TS**
Schistochlamys ruficapillus
6"(15cm)
Bill short and stubby. *Mask black.* Upperparts gray. *Sides of head, throat and breast light cinnamon.* Belly white. Tail blackish.

7. **Black-goggled Tanager   LM-FT**
Trichothraupis melanops 6"(15cm)
Forehead and face black. Crown with broad yellow stripe, usually visible. Back olive-gray. Wings and tail black. Underparts all buff, deeper on undertail coverts.

8. **Female:** No black or yellow on head. Head and back brownish, wings and tail darker brown.

9. **Black-capped Hemispingus**
MH-T
Hemispingus atropileus 6"(15cm)
Crown and sides of head black. Long eyebrow whitish (or orange in Bolivia). Back olive green. Below yellow tinged ochraceous on breast.

10. **Superciliaried Hemispingus**
MH-F
Hemispingus superciliaris
5"(13cm)
Forecrown gray to blackish. Lores black. *Eyebrow white* (or yellow in Venezuela). Above olive or grayish. Below yellow (or white in central Peru).

11. **Gray-and-gold Tanager   L-F**
Tangara palmeri   5½"(14cm)
Forehead and mask black. Above pale gray, tinged greenish on back. Wings and tail black. Below whitish, with *fringe of black spots across breast.*

12. **Fawn-breasted Tanager   LM-FT**
Pipraeidea melanonota 5"(13cm)
Crown, nape and rump bright light blue. Back and wings blackish blue. Forehead and mask black. Underparts ochraceous (or buff in some races). The eye is red in n but dark in s part of range.

MID-SIZE TANAGERS 4.

1. Common Bush-Tanager   MH-TS
Chlorospingus ophthalmicus
5"(13cm)
Crown brown or grayish. Conspicuous white spot back of eye (lacking in some races). Above olive green. *Throat whitish, spotted dusky.* Breast yellow. Belly white. Tail olive green.

2. Yellow-throated Bush-Tanager
LM-F
Chlorosphingus flavigularis
5"(13cm)
Upperparts yellowish olive. Lores gray. *Throat yellow* (only sides of throat yellow w of the Andes). Below gray.

3. Ashy-throated Bush-Tanager
M-FT
Chlorospingus canigularis
5"(13cm)
Head gray. Above olive green. Throat gray, *unspotted.* Breast band yellow. Belly whitish.

4. Dusky-bellied Bush-Tanager
LM-F
Chlorospingus semifuscus
5"(13cm)
Head dark gray. White spot back of eye in some races. Back, wings and tail dark olive. Underparts dull gray (center of belly whitish in s part of range).

5. White-shouldered Tanager
LM-FT
Tachyphonus luctuosus
4½"(12cm)
Glossy black except *large white patch on shoulder.*

6. Female: *Head gray.* Back yellowish olive. Below yellow, tinged olive on breast.

7. Plain-colored Tanager   L-FT
Tangara inornata   4½"(12cm)
Upperparts, throat and breast gray. Wings and tail black, wing coverts bright blue. Belly white.

8. Scarlet-and-white Tanager   L-F
Erythrothlypis salmoni 4½"(12cm)
Head, throat and breast flame scarlet. Back red. Wings brownish red. Belly red in center. Flanks white.

9. Female: Above uniform bronzy olive. Below whitish.

10. Rufous-throated Tanager   LM-FT
Tangara rufigula   4½"(12cm)
Head black. Back black, feathers tipped yellowish green, appearing scaled. Wings and tail black, feathers edged greenish. *Throat rufous.* Below white profusely *spotted black* on breast and sides.

11. Opal-crowned Tanager   L-FT
Tangara callophrys   5"(13cm)
Forehead purple. *Crown, sides of head and rump silvery.* Nape, back and wings black. Underparts shining purple, center of belly black. Tail black edged purple.

12. Masked Tanager   L-FT
Tangara nigrocincta   4½"(12cm)
Head and nape pale silvery blue. Mask, back and *breast black.* Wings black, coverts blue. Rump blue. Belly white. Tail black edged blue. Considered same species as Golden-hooded Tanager (170-4) in BSA.

MID-SIZE TANAGERS 5, WITH RUFOUS AROUND HEAD OR WITH PROMINENT BLUE.

Tangara TANAGERS - 164, 166, 170, 172, 310, 311.
Thlypopsis TANAGERS - 314.

1. Scrub Tanager   **LM-S**
Tangara vitriolina   5½" (14cm)
Crown rufous. Sides of head black. Above silvery green, wings often bluer. Below greenish or grayish. Belly and undertail coverts buff.

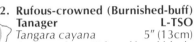

2. Rufous-crowned (Burnished-buff) Tanager   **L-TSO**
Tangara cayana   5" (13cm)
Crown rufous. Sides of head black. Nape and back buff. Wings blue. Underparts buff, tinged blue on throat and breast (or with broad black stripe down center of underparts in s part of range).

Chestnut-backed Tanager LM-FT
Tangara preciosa   5½" (14cm)
Crown, nape and upper back bright chestnut. Back and wing coverts silvery ochraceous. Underparts bluish green, vent chestnut. Wings and tail blackish, feathers edged blue.

3. Female: Crown and nape chestnut. Back, wings and tail green. Below pale silvery green.

4. Chestnut-headed Tanager LM-FT
Pyrrhocoma ruficeps   4½" (12cm)
Forehead, lores and chin black. *Head and throat chestnut.* Rest of plumage dark gray, lighter on belly.

5. Female: Back olive. Head cinnamon, no black on face. Below yellowish. Sides grayish.

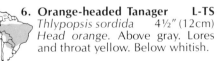

6. Orange-headed Tanager   **L-TS**
Thlypopsis sordida   4½" (12cm)
Head orange. Above gray. Lores and throat yellow. Below whitish.

7. Turquoise Tanager   **L-FT**
Tangara mexicana   4½" (12cm)
Forehead, lores, hindcrown, back, wings and tail blue. Middle of crown, *face, throat, breast* and rump *blue. Belly yellow* (white in se Brazil) spotted blue on sides.

8. Blue-necked Tanager   **LM-TS**
Tangara cyanicollis   4½" (12cm)
Head and neck blue, lores black. Throat purplish in some races. *Back black,* rump light blue or green. Wings and tail black margined blue or purple. Wing coverts bronzy gold. *Underparts black.*

9. Blue-and-black Tanager   **H-FT**
Tangara vassorii   5" (13cm)
Uniform shining purplish blue. (In Peru, crown contrasting paler blue. In s Peru and Bolivia nape patch yellow.) Narrow mask, wings and tail black.

10. Paradise Tanager   **L-FT**
Tangara chilensis   5" (13cm)
Head yellowish green. Back and tail black. Wings black, edged purple. Throat purple. *Rump red* (or red and yellow in e part of range). Wing coverts, sides of breast and belly brilliant blue. Belly black in center.

11. Beryl-spangled Tanager   **M-FT**
Tangara nigroviridis   4½" (12cm)
Forehead, back and face black. Crown and rump silvery blue. Mantle and *all underparts spotted black and silvery blue.* Wings and tail black, feathers edged dark blue.

12. Golden-naped Tanager   **M-FT**
Tangara ruficervix   4½" (12cm)
Mainly turquoise blue, more purplish in Peru. *Crown blue, hindcrown golden or orange.* Center of belly white. Tail black, feathers edged blue.

MID-SIZE TANAGERS 6, WITH PROMINENT YELLOW.

Tangara TANAGERS - 164, 166, 168, 172, 310, 311.
Chlorochrysa TANAGERS - 172, 310.
Hemithraupis TANAGERS - 314.

1. Silver-throated Tanager   LM-F
Tangara icterocephala 4½" (12cm)
Top and sides of head yellow bordered below by narrow black line. *Back striped yellow and black.* Wings and tail black, feathers edged green. Rump yellow. Throat light gray. Below yellow.

2. Emerald Tanager   L-F
Tangara florida   5" (13cm)
Forehead, chin, *spot on cheek black.* Crown, rump and center of underparts yellow. Back streaked green and black. Sides green. Wings and tail black edged greenish. ♀: No yellow crown.

3. Golden Tanager   LM-F
Tangara arthus   4½" (12cm)
Head and underparts golden yellow (or with black chin, throat and breast chestnut in some races). Prominent black *mark on cheeks. Back streaked black and gold,* rump yellow. Wings and tail black.

4. Golden-hooded Tanager   L-TS
Tangara larvata   4½" (12cm)
Forehead and mask black, area around eye blue. Rest of *head and throat yellow.* Back, wings and *breast black.* Wing coverts and rump blue. Tail black. Considered a race of Masked Tanager (166-12) in BSA.

5. Saffron-crowned Tanager   M-FT
Tangara xanthocephala
              4½" (12cm)
Crown and sides of head yellow. *Mask, chin and narrow collar black.* Back striped bluish and black. Rump and breast blue. Belly buff or grayish. Wings and tail black, feathers edged blue.

6. Gilt-edged Tanager   LM-F
Tangara cyanoventris   5" (13cm)
Crown and sides of head yellow. Above streaked black and gold. *Forehead and throat black. Below shining blue.* Wings and tail black, feathers edged green.

7. Multicolored Tanager   LM-F
Chlorochrysa nitidissima
              4½" (12cm)
Forecrown and sides of head golden yellow. Hindcrown and nape green. Patch on back glistening lemon yellow. *Black spot below ear coverts.* Throat orange yellow. Breast and belly glistening blue with black in center. ♀: Has green breast and belly.

8. Green-and-gold Tanager   L-FT
Tangara schrankii   4½" (12cm)
Forehead, chin and *sides of head black. Small crescent in front of eye greenish.* Crown, rump and center of breast and belly golden yellow. Throat and sides green. Back streaked black and green. Wing coverts tinged bluish. ♀: Crown green like back.

9. Speckled Tanager   M-F
Tangara guttata   4½" (12cm)
Crown yellowish green. Face yellow, lores black. Back green spotted black. *Below white spotted black.* Tail green.

10. Black-headed Tanager   LM-F
Tangara cyanoptera 4½" (12cm)
Head black. Back and underparts greenish yellow. Wings and tail black, feathers edged blue.

11. Female: Above greenish. Wings and tail dark brown, the feathers edged green. Cheeks and sides of body gray, tinged green. Throat and breast gray, more or less spotted dusky.

12. Yellow-backed Tanager   L-FT
Hemithraupis flavicollis
              4½" (12cm)
Above dull black, rump yellow. Wings black with *white speculum. Throat yellow.* Below white except vent yellow. ♀: Above brownish olive. *Below bright yellow,* flanks olive.

MID-SIZE TANAGERS 7, WITH PROMINENT GREEN.

Chlorochrysa TANAGERS - 170,310.
Tangara TANAGERS - 164, 166, 168, 170, 310, 311.

1. Glistening-green Tanager   LM-F
Chlorochrysa phoenicotis
                            4½"(12cm)
Shining green. Small spot back of
ear coverts gray and red.

Rufous-winged Tanager   L-F
Tangara lavinia   4½"(12cm)
Head rufous. Upper back yellow.
Lower back green. Wings with *rufous* edges making prominent
patch. Below green, center of
throat and belly bright blue.

2. Female: Mostly green above and
below. *Wing patch rufous.*

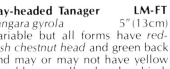

Bay-headed Tanager   LM-FT
Tangara gyrola   5"(13cm)
Variable but all forms have *reddish chestnut head* and green back
and may or may not have yellow
shoulders or yellow band on hindneck.

3. Form with green underparts.
4. Form with blue underparts.

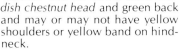

5. Green-headed Tanager   LM-FT
Tangara seledon   5"(13cm)
Head bluish green, nape and sides
of neck yellowish green. Back
black, rump orange yellow. Wing
coverts blue, primaries broadly
edged blue green. *Below shining
blue*, flanks broadly bright green.
Tail black, feathers edged green.

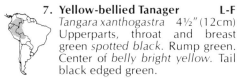

6. Red-necked Tanager   LM-F
Tangara cyanocephala   5"(13cm)
Forehead, lores, chin and mantle
black. Wing coverts black tipped
orange yellow. Lower back,
cheeks, *ear coverts and collar
scarlet* (or orange in one race).
Throat blue, underparts and lower
back green to bluish. Tail black,
feathers edged green.

7. Yellow-bellied Tanager   L-F
Tangara xanthogastra 4½"(12cm)
Upperparts, throat and breast
green *spotted black*. Rump green.
Center of *belly bright yellow*. Tail
black edged green.

8. Black-capped Tanager   M-FTS
Tangara heinei   4½"(12cm)
Crown black. Sides of head, throat
and breast shining silvery green.
Back and belly bluish. Wings and
tail black, feathers edged blue.

9. Female: Above yellowish green.
Below pale gray.

10. Metallic-green Tanager   M-FT
Tangara labradorides 4½"(12cm)
Mostly silvery bluish or greenish.
Hindcrown, nape and back black.
Wing coverts purple and green.
Forecrown, mask and chin black.
Wings and tail black, feathers
edged green. Belly gray. Vent cin-
namon.

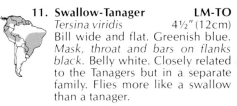

11. Swallow-Tanager   LM-TO
Tersina viridis   4½"(12cm)
Bill wide and flat. Greenish blue.
*Mask, throat and bars on flanks
black*. Belly white. Closely related
to the Tanagers but in a separate
family. Flies more like a swallow
than a tanager.

12. Female: Above grass green. *Forehead, lores and throat mottled
black and white.* Breast grass
green. Belly pale yellow.

SMALL TANAGERS

1. **Thick-billed Euphonia   LM-T**
   Euphonia laniirostris 4¼" (11cm)
   Slightly thicker bill hard to see in field. Yellow forecrown *reaches past eye*. Above blue black. Underparts bright yellow, *including throat*.
2. **Female:** Olive above. Olive yellow below. Center of belly clear yellow.
3. **Immature male:** At one stage has narrow yellow forehead.

   Blue-hooded Euphonia   LM-FT
   Euphonia musica   4¼" (11cm)
   Forehead, face and throat black. *Crown and nape light blue*. Back black, rump yellow. Breast and belly deep yellow. Tail black.
4. **Female:** Crown and nape blue. Above olive. Below yellowish.

   Golden-bellied Euphonia   L-TS
   Euphonia chrysopasta 4¼" (11cm)
   Above olive. *Lores and throat whitish*. Nape gray. Below yellow, barred olive on breast.
5. **Female:** Underparts pale gray, flanks and undertail coverts olive yellow.

6. **Chestnut-bellied Euphonia   L-FT**
   Euphonia pectoralis   4¼" (11cm)
   Upperparts, throat and breast blue black, patch at sides of breast yellow. *Belly dark chestnut*. ♀: Above olive green. Below olive yellow on sides, gray in center.

7. **Rufous-bellied Euphonia   L-FT**
   Euphonia rutiventris   4¼" (11cm)
   Upperparts, *throat and breast steel blue*. Lower breast and belly rufous ochraceous. ♀: Above olive. Below olive yellow, *center of belly gray. Vent rufous*.

8. **Violaceous Euphonia   L-T**
   Euphonia violacea   4¼" (10cm)
   Yellow forecrown reaches only to eye. Above blue black. Underparts deep yellow. Large white spots on outer two pairs of tail feathers. ♀: Olive above. Whitish spot in front of eye. Breast olive becoming yellowish on belly.

9. **Orange-bellied Euphonia   LM-FT**
   Euphonia xanthogaster 4" (10cm)
   Yellow or rufous *forecrown reaches past eye*. Above blue black. Throat and sides of head black. Below yellowish orange. ♀: Forecrown yellowish to rufous. Above bronzy olive except *nape grayish*. Below pinkish gray.

   Purple-throated Euphonia   L-TS
   Euphonia chlorotica   4" (10cm)
   Crown patch yellow *extending past eye*. Rest of upperparts and *throat blue black*. Below bright yellow. Tail blue black with large white oval patch on two outermost tail feathers.
10. **Female:** Olive green above. Olive yellow below, center of belly yellow.

11. **White-vented Euphonia   L-FT**
    Euphonia minuta   3½" (9cm)
    Yellow forehead reaches *only to* eye. Upperparts and throat blue black. Breast and belly yellow. *Undertail coverts white*. ♀: Above olive. Throat and center of belly whitish. Breast and sides of body greenish yellow.

12. **Yellow-collared Chlorophonia   L-F**
    Chlorophonia flavirostris   3½" (9cm)
    Bright grass green. Bill and legs reddish. Collar, prominent eye-ring rump, center of breast and belly golden yellow. (Collar missing in some races). Narrow chestnut band on breast sometimes not visible. ♀: All green, no yellow.

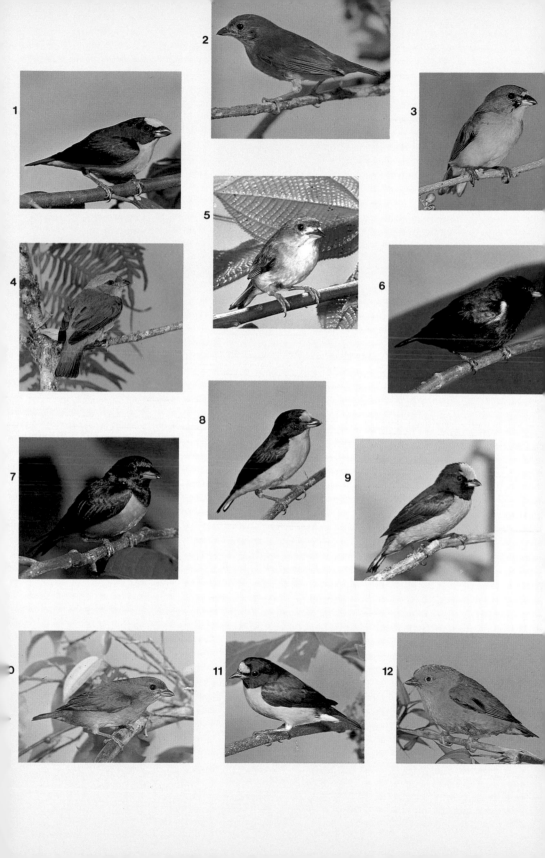

LARGE FINCHES 1.

1. Grayish Saltator   **L-TSO**
Saltator coerulescens   7½" (19cm)
Above light to dark gray. Short eyebrow white. Throat white. Prominent whiskers black. Underparts pale gray, becoming buff on belly and vent.

2. Green-winged Saltator   **LM-TS**
Saltator similis   7½" (19cm)
Crown and mantle olive (not gray). Inner flight feathers edged bright olive green. Breast and belly clay color (not grayish).

3. Buff-throated Saltator   **L-TS**
Saltator maximus   7½" (19cm)
Head gray with short white eyebrow. *Back and tail bright olive. Chin white, throat buff.* Prominent whiskers black. Breast gray. Belly buff.

4. Black-winged Saltator   **M-TS**
Saltator atripennis   7½" (19cm)
Crown black (gray w of Andes). Back olive. Wings black. Sides of head black, long eyebrow and *patch on ear coverts white.* Throat white. Breast and belly light gray. Tail black.

Golden-billed Saltator   **MH-TS**
Saltator aurantiirostris   7" (18cm)
Bill orange or red. Above gray. Forehead and sides of head black. Long streak back of eye white. Throat white. Below light gray (with broad black band across breast in some races). Tail black.

5. Female: *Upper bill black,* lower black at base, tipped reddish. Throat and streak back of eye buff instead of white.

6. Streaked Saltator   **LM-TS**
Saltator albicollis   7" (18cm)
Bill black *with yellow tip.* Above olive to grayish. Short eyebrow white. *Below white streaked gray-*

ish (or unstreaked below and breast tinged yellow from sw Colombia to w Peru).

7. Black-backed Grosbeak   **MH-TS**
Pheucticus aureoventris
     7½" (19cm)
Upperparts, throat and breast black. (Rump yellow in Venezuela and Colombia.) (Center of throat and breast yellow in s Colombia and Ecuador.) Wing feathers with much white, outer tail feathers broadly tipped white. *Belly bright yellow,* some black spotting on sides. ♀: Browner. Below yellow, spotted black especially on breast.

8. Rose-breasted Grosbeak   **LM-T**
Pheucticus ludovicianus*
     6½" (17cm)
Male in breeding plumage has black back and bright red breast but is seldom seen in S.A. Non-breeding ♂ is rather like ♀ but has reddish tinge on breast.

9. Female: *Above brown streaked black,* wing coverts tipped white. Long eyebrow and line below cheeks white. Below buff streaked dusky. Tail uniform brown.

10. Black-throated Grosbeak   **L-F**
Pitylus fuliginosus   7" (18cm)
All black. Bill bright red.

11. Slate-colored Grosbeak   **L-FT**
Pitylus grossus   6½" (17cm)
Bill heavy, *bright red.* Above dark gray. Throat white. Lores, sides of neck and band across breast black. *Below gray, paler than back.* ♀: Somewhat paler than ♂ and lacks black on neck and breast.

12. Yellow-green Grosbeak   **L-FT**
Caryothraustes canadensis
     6¼" (16cm)
Bill heavy, gray, tipped black. Above olive yellow. *Mask and chin black* bordered by bright yellow. Underparts bright yellow.

LARGE FINCHES 2.

Atlapetes BRUSH-FINCHES - 180, 321, 322.

1. **Black-headed Brush-Finch LM-FS**
Atlapetes atricapillus 7½" (19cm)
Head deep black. Above bright olive. Usually shows yellow at bend of wing. Below white, sides gray. Tail black.

2. **Stripe-headed Brush-Finch**
                                    LM-FT
Atlapetes torquatus 6½" (17cm)
Head black, *crown stripe and long eyebrow gray or white.* Back and wings olive. Throat white. Band across breast black (lacking w of Andes). Below grayish, center of belly white. Tail dusky.

3. **Yellow-throated Brush-Finch**
                                    M-TS
Atlapetes gutturalis 6½" (17cm)
Long crown streak white. Above blackish. Sides of head black. *Throat bright yellow.* Below whitish. Tail dusky.

4. **Chestnut-capped Brush-Finch**
                                    LM-FT
Atlapetes brunneinucha
                                    6½" (17cm)
Forecrown black. Crown and nape chestnut. Back and wings olive green. Sides of head black. Throat white. *Band across breast black* (lacking in w Ecuador). Below white in center, gray or olive at sides. Tail blackish.

5. **White-rimmed Brush-Finch M-F**
Atlapetes leucopis 6½" (17cm)
Crown and nape chestnut. Back, wings, tail and sides of head black. *Eye-ring and streak behind eye white.* Throat dusky gray. Below dark olive green.

6. **Pale-naped Brush-Finch H-T**
Atlapetes pallidinucha 6½" (17cm)
Forecrown cinnamon. Above dark gray. *Line down center of nape white.* Face black. Throat bright yellow. Below olive yellow. Tail blackish.

7. **Rufous-naped Brush-Finch M-TS**
Atlapetes rufinucha 6¼" (16cm)
Crown and nape chestnut (forehead and chin black in Venezuela). Above gray or dark olive or black (with prominent speculum in Colombia and Peru). Sides of head black. Underparts yellow, flanks olive. Tail dark gray.

8. **Slaty Brush-Finch MH-FT**
Atlapetes schistaceus 6¼" (16cm)
Crown and nape rufous, sides of head black. *Upperparts dark gray to blackish* (conspicuous white speculum in most of Colombia and Ecuador). Throat broadly white, with *black whisker.* Below gray. Tail black.

9. **Ochre-breasted Brush-Finch**
                                    LMH-TS
Atlapetes semirufus 6¼" (16cm)
Head, nape, throat and breast orange rufous (with center of throat white in one race in Venezuela). Back, wings and tail olive, center of belly yellow, flanks olive.

10. **Santa Marta Brush-Finch M-FTS**
Atlapetes melanocephalus
                                    6¼" (16cm)
Head and chin black, *gray patch on cheeks.* Back, wings and tail dark gray. *Underparts bright yellow.*

11. **Dusky-headed Brush-Finch M-TS**
Atlapetes fuscoolivaceus
                                    6¼" (16cm)
Above dark olive green. *Head brownish black. Distinct dusky whisker.* Below yellow, mottled olive on sides. Tail blackish.

12. **Olive-headed Brush-Finch M-TS**
Atlapetes flaviceps 6¼" (16cm)
Above olive. Wings and tail black. *Lores, eye-ring and underparts yellow.*

LARGE FINCHES 3, MID-SIZE FINCHES 1.

1. Great Pampa-Finch   LM-SO
Embernagra platensis 7½" (19cm)
Bill orange, black on ridge. Above
olive green to grayish (streaked
dusky in immatures). Wing coverts
yellowish olive. Face dusky. Below
gray, center of belly whitish.

2. Tanager-Finch   M-F
Orcothraupis arremonops
7" (18cm)
Head black, *broad crown stripe
and eyebrow whitish.* Above rufous. Below rufous except center
of belly gray. Tail blackish.

3. Red-crested Cardinal   L-SO
Paroaria coronata   6½" (17cm)
Bill yellow. *Long crest, head, throat
and stripe down breast scarlet.*
Back and wings gray. Below white.
Tail black.

4. Red-capped Cardinal   L-SW
Paroaria gularis   6¼" (16cm)
Upper bill black, lower yellowish
tipped black. *Head and chin red*
(with black stripe through eye in n
part of range). Back, wings and tail
black. Lower throat black (red in
most of Venezuela) extending as
point onto breast. Below white.
♀: like ♂. Immatures have brown
head and throat.

5. White-winged Brush-Finch
MH-TS
Atlapetes leucopterus   6" (15cm)
Crown rufous. Back, wings and
tail gray. Narrow black whisker.
*Conspicuous   wing   speculum
white.* Sides of head black, lores
white. Underparts white, sides
gray. In s Ecuador and Peru, forecrown and area around eye white.

6. Black-striped Sparrow   L-TS
Arremonops conirostris 6" (15cm)
Head gray, striped black. Back,
wings and tail grayish olive or
brownish olive. Bend of wing yellow. Below whitish, shaded gray
or brown on breast and sides.

7. Saffron-billed Sparrow   LM-TS
Arremon flavirostris   6" (15cm)
Bill yellow with black ridge. Head
black with gray crown stripe
(sometimes poorly defined). Eyebrow white. Upper back gray. Back
and wings bright olive. Below
white with *black band on breast.*

8. Orange-billed Sparrow   L-FT
Arremon aurantiirostris
5½" (14cm)
Bill orange (dusky in immatures).
Head black with gray crown stripe.
Long eyebrow white. Back and
wings olive, bend of wing yellow.
Underparts white with *black band
across breast.* Tail dark brown.

9. Pectoral Sparrow   L-FT
Arremon taciturnus 5½" (14cm)
Bill black (lower yellow in Colombia and n Venezuela). Head black,
crown streak gray. Long eyebrow
white. Back and wings bright olive,
shoulders bright yellow. Below
white with *full or partial black
band across breast* (♀ lacking). Tail
dusky.

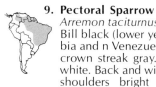

10. Golden-winged Sparrow   L-S
Arremon schlegeli   5½" (14cm)
Bill yellow. *Head all black.* Collar
white. Above olive, tinged gray on
upper back. *Shoulders yellow.*
Below white. Tail dark gray.

11. Rufous-collared Sparrow
LMH-SO
Zonotrichia capensis 5½" (14cm)
Crown streaked gray and black.
Above reddish brown streaked
black, *semi-collar rufous.* Wing
coverts tipped white. Below whitish, black patch at each side of
breast. Tail dull brown.

12. Plush-capped Finch   MH-FT
Catamblyrhynchus diadema
5" (13cm)
Bill short, stubby. *Forecrown deep
yellow.* Hindcrown and nape
black. Back, wings and tail dark
gray. Sides of head and all underparts chestnut. Resembles the
Finches but put in a separate family in RSA.

MID-SIZE FINCHES 2.

1. Great-billed (Greater Large-billed) Seed-Finch   L-TSO
Oryzoborus maximiliani 6" (15cm)
All black (with speculum in some races). *Bill extremely thick, horn color.* ♀: Above rufous brown, wings and tail darker. Below varies from reddish brown to bright cinnamon. Bill like ♂.

2. Blue-black Grosbeak   L-FT
Cyanocompsa cyanoides
                    6" (15cm)
Bill heavy, dusky. Dark blue. Forehead, eyebrow, wing coverts and spot at base of bill brighter blue. Wings and tail black.

3. Female: Uniform reddish brown.

4. Indigo Grosbeak   L-S
Cyanoloxia glaucocaerulea
                    5½"(14cm)
Bill small and stubby for a grosbeak. Bright light blue, sometimes lighter blue on wing coverts and above eye. Wings and tail black edged blue. ♀: Above dark brown, lighter brown below.

5. Olive Finch   LM-F
Lysurus castaneiceps 6" (15cm)
Olive. Crown and nape chestnut. Sides of head and throat gray. Wings and tail black.

6. Mourning Sierra-Finch   H-S
Phrygilus fructiceti 6" (15cm)
Bill yellow. Above dark gray streaked black. Wings and tail blackish. *Wing-bars white.* Throat and breast black, sides gray. Belly white. Legs light brown. ♀: Above grayish brown streaked blackish. Eyebrow and ear coverts whitish, surrounding brown cheeks. Two prominent white wing-bars. Below whitish, streaked blackish on throat and breast.

7. Plumbeous Sierra-Finch   H-SO
Phrygilus unicolor 5½" (14cm)
Uniform lead gray. Wings and tail blacker.

8. Female: Above brownish, below whitish, *heavily streaked dusky above and below.*

9. Wedge-tailed Grass-Finch   L-O
Emberizoides herbicola
          6"(15cm) extended tail + 3cm.
Above brownish streaked black. Lores and eye-ring white. Below white. *Tail long, pointed, much graduated.*

10. Long-tailed Reed-Finch   LM-SW
Donacospiza albifrons 6" (15cm)
Crown grayish brown shading to reddish brown on rump. Wings brown. Lores, eye-ring and narrow eyebrow white. Underparts tawny buff, whitish on center of belly. ♀: Crown and back streaked blackish.

11. Black-and-rufous Warbling-Finch   LM-TSO
Poospiza nigrorufa 5½" (14cm)
Above dark olive brown or grayish brown. *Long eyebrow white turning rufous behind eye.* Sides of head black. Throat rufous bordered by narrow white line. *Below rufous.*

12. Red-rumped Warbling-Finch   LM-TS
Poospiza lateralis 5" (13cm)
Crown and back gray (upper back sometimes reddish brown). *Rump rufous.* Wings black, coverts edged white. Long eyebrow white (or only streak over lores white n of Sao Paulo, Brazil). *Below whitish, sides rufous.* Tail black with prominent white on outer feathers.

RIDGELY

MID-SIZE FINCHES 3; SMALL FINCHES 1.

Catamenia SEEDEATERS - 319.
Sicalis YELLOW-FINCHES - 319, 320.

1. Pileated Finch   **L-S**
Coryphospingus pileatus
5" (13cm)
Crest red, bordered black. Above light gray. Primaries brown, edged gray. Lores and eye-ring whitish. Below white tinged grayish on breast and sides. Tail black.

2. Female: No crest. Above brownish gray. Below white, streaked dusky on breast.

3. Red-crested Finch   **L-SO**
Coryphospingus cucullatus
5" (13cm)
Crest crimson bordered black, not always visible. Eye-ring white. Above dark reddish brown, rump crimson. Underparts dark reddish. Wings and tail blackish.

4. Female: Above brownish, rump dull red. *Eye-ring, lores and throat whitish.* Underparts pinkish brown.

5. Paramo Seedeater   **MH-TS**
Catamenia homochroa 5" (13cm)
Dark slaty gray, face blacker. Bill yellow. Center of belly lighter. Vent chestnut.

6. Female: Dark brownish, streaked dusky above. Below grayish becoming buffy on belly.

7. Band-tailed Seedeater   **H-SO**
Catamenia analis   5" (13cm)
Bill yellow. Above dark slaty gray. Wings black. Area around eye blackish or gray. Tail black with *white oval patch* on each feather. Below gray, vent chestnut. Legs dusky.

8. Female: Above brownish streaked dusky. Below whitish streaked blackish. Tail like ♂.

9. Blue Finch   **L-SO**
Porphyrospiza caerulescens
5" (13cm)
Bill yellow. Dark blue. Bright blue on forehead, face, throat and rump. ♀: Above rufous brown. Below whitish, narrowly streaked blackish.

10. Saffron (Finch) Yellow-Finch
LM-TSO
Sicalis flaveola   5" (13cm)
Crown orange. Back yellowish, more or less faintly streaked dusky. Below bright yellow (or dull yellow, tinged olive on breast). Wings and tail dusky edged olive.

11. Female: Above brown broadly streaked dusky. Below whitish streaked dusky. Breast often tinged pale yellow.

Grassland Yellow-Finch   **LM-O**
Sicalis luteola   4¼" (11cm)
Above yellowish olive, streaked black. Rump olive. Eye-ring, lores and underparts bright yellow (with gray breast band in s part of range).

12. Female: Browner. Throat and breast brownish. Belly yellow.

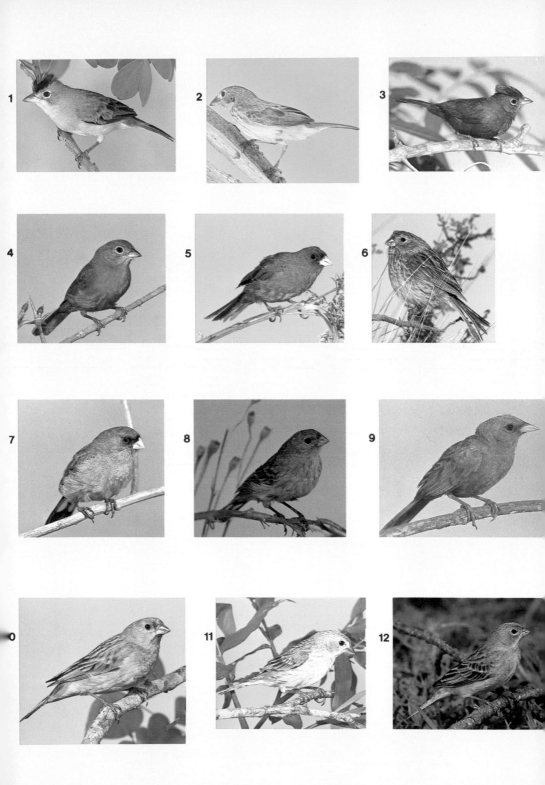

SMALL FINCHES 2.

Oryzoborus SEED-FINCHES - 182, 318.
Ammodramus SPARROWS - 322.
Carduelis SISKINS - 324.

1. Lesser Seed-Finch   **L-TS**
Oryzoborus angolensis
4½″(12cm)
Bill black, very thick at base. Head, upperparts, throat, breast, wings and tail black. Wing speculum white. *Belly chestnut* (all black w of Andes and in n Colombia).

2. Female: Brown. Bill and wings darker brown. Belly cinnamon.

3. Uniform Finch   **LM-F**
Haplospiza unicolor 4½″ (12cm)
Uniform bluish gray. Bill rather slender for a finch. ♀: Olive brown above. Below whitish, breast shaded olive and streaked dusky. Sides olive brown.

4. Slaty Finch   **MH-FT**
Haplospiza rustica 4½″ (12cm)
Uniform slaty gray. Bill rather long, slender, sharp-pointed, blackish. Similar: Plumbeous Sierra-Finch (182-7) is much larger and is pale gray below.

5. Female: Above brown. Below olive brown, faintly streaked on throat and breast. Center of belly whitish.

6. Yellow-browed Sparrow   **L-SO**
Ammodramus (Myospiza)
aurifrons 4½″ (12cm)
Above gray, streaked black. *Eyebrow and eye-ring yellow.* Area at base of lower bill yellow. Below white, tinged grayish on breast. Tail dusky brown, the feathers edged paler.

7. Grassland Sparrow   **LM-O**
Ammodramus (Myospiza)
humeralis 4½″ (12cm)
Above gray with black streaks edged chestnut. Eyebrow yellowish in front of eye and gray behind it. Below dirty white, the breast buffy gray in contrast.

8. Hooded Siskin   **LMH-TSO**
Carduelis (Spinus) magellanica
4½″(12cm)
Head and throat black. Back yellowish olive. Narrow collar and rump bright yellow. Wings black with *yellow patch.* White usually shows on inner wing feathers. Below bright yellow. Tail black.

9. Female: Above olive, bright yellow. Wings patterned like ♂. Below olive, yellower on belly.

The following three birds were treated as separate species in BSA but are here considered races of Hooded Siskin. This treatment is tentative and requires further study.
Santa Cruz Siskin, *C. santaecrucis,* back spotted black.
Saffron Siskin, *C. siemiradzkii,* back bright yellow.
Olivaceous Siskin, *C. olivaceus,* belly deep yellow.

10. Andean Siskin   **MH-SO**
Carduelis (Spinus) spinescens
4¼″(11cm)
Cap black. Above olive green. Wings with *large yellow patch.* White edges show on innermost wing feathers. Underparts olive yellow. Tail black.

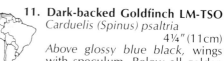

11. Dark-backed Goldfinch LM-TSO
Carduelis (Spinus) psaltria
4¼″(11cm)
Above glossy blue black, wings with speculum. Below all golden yellow. Tail black, white near base.

12. Female: Above olive. Below dull yellow. Tail brown with no white.

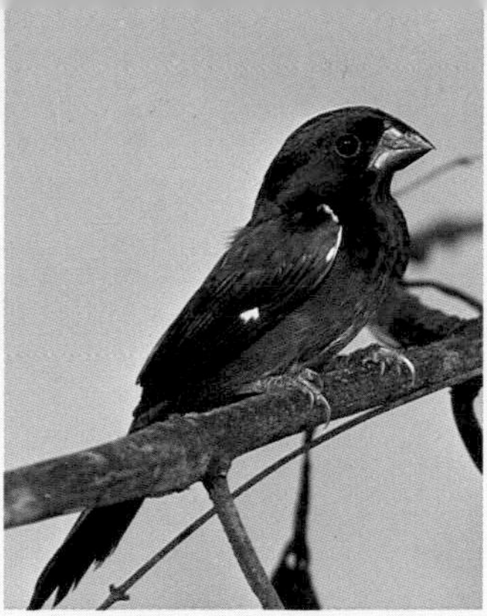
1

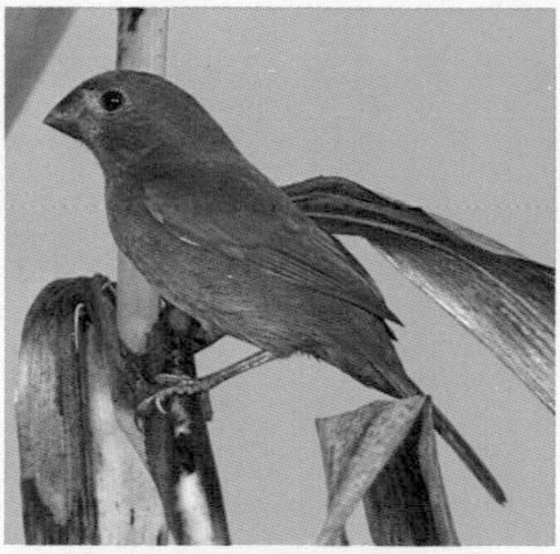
2

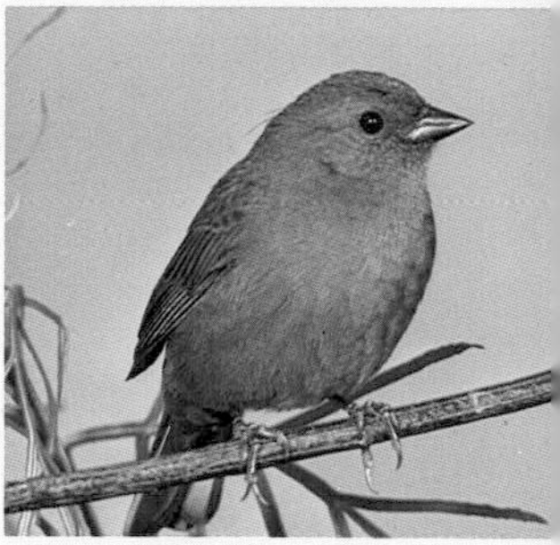
3

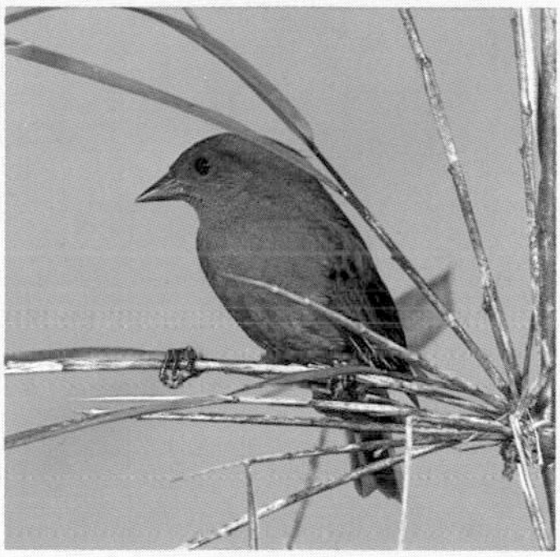
4

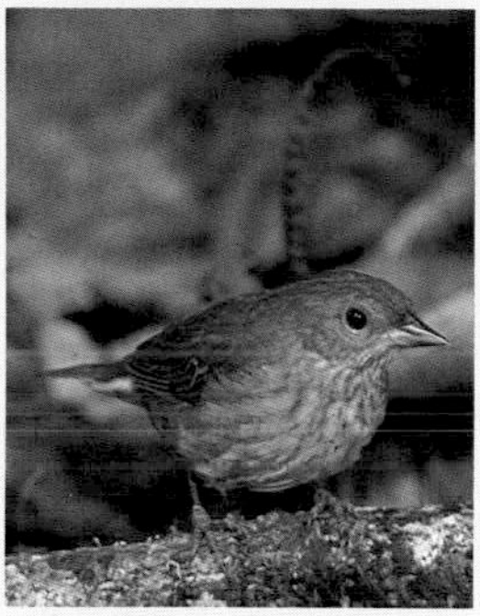
5

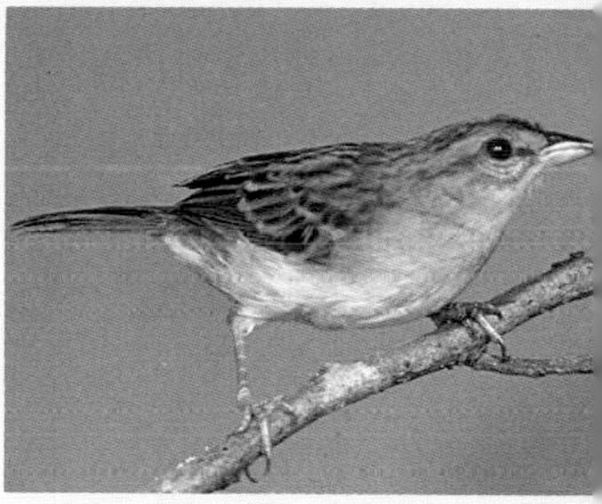
6

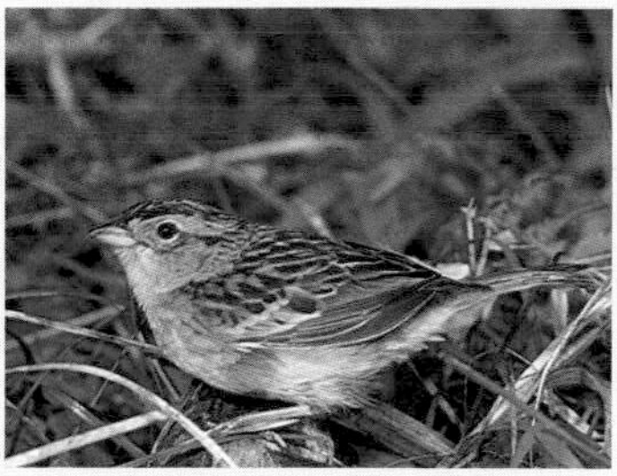
7

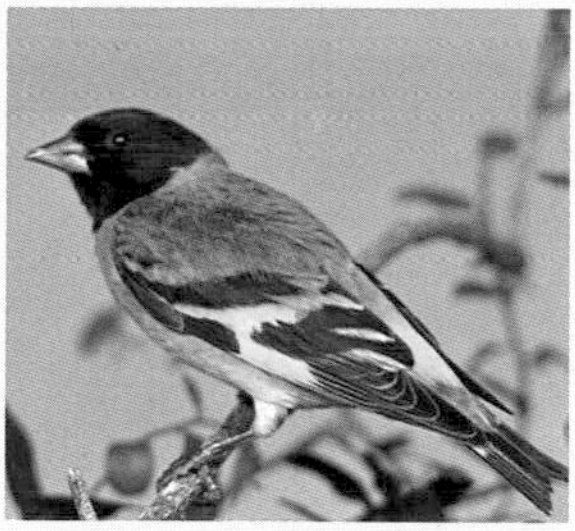
8

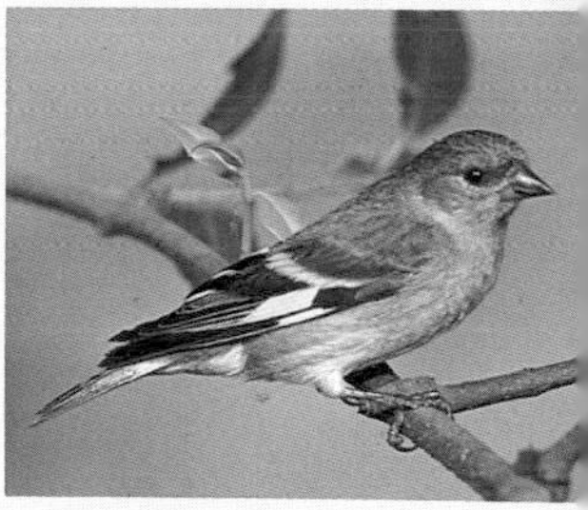
9

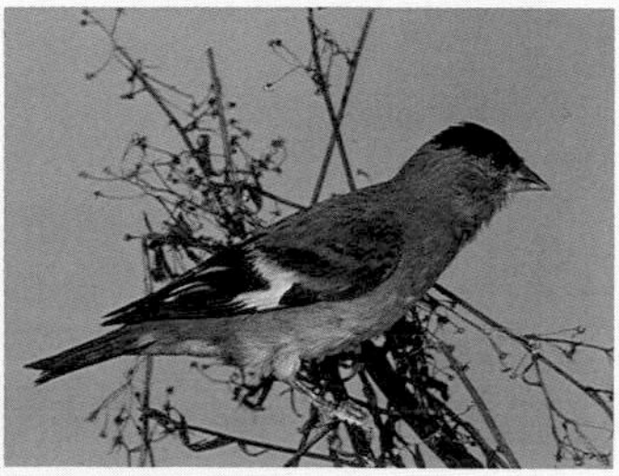
10

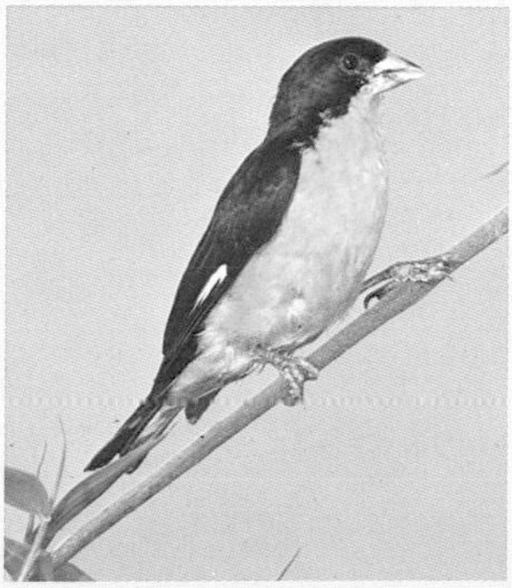
11

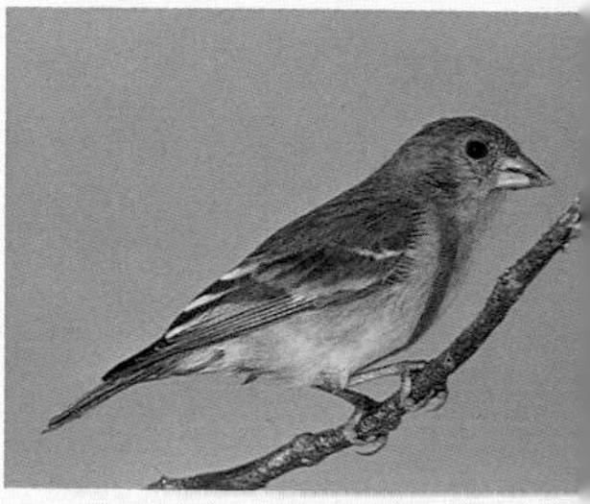
12

SMALL FINCHES 3.

Sporophila SEEDEATERS - 190, 317, 318.

Most female Seedeaters are very similar and are not described. They resemble the female Variable Seedeater (188-11) and can often be identified by the males which accompany them.

1. House Sparrow   LM-TO
Passer domesticus   4½" (12cm)
Crown gray. Above brown, streaked black. Line back of eye chestnut. Cheeks and sides of neck whitish. *Throat and breast black.* Belly gray. ♀: Grayish brown. Faint eyebrow whitish. No black on throat or breast.

2. Coal-crested Finch   L-SO
Charitospiza eucosma 4¼" (11cm)
Crown, face, throat and center of breast black. Cheek patch whitish. Back gray. Belly and sides of breast chestnut. Tail black, white near body.

Crimson Finch   L-S
Rhodospingus cruentus 4" (10cm)
Bill quite narrow, pointed. Above black. Center of crown and *underparts scarlet.*

3. Female: Above brown. Below yellowish, brownish on sides.

4. Yellow-bellied Seedeater LM-SO
Sporophila nigricollis 4¼" (11cm)
Crown, sides of head, *throat and breast black.* Back, wings and tail olive. No speculum. *Belly pale yellow.*

5. Black-and-white Seedeater
                          LMH-SO
Sporophila luctuosa 4¼" (11cm)
Bill bluish. *Upperparts,* throat, breast and tail *glossy black. Belly white.* Wing speculum prominent.

6. Gray Seedeater   LM-SO
Sporophila intermedia 4¼"(11cm)
Bluish gray (race in sw Colombia is grayish black). *Bill yellow.* Speculum white. *Patch at sides of neck white.* Center of breast and belly white. Legs black. Female: Bill black. Above grayish brown. Below buff. Toe nails black.

7. Slate-colored Seedeater   L-T
Sporophila schistacea 4¼" (11cm)
Bill bright yellow. Dark slaty gray. Patch on sides of throat white. Wing-bar, wing speculum and center of breast and belly white. Legs greenish gray.

8. Double-collared Seedeater
                          LM-SO
Sporophila caerulescens
                          4¼" (11cm)
Above dull gray to brownish gray, browner on wings and tail. *Throat and band across breast black.* Whisker and rest of underparts white. ♀: Like other ♀ seedeaters but *lower bill yellow.*

9. Variable Seedeater   L-TS
Sporophila americana 4¼" (11cm)
Bill black. Crown and back glossy black. Wings black, sometimes with double bar and/or speculum. Rump gray or white. Throat and *partial collar white. Band* (sometimes incomplete) *across breast black.* Belly white.

10. Female: Brownish. Bill blackish. Below buffy brown.

11. Rusty-collared Seedeater L-SOW
Sporophila collaris   4¼" (11cm)
Above black, *spot at sides of forehead and below eye white. Collar whitish or rusty.* Wing-bars buff. Rump whitish to cinnamon. Throat white. *Breast band black.* Belly buff to cinnamon.

SMALL FINCHES 4.

Sporophila SEEDEATERS - 188, 317, 318.
Tiaris GRASSQUITS - 317.

1. **Lined Seedeater** **L-SO**
Sporophila lineola 4" (10cm)
Crown stripe white (crown all black in some races). Above glossy black, *rump white*. Throat black. *Broad whiskers white*. Below white. Tail black.

2. **Female:** Above olive brown. Throat and breast buff contrasting with white belly.

3. **Plumbeous Seedeater** **L-O**
Sporophila plumbea 4" (10cm)
Bill black. Above blue gray. Lower part of eye-ring white. Wings and tail brownish black, the feathers edged gray. Speculum white. Throat, whiskers and belly white. Breast and sides pale gray. ♀: Light brown above, yellowish buff below, with facial area grayish white. Bill brown.

4. **Ruddy-breasted Seedeater**
LM-TSO
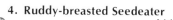
Sporophila minuta 3½" (9cm)
Back and head brownish gray. Wings brownish, speculum white but not always visible. *Rump and entire underparts, including sides of body, rufous*. Tail brownish. ♀: Above dull reddish brown. Wing coverts conspicuously pale tipped. Below buff.

5. **Chestnut-bellied Seedeater L-SO**
Sporophila castaneiventris
3½" (9cm)
Upperparts (including rump) bluish gray. Lacks prominent speculum. Throat, breast, belly and undertail coverts chestnut. Flanks gray. Tail black.

6. **Female:** Olive brown above, buffy below.

7. **Black-faced Grassquit** **L-SO**
Tiaris bicolor 3½" (9cm)
Face, throat and breast dull black. Back, wings and belly dull olive.

8. **Female:** Above gray. Below light gray. Center of belly white.

9. **Yellow-faced Grassquit LM-TSO**
Tiaris olivacea 3½" (9cm)
Forehead and face blackish. *Eyebrow and throat yellow*. Above olive. Breast black (extent of black variable). Belly olive, pale in center. ♀: Dull olive. Belly pale grayish olive. *Eyebrow and throat dull yellow*.

10. **Blue-black Grassquit** **LM-TSO**
Volatinia jacarina 3½" (9cm)
Uniform glossy blue black. Note bill is more slender and more pointed than most small finches.

11. **Female:** Above brownish. Below white *streaked brown*.

12. **Moulting Male:** Below buff scalloped dusky.

1

2

3

4

5

6

8

9

11

12

1. Lesser Rhea   **H-O**
Pterocnemia pennata   38″ (95cm)
Very like Greater Rhea (2-1) but smaller. Still *very large*. Ostrich-like. Above uniformly gray. Below whitish. Flightless.

2. Gray Tinamou   **L-F**
Tinamus tao   18″ (45cm)
Head and neck speckled white. Back and wings gray, speckled or finely barred black. Throat whitish. Below gray. Undertail coverts rufous.

3. Solitary Tinamou   **LM-F**
Tinamus solitarius   18″ (45cm)
Above brown, wings and rearparts barred black. *Sides of head and foreneck mostly ochraceous;* throat white (except in n). Gray below.

4. Black Tinamou   **M-F**
Tinamus osgoodi   17″ (42cm)
Upperparts and breast black. Throat and belly gray. Undertail coverts cinnamon.

5. Great Tinamou   **L-F**
Tinamus major   17″ (42cm)
Variable. Crown rufous to black. Back brownish. Throat white. Below grayish, heavily barred black on flanks. Center of belly white.

6. Highland Tinamou   **M-F**
Nothocercus bonapartei
             15″ (38cm)
Crown black. Back brown. Below cinnamon with wavy dusky lines.

7. Tawny-breasted Tinamou   **MH-F**
Nothocercus julius   15″ (38cm)
Head chestnut. Above brown barred black. *Throat white.* Breast brown. Belly rufous.

8. Hooded Tinamou   **M-F**
Nothocercus nigrocapillus
             13″ (33cm)
Head gray. Above light brown narrowly freckled black. Below light brown barred dusky, belly pale-spotted.

9. Cinereous Tinamou   **L-FT**
Crypturellus cinereus   12″ (30cm)
Crown and nape reddish brown or blackish. Above and below grayish brown. *No white throat.* Legs grayish.

10. Little Tinamou   **L-TS**
Crypturellus soui   9″ (22cm)
Variable. Recognize by *small size* and *lack of barring.* Above chestnut. Below rufous except throat white. Legs grayish or olive.

11. Tepui Tinamou   **M-F**
Crypturellus ptaritepui 11″ (27cm)
Above brown. Below gray. Upper bill black, *lower yellow tipped black.*

12. Undulated Tinamou   **L-T**
Crypturellus undulatus 12″ (30cm)
Very variable. Mostly grayish or olive brown, some races finely vermiculated black or barred rufescent and black. *Contrasting white throat.* Legs dull yellowish to grayish.

1. Rusty Tinamou   **L-F**
Crypturellus brevirostris
11"(27cm)
Crown chestnut. Above rufous boldly barred black. Throat and belly white. Breast bright rufous. Flanks barred black. Legs yellowish gray.

2. Bartlett's Tinamou   **L-F**
Crypturellus bartletti   10"(26cm)
Crown blackish. Above brown barred black. Throat white. Below rufous, flanks barred black. Belly whitish.

3. Variegated Tinamou   **L-F**
Crypturellus variegatus 12"(30cm)
Head blackish. Back barred black and cinnamon. Throat white. *Neck and breast bright rufous,* belly buffy. Legs greenish to yellowish brown.

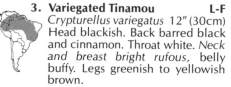

4. Black-capped Tinamou   **LM-FT**
Crypturellus atrocapillus
11"(29cm)
Cap blackish. Mostly brown above, obscurely barred or mottled black. Throat and neck rufescent, *breast dark gray,* underparts cinnamon to buff. Legs pink to bright red. ♀: More boldly barred above.

5. Red-legged Tinamou   **LM-TS**
Crypturellus erythropus
11"(29cm)
Mostly brown above, usually with back and wings barred with black. Throat usually whitish. *Breast gray.* Underparts buff to cinnamon, flanks barred black. *Legs pink to reddish.* Considered a race of *C. atrocapillus* in BSA. Includes *C. cinnamomeus, C. boucardi* and *C. saltuarius* considered separate species in BSA.

6. Yellow-legged Tinamou   **L-FT**
Crypturellus noctivagus
12"(31cm)
Cap blackish. *Broad eyebrow buffy.* Above gray. Wings and rearparts barred with black. Throat whitish. Neck and upper breast gray. Lower breast rufous. Belly buffy whitish. *Legs yellowish.*

7. Gray-legged Tinamou   **L-F**
Crypturellus duidae   12"(30cm)
Head, neck and breast rufous. Throat white. Back dark brown lightly barred blackish. Legs grayish.

8. Pale-browed Tinamou   **L-FT**
Crypturellus transfasciatus
11"(28cm)
Crown brown. Conspicuous eyebrow whitish. Back gray to brown, barred black. Throat white. Below grayish to buffy, barred on flanks. Legs pink.

9. Brazilian Tinamou   **L-F**
Crypturellus strigulosus
11"(28cm)
Above reddish brown. Throat rufous. Breast gray. Belly whitish. Legs brown. ♀: Distinctly barred blackish and ochraceous above.

10. Barred Tinamou   **L-F**
Crypturellus casiquiare 10"(26cm)
Head chestnut. Above barred black and buffy. Throat white. Sides of neck and breast gray. Belly white.

11. Choco Tinamou   **L-F**
Crypturellus kerriae
10"(25cm)
Head blackish. Above dark reddish brown. Throat grayish. Below dark brown. Legs reddish.

12. Small-billed Tinamou   **LM-TS**
Crypturellus parvirostris 8"(21cm)
Crown, sides of head and underparts gray to brownish. Back dark brown. *Bill and legs red.*

1. Tataupa Tinamou   LM-TS
Crypturellus tataupa   10"(25cm)
Crown and back dark brown. *Sides
of head, neck and breast gray.*
Throat light gray. Belly pinkish buff.
Bill and legs dark purplish red.

2. Red-winged Tinamou   LM-SO
Rhynchotus rufescens   16"(40cm)
Crown black. Above barred black
and brown. *Primaries rufous.*
Throat white. Foreneck and breast
cinnamon (most races). Underparts light grayish brown, flanks
and belly barred black.

3. Taczanowski's Tinamou   H-SO
Nothoprocta taczanowskii
13"(33cm)
Bill slender, curved. Above grayish to olive brown, spotted and
streaked black and butty. Throat
whitish, breast gray spotted whitish. Underparts buffy, obscurely
barred blackish. Legs yellow.

4. Kalinowski's Tinamou   H-SO
Nothoprocta kalinowski
14"(34cm)
Head and neck buffy very prominently spotted black. Upperparts
brownish gray marked with black
and buff. Underparts tawny buff,
barred blackish. Bill slender,
curved. Legs yellowish or grayish.

5. Ornate Tinamou   H-SO
Nothoprocta ornata   13"(33cm)
Bill slender, curved. Head and
neck buffy, prominently spotted
black. Upperparts brownish gray
marked with black and buff. Underparts tawny buff. Legs yellowish or grayish.

6. Chilean Tinamou   MH-O
Nothoprocta perdicaria 12"(30cm)
Bill curved. Above grayish or olive
brown, narrowly streaked white or
buffy. Throat white, breast grayish,
belly light buffy. Legs pale yellowish.

7. Brushland Tinamou   LM-S
Nothoprocta cinerascens
12"(32cm)
Crown mostly black. Above grayish to olive brown with conspicuous white streaks and black bars.
Sides of head and throat white,
lower throat barred black. *Breast
gray spotted white,* belly whitish.
Legs dark gray.

8. Andean Tinamou   MH-SO
Nothoprocta pentlandii
11"(27cm)
Crown blackish brown. Above
grayish to olive brown, narrowly
streaked and barred white and
black. Sides of head and throat
mottled grayish. *Breast gray, usually profusely spotted white or buff.*
Belly buffy or whitish. Legs yellow.

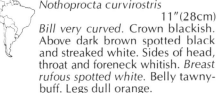

9. Curve-billed Tinamou   H-O
Nothoprocta curvirostris
11"(28cm)
Bill very curved. Crown blackish.
Above dark brown spotted black
and streaked white. Sides of head,
throat and foreneck whitish. *Breast
rufous spotted white.* Belly tawny-
buff. Legs dull orange.

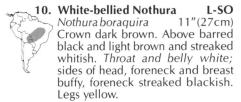

10. White-bellied Nothura   L-SO
Nothura boraquira   11"(27cm)
Crown dark brown. Above barred
black and light brown and streaked
whitish. *Throat and belly white;*
sides of head, foreneck and breast
buffy, foreneck streaked blackish.
Legs yellow.

11. Lesser Nothura   L-O
Nothura minor   7"(18cm)
Very small. Dark phase: Mostly
chestnut-rufous vermiculated with
black above. Pale buffy to tawny-
rufous below. Light phase: Above,
rufescent buff, vermiculated black.
Below light buffy. Legs yellowish.

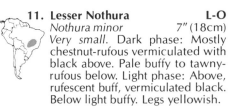

12. Darwin's Nothura   HM-O
Nothura darwinii   10"(26cm)
Very like Spotted Nothura (4-3)
but more rufous generally and
more broadly streaked below.

1. Chaco Nothura L-O
Nothura chacoensis 9" (24cm)
Like Spotted Nothura (4-3) but *buffier and paler generally.*

2. Dwarf Tinamou L-SO
Taoniscus nanus 6" (15cm)
Crown blackish. Above reddish brown spotted black. Below light buffy, *barred brown on breast and flanks.*

3. Elegant Crested-Tinamou L-SO
Eudromia elegans 15" (39cm)
Long thin crest black, curving forward. Above grayish brown to blackish with *many small white spots.* Stripe behind eye dusky, bordered above and below by white stripes. Below whitish to light buffy, heavily vermiculated and barred with black.

4. Quebracho Crested-Tinamou
 L-SO
Eudromia formosa 15" (39cm)
Long thin crest black, straight. Above grayish brown to blackish with few small white spots. Stripe behind eye dusky, bordered above and below by white stripes. Below whitish to light buffy, heavily vermiculated and barred with black.

5. Puna Tinamou H-O
Tinamotis pentlandii 16" (41cm)
Head white with black streaks. Above brown spotted white. Breast bluish gray. Belly rufous.

6. Patagonian Tinamou LM-O
Tinamotis ingoufi 14" (35cm)
Back gray spotted black. Throat whitish. Below rufous. Belly lighter.

7. Northern Screamer LM-OW
Chauna chavaria 31" (78cm)
Rather like Horned Screamer (2-2) but lacks quill. White bands above and below broad black band on neck.

8. Southern Screamer LM-OW
Chauna torquata 31" (78cm)
Rather like Horned Screamer (2-2) but lacks quill. Only base of neck black. Much white in underparts.

9. Andean Condor LMH-O
Vultur gryphus 42" (108cm)
Head and neck bare, flesh color. White neck ruff. All black with silvery patch on wings. Huge wingspan (10'). Flies on *flat* wings, primaries usually spread.

10. Lesser Yellow-headed Vulture
 L-O
Cathartes burrovianus 25" (62cm)
Very like Turkey Vulture (6-2) but bare head orange.

11. Greater Yellow-headed Vulture
 L-F
Cathartes melambrotos 32" (80cm)
Very like Turkey Vulture (6-2) but bare head yellow.

12. White-tailed Kite LM-SO
Elanus leucurus 13" (34cm)
Head white. Above gray with *black shoulder patch.* Below white. *Tail white, long, square-tipped.*

1. Pearl Kite   **L-SO**
Gampsonyx swainsonii 9" (22cm)
Forehead and sides of head yellowish buff. Crown and upperparts slaty. Collar and most of underparts white. Thighs rufous.

2. Swallow-tailed Kite   **LM-FT**
Elanoides forficatus 22" (55cm)
Head white. Above black. Below white. *Tail very long, deeply forked.*

3. Hook-billed Kite   **LM-FT**
Chondrohierax uncinatus
15" (39cm)
Strongly hooked bill. Eye pale. Gray above, coarsely barred gray and white below. (Dark phase all brownish black.) Tail with two to three pale bands. ♀: Above brown, collar tawny. *Below coarsely barred rusty and white.* Imm: Mostly brownish above, whitish below with some black barring.

4. Rufous-thighed Kite   **L-FT**
Harpagus diodon 12" (31cm)
Above gray, below pale gray. Throat whitish with *dusky central stripe.* Thighs rufous. Tail blackish with three or four gray bars. Imm: Whitish below streaked dusky.

5. Mississippi Kite   **L-O**
Ictinia mississippiensis*
13" (33cm)
Light gray, back darker gray. Tail blackish with *no white band.* Legs dusky. Wing shows pale gray patch in secondaries. Imm: Above brown streaked white. Throat white. Below white streaked rufous brown.

6. Plumbeous Kite   **L-T**
Ictinia plumbea* 13" (33cm)
Head and underparts gray. Back dark gray. Wings pointed and long *(extending beyond tail at rest).* In flight shows *large chestnut patch in primaries.* Imm: Above blackish streaked white on head and nape. Below white streaked gray.

7. Snail Kite   **L-OW**
Rostrhamus sociabilis 15" (38cm)
Slender, deeply hooked bill. Blackish except face and legs red and base of tail white. ♀ and imm: Brown above. Face white. Below white, mottled brown. Tail as in ♂.

8. Slender-billed Kite   **L-FTW**
Helicolestes hamatus 14" (35cm)
Bill slender, deeply hooked. Gray. Face and legs red. Eye whitish. *No white on tail.* Imm: Several narrow white tail bands.

9. Bicolored Hawk   **LM-FT**
Accipiter bicolor 15" (37cm)
Crown black, above dark gray. Below gray with *contrasting rufous thighs.* Tail with three pale gray bands. Imm: Varies from creamy white to rufous below, usually shows pale collar on hindneck.

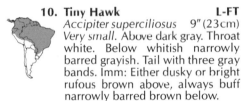

10. Tiny Hawk   **L-FT**
Accipiter superciliosus 9" (23cm)
Very small. Above dark gray. Throat white. Below whitish narrowly barred grayish. Tail with three gray bands. Imm: Either dusky or bright rufous brown above, always buff narrowly barred brown below.

11. Semicollared Hawk   **M-F**
Accipiter collaris 12" (30cm)
Small. Above sooty brown. Cheeks and more-or-less distinct collar white. Below whitish narrowly barred grayish. Imm: More coarsely barred below.

12. Gray-bellied Hawk   **L-F**
Accipiter poliogaster 18" (44cm)
Crown black. Above dark gray. Below gray. Tail with three pale gray bands. Imm: *Collar* and sides of head and neck *rufous. Below white coarsely barred and spotted black.* Tail with three gray bands.

1. Black-chested Buzzard-Eagle
LMH-SO
Geranoaetus melanoleucus
23″(58cm)
Blackish above, wing coverts paler gray. Throat whitish. *Sides of head and breast blackish.* Belly white, finely barred black. *Tail* dusky, *very short,* wedge-shaped. Imm: Generally brownish, heavily streaked and mottled below.

2. Red-backed Hawk   LMH-SO
Buteo polyosoma   19″(47cm)
Variable. Gray above (often with rufous back). White below. *Tail white with black subterminal band.* Some birds mostly slaty. Imm: Dark brown above, mottled rufous on back and wings. Below whitish streaked brown.

3. Rufous-tailed Hawk   L-FT
Buteo ventralis   21″(53cm)
Above blackish brown. Below whitish, somewhat streaked black. Thighs rufous. *Tail rufous* narrowly barred black. Dark phase all dusky black, tail rufous mottled gray. Imm: Gray, barred blackish.

4. Zone-tailed Hawk   L-TS
Buteo albonotatus   19″(47cm)
Black. Rather long tail with several pale bands. Gray from above, white from below. In flight with two-toned wings (paler flight feathers) held slightly above horizontal.

5. Swainson's Hawk   L-SO
Buteo swainsoni*   19″(47cm)
Pale phase: Dark brown above, white below, with *dark brown sides of head and band across breast.* Tail brownish gray with numerous dusky bands. Dark phase: Mostly sooty brown all over. Imm: Brown above, buffy below variably streaked brown.

6. Broad-winged Hawk   LM-T
Buteo platypterus*   15″(38cm)
Dark brown above, head lightly streaked whitish. Throat whitish. *Below barred or mottled rufous.* Tail blackish with *two or three*

prominent white bands. Underwing white. Imm: Whitish below streaked brown, tail barred.

7. White-rumped Hawk   LM-FT
Buteo leucorrhous   13″(33cm)
Black. Thighs rufous. *Rump white. Tail with few white bars.* In flight distinctive white underwing coverts contrast with black body and flight feathers. Imm: Blackish streaked rufous.

8. White-throated Hawk   MH-FTS
Buteo albigula   17″(44cm)
Above dark brown. Forehead white. *Sides of head and neck blackish.* Throat white. Below white streaked brown. Tail short, with numerous bars.

9. Short-tailed Hawk   LM-TS
Buteo brachyurus   15″(38cm)
Light phase: Dark brown above with white forehead and *blackish sides of head and neck.* White below. Underwing white. Tail short, narrowly barred dusky. Dark phase: Mostly black. Forehead white. Underwing black.

10. Gray Hawk   L-TS
Buteo nitidus   15″(38cm)
Above pale gray, lightly flecked darker. *Below* white, *narrowly barred gray.* Tail black with one or two prominent white bands. Imm: Brown above, mottled whitish and buff especially on head. Buffyish below.

11. Bay-winged Hawk   L-TSO
Parabuteo unicinctus   18″(46cm)
Dark brown. *Shoulders and thighs rufous.* Base and tip of rather long tail white. Imm: Head and underparts streaked or mottled whitish, less obvious rufous.

12. Gray-backed Hawk   LM-FT
Leucopternis occidentalis
17″(44cm)
Upperparts dark gray, *crown and nape streaked white.* Below white. Underwing mostly white. Tail white with single broad black band.

1. Mantled Hawk   LM-FT
Leucopternis polionota 21" (51cm)
Head, neck, upper back and underparts pure white. Lower back and wings slaty gray. Underwing mostly white. *Tail mostly white, with black band near base.*

2. White-necked Hawk   L-FT
Leucopternis lacernulata
18" (46cm)
Crown and hindneck white tinged pale gray. Upperparts dark slaty gray. Below white. Tail white with black base and *narrow black band near tip.*

3. Black-faced Hawk   L-F
Leucopternis melanops 14" (36cm)
Crown and hindneck whitish narrowly streaked black. Upperparts slaty black, back spotted white. Below white. Tail black with *single narrow white band.* Legs and base of bill orange.

4. White-browed Hawk   L-F
Leucopternis kuhli   13" (33cm)
Crown and hindneck blackish narrowly streaked white. Eyebrow white. Upperparts slaty black. Below white. Tail black with single narrow white band. Legs and base of bill orange.

5. Semi-plumbeous Hawk   L-F
Leucopternis semiplumbea
13" (33cm)
Above uniform slaty gray. Below white. Tail black with one (rarely two) narrow white tail band. Legs and base of bill orange.

6. Slate-colored Hawk   L-FT
Leucopternis schistacea
14" (37cm)
Uniform slaty gray. Tail black with one white band. Legs and base of bill orange-red. Imm: Belly and underwing narrowly barred white.

7. Plumbeous Hawk   L-F
Leucopternis plumbea 15" (33cm)
Uniform dark slaty gray. Tail black with one white band. Underwing coverts white. Legs and base of bill orange.

8. Barred Hawk   LM-F
Leucopternis princeps 18" (45cm)
Above black. *Throat and breast black, contrasting sharply with white belly.* Tail black with one white band. Legs and base of bill yellow.

9. Rufous Crab-Hawk   L-TSW
Buteogallus aequinoctialis
17" (43cm)
Like Savanna Hawk (6-6) but with barely visible tail band. Head and upperparts blackish brown. Below rufous, narrowly barred dusky. Wings show much rufous, especially in flight. Coastal, especially in mangroves.

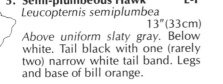

10. Great Black Hawk   L-FTS
Buteogallus urubitinga 23" (58cm)
Black. *Rump, upper tail coverts and basal half of tail white.* Base of bill and rather long legs yellow. Imm: Brownish above, buff below heavily streaked brown. Tail with numerous narrow bars.

11. Crowned Eagle   LM-TS
Harpyhaliaetus coronatus
24" (59cm)
Ashy gray. Prominent pointed crest. Tail short with single white band and tip. Imm: Browner above, nape and sides of neck buff boldly streaked dusky. Below buffy broadly streaked dusky. Tail narrowly barred.

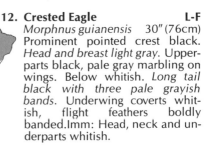

12. Crested Eagle   L-F
Morphnus guianensis 30" (76cm)
Prominent pointed crest black. *Head and breast light gray.* Upperparts black, pale gray marbling on wings. Below whitish. *Long tail black with three pale grayish bands.* Underwing coverts whitish, flight feathers boldly banded. Imm: Head, neck and underparts whitish.

1. Harpy Eagle   **LM-F**
Harpia harpyja   33" (84 cm)
Divided crest blackish. Head gray, upperparts and breast black. Belly white, thighs barred black. Long tail black with three pale gray bands. Underwing boldly banded. Imm: Head whitish.

2. Black-and-chestnut Eagle   **MH-F**
Oroaetus isidori   25" (64cm)
Black crest long, pointed. Head, *throat* and upperparts *black. Below chestnut* lightly streaked black. Tail gray, black at end. Underwing mostly chestnut with conspicuous large pale area on primaries. Imm: Above mottled. Below white.

3. Black-and-white Hawk-Eagle
     L-FT
Spizastur melanoleucus
     21" (53cm)
Head, neck and underparts white. Short crest, area around eye and upperparts black. Tail black with three grayish bands. Underwing mostly white. *Conspicuous orange at base of bill.* Legs feathered.

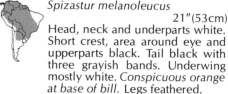

4. Ornate Hawk-Eagle   **L-F**
Spizaetus ornatus   22" (55cm)
Crown and *long crest black. Sides of head and neck bright rufous.* Upperparts black. Below *white barred black on belly.* Underwing whitish with black spotting and barring. Imm: White head, neck and underparts.

5. Black Hawk-Eagle   **L-F**
Spizaetus tyrannus   25" (62cm)
Black. Flanks and thighs narrowly barred white. *Tail long with three to four prominent whitish bands.* Underwing boldly spotted and banded black and whitish. Imm: *Eye-stripe white.*

6. Northern Harrier   **L-O**
Circus cyaneus*   18" (46cm)
Head, *upperparts and breast pale gray. Rump white.* Belly white lightly barred rufous. Tail banded light gray and dusky. ♀: Dark brown above. Below buffy streaked brown.

7. Cinereous Harrier   **LMH-O**
Circus cinereus   17" (44cm)
Above pale gray, rump white. Throat and breast gray, more or less spotted white. *Belly boldly barred rufous brown and white.* ♀: Dark grayish brown above, rump white. Throat and breast brownish.

8. Long-winged Harrier   **L-O**
Circus buffoni   19" (49cm)
Above black. Narrow eyebrow, collar and rump white. Tail banded black and silvery gray. Throat and breast black, belly white. Imm: Heavily streaked below.

9. Crane Hawk   **L-FSO**
Geranospiza caerulescens
     18" (45cm)
Mostly gray. Bill dark. In e and s *underparts barred with white.* Tail black with two white bands. Legs long, orange-red. Wings from below have *diagnostic white band near ends.*

10. Osprey   **L-W**
Pandion haliaetus*   21" (52cm)
Mostly white. *Long dark stripe through eye.* Wings and tail banded blackish. Wings long, usually "kinked" back showing *black patch at bend of wing* from below.

11. Collared Forest-Falcon   **LM-FT**
Micrastur semitorquatus
     20" (50cm)
Above blackish with *light collar.* Cheeks white to tawny, bordered below by narrow black band. Throat and below uniform white to tawny. Tail blackish with three or four visible narrow white bands. Imm: Underparts barred brown.

12. Buckley's Forest-Falcon   **L-F**
Micrastur buckleyi   17" (42cm)
Above blackish with *light collar.* Cheeks white to tawny bordered below by narrow black band. Throat and below uniform white to tawny. Tail blackish with two or three visible narrow white bars.

1. Slaty-backed Forest-Falcon   L-F
Micrastur mirandollei 15″ (36cm)
Above dark gray. No collar. *Below white.* Tail black with three narrow white bars.

2. Lined Forest-Falcon   L-F
Micrastur gilvicollis   12″ (30cm)
Like Barred Forest Falcon (8-9) (but no rufous phase). *Eye white* and belly only faintly barred. *Only one or two (not three) white tail bars.* Considered a race of Barred Forest-Falcon in BSA.

3. Plumbeous Forest-Falcon   L-F
Micrastur plumbeus 14″ (36cm)
Above gray. Below pale gray finely barred black. Tail black with *one* conspicuous white bar. Imm: Similar but with barring on sides only.

4. Black Caracara   L-FTO
Daptrius ater   16″ (43cm)
Black. Bare skin of face and throat bright orange-red. Tail black with *conspicuous white band across base.*

5. Red-throated Caracara   L-F
Daptrius americanus 19″ (49cm)
Glossy black. Bare skin of face and throat dark red. *Contrasting white belly and vent.* Tail all black. In groups, very raucous calls.

6. Chimango Caracara   L-SO
Milvago chimango 15″ (38cm)
Essentially brown. *Pale buffy patch in primaries* conspicuous in flight. Rump white. Tail buffy whitish narrowly barred dusky with broad blackish band near tip.

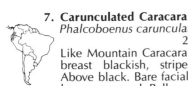

7. Carunculated Caracara   H-O
Phalcoboenus carunculatus
20″ (50cm)
Like Mountain Caracara (8-6) but breast blackish, striped white. Above black. Bare facial skin and legs orange-red. Belly pure white. Imm: Brown. Rump buff.

8. White-throated Caracara
MH-TO
Phalcoboenus albogularis
19″ (47cm)
Like Mountain Caracara (8-6) but *all of underparts white.* Above black. Bare facial skin yellow-orange. Tail black, tipped white.

9. Peregrine Falcon   LM-SO
Falco peregrinus   16″ (39cm)
Above dark gray. *Area back of eye and broad whisker black.* Below whitish or buffy. Breast and belly barred and flecked gray. Tail banded gray and blackish. Imm: Browner above, more streaked below.

10. Pallid Falcon   LM-O
Falco kreyenborgi   16″ (40cm)
Head whitish with *narrow blackish whisker* below eye. *Above clear pale gray,* conspicuously barred throughout with blackish. *Below whitish.* Underwing mostly white. Tail narrowly barred black and gray. Imm: Above brown, feathers edged rufous.

11. Orange-breasted Falcon   LM-FT
Falco deiroleucus   14″ (34cm)
Very like Bat Falcon (8-12) but larger. *Breast washed rufous.* Belly barred black and buff. Tail black with three narrow white bars.

12. Aplomado Falcon   LMH-SO
Falco femoralis   16″ (39cm)
Above gray. *Eyebrow white, narrow whisker black.* Throat and sides of neck white. Breast white streaked dusky. Upper belly black narrowly barred white. Lower belly, thighs and vent rufous. Tail narrowly banded blackish and white. Imm: Above dusky. Breast streaked black.

1. Merlin   **L-TSO**
Falco columbarius*   12" (30cm)
Bluish gray above, tinged rusty on sides of head and nape. Below whitish to buff, *prominently streaked brown.* Tail black with three gray bands, tipped white. ♀ and imm: Brownish above.

2. Little Chachalaca   **LM-TS**
Ortalis motmot   18" (44cm)
Head rufous. Above brown. Below buffy grayish. Central tail feathers olive brown, outer feathers chestnut.

3. Buff-browed Chachalaca   **L-TS**
Ortalis superciliaris   20" (50cm)
Eyebrow buffy or whitish. Head, back, throat and breast brown. Belly whitish. Outer tail feathers rufous.

4. Speckled Chachalaca   **L-TS**
Ortalis guttata   20" (49cm)
Head grayish brown. Above rufescent brown. Throat and breast dark brown *conspicuously spotted white.* Belly buffy grayish (whitish in e Brazil).

5. Chestnut-winged Chachalaca
    L-TS
Ortalis garrula   18" (45cm)
Head rufous. Back brown. *Primaries bright chestnut.* Throat and breast brownish. Belly white. Tail dark bronzy green, *outer feathers tipped white.*

6. Rufous-headed Chachalaca
    L-TSA
Ortalis erythroptera   20" (50cm)
Head and neck rufous. Breast olive. Below whitish. Tail dark green, outer feathers rufous.

7. Chaco Chachalaca   **L-TS**
Ortalis canicollis   20" (50cm)
Head gray. Back pale olive brown. Below dingy whitish. Tail dark gray, outer feathers tipped chestnut.

8. Marail Guan   **L-F**
Penelope marail   24" (60cm)
Mostly blackish brown, somewhat glossed with green. Head and neck somewhat grayer. Throat bare. Feathers of neck and breast edged whitish. Belly brown. Legs red.

9. Spix's Guan   **L-F**
Penelope jacquacu   30" (75cm)
Like Crested Guan (2-3). Above blackish, glossed green. Belly chestnut brown (duller brown in n part of range). Legs red.

10. Dusky-legged Guan   **LM-F**
Penelope obscura   30" (75cm)
Similar to Crested Guan (2-3). Quite blackish overall. Feathers of crown long. Narrow whitish eyestripe in Brazil. *Legs dusky.*

11. Baudo Guan   **LM-F**
Penelope ortoni   24" (60cm)
Crest rather short. A rather *brown* guan. Neck and breast feathers conspicuously edged whitish. Legs light red.

12. White-winged Guan   **LM-F**
Penelope albipennis   22" (56cm)
Mostly dark bronzy brown. Feathers of neck and underparts indistinctly streaked whitish. *Primaries white,* very conspicuous in flight, usually visible even when perched.

1. Rusty-margined Guan **L-F**
Penelope superciliaris 25" (63cm)
Mostly glossy blackish brown above. Narrow whitish or buffy eye-stripe. Feathers of *wing and back conspicuously edged chestnut.* Below dark grayish, breast feathers edged whitish. Lower belly cinnamon rufous.

2. Andean Guan **MH-F**
Penelope montagnii 23" (57cm)
Above bronzy olive brown. Head and neck gray, feathers edged whitish. *Flap under chin very small.* Narrow whitish eye-stripe in some races. Belly brownish. Legs red.

3. Red-faced Guan **HM-F**
Penelope dabbenei 28" (70cm)
Mostly brown. *Bare facial skin red.* Crown and sides of head mixed with whitish feathers. Feathers of shoulders and breast edged white.

4. White-browed Guan **L-SA**
Penelope jacucaca 26" (65cm)
Brown. *Conspicuous silvery white eyebrow.* Crown and hindneck blackish brown, somewhat crested. Feathers of shoulders and underparts conspicuously edged white. Belly rufous brown.

5. Chestnut-bellied Guan **L-F**
Penelope ochrogaster 26" (65cm)
Above brown. *Crown mixed brown and silvery whitish,* somewhat crested. Below rich chestnut. Feathers of back, shoulders and breast edged white.

6. White-crested Guan **L-F**
Penelope pileata 26" (65cm)
Above blackish, nape and mantle chestnut. Quite prominent *whitish crest* tinged buffy. *Underparts bright chestnut,* contrasting with glossy greenish black upperparts.

7. Band-tailed Guan **LM-F**
Penelope argyrotis 22" (56cm)
Mostly bronzy olive-brown, with *conspicuous silvery white streaking on sides of head and neck.* Feathers of back and underparts edged white. *Tail tipped rufous or buff.*

8. Common (Blue-throated) Piping-Guan **L-F**
Pipile pipile 22" (56cm)
Variable. Glossy black. Facial skin blue. Skin below chin either red or blue. *Conspicuous crest and large patch on wing white.* Breast feathers edged white in some races. Legs red. Includes Red-throated Piping-Guan, *Pipile cujubi,* listed as a separate species in BSA.

9. Black-fronted Piping-Guan LM-F
Pipile jacutinga 22" (56cm)
Glossy black. *Sides of head covered with black feathers.* Only narrow eye-ring bare, whitish. Conspicuous crest and large patch on wing white. Flap under chin red.

10. Wattled Guan **LM-F**
Aburria aburri 26" (65cm)
Black, upperparts glossed olive green to bluish. *Base of bill bright blue.* Long narrow *wattle hanging from throat yellow.* Legs bright yellow.

11. Sickle-winged Guan **LM-FT**
Chamaepetes goudotii 23" (57cm)
Above bronzy olive brown. Large bare *area on face and at base of bill bright blue.* Throat like upperparts. Below chestnut-rufous.

12. Black Curassow **L-F**
Crax alector 31" (78cm)
Glossy black. *Low, forward-curling black crest.* Base of bill yellow to red, no knob or wattles. Belly white. ♀: Has white in crest.

1. Bare-faced Curassow   **L-F**
Crax fasciolata   31" (78cm)
Black. *Base of bill yellow,* no knob or wattles. Belly and tip of tail white. ♀: Barred white above (except on neck), very broadly in Bolivia. Breast barred black and white in ne Brazil. Below rich buffy chestnut.

2. Blue-billed Curassow   **L-F**
Crax alberti   32" (82cm)
Black. Base of bill and wattles bright blue. Belly white. ♀: Wings and tail narrowly barred white, tail broadly tipped white. Lower breast barred black and white or chestnut, belly light chestnut.

3. Yellow-knobbed Curassow   **L-F**
Crax daubentoni   32" (82cm)
Black, *crest forward-curling. Base of bill, knob and wattles bright yellow.* Belly and tip of tail white. ♀: Bill black. Underparts narrowly barred black and white, except belly all white.

4. Wattled Curassow   **L-F**
Crax globulosa   32" (80cm)
Black. Base of bill, large knob and *wattles bright red.* Belly white. ♀: No knob or wattles. Belly rufous.

5. Great Curassow   **L-F**
Crax rubra   35" (85cm)
Black. Base of bill and *knob bright yellow.* Belly white. ♀: No knob. Head and neck barred black and white, otherwise all chestnut. Tail with conspicuous whitish black-bordered bands.

6. Razor-billed Curassow   **L-F**
Mitu mitu   31" (77cm)
Black. Bill and narrow *high knob above bill bright red.* Short crest. Belly chestnut. Tail tipped white. Legs red.

7. Salvin's Curassow   **L-F**
Mitu salvini   28" (72cm)
Black. Bill and knob on forehead bright red. Crest short. Belly white. Tail tipped white. Legs red.

8. Crestless (Lesser Razor-billed) Curassow   **L-F**
Mitu tomentosa   28" (71cm)
Black. *Bill red, not enlarged.* No knobs on forehead. No obvious crest. Belly chestnut. Tail tipped chestnut. Legs red.

9. Helmeted Curassow   **LM-F**
Pauxi pauxi   32" (81cm)
Black. *Large bluish knob on forehead.* Bill and legs red. Belly and tip of tail white. ♀: Black (rarely brown). Always known by knob on forehead.

10. Horned Curassow   **M-F**
Pauxi unicornis   32" (81cm)
Black. Bill red. *Conspicuous horn-like knob on forehead dark blue.* Belly and tip of tail white. Legs pinkish.

11. Nocturnal Curassow   **L-F**
Nothocrax urumutum   23" (58cm)
Bill red. Conspicuous crest blackish. *Neck and underparts rufous.* Above rufous brown with narrow wavy black barring. Skin above eye yellow, below eye gray. Tail blackish tipped whitish. Legs fleshy gray.

12. Crested Bobwhite   **LMH-SO**
Colinus cristatus   7½" (19cm)
Above brown mottled blackish. Conspicuous crest whitish. Face and throat buffy (in some races spotted black). Nape and sides of neck spotted black and white. Breast brown spotted white. Belly barred black.

1. Marbled Wood-Quail   L-F
Odontophorus gujanensis
10″(26cm)
Above mostly dark brown marked with black. *Bare orbital skin red.* Crown and short crest brown. Below dark brown, inconspicuously barred blackish and buffy. *No white spotting below.*

2. Spot-winged Wood-Quail   LM-F
Odontophorus capueira 10″(26cm)
Above brown, marked buff. Bare orbital skin red. Crown and short crest reddish brown. Tawny eye-stripe. *Wings with small white spots. Sides of head and underparts dark gray, unmarked.*

3. Rufous-fronted Wood-Quail   L-F
Odontophorus erythrops 10″(26cm)
Above dark brown marked black and buff. Bare orbital skin purplish (♀ blackish). Crown and short crest dark brown. *Forehead and sides of head chestnut-rufous.* Throat black, bordered below by *white gorget.* Below rufous.

4. Black-fronted Wood-Quail   LM-F
Odontophorus atrifrons 11″(27cm)
Above grayish brown marked buff and black. *Forehead, sides of head and throat black.* Crown and short crest rufous brown. Breast brown speckled white. Belly buffy streaked black.

5. Dark-backed Wood-Quail   M-F
Odontophorus melanonotus
10″(26cm)
Above brownish black, finely marked with rufous. Bare skin around eye brownish black. Throat and breast bright chestnut. Belly brown.

6. Chestnut Wood-Quail   M-F
Odontophorus hyperythrus
10″(26cm)
Above brown marked with black. Facial area and ear coverts white. Crown and short crest dull chestnut. *Sides of head and underparts chestnut.* ♀: Belly gray.

7. Rufous-breasted Wood-Quail M-F
Odontophorus speciosus 10″(26cm)
Above brown marked black and streaked white. Bare orbital skin bluish black. Crown and short crest dark brown. *Eye-stripe speckled*

black and white. Sides of head and throat black. *Below bright rufous.* ♀: Breast rufous. Belly gray.

8. Gorgeted Wood-Quail   H-F

*Odontophorus strophium*9″(23cm)
Above brown with fine black and whitish markings. Crown and ear coverts dark brown. *Eye-stripe, cheeks and chin whitish.* Throat black, bordered below by broad white band across breast. Below chestnut. ♀: Gray below.

9. Venezuelan Wood-Quail   M-F
Odontophorus columbianus
9″ (23cm)
Above brown marked with black and whitish. Bare orbital skin bluish black. Crown and ear coverts blackish. Inconspicuous buffy eye-stripe. *Throat white, bordered below by narrow black band.* Below brown, prominently spotted white.

10. Stripe-faced Wood-Quail   M-F
Odontophorus balliviani
10″ (26cm)
Above brown marked with black. Crown and short crest chestnut. *Stripe behind eye black, bordered above and below by tawny-buff stripes.* Throat black. Below dark chestnut, spotted white.

11. Starred Wood-Quail   L-F

Odontophorus stellatus 9″ (23cm)
Above brown marked with black. *Bare orbital skin red. Crown and crest bright rufous-chestnut.* Throat and sides of head and neck gray. Below rufous-chestnut, *breast prominently spotted white.*

12. Tawny-faced Quail   L-F

Rhynchortyx cinctus 6½″ (17cm)
Above brown marked black, but upper back dark gray. Crown brown. *Sides of head bright orange-rufous.* Narrow black stripe behind eye. Throat whitish, *breast gray,* belly light buffy. °: Stripe behind eye, white. Breast reddish brown. *Belly white boldly barred black.*

1. Pale-winged Trumpeter   **L-F**
Psophia leucoptera   21" (52cm)
Very like Gray-winged Trumpeter (2-6) but wing coverts edged bronze and *inner wing feathers whitish* instead of gray.

2. Dark-winged Trumpeter   **L-F**
Psophia viridis   21" (52cm)
Very like Gray-winged Trumpeter (2-6) but above dark brown, glossed green and inner wing feathers green instead of gray.

3. Red-legged Seriema   **L-SO**
Cariama cristata   27" (69cm)
Like Black-legged Seriema (2-7) but has prominent bushy frontal crest. Mostly gray, darker and browner above, somewhat streaked whitish below. Belly white. Primaries boldly banded black and white. Tail with black subterminal band and white tip.

4. Peruvian Thick-knee   **L-OA**
Burhinus superciliaris   14" (36cm)
Like Double-striped Thick-knee (2-8) but back unstreaked and more grayish brown.

5. White-bellied Seedsnipe   **H-O**
Attagis malouinus   10" (25cm)
Rather like Rufous-bellied Seedsnipe (4-4) but below whitish, breast scalloped with black. Throat whitish. Legs grayish.

6. Least Seedsnipe   **LMH-O**
Thinocorus rumicivorus
           6½" (17cm)
Very like Gray-breasted Seedsnipe (4-5) but much smaller (size of a Ground-Dove). Male has distinctive *vertical black band* connecting throat patch to breast band.

7. Chilean Pigeon   **LM-FT**
Columba araucana   14" (34cm)
Bill black. *Head, neck and underparts dark purplish chestnut.* Band on nape light buff, with bronzy green patch below it. Wings and tail gray, tail with blackish subterminal band and whitish tip. Legs red.

8. Scaled Pigeon   **L-FT**
Columba speciosa   11" (27cm)
Bill and orbital skin red. Head and upperparts dark purplish chestnut. Nape, neck and throat conspicuously scaled black and white becoming buff and brownish on breast and belly. Legs dark red.

9. Picazuro Pigeon   **L-TSO**
Columba picazuro   13" (32cm)
Head and underparts purplish brown. Skin around eye dark red. Upperparts and tail dark gray.

10. Bare-eyed Pigeon   **L-OA**
Columba corensis   11" (29cm)
Bill yellow, *large orbital area pale blue.* Head and underparts light pinkish brown. Above grayish brown, nape scaled whitish. Wing coverts with *white patch conspicuous both at rest and in flight.* Legs red.

11. Spot-winged Pigeon   **LMH-TS**
Columba maculosa   11" (29cm)
Mostly uniform grayish. Bill blackish. Wings brown, *conspicuously and evenly spotted and edged white.* Legs dull red.

12. Pale-vented Pigeon   **L-TS**
Columba cayennensis   11" (28cm)
Mostly purplish brown, head and rump gray. Bill black. Throat and vent white. Legs red.

1. Peruvian Pigeon   M-T
Columba oenops   11" (28cm)
Bill red tipped dark blue. Mostly purplish chestnut. Rump and belly dark gray, tail blackish. Legs dark red.

2. Ruddy Pigeon   LM-F
Columba subvinacea   11" (28cm)
Above and below purplish brown, wings darker, feathers lined dull chestnut. Short bill black. Body rather slender. Tail rather long, bronzy brown.

3. Plumbeous Pigeon   LM-F
Columba plumbea   12" (30cm)
Above purplish brown. Wings darker with *no chestnut linings.* Below paler than back. Tail rather long, bronzy brown.

4. Short-billed Pigeon   L-F
Columba nigrirostris   11" (27cm)
Back and wings bronzy brown. Wing linings dull cinnamon. Below grayish brown. Tail bronzy brown.

5. White-winged Dove   L-SOA
Zenaida asiatica   10" (26cm)
Above pale olive brown. Small black spot below ear coverts. *Large white patch on wing coverts,* showing at rest but especially conspicuous in flight. Below pale buffy grayish. Outer tail feathers tipped white.

6. Blue-eyed Ground-Dove   L-S
Columbina cyanopis   5½" (14cm)
Head rich purplish brown. Above brown, wings with dark blue spots. Below light buffy brownish, darkest on breast. Outer tail feathers black tipped white.

7. Croaking Ground-Dove   LM-SA
Columbina cruziana   6" (15cm)
Bill bright yellow or orange, tipped black. Head bluish gray. Above light grayish brown, wings prominently spotted and marked with black. Below light pinkish brown. Outer tail feathers black narrowly tipped white.

8. Purple-winged Ground-Dove L-F
Claravis godefrida   7½" (19cm)
Like Blue Ground-Dove (12-3) but wings crossed by three broad purple bands and outer tail feathers white (not black). ♀: Like ♀ Blue Ground-Dove (12-4) but has same wing pattern as ♂ and outer tail feathers broadly tipped buff.

9. Maroon-chested Ground-Dove
                    M-F
Claravis mondetoura   8" (20cm)
Bluish gray above. Wings with three broad purple bands. Outer tail feathers white. Throat whitish, breast reddish purple. Belly grayish, vent white. ♀: Reddish brown above, wings like ♂. Below brown. Outer tail feathers narrowly tipped whitish.

10. Bare-faced Ground-Dove
                  MH-SO
Metriopelia ceciliae   6½" (17cm)
Mostly brown, upperparts spotted whitish. *Bare skin around eye bright yellow orange.* Below mostly pale buffy brown. Outer tail feathers broadly tipped white.

11. Bare-eyed Ground-Dove   H-O
Metriopelia morenoi   6½" (17cm)
Mostly brown, *upperparts not spotted. Bare skin around eye bright yellow orange.* Below mostly pale buffy brown. Outer tail feathers broadly tipped white.

12. Golden-spotted Ground-Dove
                  H-O
Metriopelia aymara   7" (18cm)
Mostly light grayish brown, tinged pinkish below. *Wing coverts spotted golden. No white on wing.* Flight feathers black, base of primaries rufous. Tail rather short, black.

1. Black-winged Ground-Dove
MH-SO
Metriopelia melanoptera
8″(21cm)
Bare skin around eye yellow-orange. Above light grayish brown. *Shoulder and bend of wing white,* showing both at rest and in flight. Flight feathers black. Below light pinkish brown. Tail black.

2. Long-tailed Ground-Dove   L-O
Uropelia campestris   6½″(17cm)
Above drab brown. Bill dusky. Narrow eye-ring yellow. *Wings crossed by two white and black bands.* Below light pinkish brown, belly whiter. Tail long and graduated, outer feathers broadly tipped white. Legs orange.

3. Tolima Dove   M-FT
Leptotila conoveri   9″(24cm)
Forehead whitish, crown gray. Above dark brown, hindneck and upper back glossed purple. Throat white. *Breast dark pinkish tawny, contrasting with buffy belly.* Outer tail feathers narrowly tipped white.

4. Ochre-bellied Dove   LM-F
Leptotila ochraceiventris 9″(23cm)
Forehead pinkish white, *crown tawny brown.* Above olive brown, hindneck and upper back glossed purple. Throat white. Breast pinkish tawny, belly buff. Outer tail feathers tipped white.

5. Large-tailed Dove   M-TS
Leptotila megalura   11″(27cm)
Like White-tipped Dove (10-9) but *white throat* more extensive, extending to face.

6. Pallid Dove   L-FT
Leptotila pallida   9″(24cm)
Very like White-tipped Dove (10-9) but upperparts more rufous brown. *Head and underparts much paler over all.* Tail reddish brown.

7. Violaceous Quail-Dove   L-F
Geotrygon violacea   9″(24cm)
The only Quail-Dove without a whisker. Bill and eye-ring red. Above chestnut brown. Forehead and throat white. Breast pinkish gray. Belly white.

8. Russet-crowned Quail-Dove   L-F
Geotrygon goldmani   10″(25cm)
Like White-throated Quail-Dove (10-3) but crown rufous instead of gray and underparts more grayish, less brownish. *Crown and hindneck rufous brown.*

9. Hyacinthine Macaw   L-FT
Anodorhynchus hyacinthinus
39″(100cm)
Uniform rich blue. Underside of flight feathers and tail blackish. Eye-ring and bare skin at base of lower bill yellow.

10. Indigo Macaw   L-F
Anodorhynchus leari   29″(74cm)
Deep blue. Head and neck greenish blue. Eye-ring and bare skin at base of lower bill pale yellow.

11. Glaucous Macaw   L-F
Anodorhynchus glaucus
25″(64cm)
Mostly greenish blue. Head and underparts tinged grayish. Eye-ring and bare skin at base of lower bill pale yellow.

12. Little Blue Macaw   L-T
Cyanopsitta spixii   20″(50cm)
Blue, upperparts darker. Bare facial skin black. Head dusty bluish gray.

1. Military Macaw   **LM-FT**
Ara militaris   28" (70cm)
Mostly green. Bare facial skin whitish with narrow lines of black feathers. *Forehead red.* Flight feathers, lower back and rump blue. Tail mostly blue from above, feathers red at base.

2. Great Green Macaw   **L-F**
Ara ambigua   34" (85cm)
Mostly green, forehead red. Bare facial skin with narrow black lines. Flight feathers, lower back and rump pale blue. Tail mostly *pale blue,* but red at base.

3. Golden-collared Macaw   **L-T**
Ara auricollis   15" (38cm)
Mostly green. Bare facial skin whitish. Narrow yellow collar on hindneck (sometimes hard to see). Crown and cheeks blackish. Flight feathers blue. From above tail brownish red at base, blue toward tip.

4. Chestnut-fronted Macaw   **L-FT**
Ara severa   18" (45cm)
Mostly green. Bare facial skin white. *Narrow band on forehead chestnut.* Wings blue above, red below. Tail reddish brown tipped blue.

5. Red-bellied Macaw   **L-TO**
Ara manilata   20" (50cm)
Mostly green, tinged blue on crown and sides of head. Bare facial skin yellowish. *Center of belly dull reddish.* Feathers of underparts edged darker, giving slight scaly look. *Underside of wings and tail greenish yellow.*

6. Blue-winged Macaw   **L-FT**
Ara maracana   21" (52cm)
Mostly green, tinged blue on crown and sides of head. Bare facial skin whitish. *Forehead red.* Wings and tail blue above, olive-yellow below. Belly red.

7. Blue-headed Macaw   **L-FT**
Ara couloni   16" (40cm)
Mostly green. Head dull blue. Small bare facial area gray. Underside of flight feathers and tail yellowish. From above primaries mostly blue, tail largely brownish red.

8. Blue-crowned Parakeet   **LM-TSO**
Aratinga acuticauda   14" (35cm)
Green. *Crown blue.* Enlarged eye-ring white. Underside of tail brownish red.

9. Golden Parakeet   **L-F**
Aratinga guarouba   14" (35cm)
Golden yellow. Flight feathers green.

10. Scarlet-fronted Parakeet   **LM-FT**
Aratinga wagleri   14" (35cm)
Green. *Forecrown red.* In Ecuador and Peru bend of wing also red.

11. Red-masked Parakeet   **L-TSOA**
Aratinga erythrogenys 13" (32cm)
Green. *Most of head red.* Bend of wing and underwing coverts also red.

12. White-eyed Parakeet   **L-FT**
Aratinga leucophthalmus
    13" (33cm)
Green. Variable scattering of red feathers on head and neck, but *no red on forecrown.* Some red shows at shoulder.

1. **Dusky-headed Parakeet   L-FT**
Aratinga weddellii   10" (25cm)
Head bluish gray. Otherwise green, yellower on belly. Flight feathers and tail partly blue.

2. **Cactus Parakeet   L-SA**
Aratinga cactorum   10" (25cm)
Above green. *Throat and breast brown, contrasting with dull orange-yellow belly.*

3. **Peach-fronted Parakeet   L-TS**
Aratinga aurea   10" (25cm)
Above green. Area around eye and *forecrown orange.* Rear-crown blue. Below brownish olive, belly greenish yellow.

4. **Nanday (Black-hooded) Parakeet   MH-T**
Nandayus nenday   14" (35cm)
Head mostly black. Body mostly green, paler below, tinged blue on breast. Tail long, pointed, olive green, gray from below.

5. **Golden-plumed Parrot   H-F**
Leptosittaca branickii   14" (34cm)
Mostly green, somewhat paler below. Forehead narrowly orange, elongated feathers behind eye. *Belly washed with orange.* Underside of tail reddish.

6. **Yellow-eared Parakeet   MH-F**
Ognorhynchus icterotis
16" (40cm)
Forehead and sides of head bright yellow, contrasting with dark green upperparts. Below yellowish green. Underside of flight feathers yellowish. Underside of tail reddish.

7. **Blue-breasted   (Ochre-marked) Parakeet   L-FT**
Pyrrhura cruentata   11" (28cm)
Mostly green. Crown and nape dark brown. Band below eye to ear coverts brownish red, merging into *large orange buffy patch on sides of neck.* Shoulder red. Rump and patch on belly dull red. *Breast blue.* Tail olive above, reddish below.

8. **Blaze-winged Parakeet   L-FT**
Pyrrhura devillei   10" (25cm)
Mostly green. *Crown brown.* Breast feathers olive tipped paler. Small patch on belly reddish. *Shoulder and underwing coverts red.* Tail olive above, reddish below.

9. **Reddish-bellied Parakeet   LM-FT**
Pyrrhura frontalis   10" (26cm)
Mostly green. Ear coverts grayish brown. Forehead narrowly rufous. *Throat, sides of neck and breast broadly scalloped brownish olive and yellow.* Small patch on belly reddish. Tail above olive broadly tipped reddish, below all reddish.

10. **Pearly Parakeet   L-FT**
Pyrrhura perlata   9" (24cm)
Crown brown. Ear coverts buff. Above green. Shoulder and underwing coverts mostly red. *Throat and breast brown edged buff giving scaly appearance.* Below green. Tail dark reddish above, blackish below.

11. **Crimson-bellied Parakeet   L-F**
Pyrrhura rhodogaster   9" (22cm)
Head, neck and breast brown edged buff giving scaly appearance. Above mostly green, some blue on upper back. Shoulder and underwing coverts red. *Belly bright red.* Tail dark reddish above, blackish below.

12. **Blood-eared Parakeet   LM-FT**
Pyrrhura hoematotis   9½" (24cm)
Mostly green. *Ear coverts dull red.* Tail reddish above and below.

13. **Maroon-faced Parakeet   LM-FT**
Pyrrhura leucotis   8" (21cm)
Mostly green. Crown brown, forecrown tinged blue. Facial area maroon, *ear coverts whitish.* Breast feathers edged whitish giving scaly appearance. Shoulder, rump and patch on center of belly red. Tail reddish.

1. Santa Marta Parakeet   **M-FT**
Pyrrhura viridicata   9½"(24cm)
Mostly green. *Ear coverts maroon.*
Lower breast with scattered orange-red feathers. Shoulder and underwing coverts mixed orange and red. Tail green above, reddish below.

2. Fiery-shouldered Parakeet
            LM-FT
Pyrrhura egregia   9½"(24cm)
Like Maroon-tailed Parakeet (16-2) but has green cheeks, maroon belly and breast mostly green, feathers edged buff. Shoulder flame-orange.

3. Rock Parakeet   **L-FT**
Pyrrhura rupicola   10"(25cm)
Mostly green. Crown blackish. *Feathers of sides of neck and breast broadly edged whitish giving scalloped appearance.* Primary coverts red. Tail green above, grayish below.

4. White-breasted Parakeet   **LM-FT**
Pyrrhura albipectus   9½"(24cm)
Crown brown. Ear coverts orange-yellow. *broad white collar encircling neck* merging into yellow breast. Primary coverts red, conspicuous in flight. Otherwise mostly green. Tail mostly reddish.

5. Flame-winged Parakeet   **MH-FT**
Pyrrhura calliptera   9"(22cm)
Mostly green. Crown tinged brown. Ear coverts reddish brown. *Breast brown faintly scaled lighter. Primary coverts yellow and orange,* conspicuous in flight. Tail brownish red.

6. Rose-crowned (headed) Parakeet
            M-F
Pyrrhura rhodocephala
            9½"(24cm)
Mostly green. *Entire crown rosy red. Primary coverts white,* conspicuous in flight. Tail reddish.

7. Austral Parakeet   **M-FT**
Enicognathus ferrugineus
            12"(31cm)
Bill small, often almost concealed by facial feathers. Dull green, feathers edged dusky giving scaly appearance. Forehead, lores and patch on center of belly dull red. Tail brownish red.

8. Slender-billed Parakeet   **LM-FT**
Enicognathus leptorhynchus
            15"(38cm)
Bill slender, upper long and pointed. Dull green, feathers edged dusky giving scaled appearance. Forehead and lores rather bright red. Tail brownish red.

9. Gray-hooded Parakeet   **MH-S**
Bolborhynchus aymara   8"(20cm)
Head and nape grayish brown. Above green. *Throat and breast gray.* Belly light green.

10. Mountain Parakeet   **LMH-SO**
Bolborhynchus aurifrons
            7½"(19cm)
Mostly green. (In Peru, ♂ has forehead, lores and throat bright yellow, underparts strongly tinged yellow). *Long pointed tail.*

11. Barred Parakeet   **M-F**
Bolborhynchus lineola
            6½"(17cm)
Mostly green, paler below. *Feathers of upperparts and sides edged blackish,* giving barred appearance. Shoulder blackish. *Tail pointed but rather short.*

12. Rufous-fronted Parakeet   **H-S**
Bolborhynchus ferrugineifrons
            6½"(17cm)
Dark green, somewhat paler on rump and underparts. No barring. Forehead and lores narrowly edged rufous. Tail rather short and pointed.

1. Andean Parakeet   MH-FT
Bolborhynchus orbygnesius
                        6½"(17cm)
Dark green, somewhat paler on
rump and below. *No barring.* Tail
rather short and pointed.

2. Blue-winged Parrotlet   L-TSO
Forpus xanthopterygius
                        4½"(12cm)
Green, somewhat paler below.
Rump and wing coverts blue. Bill
horn-colored, dusky at base of
upper bill. ♀: Blue replaced by
green.

3. Yellow-faced Parrotlet   LM-SA
Forpus xanthops   5½"(14cm)
Crown and face bright yellow.
Stripe behind eye and nape bluish
gray. Above greenish gray. Wing
coverts and rump dark blue. Below
greenish yellow.

4. Plain Parakeet   L-T
Brotogeris tirica   9"(23cm)
Green, brighter and more yellowish on head and below. Wing coverts brownish olive. Tail quite long,
pointed.

5. Gray-cheeked Parakeet   L-FSA
Brotogeris pyrrhopterus 8"(20cm)
Crown pale blue. Sides of head
and throat pale gray. Otherwise
green, paler and yellower below.
Primary coverts blue, underwing
coverts orange.

6. Orange-chinned Parakeet   L-T
Brotogeris jugularis   7"(18cm)
Green. Crown tinged brown or
bluish. Small chin spot orange
(hard to see in field). *Shoulders
brown.* Underwing coverts yellow.

7. Golden-winged Parakeet   L-T
Brotogeris chrysopterus 7"(18cm)
Green, darker on back and wings.
Faint chin spot orange (very hard
to see in field). Primary coverts orange (usually hidden at rest, but
conspicuous in flight). Underwing
coverts green.

8. Tui Parakeet   L-T
Brotogeris sanctithomae 6"(15cm)
Like Cobalt-winged Parakeet (16-
5) but no orange chin spot. *Conspicuous yellow forecrown.* (In
lower Amazon also a yellow streak
below eye). Flight feathers green
above.

9. Tepui Parrotlet   M-F
Nannopsittaca panychlora
                        5"(13cm)
Green. Around eye yellowish. *Tail
short and square.*

10. Sapphire-rumped Parrotlet   L-F
Touit purpurata   6¼"(16cm)
Mostly green, paler below. Crown
brown (green in nw part of range).
Lower back and rump blue. Tail
mostly violet-red, central feathers
green.

**11. Brown-backed (Black-eared)
Parrotlet   M-F**
Touit melanonota   5½"(14cm)
Mostly green, paler below. *Mantle
blackish brown.* Tail mostly red,
tipped blackish, central feathers
green.

12. Scarlet-shouldered Parrotlet L-F
Touit huetii   6"!15cm)
Mostly green, paler and yellower
below. *Forehead and front of face
dark blue. Upperwing coverts dark
blue.* Underwing coverts and patch
on sides of breast red. Tail mostly
purplish red, tipped black, central
feathers green. Vent yellow.

1. Red-winged Parrotlet **L-F**
Touit dilectissima 6½" (17cm)
Mostly green, paler and yellower
below. *Forecrown blue,* hindcrown brownish. Lores and streak
below eye red. *Bend of wing and
part of wing coverts red* (green in
♀). *Tail mostly yellow* tipped black,
central feathers green.

2. Golden-tailed Parrotlet **L-F**
Touit surda 6¼" (16cm)
Mostly green, paler and yellower
below. Forehead and facial area
yellowish buffy. *Tail mostly greenish yellow* tipped black, (♀ tipped
green).

3. Spot-winged Parrotlet **M-F**
Touit stictoptera 6¼" (16cm)
Green, somewhat paler and yellower below. *Wing coverts brown
tipped whitish* with orange patch
in middle. ♀: Face yellowish,
wings green somewhat spotted
blackish.

4. Black-headed Parrot **L-F**
Pionites melanocephala 9" (23cm)
Crown black. Back green. *Throat,
sides of head and collar orange-
yellow. Below white,* sides of belly
and thighs orange-yellow.

5. White-bellied Parrot **L-F**
Pionites leucogaster 9" (23cm)
*Entire head, neck and throat yel-
low-orange.* Back green. *Below
white,* sides of belly and thighs
green.

6. Red-capped Parrot **LM-F**
Pionopsitta pileata 9" (22cm)
Green. *Crown and stripe below
eye red.* Bend of wing and primary
coverts blue. Outer tail feathers
mostly blue. ♀: Lacks red.

7. Brown-hooded Parrot **L-F**
Pionopsitta haematotis 8" (21cm)
Mostly green. Head brown (or pink
in s part of range). Small red spot
on ear coverts. Breast brownish
olive with red band. Underwing
coverts blue.

8. Caica Parrot **L-F**
Pionopsitta caica 9" (23cm)
*Entire head blackish, collar on
hindneck tawny.* Throat and breast
brownish olive. Otherwise mostly
green. Tail green, inner webs yellow.

9. Orange-cheeked Parrot **L-F**
Pionopsitta barrabandi 10" (25cm)
Head and nape blackish with *large
orange patch on cheeks.* Breast
yellowish olive. Otherwise mostly
green. Shoulders orange. Underwing coverts red.

10. Saffron-headed Parrot **L-F**
Pionopsitta pyrilia 9½" (24cm)
Entire head golden yellow. Breast
yellowish olive. Otherwise mostly
green. Shoulders yellow-orange.
Bend of wing, underwing coverts
and sides of body red.

11. Black-winged (eared) Parrot
MH-F
Hapalopsittaca melanotis
9½" (24cm)
Mostly dark green. Ear coverts
black. *Wings mostly black.* Tail
broadly tipped dark violet-blue.

12. Rusty-faced Parrot **MH-F**
Hapalopsittaca amazonina
9" (23cm)
Variable. Back green. Facial area
reddish (yellowish in Central Andes
of Colombia). Crown tinged bluish
(reddish in Ecuador). *Shoulder red.*
Tail brownish red tipped dark violet-blue.

1. **Vulturine Parrot**   L-F
Gypopsitta vulturina   9″ (23cm)
Head bare, black, bordered behind by *bright yellow collar.* Otherwise mostly green. Breast yellowish olive. Shoulder orange.
Bend of wing red. Imm: Head
feathered, yellowish green.

2. **Short-tailed Parrot**   L-T
Graydidascalus brachyurus
                        9½″ (24cm)
All green, paler below. Wing
feathers edged yellow. *Extremely
short tail* (readily apparent in field).

3. **Blue-headed Parrot**   L-FT
Pionus menstruus   11″ (26cm)
Head and neck deep blue, ear
coverts blackish. Otherwise green.
Base of bill reddish. Bare eye-ring
dusky. Base of tail and vent red.

4. **Red-billed Parrot**   LM-FT
Pionus sordidus   10″ (25cm)
Bill all red. Mostly olive green,
feathers of head edged blue. *Bare
eye-ring whitish. Eye pale yellow.*
Patch of blue on lower throat and
breast. Vent and base of tail red.

5. **Scaly-headed Parrot**   L-FT
Pionus maximiliani   11″ (27cm)
Bill yellowish. Dull green. Feath-
ers, especially on head, edged
dusky giving scaly appearance.
Bare eye-ring white. Vent red.

6. **Plum-crowned Parrot**   M-F
Pionus tumultuosus   10″ (25cm)
Bill olive yellow. Head and neck
plum color (crown whitish in some
races) darkening to purple on
breast. Back and belly green. Vent
red. Base of outer tail feathers reddish.

7. **White-capped Parrot**   MH-F
Pionus seniloides   10″ (25cm)
Head white, scaled dusky on sides
and nape. Above green. Breast
brown. Belly reddish.

8. **Bronze-winged Parrot**   M-FT
Pionus chalcopterus   10″ (25cm)
A very dark parrot. Bill whitish.
Above dark bronzy green. Throat
white. Breast pink. Belly dark
bronzy brown. Tail blue, red at
base.

9. **Dusky Parrot**   L-F
Pionus fuscus   9″ (23cm)
A very dark parrot. Bill dusky with
a red spot near base. Above bronzy
brown, sides of head streaked
whitish. Below reddish brown,
tinged purple on belly. Tail blue,
red at base.

10. **Red-spectacled Parrot**   L-FT
Amazona pretrei   12″ (31cm)
Mostly green, feathers distinctly
edged black giving scaly look. *Forecrown, facial area, shoulder and
primary coverts red.* Tail tipped
yellowish.

11. **Alder Parrot**   LM-FT
Amazona tucumana   12″ (29cm)
Mostly green. *Feathers broadly
edged black.* Small area on forehead red. Primary coverts (not
shoulder) red. Thighs orange (not
red).

12. **Red-lored Parrot**   L-FT
Amazona autumnalis
                        12½″ (31cm)
Forehead red, crown purplish in
nw Brazil. Body green. Feathers of
nape and sides of neck edged
dusky. Red speculum.

1. Blue-cheeked Parrot   **L-F**
Amazona brasiliensis   12" (31cm)
Three separate races may be three species. All mostly green. In Guianas crown yellow, sides of head blue. Speculum orange. In e Brazil crown red, sides of head greenish blue. Speculum red. Tail with red band. In se Brazil crown red, sides of head purple. No speculum. Tail with red band and yellow tip.

2. Festive Parrot   **L-FT**
Amazona festiva   14" (34cm)
Green, neck feathers edged black. *Band on forehead and lores dark red.* Head tinged blue. Lower back and rump red (hard to see except when flying).

3. Yellow-faced Parrot   **L-TS**
Amazona xanthops   10" (26cm)
Head and neck mostly yellow. Back and wings green. Below mostly yellow, tinged green on breast with *orange patch on sides.* Imm: Yellow restricted to crown and face.

4. Yellow-shouldered Parrot   **L-TSA**
Amazona barbadensis 13" (31cm)
Mostly green, feathers quite strongly edged blackish. *Forecrown and lores white,* top of crown and face yellow. *Bend of wing yellow.* Red speculum.

5. Yellow-headed Parrot   **L-FTO**
Amazona ochrocephala
            13" (32cm)
Mostly green, feathers of hindneck edged dusky. *Forecrown yellow.* Bend of wing and speculum red.

6. Orange-winged Parrot   **L-FT**
Amazona amazonica 12" (30cm)
Mostly green. Forecrown and cheeks yellow. *Lores and narrow stripe over eye blue.* Orange speculum. No shoulder patch.

7. Scaly-naped Parrot   **MH-F**
Amazona mercenaria 12" (30cm)
Green. Nape, hindcrown and breast feathers noticeably edged blackish. Bend of wing orange. Red speculum (usually absent Venezuela to Ecuador). *Tail with red median band, tipped pale green.*

8. Mealy Parrot   **L-F**
Amazona farinosa   15" (38cm)
Green, usually with powdery look above. Patch on crown yellow (sometimes mixed with red or green). Feathers of hindneck edged blackish. Bend of wing and speculum red. Outer half of tail pale greenish yellow.

9. Vinaceous-breasted Parrot LM-F
Amazona vinacea   13" (33cm)
Bill dull reddish, tipped horn color. Mostly green, feathers strongly edged blackish. *Lores red.* Hindneck pale blue. *Lower throat and breast reddish purple.* Bend of wing and speculum red.

10. Red-fan Parrot   **L-F**
Deroptyus accipitrinus 13" (33cm)
Head brown streaked white, *crown white* (brown s of Amazon). *Long erectile feathers on nape* and hindneck red, tipped blue. Back and wings green. Feathers of breast and belly red broadly tipped blue. Underside of long tail black.

11. Blue-bellied Parrot   **LM-F**
Triclaria malachitacea 9" (24cm)
All green. Patch on center of breast and belly blue. Long, rounded tail. ♀: Lacks patch on center of breast and belly.

12. Dwarf Cuckoo   **L-TS**
Coccyzus pumilus   8" (20cm)
Bill black. Crown and nape gray. *Throat and breast rufous.* Back grayish brown. Belly white. Tail black with narrow white tip.

1. Ash-colored Cuckoo **L-TS**
Coccyzus cinereus 9″ (22cm)
Bill black. Above brown. *Throat and breast gray brown.* Belly white. Tail with narrow white tip.

2. Pearly-breasted Cuckoo **L-TS**
Coccyzus euleri 9″ (23cm)
Very like Yellow-billed Cuckoo (18-5) but somewhat smaller and has *no rufous on flight feathers.*

3. Mangrove Cuckoo **L-TS**
Coccyzus minor 11″ (28cm)
Like Yellow-billed Cuckoo (18-5) but is *buffy below* and has well-marked *black ear coverts.* No rufous in wing.

4. Gray-capped Cuckoo **L-TS**
Coccyzus lansbergi 9″ (22cm)
Bill black. *Crown gray. Above rufous brown.* Below deep buff. Tail black, outer feathers tipped white.

5. Black-bellied Cuckoo **L-F**
Piaya melanogaster 13″ (33cm)
Rather like Squirrel Cuckoo (18-1) but *crown gray,* bill red, lores yellow. Breast and *belly black.* Tail shorter.

6. Greater Ani **LMH-TSW**
Crotophaga major 16″ (41cm)
Very like Smooth-billed Ani (18-8) but much larger. *Eye conspicuously whitish.*

7. Pheasant Cuckoo **L-FT**
Dromococcyx phasianellus
14″ (35cm)
Crown and crest rufous. Long *white stripe back of eye.* Above dark brown. Wing coverts edged buff. *Throat* and *breast* buff *spotted dusky.* Belly white. *Tail long and very broad. Uppertail coverts plume-like,* almost as long as tail itself.

8. Pavonine Cuckoo **LM-F**
Dromococcyx pavoninus
9″ (23cm)
Crown and crest rufous. Long *buffy stripe* back of eye. Above blackish. Wing coverts edged buff. *Throat and breast uniform buffy brown.* Belly white. Tail rather long and broad.

9. Rufous-vented Ground-Cuckoo **L-T**
Neomorphus geoffroyi 17″ (43cm)
Prominent flat crest. Above bronzy. Below grayish to buffy with narrow *black band across breast.* Tail long. Terrestrial. Includes Scaled Ground-Cuckoo, *N. squamiger,* considered a separate species in BSA.

10. Banded Ground-Cuckoo **L-F**
Neomorphus radiolosus
17″ (43cm)
Crest long, flat. Back blackish, barred buffy. Below broadly banded black and buffy. Tail long, purplish. Terrestrial.

11. Rufous-winged Ground-Cuckoo **L-F**
Neomorphus rufipennis
17″ (43cm)
Head, crest, neck, back and breast blackish. *Bare skin around eye red.* Throat and belly brownish. Tail long, purplish. Terrestrial.

12. Red-billed Ground-Cuckoo **L-F**
Neomorphus pucheranii
17″ (43cm)
Crest blue. Above olive to blackish. *Bare skin around eye red.* Breast ashy gray with narrow black band. Below whitish. Terrestrial.

1. **Barn Owl** **LMH-O**
Tyto alba 14″ (36cm)
Appears whitish. Above light brownish with white dots. *Large white disks around eyes* surrounded by dusky rims. Below whitish with small dusky spots.

2. **Vermiculated Screech-Owl LM-F**
Otus guatemalae 7½″ (19cm)
Like Tropical Screech-Owl (20-2) but few, if any, streaks on underparts, looking mottled.

3. **West Peruvian Screech-Owl**
LMH-TO
Otus roboratus 8″ (21cm)
Like Tropical Screech-Owl (20-2) but *center of belly white.*

4. **Long-tufted Screech-Owl LM-F**
Otus atricapillus 9″ (23 cm)
Like Tropical Screech-Owl (20-2) but ear tufts longer. Crown and ear tufts streaked black.

5. **Rufescent Screech-Owl M-F**
Otus ingens 10″ (25cm)
Rather like Tropical Screech-Owl (20-2) but ear tufts short and eye dark. Above tawny olive vermiculated dusky. Partly concealed white collar. *Below buffy or whitish streaked brown.* In rufous phase general tone is rufous brown.

6. **Tawny-bellied Screech-Owl L-F**
Otus watsonii 8″ (21cm)
Rather like Tropical Screech-Owl (20-2) but long ear tufts black and *eyebrow rufous.* Below tawny streaked black on breast.

7. **Bare-shanked Screech-Owl M-F**
Otus clarkii 9″ (22cm)
Eye yellow. Rufous brown above. Ear tufts short. Below buffy brown spotted *whitish on breast.* Legs bare, but hard to see.

8. **White-throated Screech-Owl**
H-F
Otus albogularis 10″ (25cm)
Eye yellow. Rather like Tropical Screech-Owl (20-2) but sooty brown above with fine buff spots. Ear tufts very small. *Throat conspicuously white.* Belly buffy, lightly streaked dusky.

9. **Crested Owl L-F**
Lophostrix cristata 14″ (37cm)
Forehead, eyebrow and *very long ear tufts white.* Above sooty brown with fine buff spots. Face chestnut. Large white spots on wing coverts. Below buffy brown.

10. **Great Horned Owl LMH-FTS**
Bubo virginianus 19″ (48cm)
Large, widely spaced ear tufts. Eye yellow. Above dark brown mottled buff and gray. Face cinnamon. Throat white. Below whitish barred brown.

11. **Tawny-browed Owl LM-F**
Pulsatrix koeniswaldiana
15″ (38cm)
Like Spectacled Owl (20-1) but "spectacles" light buffy (not white).

12. **Band-bellied Owl L-F**
Pulsatrix melanota 16″ (40cm)
Rather like Spectacled Owl (20-1) but face rufous. Above dark brown, lightly spotted buff. Throat sooty brown bordered below by white band. Breast and belly whitish, barred rufous and brown.

1. Least Pygmy-Owl **L-FT**
Glaucidium minutissimum
5½"(14cm)
Like Andean Pygmy-Owl (20-4) but crown with tiny white spots (not streaked). Back unspotted.

 2. Austral Pygmy-Owl **LM-TS**
*Glaucidium nanum** 6½" (17cm)
Like Andean Pygmy-Owl (20-4). Many white spots on wing coverts. Tail narrowly barred.

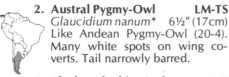 **3. Black-and-white Owl** **L-F**
Ciccaba nigrolineata 16" (40cm)
No ear tufts. Bill and toes yellow. *Face disks black outlined by mottled white.* Above sooty black. Below white narrowly barred black. Tail black narrowly barred white.

4. Black-banded Owl **L-F**
Ciccaba huhula 14" (36cm)
No ear tufts. Bill and toes yellow. Face disks black, dully outlined by mottled white. Above and below black narrowly banded white everywhere.

5. Mottled Owl **LM-FT**
Ciccaba virgata 13" (32cm)
No ear tufts. Eye brown. Face disks black sharply outlined whitish. Above and breast dark brown everywhere finely dotted and barred with white or reddish buff. *Belly buff broadly streaked dark brown.* Tail black with four whitish bars.

6. Rufous-banded Owl **MH-F**
Ciccaba albitarsus 14" (34cm)
No ear tufts. Face disks black strongly outlined white. Above brown spotted and barred tawny. Below bright orange tawny spotted with silvery white. Tail banded.

7. Rusty-barred Owl **LM-F**
Strix hylophila 14" (34cm)
No ear tufts. Eye brown. Above dark brown banded buff. Facial area buff barred blackish. *Below brown, barred rufous on breast, white on belly.*

8. Rufous-legged Owl **LM-F**
Strix rufipes 13" (33cm)
No ear tufts. Eye brown. Facial area rufous. *Eyebrows, lores and throat white.* Above brown narrowly barred white. Below boldly banded white and blackish.

 9. Striped Owl **L-O**
Rhinoptynx clamator 14" (36cm)
Prominent long black ear tufts. Face disks whitish rimmed black. Above tawny buff striped black. *Below buff, strongly striped black.*

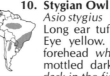 **10. Stygian Owl** **LMH-FT**
Asio stygius 16" (40cm)
Long ear tufts set close together. Eye yellow. Above dark brown, forehead *whitish.* Below heavily mottled dark brown. *Looks very dark in the field.*

 **11. Short-eared Owl** **LMH-O**
Asio flammeus 14" (36cm)
Small ear tufts often not visible in the field. Eye yellow. Above and below mostly tawny brown striped dark brown. Eyebrow and lores whitish. Often day-flying, low over open country.

 12. Buff-fronted Owl **MH-F**
Aegolius harrisii 7½" (19cm)
No ear tufts. Eye yellow. Above dark brown, wings and tail spotted white. *Prominent forecrown yellowish buff.* Entire underparts and collar yellowish buff. Tail blackish with two broken white bars and white tip.

1. Great Potoo **L-FT**
.*Nyctibius grandis* 18″ (46cm)
Like gray phase of Common Potoo
(20-6) but larger and paler. Eye
brown instead of yellow. All light
grayish. Tail long, marbled gray,
brown and black and with numerous dusky bars.

2. Long-tailed Potoo **L-F**
Nyctibius aethereus 17″ (43cm)
Very like brown phase of Common Potoo (20-6). Tail strongly
graduated, central feathers pointed. Row of black spots across
breast.

3. White-winged Potoo **LM-F**
Nyctibius leucopterus 9″ (23cm)
Like brown phase of Common
Potoo (20-6) but much smaller with
much shorter tail and crown heavily spotted black. *Broad white
band across closed wing.*

4. Rufous Potoo **L-F**
Nyctibius bracteatus 8″ (21cm)
Smaller than other potoos. Mostly
cinnamon-rufous. *Conspicuous
large white-edged spots on shoulders and belly.*

**5. Short-tailed (Semi-collared)
Nighthawk** **LM-FT**
Lurocalis semitorquatus 8″ (21cm)
Above blackish sprinkled with gray
and rufous spots. Throat white.
Breast blackish with rufescent or
gray spots. Belly rufous barred
blackish. Wings long and pointed,
no white band across primaries.
Tail very short.

6. Least Nighthawk **L-SO**
Chordeiles pusillus 5½″ (14cm)
The smallest Nighthawk. Grayish
brown vermiculated blackish and
speckled rufous. Throat and vent
white. Breast and belly white
barred dark brown. In flight shows
prominent whitish trailing edge to
wings.

7. Sand-colored Nighthawk **L-OW**
Chordeiles rupestris 8″ (20cm)
Above light sandy grayish streaked
brown and buffy. Below white,
band across breast mottled sandy-
grayish. *Tail mostly white, tipped
black.* In flight inner flight feathers
white, outer primaries black, no
bar. Often on sand bars in rivers.

8. Lesser Nighthawk **L-O**
Chordeiles acutipennis 7″ (18cm)
Above grayish speckled black.
Throat white. Below narrowly
banded buff and dark brown. Tail
blackish banded buff with white
subterminal band. In flight shows
white band *near middle* of wing
feathers. Usually flies low.

9. Common Nighthawk **L-T**
Chordeiles minor* 8″ (20cm)
Very like preceding but in flight
shows white wing-band *less* than
halfway from the bend of the wing
to the tip. Usually flies high. In
most of South America occurs only
as winter migrant from North
America.

10. Band-tailed Nighthawk **L-OW**
Nyctiprogne leucopyga
6¼″ (16cm)
Mostly blackish. Belly barred
whitish and black. Small white
patch on either side of throat. *No
band across wings.* Rather long
notched tail, blackish, crossed by
single broad white band near base.

11. Nacunda Nighthawk **L-O**
Podager nacunda 10″ (26cm)
Above sandy brown vermiculated
with black. Throat patch white.
Breast brown vermiculated with
blackish. *Belly white.* Conspicuous white band across primaries.
Tail broadly tipped white. Usually
flies high over open country.

12. Ocellated Poorwill **L-F**
Nyctiphrynus ocellatus
7½″ (19cm)
Mostly dark reddish brown (blackish in w Colombia and Ecuador).
Bar on throat and *spots on belly
white.* No wing band. Outer tail
feathers tipped white (all of tail
white in w Colombia and Ecuador). Rarely leaves forest.

1. Chuck-Wills-Widow   LM-FT
Caprimulgus carolinensis*
10"(26cm)
Rather like Pauraque (20-9) but *no white in wing.* Eyebrow buffy. Narrow band across throat extends to below cheeks. Three outer tail feathers white (♀ buff) on inner webs, tipped buff. Rest of tail feathers rufous.

2. Rufous Nightjar   L-TS
Caprimulgus rufus   9"(24cm)
Rather like Pauraque (20-9) but more rufescent. Tail has large buff patches on underside (♀ lacking). No white wing-bar in flight.

3. Silky-tailed Nightjar   L-T
Caprimulgus sericocaudatus
11"(27cm)
In shape like Pauraque (20-9) but narrow collar tawny. Band across throat buff. Below brown mixed with whitish. *Tail rounded with wide diagonal white (♀ rufous) band across tip.*

4. Band-winged Nightjar   MH-TSO
Caprimulgus longirostris
9"(22cm)
In shape like Pauraque (20-9). Above black spotted chestnut and white. *Collar chestnut.* In flight shows conspicuous white band across primaries. Outer tail feathers broadly tipped white (♀ lacking).

5. White-winged Nightjar   L-TSO
Caprimulgus candicans 8"(21cm)
In shape like Pauraque (20-9) but mostly pale grayish. Belly, underwing coverts and outer tail feathers white. In flight shows prominent white band across wing. ♀: Buff where ♂ is white.

6. Spot-tailed Nightjar   L-TSO
Caprimulgus maculicaudus
7½"(19cm)
In shape like Pauraque (20-9) but *head* mostly *black with conspicuous buffy eyebrow* and rufous collar. Above brown faintly banded dusky. Wings spotted light buff. Throat buffy, *breast blackish with large whitish spots.* Belly tawny. Tail broadly tipped white (♀ lacking).

7. Cayenne Nightjar   L-OA
Caprimulgus maculosus
8"(20cm)
A dark nightjar. Primaries black with white spot on inner web of four outermost feathers. Outermost tail feather virtually uniform, next two tipped white.

8. Blackish Nightjar   L-SO
Caprimulgus nigrescens
7½"(19cm)
Upperparts and breast black heavily spotted buff. Wings black with small white patch on inner web of two primaries. *White band on throat.* Belly finely barred black and buff. Tail blackish, some feathers tipped white.

9. Roraiman Nightjar   M-TSO
Caprimulgus whiteleyi 8"(20cm)
Mostly brownish black dotted rufous. Patch on sides of throat white. Below barred black and buff. White band on three outer primaries.

10. Pygmy Nightjar   L-SO
Caprimulgus hirundinaceus
6½"(17cm)
The smallest true nightjar. *Pale grayish brown generally.* Conspicuous white band across primaries. Outer tail feathers tipped white.

11. Scissor-tailed Nightjar   LM-TS
Hydropsalis brasiliana 15"(38cm)
♀: 11" (27cm)
Grayish brown above marked with black and buff. Rufous collar on hindneck. Below brownish, barred dusky, belly more buffy. No white wing-band. *Outer tail feathers greatly elongated,* whitish at tip and along inner web. ♀: Lacks tail streamers, but outer feathers still longest; tail grayish brown with blackish bars.

12. Swallow-tailed Nightjar   H-FT
Uropsalis segmentata 25"(65cm)
♀: 9" (22cm)
Mostly blackish. *No collar on hindneck,* or pale band on primaries. Small white band across lower throat. *Outer tail feathers very long,* straight, blackish. ♀: *Tail normal,* slightly forked, blackish barred rufous.

1. Lyre-tailed Nightjar M-FT
Uropsalis lyra 30"(75cm)
♀: 10"(25cm)
Mostly blackish brown marked with rufous. Collar rufous. *Outer tail feathers enormously elongated,* black, tipped white. ♀: Tail normal length, blackish barred rufous.

2. Long-trained Nightjar LM-FT
Macropsalis creagra 27"(68cm)
♀: 8" (20cm)
Mostly blackish. Collar pale rufous. *Outer tail feathers very long,* mostly white on inner web. ♀: Tail normal.

3. Sickle-winged Nightjar L-SW
Eleothreptus anomalus 7"(18cm)
Mostly grayish marked with black. Throat blackish. *Peculiar wing shape* with outer primaries curved inward, tipped white. Inner primaries somewhat longer than outer ones. Tail very short, buffy brown barred blackish, tipped whitish.

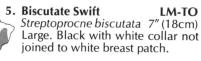

4. White-collared Swift LMH-TO
Streptoprocne zonaris 7½"(19cm)
Large. Blackish with conspicuous *white collar.* Tail slightly forked. Imm: Collar reduced or lacking.

5. Biscutate Swift LM-TO
Streptoprocne biscutata 7" (18cm)
Large. Black with white collar not joined to white breast patch.

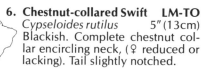

6. Chestnut-collared Swift LM-TO
Cypseloides rutilus 5"(13cm)
Blackish. Complete chestnut collar encircling neck, (♀ reduced or lacking). Tail slightly notched.

7. Tepui Swift LM-TO
Cypseloides phelpsi 6"(15cm)
Sooty black. Cheeks, chin, throat, breast and broad collar rufous. Tail forked.

8. Great Dusky Swift L-TO
Cypseloides senex 7"(18cm)
Uniform sooty brown. Forecrown, face and throat grizzled whitish. Tail square.

9. Sooty Swift LM-TO
Cypseloides fumigatus 6¼"(16cm)
Brownish black, forecrown and throat grizzled whitish. *Little or no white on face.*

10. Spot-fronted Swift M-TO
Cypseloides cherriei 5"(13cm)
Sooty black. *Quite conspicuous white spots* in front of eye and behind eye. Short square tail.

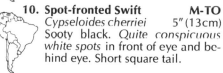

11. White-chinned Swift LM-TO
Cypseloides cryptus 5½"(14cm)
Sooty brown. Inconspicuous small whitish chin spot. Short square tail.

12. White-chested Swift LM-TO
Cypseloides lemosi 6"(15cm)
Blackish brown. *Conspicuous white triangular patch on breast,* pointing towards belly. Tail slightly forked. Imm: Little or no white on breast.

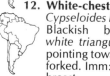

13. Chapman's Swift L-TO
Chaetura chapmani 5"(13cm)
Black above glossed with blue or green, especially on wings. Rump dark brown, contrasting only slightly from back. *Below uniform sooty gray.*

1. Chimney Swift **LM-TO**
*Chaetura pelagica** 5½" (14cm)
Above uniform dark sooty olive, rump only slightly paler. Below uniform grayish brown, but *throat distinctly paler.*

2. Vaux's Swift **LM-TO**
Chaetura vauxi 4" (10cm)
Above black with contrasting grayish brown rump. Below grayish brown, *contrasting strongly with whitish throat* and upper breast.

3. Gray-rumped Swift **LM-TO**
Chaetura cinereiventris
4½" (11cm)
Above glossy black with *sharply contrasting gray rump.* Tail rather long, blackish. Below gray, throat paler gray.

4. Pale-rumped Swift **L-TO**
Chaetura egregia 4½" (12cm)
Above glossy black. *Rump whitish* (not gray). Dark sooty gray below.

5. Band-rumped Swift **L-TO**
Chaetura spinicauda 4" (10cm)
Blackish above with *narrow but conspicuous* (contrasting sharply) *whitish band across rump.* Below dark gray, blackest on belly, with throat notably paler.

6. Ashy-tailed Swift **LM-TO**
Chaetura andrei 5½" (14cm)
Dusky brown above with contrasting pale brownish gray rump. Below dark sooty brown, *contrasting strongly with pale gray throat.* Rather short tail.

7. Short-tailed Swift **L-O**
Chaetura brachyura 4" (10cm)
Mostly black. Rump and tail contrastingly light grayish brown. *Tail very short.*

8. White-tipped Swift **MH-TO**
Aeronautes montivagus
4½" (12cm)
Sooty black with conspicuous white patch on throat and breast. Center of belly whitish. Tail notched, *tipped white* (more obvious from above).

9. Andean Swift **MH-O**
Aeronautes andecolus 5" (13cm)
Above brown. White collar around hindneck. White band across rump. Below white. Tail rather long, forked.

10. Lesser Swallow-tailed Swift L-TO
Panyptila cayennensis 4½" (12cm)
Mostly black. Throat and breast white, extending as collar around hindneck. Small white spot on lores. White patch on either side of rump. *Tail long and deeply forked* (but usually held closed when looks pointed).

11. Pygmy Swift **L-TO**
Micropanyptila furcata 3½" (9cm)
Very small. Mottled brownish breast band. Small white spots on sides of base of tail (hard to see). Tail deeply forked.

12. Fork-tailed Palm-Swift **L-SO**
Reinarda squamata 4½" (12cm)
Blackish brown above. Whitish mottled with brown below. *Tail very long and deeply forked,* but usually held closed so looks pointed. Almost always near palms. Very fast stiff wingbeats.

1. Blue-fronted Lancebill **LM-FT**
Doryfera johannae 4¼" (11cm)
Bill 2x head, thin. Like Green-fronted Lancebill (32-3) but smaller, darker and bill shorter. Looks mostly blackish.

2. Saw-billed Hermit **LM-F**
Ramphodon naevius 6¼" (16cm)
Bill 2x head, heavy, hooked at end, lower mandible yellow. Above dark coppery olive. Buff streak back of eye. Cheeks rufous. Below buff *streaked dusky*. Black streak down center of throat. ♀: Lacks hook on bill.

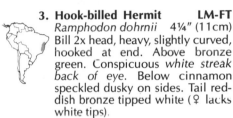

3. Hook-billed Hermit **LM-FT**
Ramphodon dohrnii 4¼" (11cm)
Bill 2x head, heavy, slightly curved, hooked at end. Above bronze green. Conspicuous *white streak back of eye*. Below cinnamon speckled dusky on sides. Tail reddish bronze tipped white (♀ lacks white tips).

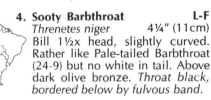

4. Sooty Barbthroat **L-F**
Threnetes niger 4¼" (11cm)
Bill 1½x head, slightly curved. Rather like Pale-tailed Barbthroat (24-9) but no white in tail. Above dark olive bronze. *Throat black, bordered below by fulvous band.*

5. Bronze-tailed Barbthroat **L-F**
Threnetes loehkeni 4½" (12cm)
Bill 2x head, slightly curved. Very like Pale-tailed Barbthroat (24-9) but *tail uniformly dark bronze.*

6. Great-billed Hermit **L-F**
Phaethornis malaris 6¼" (16cm)
Bill 2x head, rather heavy, slightly curved. Very like Long-tailed Hermit (22-1) but *bill heavier.*

7. Needle-billed Hermit **L-F**
Phaethornis philippi 5½" (14cm)
Bill 2x head. Very like Tawny-bellied Hermit (22-2) except bill straight instead of curved.

8. Dusky-throated Hermit **LM-F**
Phaethornis squalidus 4¼" (11cm)
Bill 1½x head, curved. Crown dusky brown. Above dull olive. Streak behind eye and whisker whitish, ear coverts black. *Throat dusky. Below grayish.* Tail olive, Rather like Scale-throated Hermit (22-3).

9. Buff-bellied Hermit **L-FT**
Phaethornis subochraceus
4½" (12cm)
Bill 1½x head, curved. Crown dark coppery, feathers edged buffy. Above dull olive. Grayish below. Belly buff.

10. Cinnamon-throated Hermit **L-TS**
Phaethornis nattereri 4½" (12cm)
Bill 2x head, curved. Like Planalto Hermit (22-5) but smaller and all except four central tail feathers tipped buff instead of white.

11. Maranhão Hermit **L-TS**
Phaethornis maranhaoensis
3½" (9cm)
Resembles Planalto Hermit (22-5), but much smaller. Darker and tawnier below. Tail blackish at base (not rufous or coppery).

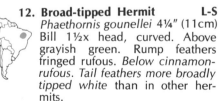

12. Broad-tipped Hermit **L-S**
Phaethornis gounellei 4¼" (11cm)
Bill 1½x head, curved. Above grayish green. Rump feathers fringed rufous. *Below cinnamon-rufous. Tail feathers more broadly tipped white* than in other hermits.

1. White-browed Hermit   L-F
Phaethornis stuarti   3½" (9cm)
Bill 1½x head, curved. Like Reddish Hermit (22-12) but no black on breast. Uniform rich rufous underparts. Side tail feathers tipped whitish (not rufous). Tail green.

2. Gray-chinned Hermit   LM-F
Phaethornis griseogularis
3½" (9cm)
Bill 1½x head, curved. Like Reddish Hermit (22-12) but no black on breast and center of throat grayish. Central part of tail feathers black and side tail feathers *tipped cinnamon.*

3. Minute Hermit   LM-FT
Phaethornis idaliae   3" (8cm)
Bill 1¼x head, curved, thin. Like Reddish Hermit (22-12) but has green upper tail coverts, black chin and no black on breast. Belly dark gray. ♀: Uniform buff below.

4. Buff-tailed Sicklebill   L-T
Eutoxeres condamini   5" (13cm)
Bill (chord) 1¼x head, *very strongly curved,* heavy. Very like Whitetipped Sicklebill (24-1) but *three outer tail feathers mostly buff* with white tips. Small blue patch on sides of neck usually hard to see.

5. Scaly-breasted Hummingbird L-T
Phaeochroa cuvierii   4½" (12cm)
Bill = head, straight, base of lower mandible reddish. Above dull bronzy green. *Below mostly grayish buffy with numerous green spots* giving scaled look. Tail bronzy green, outer feathers broadly tipped white.

6. Rufous-breasted Sabrewing M-TS
Campylopterus hyperythrus
4½" (12cm)
Bill = head, straight. Above shining bronzy green. Spot behind eye and underparts uniform rufous. Tail golden bronze above, cinnamon rufous below.

7. Buff-breasted Sabrewing   M-TS
Campylopterus duidae
4½" (12cm)
Bill = head, straight. Above shiny bronzy green. Spot behind eye rufous. Underparts drab buff.

8. White-tailed Sabrewing   LM-F
Campylopterus ensipennis
5½" (14cm)
Bill = head, curved. Mostly glittering green. Throat glittering violet. All but central tail feathers mostly white. ♀: Grayer below with white streak below eye.

9. Santa Marta Sabrewing   MH-FS
Campylopterus phainopeplus
5½" (14cm)
Bill = head, curved. Mostly glittering green. *Crown, throat* and breast glittering blue. *Tail blue-black.* ♀: Shining green above. Gray below. Tail green with outer feathers tipped gray.

10. Napo Sabrewing   L-F
Campylopterus villaviscensio
5" (13cm)
Bill 1¼x head, curved. Crown glittering golden green. Above shining bronzy green. *Throat and breast glittering violet-blue.* Belly gray with green spangles. Tail dark blue. ♀: *Dull gray below.* Outermost tail feathers narrowly tipped gray.

11. Swallow-tailed Hummingbird
L-SO

Eupetomena macroura   6" (15cm)
Bill = head. Head, neck and breast violet-blue, rest of plumage shining or bronzy green. *Tail long, deeply forked, dark blue.*

12. Black Jacobin   LM-FTS
Melanotrochilus fuscus
4¼" (11cm)
Bill = head. Black except rump and wing coverts bronzy olive. All but central tail feathers white tipped black. ♀: Chestnut band on sides of throat, feathers of upperparts fringed chestnut, only outer tail feathers white.

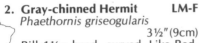

1. Brown Violetear   LM-TS
Colibri delphinae   4½" (12cm)
Bill ¾x head. Mostly brown, tinged rufous on rump. Patch on *ear coverts violet*. Throat glittering green, bordered by whitish whisker. Tail bronzy olive with dull coppery purple subterminal band.

2. Green Violetear   MH-TO
Colibri thalassinus   4¼" (11cm)
Bill = head. Very like Sparkling Violetear (34-2) but is much smaller and has no purple on breast or belly. *Tail with dusky bar near end.*

3. Green-breasted Mango   L-TS
Anthracothorax prevostii
4½" (12cm)
Bill 1¼x head. Very like Blackthroated Mango (24-3) but black stripe on underparts does not extend below breast. Belly all shining green.

4. Fiery-tailed Awlbill   L-FT
Avocettula recurvirostris
3½"(9cm)
Bill upturned at tip, shorter than head. Above shining green. Throat and breast glittering green. *Center of belly black.* Tail violet above, coppery below. ♀: White below with black stripe down center of throat and breast. Tail tipped white.

5. Ruby-topaz Hummingbird   L-TS
Chrysolampis mosquitus   3"(8cm)
Bill ¾x head. *Crown and nape glittering red.* Back, wings and line back of eye dark brown. *Throat and breast glittering orange.* Belly brown. ♀: Above coppery green. Below smoky gray. Tail olive with black band and white tip.

6. Violet-headed Hummingbird
LM-FTS
Klais guimeti   3½" (9cm)
Bill ½x head. *Entire head and throat shining violet-blue. Small spot behind eye white.* Otherwise shining green above, grayish flecked with green below. Tail green with dusky band and whitish tip. ♀: Lacks violet-blue. Crown bluish green, otherwise green above, grayish below.

7. Purple- (Black-) Breasted Plovercrest   LM-FT
Stephanoxis lalandi   3½"(9cm)
Bill ½x head, thin. *Conspicuous long thin crest black.* Spot behind eye white. Above shining green. Below glittering purple in center, gray on sides. ♀: Lacks crest.

8. Dot-eared Coquette   LM-TS
Lophornis gouldii   2¾"(7cm)
Bill ½x head, red, tipped black. Mostly green. *Long plumes from cheeks white,* tipped green. *White band across rump.* Tail rufous. ♀: Like ♀ Tufted Coquette (30-12).

9. Frilled Coquette   LM-TS
Lophornis magnifica   2¾"(7cm)
Bill ½x head, red, tipped black. Mostly green. *White plumes, tipped green, look like a fan covering sides of neck. White band across rump.* ♀: Throat rufous, rest of underparts bronzy green.

10. Rufous-crested Coquette   LM-TS
Lophornis delattrei   2¾"(7cm)
Bill ½x head, red, tipped black. *Crown and crest rufous. No cheek plumes.* Mostly green, white band across rump. Tail mostly rufous. ♀: Lacks ornamentation. Tail cinnamon with broad black band near end.

11. Spangled Coquette   LM-S
Lophornis stictolopha   2¾"(7cm)
Bill ½x head, red, tipped black. *Crest red, feathers tipped black.* Throat green. No cheek plumes. Mainly bronzy green with white rump band. Tail reddish. ♀: *Throat whitish.* Tail greenish tipped grayish.

12. Festive Coquette   L-TS
Lophornis chalybea   3"(8cm)
Bill ¾x head, black. *Long cheek plumes green.* Above shining green. Rump band white. Below grayish. Tail purple. ♀: Lacks plumes and has broad white whiskers.

1. **Peacock Coquette**   **M-F**
Lophornis pavonina   3½" (9cm)
Bill ½x head. *Cheek plumes green with large black spots.* Above bronzy green, white band across rump. Throat black. Below dark green. Tail bronzy green. ♀: Bronzy green, throat and breast white *streaked blackish.*

2. **Wire-crested Thorntail**   **LM-FT**
Popelairia popelairii   4½" (12cm)
Bill ½x head. *Crest of very long wire-like feathers.* Above bronzy green, white band across rump. Below black. Tail very long, feathers narrow, pointed. ♀: No crest. Coppery green above, black below. Whiskers and rump band and flank patch white. Tail normal.

3. **Black-bellied Thorntail**   **L-FT**
Popelairia langsdorffi   5" (13cm)
Bill ¾x head. Above bronzy green, band across rump white. Throat and breast glittering green. *Belly black.* Tail very long, wire-like. ♀: Throat black. *Whiskers,* rump band and flank patch *white.* Tail normal.

4. **Coppery Thorntail**   **L-FT**
Popelairia letitiae   4" (10cm)
Bill ¾x head. Head, throat and breast glittering golden green. *Above shining reddish brown,* rump band white. Belly green. Tail wire-like.

5. **Green Thorntail**   **L-FT**
Popelairia conversii   4" (10cm)
Bill ¾x head. Green, rump coppery, band white. *Blue spot on breast.* Tail long, wire-like. ♀: Green above, blackish below. Whiskers, rump band and flank patch white. Tail normal.

6. **Racket-tailed Coquette**   **L-FT**
Discosura longicauda   4" (10cm)
                          ♀ 2½" (6½cm)
Bill ½x head. Head and throat green. Back and sides bronzy green, rump band buff. Below blackish spotted coppery. *Tail very long, deeply forked, outer feathers ending in rackets.* ♀: Tail normal.

7. **Coppery Emerald**   **LM-TS**
Chlorostilbon russatus   3" (8cm)
Bill ½x head. Very small. Above coppery green. Below green. Tail golden coppery on upper surface, dusky beneath. ♀: Grayish below. Tail coppery with darker subterminal band.

8. **Narrow-tailed Emerald**   **MH-TS**
Chlorostilbon stenura   3" (8cm)
Bill ¾x head. Above shining green. Below all green. *Tail shining green.* ♀: Green above, whitish below. White streak behind eye. Ear patch blackish. Tail shining green with blackish band near end and *broad white tip.* Occurs usually over 1900 meters.

9. **Green-tailed Emerald**   **LM-TS**
Chlorostilbon alice   3" (8cm)
Bill ¾x head. Above shining green. Below green. *Tail shining green.* ♀: Tail with *small white tip.* Usually under 1800 meters. The most common of the three green-tailed Emeralds.

10. **Short-tailed Emerald**   **LM-TS**
Chlorostilbon poortmanni
                          3½" (9cm)
Almost identical to two preceding shining green-tailed species and probably not safely distinguished in field. Occurs mostly at 800–2100 meters elevation.

11. **Long-tailed Woodnymph**   **L-FT**
Thalurania watertonii   5" (13cm)
Bill = head. Rather like Fork-tailed Woodnymph (28-7) but *tail longer and more deeply forked.* Crown shining green. *Back glittering purple.* Tail blue-black. ♀: Very like ♀ Fork-tailed Woodnymph (28-8) but tail longer and more forked.

12. **Sapphire-throated Hummingbird**
Lepidopyga coeruleogularis **L-S**
                          3½" (9cm)
Bill = head, lower mandible flesh color. All shining green except *throat and breast glittering violet blue.* Tail blackish, forked. ♀: Below white with green spangles on sides. Outer tail feathers tipped whitish.

1. Sapphire-bellied Hummingbird
L-S

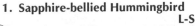

Lepidopyga lilliae 3½" (9cm)
Bill = head, lower bill flesh color.
Above shining green. Throat glittering purple. Breast shining blue-green. *Belly glittering deep blue.*

2. Golden-tailed Sapphire **LM-TS**
Chrysuronia oenone 4¼" (11cm)
Bill = head, *lower bill pink,* tipped black. Very like Blue-headed Sapphire (26-2) but head more purple and tail shining golden copper.

3. Violet-capped Hummingbird
LM-F

Goldmania violiceps 4" (10cm)
Bill ¾x head, lower bill pinkish tipped black. Mostly bright shining green, with *contrasting bright violet blue crown.* Tail rich chestnut tipped golden bronzy. ♀: Green above. Below white with gray spots on throat and green spots on sides. Tail tipped whitish.

4. Pirre Hummingbird **L-F**
Goethalsia bella 4" (10cm)
Bill ¾x head. Mostly green. *Forehead, lores and chin rufous chestnut. Conspicuous patch in wing and outer tail feathers cinnamon.* Vent white. ♀: Forehead green. Breast whitish, below cinnamon buff.

5. Tepui Goldenthroat **M-SO**
Polytmus milleri 5" (13cm)
Bill = head, curved. Rather like White-tailed Goldenthroat (28-11) but *bill all black and no white at eye.* Above golden bronze. Below glittering golden green. Tail broadly white at base and on tips.
♀: Smaller. Throat and breast white, spotted green. Belly grayish.

6. Buffy Hummingbird **L-SA**
Leucippus fallax 4" (10cm)
Bill 1¼x head, lower bill pinkish tipped black. Above dull dusty green. *Below uniform buff,* white on center of belly and vent. Tail olive green, broadly tipped white.

7. Tumbes Hummingbird **L-A**

Leucippus baeri 4¼" (11cm)
Bill 1¼x head. Crown dull brownish. Above dusty dull green. *Below pale gray with no spotting.* Tail mostly gray with black subterminal band.

8. Spot-throated Hummingbird **L-A**
Leucippus taczanowskii
4½" (12cm)
Bill 1¼x head, rather heavy, black. Above dull dusty green. White spot behind eye. Below pale gray, *throat with small but conspicuous green spots.* Tail dull olive green.

9. Olive-spotted Hummingbird
LM-SA

Leucippus chlorocercus 4" (10cm)
Bill = head. Above dull dusty green. Small white spot behind eye. *Below* grayish white inconspicuously *spotted and mottled with dull green.* Tail green, outer feathers tipped grayish.

10. Many-spotted Hummingbird
L-SA

Taphrospilus hypostictus 5" (13cm)
Bill 1¼x head. Above shining green. Small white spot behind eye. *Below white thickly spotted with green* except on center of belly. Tail blue green, not forked.

11. Green-and-white Emerald (Hummingbird) **LM-TS**

Amazilia viridicauda 4¼" (11cm)
Bill 1¼x head. Above shining green. *Below white, sides of body broadly green.* Tail green tipped white, tips broader towards sides.

12. White-bellied Hummingbird
MH-TS

Amazilia chionogaster 4¼" (11cm)
Bill 1¼x head. Above shining green. Below white, sides of body green. Tail bronzy green with *outer feather entirely white.*

1. Tachira Emerald L-T
Amazilia distans 3½" (9cm)
Bill 1¼x head, slightly curved, lower red at base. Very like Glittering-throated Emerald (26-9) but crown glittering blue-green and breast glittering blue. Throat blue, spotted white. Line down center of underparts gray on belly.

2. Sapphire-spangled Emerald L-TS
Amazilia lactea 3½" (9cm)
Bill 1¼x head, lower bill flesh color, tipped black. Like Glittering-throated Emerald (26-9) but throat and breast glittering violet-blue, the feathers edged gray. *Broad line down center of belly white.*

3. Blue-chested Emerald (Hummingbird) L-T
Amazilia amabilis 3½" (9cm)
Bill 1¼x head. Like Purple-chested Emerald (26-12) but crown glittering green and *breast glittering violet blue* (not green). Belly gray. Tail blackish. ♀: Black disks on throat.

4. Andean Emerald M-TS
Amazilia franciae 4" (10cm)
Bill 1¼x head, base of lower bill flesh color. Crown glittering blue. Sides of head and neck glittering green. Above shining green. *Rump and tail bright coppery. Below pure white,* some green on sides of breast and flanks.

5. Green-bellied Emerald (Hummingbird) LM-TS
Amazilia viridigaster 4" (10cm)
Bill 1¼x head. Like Steely-vented Emerald (26-11) but tail shining purple or purplish chestnut (not blue black). *Rump bronzy brown.*

6. Chestnut-bellied Emerald (Hummingbird) M-TS
Amazilia castaneiventris 4" (10cm)
Bill 1¼x head, pink with dark tip. Like Rufous-tailed Emerald (26-6) but above shining reddish bronzy (not bronzy green) and *belly rich chestnut (not gray).*

7. Amazilia Emerald (Hummingbird) LM-TOA
Amazilia amazilia 4" (10cm)
Bill 1¼x head, red, tipped dusky. Above bronzy green. *Rump and tail rufous.* Throat glittering green. *Below white, broadly rufous on sides* (breast glittering bluish green in interior s Ecuador and n Peru).

8. Bronze-tailed Plumeleteer L-FT
Chalybura urochrysia 4" (10cm)
Bill 1¼x head, black. Like White-vented Plumeleteer (28-1) but rump and tail greenish bronzy. *Feet pink.*

9. Sombre Hummingbird L-TS
Aphantochroa cirrhochloris 4" (10cm)
Bill ¾x head, black. Above light grayish green. Below dull gray, throat and breast inconspicuously spotted pale green. Tail bronzy black.

10. Blossomcrown M-F
Anthocephala floriceps 3" (8cm)
Bill ¾x head, black. *Forecrown buffy white,* rearcrown more chestnut. Above shining green. White spot behind eye. Rump and tail bronzy green, tail broadly tipped white. Below uniform grayish buff. ♀: Crown brownish.

11. Ecuadorian Piedtail L-FT
Phlogophilus hemileucurus 3" (8cm)
Bill ¾x head. Above shining green. Below white, throat and belly spotted green, *band of immaculate white from sides of neck across breast.* Tail dark blue green, white at base, and broadly tipped white.

12. Peruvian Piedtail L-F
Phlogophilus harterti 3" (8cm)
Bill ¾x head. Above shining green. *Underparts whitish,* pale buff on breast. Tail rounded, central feathers like back but with large blackish area near end, outer feathers buff with broad black diagonal band.

1. Violet-fronted Brilliant   M-FT

Heliodoxa leadbeateri   5″ (13cm)
Bill = head. Like Green-crowned Brilliant (34-5) but *crown glittering violet,* (no spot on throat). Tail mostly black. ♀: Like ♀ Green-crowned Brilliant (34-6).

2. Velvet-browed Brilliant   M-TSO

Heliodoxa xanthogonys
4¼″ (11cm)
Bill = head. *Lower bill orange at base.* Like Green-crowned Brilliant (34-5) but center of crown golden green, rest of crown black. Spot on throat blue. ♀: Like ♀ Green-crowned Brilliant (34-6) but belly coppery green.

3. Pink-throated Brilliant   L-F

Heliodoxa gularis   4½″ (12cm)
Bill = head. Shining green. *Spot on throat glittering pink.* Some white on center of breast. Center of belly gray. Vent white, prominent. ♀: Has white whisker.

4. Rufous-webbed Brilliant   L-F

Heliodoxa branickii   4½″ (12cm)
Bill = head. Dark shining green. *Throat patch glittering rosy red. Rufous edges on primaries.* Tail dark blue, forked.

5. Scissor-tailed Hummingbird M-F

Hylonympha macrocerca
♂ 8″ (20cm)   ♀ 5″ (13cm)
Bill = head, rather heavy. Crown glittering violet. Face black. Above shining dark green. Throat and breast glittering green. Belly blackish. *Tail black, very long, deeply forked.* ♀: Throat and breast white spotted green. *Belly rufous chestnut.* Tail normal length, outer feathers tipped white.

6. Crimson Topaz   L-F

Topaza pella   7½″ (19cm)
Bill = head, rather heavy. Head black. Back purple, rump golden. Throat glittering yellow, outlined in black. Below glittering crimson. Tail rufous, *two feathers greatly elongated, crossing* ♀: Green, throat red. Tail shorter, rufous.

7. Fiery Topaz   L-F

Topaza pyra   8″ (20cm)
Bill = head, rather heavy. Head black. Back purple, rump green. Throat glittering golden green, outlined in black. Breast and belly glittering orange-red. Tail mostly blackish, *two feathers greatly elongated, crossing.* ♀: Green, throat reddish. Tail shorter, no rufous.

8. Andean Hillstar   H-O

Oreotrochilus estella   5″ (13cm)
Bill = head. Above dull green. Throat green or violet, bordered below by narrow black line. *Below white, narrow chestnut stripe down center.* Tail white, central and outer feathers black. ♀: Throat white spotted green. Below grayish.

9. White-sided Hillstar   H-O

Oreotrochilus leucopleurus
5″ (13cm)
Bill = head. Head and throat green or violet, bordered below by narrow black line. Back dull green. *Below white with broad black stripe down center.* Tail central and outer feathers black, rest white. ♀: Throat white, spotted green. Below grayish.

10. Black-breasted Hillstar   H-O

Oreotrochilus melanogaster
4¼″ (11cm)
Bill = head. Above dark shining green. *Throat and sides of neck glittering emerald green. Below black,* sides browner. Tail blackish. ♀: Throat white spotted green. Tail dark, tipped white.

11. Wedge-tailed Hillstar   H-O

Oreotrochilus adela   5″ (13cm)
Bill 1¼x head. Above dull green, crown brownish. Throat and sides of neck glittering emerald green. *Below black, sides broadly chestnut.* Tail brown. ♀: Throat white, heavily spotted blackish. Below cinnamon.

12. Giant Hummingbird   H-TS

Patagona gigas   9″ (22cm)
Bill 1½x head. *Very large,* in flight more resembling a swift than a hummingbird. Above olive brown, *rump contrastingly whitish.* Below uniform dull cinnamon, vent white. Tail forked, bronzy olive.

1. **White-tufted Sunbeam** **H-TS**
Aglaeactis castelnaudii 5" (13cm)
Bill 1¼x head. Like Shining Sunbeam (34-9) but *underparts dark
brown with white patch on center
of breast.* Rump purple (not green
as in Shining Sunbeam).

2. **Purple-backed Sunbeam** **H-TS**
Aglaeactis aliciae 5" (13cm)
Bill = head. Rather like Shining
Sunbeam (34-9) but lores, chin,
band across upper breast, lower
belly and vent all white. *Lower
back and rump glittering purple.*

3. **Black-hooded Sunbeam** **H-TS**
Aglaeactis pamela 4½" (12cm)
Bill = head. Black. Lower back and
rump glittering green. Patch on
center of breast white. Tail bright
coppery rufous.

4. **Black Inca** **M-FT**
Coeligena prunellei 5½" (14cm)
Bill 1½x head. Mostly black, throat
and shoulders glittering blue and
*conspicuous white patch on each
side of breast.*

5. **Golden-bellied Starfrontlet**
MH-FTS
Coeligena bonapartei 5" (13cm)
Bill 1½x head. Above shining
green, *becoming glittering orange
on rump.* Wings with *prominent
rufous patch on coverts. Large violet patch on throat.* Breast glittering green. Belly orange. ♀: Throat
and breast buffy with small green
spots. Belly cinnamon.

6. **Dusky Starfrontlet** **H-F**
Coeligena orina 5½" (14cm)
Bill 1¼x head. *Uniform dark shining green,* spot on throat glittering
blue.

7. **Blue-throated Starfrontlet**
MH-FTS
Coeligena helianthea 5" (13cm)
Bill 1¼x head. *Mostly greenish
black.* Forehead glittering green.
Rump glittering blue green. Blue
patch on throat. *Belly rosy violet.*
♀: Shining green above. Below
cinnamon, spotted green on sides.
Belly with spots of glittering rosy
violet.

8. **Violet-throated Starfrontlet**
M-FT
Coeligena violifer 6" (15cm)
Bill 1½x head. Above bronzy
green. Crown black. *Rump and
tail rufous.* Throat and breast
green, *glittering violet patch on
throat.* Band of white across breast
(lacking in Bolivia). Belly cinnamon. ♀: Crown green and no
throat patch.

9. **Rainbow Starfrontlet** **MH-FTS**
Coeligena iris 5" (13cm)
Bill 1½x head. Crown changing
from green to fiery orange to violet. Back bronzy green. Throat
and breast glittering green with
patch of blue on throat. *Rump,
belly, wings and tail all rufous
chestnut.*

10. **Green-backed Firecrown** **LM-TS**
Sephanoides sephaniodes
4¼" (11cm)
Bill = head. Above dark green.
Crown glittering red. Below whitish speckled green. ♀: Lacks red
crown.

11. **Chestnut-breasted Coronet** **M-FT**
Boissonneaua matthewsii
4½" (12cm)
Bill = head. Above shining green.
Generally similar to Buff-tailed
Coronet (36-9) but *below chestnut*
thickly speckled with glittering
green disks. Tail mostly chestnut
tipped and edged green. ♀: Throat
buff spotted green.

12. **Velvet-purple Coronet** **LM-FT**
Boissonneaua jardini 4½" (12cm)
Bill = head. *Forecrown, throat and
most of underparts glittering purple.* Head and breast black. Broad
whisker rufous. Above glittering
blue-green. Tail mostly white
edged and tipped black, central
feathers also black. ♀: Breast and
belly mixed with green.

1. Orange-throated Sunangel
MH-TS

Heliangelus mavors 4¼" (11cm)
Bill ½x head. Above, including tail, shining green. Face black. Small forehead, *throat and breast glittering reddish orange,* bordered below by broad cinnamon buff breast band. Center of belly buff, sides green. ♀: Throat buff spotted dusky.

2. Merida Sunangel **MH-FT**
Heliangelus spencei 4" (10cm)
Bill ½x head. Very like Amethyst-throated Sunangel (38-7) but outer tail feathers dull blackish (not blue black). ♀: Throat black.

3. Gorgeted Sunangel **M-FT**
Heliangelus strophianus 4" (10cm)
Bill ½x head. Very like Amethyst-throated Sunangel (38-7) but belly dark gray instead of buff and tail all steel blue, larger and noticeably forked. ♀: Throat blackish streaked white.

4. Purple-throated Sunangel
MH-FTS

Heliangelus viola 4½" (12cm)
Bill ½x head. Very like Tourmaline Sunangel (38-8) but breast and belly all glittering green (belly not dusky). Forehead glittering blue green. ♀: Lacks purple throat.

5. Black-breasted Puffleg **H-TS**
Eriocnemis nigrivestis 3½" (9cm)
Bill = head. *Blackish.* Rump shining dark blue. Throat and vent glittering violet blue. White leg puffs conspicuous. ♀: Mostly shining bronzy green. Rump glittering blue green. Throat glittering light blue.

6. Turquoise-throated Puffleg **H-TS**
Eriocnemis godini 4" (10cm)
Bill = head. Like Glowing Puffleg (36-2) but back is lighter green and underparts more emerald green.

7. Blue-capped Puffleg **MH-FT**
Eriocnemis glaucopoides
3½" (9cm)

Bill = head. *Forecrown glittering blue.* Above shining green. Below glittering golden green, bluer on belly. Vent glittering violet-blue. Conspicuous white leg puffs. Tail forked, blue-black. ♀: Shining green above. Below uniform cinnamon.

8. Emerald-bellied Puffleg **M-FT**
Eriocnemis alinae 3½" (9cm)
Bill = head. Above bronzy green. Forehead and most of underparts glittering green. *Oval patch on center of breast white.* Large white leg puffs. Tail short, slightly forked, green.

9. Black-thighed Puffleg **H-S**
Eriocnemis derbyi 4" (10cm)
Bill = head. Mostly shining coppery green. Upper tail coverts glittering green, contrasting with short, slightly forked black tail. Vent glittering green. *Leg puffs black.* ♀: Throat and breast white spotted green. *Leg puffs mixed black and white.*

10. Hoary Puffleg **LM-F**

Haplophaedia lugens 4" (10cm)
Bill = head. Like Greenish Puffleg (36-6) but *underparts dark gray,* feathers of throat and breast edged whitish. Leg puffs white.

1. Black-tailed Trainbearer MH-SO
Lesbia victoriae   10" (25cm)
Bill ½x head. Very like Green-tailed Trainbearer .(38-4) but *tail mostly black (instead of greenish)* and *much longer,* about twice the length of the body. ♀: Below white, speckled green. Tail as in ♂ but much shorter.

2. Red-tailed Comet   H-S
Sappho sparganura   7½" (19cm)
Bill = head. Shining green, back purple. Throat glittering golden green. Below shining green. *Tail about as long as body, deeply forked, glittering rosy red.* ♀: Above shining green. Throat buffy spotted green. Below white. Tail shorter.

3. Bronze-tailed Comet   MH-TS
Polyonymus caroli   5" (13cm)
Bill = head. Bronzy green. *Patch on throat and breast glittering rosy violet.* Tail rather long, forked, outer web of outer feather whitish. ♀: Throat spotted glittering orange. Belly grayish spotted green.

4. Black-backed Thornbill   H-TS
Ramphomicron dorsale 4" (10cm)
Bill ⅓x head. Like Purple-backed Thornbill (38-11) but *back black* and throat glittering olive. Below dark gray mottled green and white. ♀: Rather like ♀ Purple-backed Thornbill (38-12) but spotted below only on throat and flanks.

5. Black Metaltail   MH-TSO
Metallura phoebe   5" (13cm)
Bill ¾x head. *Brownish black.* Throat patch glittering green. Small white spot behind eye. Tail shining purple or gold, golden copper below.

6. Coppery Metaltail   H-TS
Metallura theresiae   4" (10cm)
Bill ½x head. *Mostly reddish coppery green,* reddest on head. Throat patch glittering green. Small white spot behind eye. Tail shining blue-green, green below.

7. Scaled Metaltail   MH-TS
Metallura aeneocauda 4¼" (11cm)
Bill ¾x head. Mostly bronzy green. Throat patch glittering green. Small white spot behind eye. *Feathers of underparts green, narrowly tipped buffy giving scaly appearance.* Tail blue or coppery. Below bronzy green. ♀: Throat whitish.

8. Violet-throated Metaltail H-SOA
Metallura baroni   4¼" (11cm)
Bill ½x head. Mostly dark bronzy green. *Patch on throat and center of breast glittering violet purple.* Tail green or purple, below green.

9. Fire-throated Metaltail   H-TS
Metallura eupogon   4" (10cm)
Bill ½x head. Mostly bronzy green. *Throat patch glittering fiery red.* Tail blue or coppery, below green.

10. Viridian Metaltail   H-TSO
Metallura williami   4" (10cm)
Bill ¾x head. Coppery green. Throat patch glittering green (black in s Ecuador). Small white spot behind eye. *Tail blue or green, below coppery.* ♀: Throat and breast cinnamon buffy lightly spotted green, lower underparts spotted whitish.

11. Perija Metaltail   MH-T
Metallura iracunda   4¼" (11cm)
Bill ½x head. *Mostly black,* strongly glossed with coppery greenish. Crown dark shining green. Throat patch glittering green. *Tail glittering purplish red* (above and below).

12. Rufous-capped Thornbill MH-FT
Chalcostigma ruficeps   4" (10cm)
Bill ½x head. *Crown rufous.* Above bronzy green. Rather short tail bronzy olive. Narrow throat patch glittering blue-green, becoming golden green. *Below buffy, spotted green.*

1. Olivaceous Thornbill   H-O

Chalcostigma olivaceum
5½"(14cm)
Bill ½x head. *Mostly uniform grayish olive.* Narrow throat patch glittering green, becoming golden violet and then violet-red. Rather long tail shining olive green.

2. Blue-mantled Thornbill   H-O

Chalcostigma stanleyi 4½" (12cm)
Bill ½x head. Crown dusky greenish blue. *Back purplish blue.* Narrow throat patch glittering green, becoming violet-blue. Below bronzy green. Tail rather long, blueblack.

3. Bronze-tailed Thornbill   H-O

Chalcostigma heteropogon
4½"(12cm)
Bill ½x head. Mostly bronzy green. Rump more coppery. *Tail quite long slightly forked, coppery bronze.* Narrow throat patch glittering green becoming rosy violet.

4. Rainbow-bearded Thornbill

H-SO
Chalcostigma herrani 4"(10cm)
Bill ½x head. Crown rufous. Above bronzy green. Rump reddish coppery. *Narrow throat patch glittering green becoming orange* and then red. Tail rather long, outer feathers broadly tipped white. ♀: Buffy brown below (no throat patch), spotted green on breast and sides.

5. Bearded Helmetcrest   H-O

Oxypogon guerinii 4¼" (11cm)
Bill ⅓x head. *Conspicuous long crest and long beard white.* Face black, collar white. Above greenish. Below buffy. ♀: Lacks crest and beard. Above bronzy olive with whitish collar.

6. Bearded Mountaineer   H-O

Oreonympha nobilis 6"(15cm)
Bill 1¼x head. Crown maroon bordered by violet-blue. Above olive. *Below white with narrow throat patch glittering green.* Tail long, deeply forked, mostly white. ♀: Tail shorter.

7. Mountain Avocetbill   H-FT

Opisthoprora euryptera 4"(10cm)
Bill ½x head, *slightly upturned at tip.* Above shining green. White spot behind eye. *Below white thickly spotted green.* Tail blueblack, narrowly tipped white.

8. Gray-bellied Comet   H-TO

Tephrolesbia griseiventris
6"(15cm)
Bill = head. Above shining bronzy green. Large throat patch glittering blue. Below pale gray. Tail very long and deeply forked, mostly blue.♀: Lacks throat patch and has shorter tail.

9. Hooded Visorbearer   M-S

Augastes lumachellus 4"(10cm)
Bill = head. Bronzy green. Forehead and throat glittering golden green. Crown and sides of head and neck velvety black. *Pointed spot of glittering red below throat.* Breast band white. Tail glittering golden bronzy above, golden orange below. ♀: Lacks black on head.

10. Hyacinth Visorbearer   M-S

Augastes scutatus 3"(8cm)
Bill = head. Above bronzy green. Forehead and throat glittering golden green edged black. Sides of neck purplish blue. Breast band white. Belly dark blue. Tail glittering bronzy green. ♀: Lacks black on head.

11. Black-eared Fairy   L-FT

Heliothryx aurita 4"(10cm)
Bill = head. Very like Purplecrowned Fairy (30-11) but crown green (not purple).

12. Horned Sungem   L-SO

Heliactin cornuta 4"(10cm)
Bill ½x head. Above golden green. "Horns" on sides of crown glittering red, usually not conspicuous. *Sides of head and throat black. Below white.* Tail long, strongly graduated, mostly white. ♀: Lacks "horns" and has no black on head. Tail shorter, with diagonal black band near base.

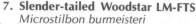

1. Marvelous Spatuletail   H-FT
Loddigesia mirabilis   4½" (12 cm)
Bill ½x head. Crown and crest glittering purple. Back bronzy green. Throat glittering blue. *Below white with black stripe down center.* Tail greatly lengthened, *ending in large purple rackets.* ♀: Tail shorter, rackets smaller.

2. Stripe-breasted Starthroat
LM-TSO
Heliomaster squamosus 5" (13 cm)
Bill 2x head. Above green. Throat glittering violet-red. Below greenish black with *white line down center.* ♀: Throat blackish, feathers edged white.

3. Blue-tufted Starthroat   L-TSO
Heliomaster furcifer   5" (13 cm)
Bill 1½x head. Crown glittering green. Above green. Throat glittering violet-red. *Long tufts on sides of neck, entire underparts glittering blue.* Tail forked. ♀: *White stripe below eye.* Below pale gray, sides spotted green. Tail shorter.

4. Oasis Hummingbird   LM-SA
Rhodopis vesper   5" (13 cm)
Bill 2x head, curved. Above shining green, rump rufous. Throat glittering violet-red. Below whitish. Tail long, deeply forked. ♀: Lacks red on throat. Tail shorter, rounded.

5. Peruvian Sheartail   LM-SA
Thaumastura cora 4" (10 cm) + tail
Bill ½x head. Above shining green. *Throat* glittering *violet-red. Breast white.* Belly light grayish spotted green on sides. *Tail very long, deeply forked, mostly white.* ♀ Below all whitish. Tail short.

6. Purple-throated Woodstar
LM-FT
Philodice mitchellii   3" (8 cm)
Bill ⅔x head. Above bronzy green. Throat and sides of neck glittering violet-red. Breast white. Belly green, *flanks broadly chestnut.* Tail purplish, forked. ♀: Throat whitish. Breast dusky. *Below rufous chestnut.*

7. Slender-tailed Woodstar LM-FTS
Microstilbon burmeisteri
2¾" (7 cm)
Bill ½x head. Above dark shining green. *Throat glittering violet-red.* Below gray, breast and flanks spotted green. *Tail long, deeply forked.* White patch on sides of rump. ♀: *White stripe behind eye.* Below cinnamon. Tail short, mostly cinnamon, black band near end.

8. Amethyst Woodstar   L-TS
Calliphlox amethystina   3" (8 cm)
Bill ¾x head. Above shining green. White spot behind eye. *Throat glittering ruby red. Breast white. Below gray, speckled green.* Tail long, deeply forked. ♀: Throat buffy flecked red. Below cinnamon. Tail not forked.

9. Purple-collared Woodstar
LM-SO
Myrtis fanny   3" (8 cm)
Bill = head. Above bronzy green. *Throat and sides of neck glittering blue,* bordered below with a violet band. Below whitish. Tail fairly long, forked. ♀: Lacks blue throat. Tail short, blackish, tipped white.

10. Chilean Woodstar   L-OA
Eulidia yarrellii   3" (8 cm)
Bill ¾x head. Above green. *Throat glittering violet-red. Below white.* Tail forked. ♀: No red throat. *Underparts buffy.* Tail short, black, broadly tipped white.

11. Short-tailed Woodstar   L-SA

Myrmia micrura   2¾" (7 cm)
Bill ¾x head. Above pale green. Whitish whisker. Throat and sides of neck glittering violet-red. Below whitish. *Tail black, very short.* ♀: Below buff. Tail tipped white.

12. White-bellied Woodstar MH-TS
Acestrura mulsant   3" (8 cm)
Bill = head. Above dark green. *White stripe behind eye.* Throat glittering violet-red, bordered below by white band. Breast green. *Belly broadly white. Tail short,* forked. ♀: Below buffy. Tail short with black band near end.

1. Little Woodstar L-TS
Acestrura bombus 2¾" (7cm)
Bill ⅓x head. Bronzy green. *Stripe behind eye buff. Throat glittering violet-red bordered below by buff band across breast. Tail forked* ♀: Cinnamon buffy below. Tail short, mostly cinnamon with black band near end.

2. Gorgeted Woodstar M-FTS
Acestrura heliodor 2¾" (7cm)
Bill ½x head. Above bluish green. Small white spot behind eye. *Throat glittering violet red.* Breast white. Belly green. Tail forked. ♀: Rump rufous. Below uniform cinnamon. Tail not forked.

3. Esmeraldas Woodstar L-TS
Acestrura berlepschi 2¾" (7cm)
Bill ½x head. Bronzy green. *Stripe behind eye and breast band white. Throat glittering violet-red.* ♀: White below.

4. Rufous-shafted Woodstar LM-TS
Chaetocercus jourdanii 2¾" (7cm)
Bill ½x head. Above bronzy green. Small white spot behind eye. *Throat and sides of neck glittering rosy red,* bordered below by white band. Below dark green. Tail forked. ♀: Throat buff. Breast green. Belly cinnamon buff. Tail cinnamon with black band near end.

5. Crested Quetzal M-F
Pharomachrus antisianus
11" (28cm)
Bill yellow. Frontal crest bushy. Upperparts, throat and breast green. Belly red. Tail central feathers black, outers all white. ♀: Bill blackish. Head brown. Above green. Below mostly brown. Belly and vent red. Tail barred black and white.

6. White-tipped Quetzal M-FT
Pharomachrus fulgidus 11" (28cm)
Bill yellow. Upperparts, throat and breast green. Belly red. Tail black, outers tipped white. ♀: Bill blackish. Head brown. Above green. Below mostly brown. Belly and vent red. Outer tail feathers tipped white and barred on both webs.

7. Golden-headed Quetzal LM-F
Pharomachrus auriceps
12" (30cm)
Bill yellow. Upperparts, throat and breast green. Belly red. *Tail all black.* ♀: Bill brown, ridge black. Above green. Below brown. Tail all black.

8. Pavonine Quetzal L-F
Pharomachrus pavoninus
12" (30cm)
Bill red. Upperparts, throat and breast green. Belly red. Undertail all black. ♀: Bill black, red at base. Head brown. Above bronzy green. Below brown, mottled green on breast.

9. Slaty-tailed Trogon L-FT
Trogon massena 11" (28cm)
Bill reddish. Eye-ring orange. Face and throat black. Upperparts and breast green. Wing coverts finely lined white. Breast red. *Underside of tail black* ♀: Gray with red belly.

10. Black-tailed Trogon LM-F
Trogon melanurus 11" (27cm)
Like Collared Trogon (40-3) but underside of tail all blackish. ♀: Gray with red belly.

11. Blue-tailed Trogon LM-F
Trogon comptus 11" (27cm)
Bill yellow. Eye conspicuously bluish white. *No eye-ring.* Upperparts and breast greenish blue. *No white band on breast.* Tail bluish. ♀: Gray with red belly.

12. Blue-crowned Trogon L-FT
Trogon curucui 9" (24cm)
Bill greenish. Back green. *Crown and breast blue with indistinct white bar.* Belly red. Outer tail feathers barred black and white. ♀: Like ♀ Surucua Trogon (40-1) but outer tail feathers broadly barred white.

1. **Belted Kingfisher**   **LM-TSW**
Ceryle alcyon   11" (27cm)
Like Ringed Kingfisher (42-1) but
breast and belly white with gray
(♀ chestnut) band across breast.

2. **Chestnut Jacamar**   **L-T**
Galbalcyrhynchus leucotis
7½" (19cm)
Bill heavy, pink, tipped dusky.
Crown, wings and tail blackish.
Body chestnut. *Ear coverts white
in w part of range.*

3. **Brown Jacamar**   **L-FT**
Brachygalba lugubris   6¼" (16cm)
Above brown. Rump, wings and
tail black. Throat light brown.
Breast brown. *Belly white or pale
buff.*

4. **Pale-headed Jacamar**   **L-TS**
Brachygalba goeringi   6¼" (16cm)
Crown and nape brownish white.
Back, wings and tail dark brown.
Throat white. Breast brown. Belly
white, crossed by rufous band.

5. **Dusky-backed Jacamar**   **L-FT**
Brachygalba salmoni   6¼" (16cm)
Above glossy blackish brown.
Throat white. Breast blackish. Belly
rufous. ♀: Throat pale buff.

6. **White-throated Jacamar**   **L-FT**
Brachygalba albogularis
6¼" (16cm)
Above blackish. *Sides of head and
throat white.* Breast and sides
blackish. Belly rufous.

7. **Three-toed Jacamar**   **L-FT**
Jacamaralcyon tridactyla
6¼" (16cm)
*Whole head chestnut streaked
buffy.* Back blackish. Breast and
belly white, sides dusky.

8. **Green-tailed Jacamar**   **L-FT**
Galbula galbula   8" (20cm)
Above metallic green. Throat white
(♀ buff). Breast green. Belly rufous. *Tail green above, blackish
below.*

9. **Bluish-fronted Jacamar**   **L-FT**
Galbula cyanescens   8" (21cm)
Very like White-chinned Jacamar
(42-10) but *crown blue* instead of
brown.

10. **Coppery-chested Jacamar**   **M-FT**
Galbula pastazae   9" (23cm)
Like Rufous-tailed Jacamar (42-9)
but crown blue and prominent eye-
ring orange.

11. **Bronzy Jacamar**   **L-FT**
Galbula leucogastra   8" (21cm)
A very dark Jacamar. Head dark
bronzy. Back and breast purplish
bronze. Throat and belly white
(buff in ♀). Tail bronzy, outer
feathers edged and tipped white.

12. **Great Jacamar**   **L-F**
Jacamerops aurea   11" (28cm)
Bill heavy, curved. Upperparts and
throat shining green. Narrow white
band below throat (lacking in ♀).
Below rufous. Tail bluish green
above, green below.

1. **White-necked Puffbird** L-TS
Notharchus macrorhynchus
9"(23cm)
Bill heavy, hooked. Upperparts, line through eye and breast band black. Forehead, cheeks, collar, throat and belly white (belly buff in s part of range).

2. **Black-breasted Puffbird** L-FT
Notharchus pectoralis 7½"(19cm)
Mostly bluish black. Large patch on ear coverts white. Below white with broad breast band black.

3. **Brown-banded Puffbird** L-FT
Notharchus ordii 7½"(19cm)
Upper parts and narrow breast band black. Cheeks, throat and narrow forehead white. Lower breast brown. Belly white, flanks barred black. Tail black, tipped white.

4. **Pied Puffbird** L-FT
Notharchus tectus 5½"(14cm)
Crown black speckled white. Long eyebrow white. Above black with white patch on wing. Below white with broad black band across breast.

5. **Collared Puffbird** L-F
Bucco capensis 7"(18cm)
Bill orange, ridge black. Head and face bright cinnamon rufous. Back brown narrowly banded black. *Collar and breast band black.* Throat white. Belly pale buff. Tail rufous, narrowly barred black.

6. **Barred Puffbird** L-F
Nystalus radiatus 8"(20cm)
Bill grayish. *Above brown, barred black,* collar on hindneck buff. *Below buff narrowly barred black.* Tail rufous barred black.

7. **Striolated Puffbird** L-FT
Nystalus striolatus 8"(20cm)
Above dark brown. Collar buff. Throat and belly white. *Breast buff streaked black.* Tail black barred cinnamon.

8. **Russet-throated Puffbird** L-TSO
Hypnelus ruficollis 9"(23cm)
Above brown, spotted whitish. Cheeks white. Narrow collar white. *Below buff with one or two black bars across breast.*

9. **White-chested Puffbird** L-F
Malacoptila fusca 7½"(19cm)
Rather like Crescent-chested Puffbird (44-5) but no black band on breast. Bill orange with black ridge and tip. Whiskers white. Belly whitish.

10. **Semi-collared Puffbird** L-F
Malacoptila semicincta
7½"(19cm)
Rather like Crescent-chested Puffbird (44-5) but bill orange and has a *rusty collar on hindneck.* No black band on breast. Belly whitish.

11. **Black-streaked Puffbird** LM-FT
Malacoptila fulvogularis 9"(23cm)
Head black narrowly streaked whitish. Back brown streaked buff. Whiskers white. *Throat and breast uniform buff with no white crescent.* Belly white heavily streaked black.

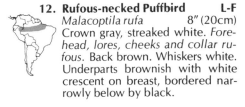

12. **Rufous-necked Puffbird** L-F
Malacoptila rufa 8"(20cm)
Crown gray, streaked white. *Forehead, lores, cheeks and collar rufous.* Back brown. Whiskers white. Underparts brownish with white crescent on breast, bordered narrowly below by black.

1. Lanceolated Monklet   **LM-F**
Micromonacha lanceolata
                 5"(13cm)
Bill short, rather thick. *Forehead and lores white.* Above brown, feathers fringed buff. *Below white streaked black.* Tail short.

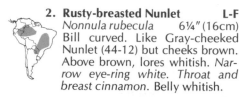

2. Rusty-breasted Nunlet   **L-F**
Nonnula rubecula   6¼"(16cm)
Bill curved. Like Gray-cheeked Nunlet (44-12) but cheeks brown. Above brown, lores whitish. *Narrow eye-ring white. Throat and breast cinnamon.* Belly whitish.

3. Fulvous-chinned Nunlet   **L-F**
Nonnula sclateri   6"(15cm)
Bill curved. Rather like Gray-cheeked Nunlet (44-12) but cheeks not gray. Forehead, lores and chin buff.

4. Brown Nunlet   **L-F**
Nonnula brunnea   6"(15cm)
Rather like Gray-cheeked Nunlet (44-12) but *above all dull brown.* Forehead and *underparts dull cinnamon.*

5. Chestnut-headed Nunlet   **L-F**
Nonnula amaurocephala
                 6"(15cm)
Rather like Gray-cheeked Nunlet (44-12) but entire head and sides of neck deep rufous chestnut.

6. White-faced Nunbird   **M-F**
Hapaloptila castanea   10"(25cm)
Bill heavy, black. Crown and sides of head gray, otherwise olive brown above. *Forehead, lores and throat white* outlined in black. *Below rufous chestnut.*

7. Black Nunbird   **L-FT**
Monasa atra   10"(26cm)
Like Black-fronted Nunbird (44-2) but *wing coverts broadly edged white.*

8. Orange-fronted Barbet   **LM-FT**
Capito squamatus   6¼"(16cm)
Forecrown orange. Crown and nape white. Above blue black. Below whitish tinged yellow on breast. ♀: Throat and breast black. Feathers on back fringed white.

9. White-mantled Barbet   **LM-F**
Capito hypoleucus   6¼"(16cm)
Forecrown red. Crown and nape white. Back blue black. Throat white. Breast buffy. Belly yellow, paler in center.

10. Five-colored Barbet   **L-F**
Capito quinticolor   6¼"(16cm)
Crown and nape red (♀ black streaked yellow). Above black with yellow wing-bars. Throat white. *Breast and belly orange.* Flanks olive mottled black.

11. Black-girdled Barbet   **L-F**
Capito dayi   6¼"(16cm)
Crown red (♀ black). Back black with white patch in center. *Throat and cheeks tawny olive,* finely barred black. Below buffy to yellowish. Vent red.

12. Scarlet-hooded Barbet   **LM-TS**
Eubucco tucinkae   5½"(14cm)
Crown and sides of head red. Back golden olive. Collar yellowish. Throat yellow. Breast orange. ♀: Crown and face red like ♂.

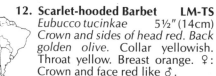

1. **Versicolored Barbet** **M-FT**

Eubucco versicolor 5½" (14cm)
Head red, bordered by blue band.
Whisker blue or yellow. Back and
tail green. Below yellowish. ♀:
Head and throat blue. Crescent on
breast red.

2. **Toucan Barbet** **LM-F**
Semnornis ramphastinus
6½" (17cm)
Bill heavy, yellow, tipped dusky.
Crown black. *Eyebrow white.*
Above brown. Rump yellow.
Cheeks, throat, breast and vent
gray. Belly red.

3. **Groove-billed Toucanet** **M-F**
Aulacorhynchus sulcatus
13" (33cm)
Mainly green. *Bill mostly red and
black,* narrow white line at base.
Area around eye blue. Throat blue
gray.

4. **Yellow-billed Toucanet** **LM-F**
Aulacorhynchus calorhynchus
13" (33cm)
Green, throat bluish. Rather like
Emerald Toucanet (48-11) but with
no chestnut in the tail. *Upper bill
mostly yellow,* lower mostly black.
Narrow white line at base of bill.

5. **Chestnut-tipped Toucanet** **LM-F**
Aulacorhynchus derbianus
14" (35cm)
Green. Like Crimson-rumped Toucanet (48-10) but rump not red.
Bill black tipped dark red, white
line at base. *Area around eye and
nape blue.* Throat bluish white.

6. **Blue-banded Toucanet** **M-F**

Aulacorhynchus coeruleicinctis
15" (37cm)
Green. Bill leaden gray (no white
line at base). Short line behind eye
bluish white. Rump dark red.
Throat white. Breast band blue.
Central tail feathers tipped chestnut.

7. **Yellow-browed Toucanet** **M-F**

Aulacorhynchus huallagae
15" (37cm)
Green. Bill leaden gray with narrow white line at base. *Line behind eye yellow.* Throat whitish.
Blue band across belly. Central tail
feathers tipped chestnut.

8. **Chestnut-eared Araçari** **L-FT**

Pteroglossus castanotis 17" (42cm)
Bill black, upper with *brown stripe
and yellow "teeth".* Crown and
breast black. Above dark green.
Rump red. Throat, cheeks and collar chestnut. Below yellow, with
single red band across belly.

9. **Black-necked Araçari** **L-FT**
Pteroglossus aracari 16" (40cm)
Like Many-banded Araçari (48-5)
but lacks black band across breast
and *band across belly is all red.*

10. **Green Araçari** **L-FT**
Pteroglossus viridis 11" (28cm)
Upper bill red with yellow on
ridge, lower black with red at base.
Back, wings and tail greenish.
Head and throat black (♀ chest-
nut). Rump crimson. *Below yel-
low, no bands.*

11. **Lettered Araçari** **L-FT**
Pteroglossus inscriptus 11" (28cm)
*Bill yellowish with black ridge and
tip.* (Lower bill black in nw part of
range). Above greenish, rump red.
Underparts yellow. ♀: Crown
black, (sides of head, neck and
throat chestnut).

12. **Red-necked Araçari** **L-F**

Pteroglossus bitorquatus
13" (33cm)
Back, wings and tail slaty green.
Upper bill yellow, lower white with
black at tip (or lower all black in
one race). Head blackish. *Nape,
mantle and rump red.* Throat
chestnut edged black below. Broad
breast band red. Belly yellow.

1. Brown-mandibled Araçari   L-FT
Pteroglossus mariae   15" (38cm)
Very like Ivory-billed Araçari (48-6) but lower bill brown with lighter tip.

2. Curl-crested Araçari   L-FT
Pteroglossus beauharnaesii
17" (44cm)
Upper bill blackish, lower white. *Crown shiny black.* Face and throat yellowish white with black dots. Mantle and rump red. Wings, tail and center of back dull green. *Below yellow with red band across belly.*

3. Yellow-eared Toucanet   LM-F
Selenidera spectabilis   14" (36cm)
Upper bill greenish gray, lower black. Above olive green. Crown, nape and underparts glossy black. *Ear coverts bright yellow.* Tail slaty. ♀: Crown and nape chestnut. Lacks yellow ear coverts.

4. Guianan Toucanet   L-F
Selenidera culik   12" (30cm)
Bill black, red at base. Head, neck and underparts mostly black. *Ear coverts and collar yellow.* Back olive green. Wings and tail slaty. ♀: Chestnut collar and all gray underparts.

5. Golden-collared Toucanet   L-F
Selenidera reinwardtii   12" (30cm)
Bill *dark red, black at tip.* Back, wings and tail olive green. Head and underparts black with *yellow ear coverts and collar.* ♀: Head and underparts chestnut.

6. Tawny-tufted Toucanet   L-F
Selenidera nattereri   12" (30cm)
Bill dark red with irregular black markings. Back, wings and tail olive green. Head and underparts black with *yellow ear coverts tipped tawny.*

7. Spot-billed Toucanet   L-F
Selenidera maculirostris
12" (30cm)
Upper bill black with broad olive tip (or whitish with black ridge and three black spots in n part of range). Head and underparts black (♀ chestnut). *Ear coverts and collar yellow.* Back, wings and tail olive green.

8. Saffron Toucanet   L-FT
Baillonius bailloni   15" (37cm)
Bill olive, red at base. *Above dark olive green,* forecrown yellowish. Rump red. *Underparts yellow.*

9. Plate-billed Mountain-Toucan
M-F
Andigena laminirostris 19" (47cm)
Bill black with red base and *raised pale yellow plate at base of upper bill.* Crown and nape black. Above bright olive brown. Rump yellow. *Underparts light blue,* patch on sides of breast yellow.

10. Gray-breasted Mountain-Toucan
H-F
Andigena hypoglauca 19" (48cm)
Bill mostly red, yellow at base. Lower tipped black. Crown black. Above brownish olive, rump yellow. *Collar and underparts blue gray.* Tail black tipped chestnut.

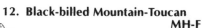

11. Hooded Mountain-Toucan   H-F
Andigena cucullata   20" (50cm)
Bill mostly olive green with tip and spot at base black. Above brownish olive. Crown black, nape light blue. *Throat and breast blackish.* Belly blue gray. Tail gray.

12. Black-billed Mountain-Toucan
MH-F
Andigena nigrirostris   21" (52cm)
Bill black. Crown and nape black. Back olive brown. Rump yellow. *Cheeks and throat white. Rest of underparts light blue.* Vent red.

1. **Yellow-ridged Toucan** **L-FT**
Ramphastos culminatus
18"(45cm)
Very like Citron-throated Toucan
(48-3) but *throat and breast white*
instead of yellow. Bill mostly black
with yellow ridge and tip.

2. **Red-breasted Toucan** **L-FT**
Ramphastos dicolorus 18"(45cm)
Bill green, black at base. Upperparts black. Throat yellow. Breast
orange. Below all red. Thighs and
tail black.

3. **Choco Toucan** **L-FT**
Ramphastos brevis 19"(47cm)
Very like Keel-billed Toucan (48-
2) but *upper bill mostly yellow
with green along ridge* and black
at base. Lower bill black.

4. **Chestnut-mandibled Toucan L-FT**
Ramphastos swainsonii 22"(56cm)
Very like Keel-billed Toucan (48-
2) but upper bill mostly yellow,
tinged green on ridge, dark chestnut at base. Lower bill dark chestnut tipped black.

5. **Black-mandibled Toucan** **LM-FT**
Ramphastos ambiguus 23"(58cm)
Very like Keel-billed Toucan (48-
2) but upper bill mostly yellow,
black at base. Lower bill black.

6. **Red-billed Toucan** **L-FT**
Ramphastos tucanus 22"(56cm)
Rather like Citron-throated Toucan (48-3) but bill dark red, upper
yellow on ridge and at base, lower
gray at base. *Throat and breast
white.* Belly black. A local race
with bill light orange-red instead
of dark red was carried as Orange-
billed Toucan, *Ramphastos aurantiirostris* in BSA.

7. **Cuvier's Toucan** **LM-F**
Ramphastos cuvieri 20"(50cm)
Like Citron-throated Toucan (48-
3) but throat and breast extensively white. Ridge and base of bill
yellowish green.

8. **White-bellied Piculet** **L-TS**
Picumnus spilogaster 3"(8cm)
Forecrown red, hindcrown black
spotted white. Above brown.
Below white with a few brown
spots or streaks on sides. ♀: Crown
all black spotted white.

9. **Ochraceous Piculet** **L-TS**
Picumnus limae 3"(8cm)
Forecrown red, hindcrown black
spotted white. Above light brown.
Cheeks whitish flecked dusky.
Throat whitish. Below yellowish.
♀: Crown all black, spotted white.

10. **Grayish Piculet** **M-TS**
Picumnus granadensis 3"(8cm)
Crown black, *spotted yellow in
front,* white behind. Above brown-
ish gray. Below grayish white. ♀:
Crown black all spotted white.

11. **Black-dotted Piculet** **L-FT**
Picumnus nigropunctatus
3"(8cm)
Crown black, streaked red. Above
yellowish olive, feathers with black
bar giving scaled appearance. Underparts pale yellow, barred black
on throat and *spotted black below.*

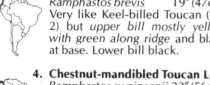

1. **Golden-spangled Piculet   LM-FT**
Picumnus exilis   3″ (8cm)
Crown black, spotted red in front,
white behind (♀ all spotted white).
*Above olive, spotted pale yellow
and black.* Underparts yellowish
barred black.

2. **Bar-breasted Piculet   L-F**
Picumnus borbae   3″ (8cm)
Crown black, spotted red in front,
white behind (♀ all spotted white).
Above olive. Throat whitish. Below
yellowish *barred black on breast
and streaked black on belly.*

3. **Gold-fronted Piculet   L-FT**
Picumnus aurifrons   2¾″ (7cm)
Crown dark brown, spotted orange in front, white behind (♀ all
spotted white). *Above barred yellow and olive* (or plain olive in w
Brazil). Below yellowish white,
barred black (in Peru and Brazil,
belly streaked black).

4. **Ochre-collared Piculet   L-F**
Picumnus temminckii   3″ (8cm)
Above brownish. *Cheeks and collar bright buff.* Below white with
broad black bars.

5. **Ocellated Piculet   LM-F**
Picumnus dorbygnianus 3″ (8cm)
Above grayish brown obscurely
spotted white (or back feathers
edged pale gray in Peru). Below
white, *feathers centered black giving scaled appearance.*

6. **Ecuadorian Piculet   L-TS**
Picumnus sclateri   3″ (8cm)
Forecrown black dotted yellow,
hindcrown dotted white. Above
brown, faintly barred whitish.
Below white heavily barred black.

7. **Speckle-chested Piculet   LM-F**
Picumnus steindachneri 3″ (8cm)
Above brownish gray scaled paler.
Throat whitish. *Breast black, spot-
ted white.* Belly banded black and
white.

8. **Varzea Piculet   L-TW**
Picumnus varzeae   4¼″ (11cm)
Brown. Underparts sparsely dot-
ted white.

9. **Spotted Piculet   L-S**
Picumnus pygmaeus   4″ (10cm)
Brown, spotted white above and
thickly spotted white below.

10. **Orinoco Piculet   L-TS**
Picumnus pumilus   3½″ (9cm)
Above plain olive, forecrown black
dotted yellow (♀ dotted white).
Hindcrown pale brown dotted
white. *Below yellowish narrowly
barred black.*

11. **Chilean Flicker   LM-TSO**
Colaptes pitius   12″ (30cm)
Crown gray. Cheeks and throat
whitish. Whisker red. Back blackish barred buff. *Rump white. Below
barred black and white.* Tail black
barred on edges.

12. **Campo Flicker   M-TO**
Colaptes campestris   11″ (28cm)
Like Field Flicker (50-8) but *throat
black* instead of white. Tail black,
outer feathers barred.

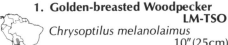

1. Golden-breasted Woodpecker LM-TSO
Chrysoptilus melanolaimus
10″(25cm)
Like Green-barred Woodpecker (52-1) but *sides of head black*. Back black barred yellowish white. Breast strongly shaded orange. Belly whitish, spotted black.

2. Black-necked Woodpecker LM-TS
Chrysoptilus atricollis 10″ (25cm)
Crown gray, nape red. Above olive barred black. *Sides of head white. Neck, throat and breast black.* Whisker red (♀ lacking). Below whitish barred black.

3. Yellow-throated Woodpecker L-F
Piculus flavigula 8″ (20cm)
Crown, nape and whisker red. Back olive. Face and neck yellow. *Throat yellow* (or red in se Brazil). *Below white conspicuously scalloped olive.* ♀: Only nape red. No whisker.

4. White-throated Woodpecker L-F
Piculus leucolaemus 8″ (20cm)
Crown and whisker red. Above olive. Face and neck yellow. *Throat white.* Breast olive spotted whitish. Belly yellowish barred dusky. ♀: Whisker yellow.

5. White-browed Woodpecker L-F
Piculus aurulentus 8½″ (21cm)
Crown and nape red. *Face gray bordered white above and below.* Back olive. Throat yellow. Below banded olive and white. ♀: Only nape red. Crown olive.

6. Golden-green Woodpecker L-FT
Piculus chrysochloros 8½″ (21cm)
Very like Golden-olive Woodpecker (52-3) but crown all red (♀ olive green), face dark gray (instead of white) and has *narrow yellow line under eye*. Back olive. Underparts barred yellowish and olive.

7. Pale-crested Woodpecker L-T
Celeus lugubris 8½″ (21cm)
Crest and throat yellow. Back black barred yellow. Below brown, feathers edged chestnut in some races.

8. Scale-breasted Woodpecker L-FT
Celeus grammicus 8½″ (21cm)
Very like Chestnut Woodpecker (50-3) but barred black on back (or almost unbarred in Colombia and Ecuador). *Rump yellow.* Underparts obviously scaled black. Tail black. ♀: No whisker.

9. Waved Woodpecker L-FT
Celeus undatus 8½″ (21cm)
Rather like Chestnut Woodpecker (50-3) but upperparts (including rump) with broad wavy black bars. Underparts regularly barred black. Tail rufous barred black. ♀: No whisker.

10. Cream-colored Woodpecker L-FT
Celeus flavus 9½″ (24cm)
Head, prominent crest, back, rump and underparts *all light yellow.* Whisker red. Wings show much brown and chestnut. Tail black. ♀: No whisker.

11. Rufous-headed Woodpecker L-F
Celeus spectabilis 10″ (26cm)
Head light chestnut. Line from behind eye to crest red. Body buff spotted black, rump unspotted. Wings chestnut. *Throat and breast black.* ♀: No whisker.

12. Ringed Woodpecker L-FT
Celeus torquatus 10″ (26cm)
Head cinnamon. Whisker red. *Collar and breast black.* Back and rump chestnut. *Below buff* (or back, wings and belly barred black in Guianas and e Venezuela). Tail chestnut barred black. ♀: No whisker.

1. Black-bodied Woodpecker L-TS
Dryocopus schulzi   12" (29cm)
Like Lineated Woodpecker (50-1)
but *all black below* with a few dull
white bars at sides.

2. Helmeted Woodpecker   LM-F
Dryocopus galeatus   11" (27cm)
*Forehead, throat and sides of head
buff.* Long crest, nape and whisker
crimson. Back, wings and tail
black. Rump whitish. Underparts
regularly barred black and buff.

3. Acorn Woodpecker   MH-T
Melanerpes formicivorus
                        9" (22cm)
Face white. Crown red. Above and
throat black. *Prominent white
patch on primaries.* Rump white.
Belly white streaked black. *Melanerpes* Woodpeckers do not have
red whisker.

4. Red-fronted Woodpecker   L-TS
Melanerpes rubrifrons   7" (18cm)
Differs from Yellow-tufted Woodpecker (50-11) only in no white
and yellow band on nape. Is now
considered a sub-species of *Melanerpes cruentatus.*

5. Yellow-fronted Woodpecker I-T
Melanerpes flavifrons 6½" (17cm)
Forecrown and throat yellow. Nape
scarlet. Above black. Rump white.
Breast olive. Belly red, sides barred
black and white.

6. Black-cheeked Woodpecker L-FT
Melanerpes pucherani 6½" (17cm)
Crown, nape and center of belly
red. *Cheeks black. Above mostly
black narrowly barred white.* Rump
white. Below buffy whitish barred
black on sides of belly.

7. Golden-naped Woodpecker L-FT
Melanerpes chrysauchen
                        6½" (17cm)
Crown and center of belly red.
Nape yellow. Cheeks black. Rump
and *center of back white.* Below
buffy grayish barred black on
breast and sides of belly. Wing
coverts and tail black. ♀: Mid-
crown black.

8. White-fronted Woodpecker
                        LM-S
Trichopicus cactorum 6¼" (16cm)
Forecrown and below eye white.
Crown, face and wing coverts
black. Back black with white line
down center. Throat yellow. Below
pale smoky gray.

9. White-spotted Woodpecker
                        LM-F
Veniliornis spilogaster 6¼" (16cm)
Crown brown streaked red (♀
white). Above barred olive and
yellow. *Broad line behind eye and
whisker white.* Throat white,
streaked gray. Below gray, spotted
white. Tail black with pale bars.
Veniliornis Woodpeckers do not
have red whisker.

10. Dot-fronted Woodpecker   LM-F
Veniliornis frontalis   6¼" (16cm)
Like Little Woodpecker (52-10) but
crown dotted white, back spotted
yellowish and tail brown barred
buffy. ♀: Gray nape instead of red
as in ♂.

11. Yellow-eared Woodpecker LM-F
Veniliornis maculifrons 6" (15cm)
Forecrown brown, streaked whitish. Hindcrown red. Nape and
sides of head yellow. Back olive.
Below white barred dusky. Tail
black barred brownish.

12. Golden-collared Woodpecker
                        L-FT
Veniliornis cassini   5½" (14cm)
Like Red-stained Woodpecker (52-
5) but *rump not red* and tail
notched white on edges instead of
all blackish.

1. Blood-colored Woodpecker L-TS
Veniliornis sanguineus 5" (13cm)
Above crimson. Below gray, barred white. Tail black. ♀: Crown brown, pale-spotted.

2. Bar-bellied Woodpecker H-F
Veniliornis nigriceps 7½" (19cm)
Crown and nape red. Back olive tinged red in places. *Below barred dark olive and whitish.* Tail black, outer feathers barred. ♀: Crown and nape black.

3. Checkered Woodpecker L-TS
Picoides mixtus 6" (15cm)
Crown brownish black. *Red spot at sides of nape.* Long white line back of eye. Back, wings and tail barred. Below white streaked black. ♀: Lacks red spot at sides of nape.

4. Striped Woodpecker LM-TS
Picoides lignarius 6" (15cm)
Crown black, sides of nape red. Broad line behind eye white. Back barred black and white. Below white streaked black. Tail blackish, barred brownish. ♀: Lacks red on nape.

5. Guayaquil Woodpecker L-F
Campephilus gayaquilensis
12½" (32cm)
Crest, top and sides of head crimson. Small black and white spot on cheek. White lines down sides of neck join in a "V" on back. Throat, neck, back, wings and tail black. Rump barred brownish black and buff. ♀: Very like ♀ Crimson-crested Woodpecker (50-2) but browner.

6. Cream-backed Woodpecker LM-FT
Campephilus leucopogon
11" (28cm)
Head and neck red with black streak on cheek. Above and below black, *center of back buff.* ♀: Crown and crest black, streak below eye white.

7. Red-necked Woodpecker L-F
Campephilus rubricollis
12" (30cm)
Entire head and neck red. Back, wings and tail all black, *Below chestnut.* ♀: Line under eye white.

8. Robust Woodpecker LM-F
Campephilus robustus
12½" (32cm)
Entire head and neck red. Back whitish. Wings and tail black. *Below barred black and white.* ♀: White line below eye.

9. Powerful Woodpecker MH-F
Campephilus pollens 12½" (32cm)
Crown red, sides of head black. Broad white stripes down neck form "V" on back. *Rump white. Throat black.* Below barred buff and black. ♀: Crown black.

10. Crimson-bellied Woodpecker LM-F
Campephilus haematogaster
13" (33cm)
Crown and hindneck red. Ear coverts black bordered above and below by buff lines. Rump red. Throat black, below red. ♀: *Belly red, lined blackish.*

11. Magellanic Woodpecker LM-F
Campephilus magellanicus
14" (36cm)
Long recurved crest and head red. Rest of plumage all black except some white in wing. ♀: Head and crest black, only base of bill red.

1. Long-tailed Woodcreeper   L-F
Deconychura longicauda
8" (20cm)
Bill ¾x head, slender, straight. Above brown, crown streaked buff. *Buffy eyebrow* and throat. *Rump brown.* Below brown, *streaked* (spotted w of Andes) *buffy on breast; tail noticeably long.*

2. Spot-throated Woodcreeper L-F
Deconychura stictolaema
6¼" (16cm)
Bill ¾x head. Above brown but *rump rufous.* Crown streaked buff. Eyebrow buffy. Throat and breast brown spotted buff.

3. Scimitar-billed Woodcreeper
L-TS
Drymornis bridgesii   12" (30cm)
Bill 2x head, curved. Above bright rufous. Long eyebrow and whisker white. Below buffy whitish, *boldly streaked dusky.* Often on ground.

4. Long-billed Woodcreeper   L-FT
Nasica longirostris   13" (33cm)
Bill 2x head, almost straight, whitish. Crown dark brown narrowly streaked buff. Long eyebrow white. Above chestnut, streaked on nape and upper mantle. Throat white. Below light brown, boldly streaked white on breast.

5. Cinnamon-throated
Woodcreeper   L-FT
Dendrexetastes rufigula 9" (23cm)
Bill ¾x head, heavy, horn color. Mostly brown, paler below. Breast with faint whitish black-edged streaks (streaks obvious in Guianas and n Brazil).

6. Red-billed Woodcreeper   L-FT
Hylexetastes perrotii   11" (28cm)
Bill = head, heavy, dark red. Brown, somewhat paler below. Narrow gray line below eye. Whisker brown. Throat whitish. Race in Guianas and n Brazil has light dusky bars on belly.

7. Bar-bellied Woodcreeper   L-F
Hylexetastes stresemanni
10" (26cm)
Bill = head, heavy, red. Above brown. Below pale brown *streaked buffy on throat and breast* and barred black on belly.

8. Strong-billed Woodcreeper
LMH-F
Xiphocolaptes promeropirhynchus 11½" (28cm)
Rather like White-throated Woodcreeper (56-1). *Bill = head, very heavy,* slightly curved, horn color. Above rufous brown, streaked buff on crown and nape. *Eyebrow and stripe under eye white.* Throat whitish. Whisker dusky. Below brown streaked dusky.

9. Snethlage's Woodcreeper   L-F
Xiphocolaptes franciscanus
10" (26cm)
Like White-throated Woodcreeper (56-1) but lower bill light gray instead of black and crown not streaked. *White stripe under eye conspicuous.*

10. Moustached Woodcreeper   L-FT
Xiphocolaptes falcirostris
10" (26cm)
Bill = head. Like White-throated Woodcreeper (56-1) but bill more slender and horn color (not black). Streak under eye is golden buff. Underparts pale brown.

11. Great Rufous Woodcreeper L-TS
Xiphocolaptes major   12" (30cm)
Very large. Bill 1¼x head, heavy, slightly curved, blackish. *Uniform bright rufous.* Throat whitish. Breast faintly streaked whitish. Belly faintly barred blackish.

12. Concolor Woodcreeper   L-F
Dendrocolaptes concolor
10" (26cm)
Bill = head. Like Barred Woodcreeper (58-1) but bars either missing or very faint. Separate from Plain-brown Woodcreeper (58-3) by no gray on sides of head.

MINERS (Bill about ¾x head, somewhat curved. Terrestrial. Wing band visible only in flight)

1. Hoffmanns' Woodcreeper   L-F
Dendrocolaptes hoffmannsi
11"(27cm)
Bill = head, heavy, black. Brown with reddish tinge on crown, contrasting with back. Breast shaded olivaceous, very narrowly streaked buff.

2. Planalto Woodcreeper   LM-F
Dendrocolaptes platyrostris
10"(26cm)
Bill ¾x head, horn color. Much like White-throated Woodcreeper (56-1) but bill much smaller and horn color instead of black.

3. Elegant Woodcreeper   L-F
Xiphorhynchus elegans 8"(20cm)
Bill ¾x head, lower dusky. Like Spix's Woodcreeper (56-6) race with spots on breast. *Back quite prominently spotted buff.*

4. Dusky-billed Woodcreeper L-FTS
Xiphorhynchus eytoni 10"(25cm)
Bill 1¼x head, black except base of lower bill pale. Like Buff-throated Woodcreeper (56-4) but *upper back boldly streaked white* and white streak back of eye prominent. *Throat whitish.* Below brown, streaked white on breast.

5. Black-striped Woodcreeper   L-F
Xiphorhynchus lachrymosus
9"(23cm)
Bill 1¼x head, heavy. *Above blackish boldly streaked buffy white.* Throat *whitish.* Below whitish *boldly streaked black.*

6. Lineated Woodcreeper   L-F
Lepidocolaptes albolineatus
7½"(19cm)
Bill = head, slender, curved, pale. Like Spot-crowned Woodcreeper (58-9) with streaks below. *Crown with no streaks or very small spots.* Above uniform reddish brown. Throat buff. Below streaked with black-bordered buff marks.

7. Brown-billed Scythebill   M-F
Campylorhamphus pusillus
10"(25cm)
Bill 1½x head, much curved, light brown. Like Black-billed Scythebill (54-11) but bill not as long. Above and below brown streaked buffy. Crown blackish. Throat buffy.

8. Curve-billed Scythebill   L-F
Campylorhamphus procurvoides
9"(24cm)
Bill 2x head, much curved, brownish. Very like Red-billed Scythebill (54-12) but most of back unstreaked and bill brownish instead of reddish.

9. Campo Miner   L-O
Geobates poecilopterus 4"(10cm)
Above brown. Throat white, below buff, streaked dusky on breast. Wings brown with rufous band. Tail rufous, tipped black.

10. Grayish Miner   LM-OA
Geositta maritima   4½"(12cm)
Bill slender. Above pale sandy gray. Below whitish, flanks buffy. Wings uniform gray (no band). Tail blackish, edged white.

11. Coastal Miner   L-OA
Geositta peruviana   5"(13cm)
Above light grayish brown. Below whitish. *Spread wings with cinnamon-buff band.* Tail brown and rusty, edged white.

12. Dark-winged Miner   H-O
Geositta saxicolina   5½"(14cm)
Above reddish brown. Wings uniform dusky *(no band).* Throat white, below pale buffy. Rump and tail buff, broadly tipped blackish.

1. Creamy-rumped Miner   H-O
Geositta isabellina   6" (15cm)
Above sandy brown. *No rufous band on wings.* Rump white, end of tail black. Below dull white.

2. Rufous-banded Miner   H-O
Geositta rufipennis   6" (15cm)
Bill ½x head, almost straight. Above light grayish brown. *Wings show bold rufous band* when spread. Throat white, below pale buffy grayish. *Flanks rufous.* Tail cinnamon-rufous broadly tipped black.

3. Puna Miner   H-O
Geositta punensis   5½" (14cm)
Grayish brown above. Wings show tawny band when spread. Rump creamy buff. Below creamy whitish, *no dusky breast streaking.*

4. Common Miner   LMH-O
Geositta cunicularia   6" (15cm)
Above grayish brown. Wings show tawny band when spread. Whitish below, breast streaked dusky. *Rump and base of tail creamy buff.* End of tail black.

5. Short-billed Miner   H-O
Geositta antarctica   5½" (14cm)
Bill ½x head, almost straight. Grayish brown above. Whitish below, breast sparsely streaked dusky. Spread wing band dull tawny.

6. Slender-billed Miner   H-O
Geositta tenuirostris   6½" (17cm)
Bill = head, slender, curved. Above sandy brown, eyebrow buffy. Below buffy whitish, *breast streaked dusky.* Spread *wings with chestnut band.* Short tail blackish, rufous on sides.

7. Thick-billed Miner   M-SO
Geositta crassirostris   6" (15cm)
Bill heavy, nearly straight. Brown above, eyebrow whitish. Throat whitish, underparts pale grayish. Spread wings with chestnut band. Tail brown and *rufous with broad black band near tip.*

8. White-throated Earthcreeper   H-SO
Upucerthia albigula   7" (18cm)
Bill = head, quite curved. Dark brown above. Obvious yellowish buff eyebrow. Throat white, feathers edged brown giving streaked look. Below pale yellowish buff, deeper on flanks.

9. Buff-breasted Earthcreeper   H-SO
Upucerthia validirostris 8" (20cm)
Bill 1¼x head, curved. Above light brown, with faint cinnamon eyebrow. *Below uniform buffy,* throat whiter. Spread wings with cinnamon band. Tail brown, cinnamon on sides.

10. Plain-breasted Earthcreeper   H-SO
Upucerthia jelskii   6½" (17cm)
Bill 1¼x head, curved. Above light brown with faint cinnamon eyebrow. Throat white. Below whitish, breast faintly streaked dusky.

11. Striated Earthcreeper   H-SO
Upucerthia serrana   7½" (19cm)
Bill 1¼x head, curved. Dark brown above, eyebrow white. Below whitish, *breast feathers edged dusky giving distinct streaked look.* Wings and tail chestnut brown.

12. Rock Earthcreeper   H-SO
Upucerthia andaecola   7" (18cm)
Bill 1¼x head, *only slightly curved.* Dark brown above, eyebrow tawny. Rump and upper tail coverts tinged rufescent. Below white, belly tinged brownish. Spread wings blackish with chestnut band. *Tail all rufous.*

Cinclodes are terrestrial birds of high rocky slopes or seacoasts.

1. Straight-billed Earthcreeper
H-SO
Upucerthia ruficauda 7" (18cm)
Bill 1¼x head, almost straight. Above brown, *eyebrow white.* Rump and upper tail coverts tinged rufescent. Below white, *breast and belly lightly streaked rufous.* Spread wings show pale rufous band. Tail rufous and black.

2. Chaco Earthcreeper
L-SO
Upucerthia certhioides
6¼" (16cm)
Bill 1¼x head, only slightly curved at tip. Brown above. *Forehead and sides of head rufous.* Throat white, below light grayish brown. Flanks tinged brownish.

3. Bolivian Earthcreeper
MH-TS
Upucerthia harterti 6" (15cm)
Bill 1¼x head, only slightly curved. Crown dark brown, eyebrow buffy whitish. Above brown, more rufous on rump, wings and tail. Throat white, below grayish white, tinged brown on flanks.

4. Band-tailed Earthcreeper
L-SO
Eremobius phoenicurus
6¼" (16cm)
Bill 1¼x head, almost straight. Eyering and eyebrow white. Above light grayish brown. Throat white. Below buffy grayish, faintly streaked whitish on breast. *Base of tail chestnut,* outer half black.

5. Crag Chilia
MH-S
Chilia melanura 7½" (19cm)
Bill straight. Above brown. *Lower back, rump and upper tail coverts rufous chestnut.* Throat and breast white, merging into gray belly. Tail black.

6. Stout-billed Cinclodes
H-O
Cinclodes excelsior 8" (20cm)
Brown above. Long eyebrow white. Spread wings show whitish band. Throat whitish, below light brown. Tail brown, edges and corners pale brown.

7. Blackish Cinclodes
L-OW
Cinclodes antarcticus 8" (20cm)
Uniform smoky grayish brown. No eye-stripe; *no* band on wing.

8. Dark-bellied Cinclodes
LM-OW
Cinclodes patagonicus
7½" (19cm)
Bill slightly curved. Long eyebrow white. Above dark brown. Throat whitish, *below dark grayish brown faintly streaked white.* Wings with buffy bar. Tail brown with pale corners.

9. Gray-flanked Cinclodes
LM-OW
Cinclodes oustaleti 6¼" (16cm)
Bill slightly curved. Above dark brown. Long eyebrow and throat whitish. Below gray streaked white. *Center of belly whitish.*

10. Bar-winged Cinclodes
LMH-OW
Cinclodes fuscus 6½" (17cm)
Bill ¾x head, slender, slightly curved. Brown above. Long eyebrow white. Throat whitish, below mostly light buffy brown. Spread wings show rufous, buff or whitish band. Tail brown, edged cinnamon.

11. White-bellied Cinclodes
H-OW
Cinclodes palliatus 8" (20cm)
Above grayish brown. *No white eyebrow.* Broad blackish streak through eye. Bold white band shows on open wing. Below pure white. Tail corners pure white.

12. Seaside Cinclodes
L-W
Cinclodes nigrofumosus 8" (20cm)
Easily recognized in its *rocky coastal habitat.* Mostly dark brown. Eyebrow white. Throat and streaks on underparts white. Tail blackish, outer feathers tipped buff.

1. Canebrake Ground-creeper   LM-FT
Clibanornis dendrocolaptoides
7½"(19cm)
Above brown. Crown, nape and tail chestnut. Eye-stripe grayish. *Throat and sides of neck white spotted black.* Below light brownish gray, brown on sides and vent.

2. Lesser Hornero   L-SO
Furnarius minor   5½" (14cm)
Like Pale-legged Hornero (60-8) but crown and upperparts brown. Legs reddish gray. Wings with buffy patch in flight.

3. Crested Hornero   L-S
Furnarius cristatus   6" (15cm)
Rather like Pale-legged Hornero (60-8) but crested and has no eyebrow. Pale brown above. Throat and center of belly white. Tail rufous.

4. Des Murs' Wiretail   LM-F
Sylviorthorhynchus desmursii
5½" (14cm) plus elongated tail. Above reddish brown. Below whitish. *Two elongated tail feathers very narrow, black, as long as head and body.*

5. Thorn-tailed Rayadito   LM-FT
Aphrastura spinicauda 3½" (9cm)
Head blackish with *conspicuous long buff eye-stripe.* Above brown, rump more rufous. Wings blackish with two cinnamon bars. Below white. Tail black and rufous ending in bare shafts about 1 cm long.

6. Andean Tit-Spinetail   H-S
Leptasthenura andicola
5½" (14cm)
Bill very small. Crown black streaked rufous. Prominent white eyebrow. Back dark brown streaked white. Throat whitish, *below brownish gray heavily streaked white.*

7. Streaked Tit-Spinetail   H-S
Leptasthenura striata 5½" (14cm)
Crown black streaked rufous. *No eye stripe.* Back dark brown streaked buff. Rump dark brown, unstreaked. Below dull grayish white, *almost unstreaked.*

8. Rusty-crowned Tit-Spinetail H-S
Leptasthenura pileata 5½" (14cm)
Crown solid rufous (no streaking). Eye stripe whitish. Back dark brown streaked white. Below grayish, distinctly streaked with whitish, except on belly.

9. White-browed Tit-Spinetail H-S
Leptasthenura xenothorax
5½" (14cm)
Crown rufous, unstreaked. *Conspicuous white eye-stripe.* Back blackish narrowly striped white. *Throat sharply streaked black and white.* Below gray.

10. Striolated Tit-Spinetail   LM-TS
Leptasthenura striolata 5½" (14cm)
Crown brown streaked black. Narrow buffy eye-stripe. Back brown streaked blackish. *Below pale buffy,* unstreaked.

11. Tufted Tit-Spinetail   L-S
Leptashenura platensis
5½"(14cm)
Crested. Crown brown, lightly streaked pale cinnamon. Back plain grayish brown. Throat white, *uniformly spotted black.* Below buffy.

12. Brown-capped Tit-Spinetail
MH-S
Leptasthenura fuliginiceps
5½"(14cm)
Crown chestnut. Back brown. Throat white, below pale buffy or grayish, unstreaked. Wings and tail rufous.

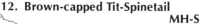

1. Tawny Tit-Spinetail   **H-TS**
Leptasthenura yanacensis
6" (15cm)
Above tawny brown, forecrown
and rump rufous. Eyebrow buff.
Below uniform tawny buff. Tail rufous.

2. Araucaria Tit-Spinetail   **LM-FT**
Leptasthenura setaria   6½" (17cm)
Crested. Crown black streaked
white. Above bright chestnut.
*Throat and breast white conspicu-
ously dotted dusky.* Below dull
buffy. Tail *very* long, mostly rufous.

3. Itatiaia Spinetail   **H-SO**
Oreophylax moreirae   6½" (17cm)
Upperparts brown, somewhat
darker on crown and slightly rufous on tail. Throat ochraceous,
below whitish.

4. Buff-browed Spinetail   **M-FT**
Synallaxis superciliosa 6½" (16cm)
Like Rufous-capped Spinetail (66-
2) but *forecrown olive.* Underparts
whitish instead of buffy.

5. Gray-browed Spinetail   **L-FT**
Synallaxis poliophrys   5" (13cm)
Rather like Azara's Spinetail (64-6)
but with whitish eyebrow and tail
much shorter.

6. Dusky Spinetail   **L-S**
Synallaxis moesta   6" (15cm)
Like Dark-breasted Spinetail (64-
9) but *tail rufous chestnut.* No
white on throat.

7. Cinereous-breasted Spinetail L-S
Synallaxis hypospodia   6" (15cm)
Like Chicli Spinetail (64-10) but
forehead brownish gray and underparts darker gray.

8. Silvery-throated Spinetail   **H-TS**
Synallaxis subpudica   6½" (17cm)
Like Chicli Spinetail (64-10) but
forecrown and center of belly
grayish. *Tail grayish brown, very
long.*

9. White-bellied Spinetail   **L-T**
Synallaxis propinqua   6" (15cm)
Above brown, tinged rufescent.
Wing coverts and tail rufous.
Throat silvery gray, *breast ashy
gray, center of belly white.*

10. Gray-bellied Spinetail   **LM-F**
Synallaxis cinerascens   5" (13cm)
Above uniform olivaceous brown.
Most of wings and tail rufous, *no
rufous on crown.* Upper throat
black, lower throat white. Below
uniform, rather dark, gray.

11. Blackish-headed Spinetail   **L-FT**
Synallaxis tithys   5½" (14cm)
*Only spinetail with black fore-
crown and face.* Above olive
brown. Wing coverts cinnamon,
but *no rufous on crown.* Throat
black speckled white. Below light
gray. Tail light dusky.

12. Stripe-breasted Spinetail LM-FT
Synallaxis cinnamomea 6" (15cm)
Head and back dark reddish
brown, wing coverts chestnut.
Throat streaked black and white.
Below brown streaked buff. Tail
dark brown.

1. Chestnut-throated Spinetail L-FT
Synallaxis cherriei   5" (13cm)
Very like brown backed forms of
Ruddy Spinetail (64-5) but *throat
dull chestnut,* not black.

2. Necklaced Spinetail   L-S
Synallaxis stictothorax 4½" (12cm)
Forehead streaked black and white.
Above brownish, wing coverts rufous. Eyebrow white. Below white,
*breast   conspicuously   streaked
dusky.*

3. Russet-bellied Spinetail   MH-T
Synallaxis zimmeri   6" (15cm)
Crown gray, becoming grayish rufescent on back and rufous on
rump.   Throat   gray,   vaguely
streaked whitish. *Below bright
cinnamon-rufous.*

4. Red-shouldered Spinetail   L-S
Gyalophylax hellmayri 6" (15cm)
Above light brownish gray. Neck
and sides of breast buffy brown.
Wing coverts bright rufous. *Throat
dull black.* Below light grayish,
center of belly buffy. Tail dusky.

5. Hoary-throated Spinetail   L-SO
Poecilurus kollari   5½" (14cm)
Like   White-whiskered   Spinetail
(66-4) but lores and cheeks pale
gray. Throat black lightly speckled
white. Tail all rufous without black
at end.

6. Ochre-cheeked Spinetail   L-FT
Poecilurus scutatus   5" (13cm)
Above grayish brown, wings and
tail rufous. *Lores and eyebrow
white,* eyebrow becoming buff behind eye. Cheeks and sides of neck
ochraceous. *Throat white,* bordered below by *narrow black
patch.* Below dull ochraceous,
center of belly white.

7. Sulphur-bearded Spinetail L-SW
Cranioleuca sulphurifera
                       5½" (14cm)
Above light brown. Eyebrow and
cheeks dull cinnamon. *Small but
prominent bright yellow patch on
center of throat.* Below mostly
whitish, *obscurely mottled gray on
breast.* Tail mostly rufous.

8. Gray-headed Spinetail   L-TS
Cranioleuca semicinerea
                       5" (13cm)
Head and neck pale gray. Back
and wings all chestnut. Below pale
buffy gray.

9. Crested Spinetail   LM-FT
Cranioleuca subcristata
                       5½" (14cm)
Like Streak-capped Spinetail (66-
9) but has no whitish eyebrow and
throat. *Crown dull olive brown,*
streaked blackish. Tail rufous.

10. Ash-browed Spinetail   M-F
Cranioleuca curtata 5½" (14cm)
Like Streak-capped Spinetail (66-
9) but *forehead is olivaceous.*
Crown is unstreaked chestnut and
eyebrow is gray instead of whitish.

11. Tepui Spinetail   M-FT
Cranioleuca demissa 5½" (14cm)
Crown all chestnut, unstreaked.
Back olive brown. Wings and tail
rufous. *Eyebrow and underparts
grayish.*

12. Pallid Spinetail   LM-FT
Cranioleuca pallida   5" (13cm)
Forehead whitish spotted black.
Above light reddish brown. *Bold
eyebrow white.* Below whitish.

1. Line-cheeked Spinetail   MH-TS

Cranioleuca antisiensis
6¼" (16cm)
Crown, wings and tail rufous. Back olivaceous brown or gray. *Bold eyebrow white,* ear coverts streaked whitish and black. Throat and breast white, belly dull brownish or grayish.

2. Marcapata Spinetail   H-F
Cranioleuca marcapatae
6¼" (16cm)
Above rufous. Sides of crown blackish. *Short whitish eyebrow.* Sides of head buffy grayish. Throat whitish, below pale grayish.

3. Light-crowned Spinetail   MH-F
Cranioleuca albiceps 5½" (14cm)
Crown and nape white or buffy, contrasting with blackish sides of head. Above rufous. Below gray.

4. Creamy-crested Spinetail   H-TS
Cranioleuca albicapilla
6¼" (16cm)
Forehead whitish, becoming cinnamon-buff on crown. Back olive-brown, wings and tail rufous. Short eyebrow and throat white. Below whitish, flanks and vent tinged olive.

5. Scaled Spinetail   L-F
Cranioleuca muelleri 5½" (14cm)
Crown rufous, forehead olive streaked buff. Eyebrow buff. Back brown. Wings and tail rufous. Underparts buffy olive scaled blackish.

6. Speckled Spinetail   L-F

Cranioleuca gutturata 5" (13cm)
Crown chestnut. Above olive brown. Wings and tail rufous. Narrow buff eyebrow. Chin yellowish. *All of underparts and sides of neck buffyish, distinctly speckled with dusky.*

7. Great Spinetail   MH-F

Siptornopsis hypochondriacus
6½" (17cm)
Bill black, rather thin and long. Above light brown, shoulders rufous. Long eyebrow and underparts white with band of dusky streaks across breast.

8. Ochre-browed Thistletail
MH-SO
Schizoeaca coryi   6½" (17cm)
Like White-chinned Thistletail (64-2) but long eyebrow, chin and sides of head cinnamon (not gray or white). Underparts grayish.

9. Mouse-colored Thistletail H-SO
Schizoeaca griseomurina
7" (18cm)
Very like White-chinned Thistletail (64-2) but lacks eyebrow. Has whitish eye-ring.

10. Eye-ringed Thistletail   MH-SO
Schizoeaca palpebralis 7" (18cm)
Like White-chinned Thistletail (64-2) but has *very prominent white eye-ring.* Chin orange-rufous (not white).

11. Puna Thistletail   H-SO
Schizoeaca helleri   7" (18cm)
Resembles White-chinned Thistletail (64-2) but eyebrow gray and prominent eye-ring white. Chin orange-rufous.

12. Black-throated Thistletail
MH-SO
Schizoeaca harterti   6½" (17cm)
Differs from all other thistletails in *throat black,* narrowly streaked white. Eye-ring and eyebrow whitish.

1. **Lesser Canastero** **LMH-SO**
Asthenes pyrrholeuca 6" (15cm)
Above uniform light grayish brown, wing coverts somewhat rufescent. Short whitish eyebrow. Throat orange-rufous (sometimes lacking). Below whitish. Tail rather long, center feathers brown, outer feathers rufous.

2. **Creamy-breasted Canastero**
MH-SO
Asthenes dorbignyi 6" (15cm)
Above light brown (darker grayish brown in Peru). *Wing coverts and rump rufous. Tail black,* edged rufous. Throat chestnut. Below whitish, *strongly rufescent on flanks* and vent.

3. **Chestnut Canastero** **H-SO**
Asthenes steinbachi 6" (15cm)
Above light drab brown. Rump cinnamon. Throat whitish edged dusky. *Below dull gray.* Tail brown, outer feathers bright cinnamon.

4. **Berlepsch's Canastero** **H-SO**
Asthenes berlepschi 6½" (17cm)
Above light brown. Rump rufous. *Wing coverts edged rufous.* Throat chestnut. Below whitish to buffy, strongly rufescent on flanks and vent.

5. **Short-billed Canastero** **L-S**
Asthenes baeri 5½" (14cm)
Bill short, rather heavy. Above light grayish brown, wing coverts rufous. Grayish eyebrow. Below whitish. Tail rather short, outer feathers rufous.

6. **Patagonian Canastero** **L-S**
Asthenes patagonica 5¼" (14cm)
Above light grayish brown. *Chin checkered black and white.* Below light grayish, tinged buff on belly. *Tail quite short, blackish,* narrowly edged rufous.

7. **Dusky-tailed Canastero** **LM-S**
Asthenes humicola 6" (15cm)
Above grayish brown. Wing coverts rufous. *Tail blackish.* Short narrow eyebrow white. *Throat white dotted black.* Below whitish *with gray flecks giving streaked look.*

8. **Cordilleran Canastero** **MH-O**
Asthenes modesta 5½" (14cm)
Above light sandy to dark grayish brown. Wing coverts tinged rufescent. Eyebrow whitish. Chestnut throat usually present. Below grayish white, finely streaked dusky on lower throat and breast. Rather fan-shaped *tail looks mostly rufous,* black on inner webs.

9. **Cactus Canastero** **LM-S**
Asthenes cactorum 6" (15cm)
Above light to darker grayish brown, wing coverts tinged rufous. Eyebrow whitish. Throat buff. Tail brown, outer feathers cinnamon.

10. **Canyon Canastero** **MH-S**
Asthenes pudibunda 6" (15cm)
Above reddish brown. Throat rufous. *Below gray. Tail rufous,* central feathers darker. A distinctive, dark-looking canastero.

11. **Rusty-fronted Canastero** **H-S**
Asthenes ottonis 6" (15cm)
Forehead narrowly cinnamon-rufous. *Above rather dark brown,* wing coverts rufous. Throat buffy. *Below light gray,* flanks and vent buffy. *Long tail mostly rufous.*

12. **Streak-backed Canastero** **H-SO**
Asthenes wyatti 6" (15cm)
Above brown *streaked dusky. Wing patch rufous.* Narrow buffy or whitish eyebrow. Throat rufous or buffy. Below buffy brownish, vaguely streaked dusky on breast (especially sides). Tail brown, outer feathers dull rufous.

1. Austral Canastero   **LM-O**

Asthenes anthoides   6" (15cm)
Above olive grayish *heavily streaked black.* Wing coverts mostly rufous. Throat dull yellow or cinnamon-rufous. Below buffy, breast usually with dusky streaking or scaling. Tail brown, outer feathers blackish at base, *broadly tipped cinnamon rufous.*

2. Cordoba Canastero   **M-S**

Asthenes sclateri   6¼" (16cm)
Above reddish brown, lightly streaked black. Wings rufous. Below buffy grayish. Outer tail feathers tipped rufous.

3. Streak-throated Canastero **H-O**

Asthenes humilis   6" (15cm)
Above brown, crown and back vaguely streaked blackish. Narrow whitish eyebrow. Throat cinnamon. Below whitish, *prominently streaked dusky on lower throat and breast.* Tail mostly brown.

4. Hudson's Canastero   **L-O**

Asthenes hudsoni   6½" (17cm)
Above brown streaked black. Throat pale yellow. Below pale buffy brownish, streaked blackish, especially on flanks. Young birds are apparently heavily streaked below. Tail blackish, edged and broadly tipped buffy brown.

5. Junin Canastero   **H-O**

Asthenes virgata   6½" (17cm)
Above brown streaked white. Wing coverts rufous. Rump plain brown. Throat cinnamon. Below whitish lightly streaked dusky.

6. Scribble-tailed Canastero **H-SO**
Asthenes maculicauda 6½" (17cm)
Forecrown chestnut. Above blackish brown streaked with yellowish buff. No throat patch. Below whitish, breast streaked dusky. Tail brown, *irregularly lined and spotted with black.*

7. Many-striped Canastero **H-SO**

Asthenes flammulata 6¼" (16cm)
Above blackish brown streaked white, crown streaked rufous. Wing coverts rufous. Throat white, (rufous chin spot in Colombia and Ecuador). Below whitish, *streaked dusky.* Tail dark brown, outer feathers broadly tipped cinnamon.

8. Line-fronted Canastero   **H-SO**

Asthenes urubambensis 7" (18cm)
Forehead lightly streaked buff and brown. Above plain brown; (in n and cen. Peru narrowly streaked buff on crown and back). *Long eyebrow white.* Below whitish streaked dusky. *Tail long, feathers very pointed,* all brown.

9. Bay-capped Wren-Spinetail
                  L-SOW

Spartanoica maluroides 5" (13cm)
Crown rufous. Above light brown *boldly streaked black.* Wings blackish, with single buff bar. Below white, breast and flanks tinged brown. Tail mostly chestnut brown, *central feathers very long and pointed.*

10. Orinoco Softtail   **L-FT**

Thripophaga cherriei   6" (15cm)
Above olive brown, wings more rufous. *Throat bright orange rufous.* Sides of head and neck and underparts olive brown, *streaked buffy.* Tail rufous-chestnut.

11. Plain Softtail   **L-FT**

Thripophaga fusciceps 6½" (17cm)
Uniform light buffy brown above. Wings and tail cinnamon rufous. Indistinct whitish eyebrow. Below light brown.

12. Russet-mantled Softtail **H-TS**

Thripophaga berlepschi
              6½" (17cm)
Crown light olive-brown. Above cinnamon rufous, rump more olivaceous. Throat buffy cinnamon. *Breast cinnamon-rufous,* contrasting with light olive-brown belly.

THORNBIRDS build enormous stick nests in trees.

1. **Little Thornbird**   **L-S**
Phacellodomus sibilatrix
          4½" (12cm)
Above brown, forehead narrowly
chestnut. Broad eyebrow gray.
Rump tinged rufous. Below whitish. Outer tail feathers cinnamon-
rufous.

2. **Rufous-fronted Thornbird**   **L-SO**
Phacellodomus rufifrons 6"(15cm)
Forecrown rufous (dull brown in
Venezuela and Colombia). Above
dull brown, *wings and tail like
back.* Indistinct whitish eyebrow.
Below whitish, sides and vent dull
buffy olive.

3. **Streak-fronted Thornbird**   **H-SO**
Phacellodomus striaticeps
          6" (15cm)
*Forecrown streaked rufous and
grayish.* Above, including most of
wings, dull brown. *Rump rufous.*
Below dull whitish. Central tail
feathers brown, outer ones cinnamon tipped dusky.

4. **Red-eyed Thornbird**   **L-FT**
Phacellodomus erythrophthalmus
          7"(18cm)
Above reddish brown, forecrown
rufous. Eye red. *Throat and breast
rufous.* Below brown. Tail rufous-
chestnut.

5. **Yellow-eyed (Greater) Thornbird**
          L-S
Phacellodomus ruber 7½"(19cm)
Eye yellow. Above reddish brown;
crown, wings and tail more rufous. Whitish below, tinged gray
on breast.

6. **Freckle-breasted Thornbird** **L-TS**
Phacellodomus striaticollis
          7" (18cm)
Crown chestnut. Above brown.
Throat white. *Breast orange ru-
fous, feathers tipped white, giving
spotted effect.* Belly buffy whitish.
Tail dark chestnut.

7. **Chestnut-backed Thornbird**
          MH-TS
Phacellodomus dorsalis
          7½" (19cm)
Crown dull rufous. *Back and much
of wings chestnut.* Rump olive
brown. Throat and sides of neck
white. *Breast orange-rufous, feathers tipped white, giving spotted effect.* Belly whitish. Tail chestnut.

8. **Lark-like Brushrunner**   **L-SO**
Coryphistera alaudina   6"(15cm)
Conspicuous crest mostly blackish. Above buffy brown, back
streaked blackish. *Patch below eye
white, ear coverts cinnamon.*
Below white, *broadly streaked light
rufous.* Tail orange rufous, central
feathers blackish.

9. **Spectacled Prickletail**   **M-FT**
Siptornis striaticollis   4" (10cm)
Bill short. Reddish brown above,
wing coverts and tail more chestnut. *Short but conspicuous white
eyebrow.* Below light brownish
streaked white on throat and
breast.

10. **Double-banded Graytail**   **L-FT**
Xenerpestes minlosi   4"(10cm)
Dark gray above. *Narrow eyebrow,
lores and two wing-bars whitish.*
Below creamy whitish. Tail gray.

11. **Equatorial Graytail**   **L-FT**
Xenerpestes singularis   4"(10cm)
Forehead rufous. Above dark gray,
crown streaked rufous. Wing bars
not prominent. Below pale yellowish conspicuously streaked
blackish. Tail gray.

12. **Orange-fronted Plushcrown** **L-FT**
Metopothrix aurantiacus 4"(10cm)
Forehead and throat orange. Above
light olive-brown, narrow yellowish eye-ring and pale eye-stripe.
Below grayish buffy tinged yellow
on breast. *Legs bright yellow.*

1. **Roraiman Barbtail** M-F
Premnoplex adusta 5½" (14cm)
Crown dark brown. *Ear coverts black, enclosed by rufous-chestnut eyebrow and collar on hindneck.* Above dark chestnut brown. Throat white, below streaked buffy and blackish. Tail dark chestnut, spines protruding.

2. **Rusty-winged Barbtail** M-F
Premnoplex guttuligera
5½"(14cm)
Above brown, wings and tail more rufous. Eyebrow and streaking on nape and upper back buffy. Throat pale buffy. Below brown, breast with *many large buff spots becoming streaks on belly.*

3. **White-throated Barbtail** LM-F
Premnoplex tatei 5½" (14cm)
Like Spotted Barbtail (68-9) but throat white and underparts streaked brown and whitish.

4. **Point-tailed Palmcreeper** L-T
Berlepschia rikeri 8" (20cm)
Woodcreeper-like. *Head, upper back, all of underparts boldly streaked black and white.* Contrasting bright rufous-chestnut mantle and tail. Climbs trunks of trees.

5. **Rufous Cacholote** L-S
Pseudoseisura cristata 8" (20cm)
Uniform cinnamon rufous, slightly paler below. *Conspicuous crest* somewhat grayer. Eye light yellow.

6. **Brown Cacholote** L-S
Pseudoseisura lophotes
9½"(24cm)
Conspicuous crest dark brown. Eye light yellow. Above somewhat rufescent brown, rump and tail rufous. Throat rufous, below rufescent brown.

7. **White-throated Cacholote** L-S
Pseudoseisura gutturalis 9" (23cm)
Above, including *conspicuous crest, grayish sandy brown.* Eye light yellow. *Throat white, black patch on upper breast.* Below grayish sandy brown. Tail darker.

8. **Striped Foliage-gleaner (Woodhaunter)** L-F
Hyloctistes subulatus 6½" (17cm)
Above brown, with narrow buff streaks on crown and back (streaking much reduced w of Andes). Throat buffy, below brownish with *blurry buff streaking.* Wings rufous brown, tail cinnamon-rufous.

9. **Chestnut-winged Hookbill** L-F
Ancistrops strigilatus 6½" (17cm)
Bill heavy, hooked. Above brown *sharply streaked buffy, contrasting with bright chestnut wings and* cinnamon rufous tail. *Below pale yellowish buff* streaked with dusky olive.

10. **Peruvian Recurvebill** L-F
Simoxenops ucayalae 7½" (19cm)
Lower bill upcurved. Eyebrow and streaking on sides of neck cinnamon rufous. Above rufous brown. Below cinnamon-rufous. Immature has feathers below broadly edged black, giving bold scaly look.

11. **Bolivian Recurvebill** LM-F
Simoxenops striatus 7" (18cm)
Lower bill obviously upcurved. Above rufous brown with buff streaks on back. Rump rufous. Throat rufous, below brownish.

12. **Scaly-throated Foliage-gleaner** LM-F
Anabacerthia variegaticeps
6"(15cm)
Resembles Montane Foliage-gleaner (62-12) but *eye-ring and eye stripe bright cinnamon.* Breast brown with broad blurry whitish streaks. Tail bright rufous.

1. White-browed Foliage-gleaner
LM-F

Anabacerthia amaurotis 6" (15cm)
Above brown. *Broad eyebrow white.* Throat white. Below light brown with large white spots on breast. Tail bright rufous.

2. Neblina Foliage-gleaner   M-F

Philydor hylobius   6¼" (16cm)
Rather like Black-capped Foliage-gleaner (62-11) but ear coverts all brown and general color darker.

3. Rufous-rumped Foliage-gleaner
L-F

Philydor erythrocercus   6" (15cm)
Above olive brown. *Rump and tail rufous.* Long eyebrow buff. Below pale yellowish buff. (W of Andes chestnut brown above with buff eyebrow and *contrasting slaty wings;* below cinnamon buffy).

4. Russet-mantled Foliage-gleaner
L-F

Philydor dimidiatus   6" (15cm)
Like Cinnamon-rumped Foliage-gleaner (62-10) but *back much brighter cinnamon-brown.* Rump and tail dark rufous. Wings brown.

5. Ochre-breasted Foliage-gleaner
L-F

Philydor lichtensteini 6¼" (16cm)
Crown, nape and ear coverts grayish. Broad eyebrow ochraceous. Back dull brownish. Wings and tail rufous. Below buffy ochraceous.

6. Chestnut-winged Foliage-gleaner
L-F

Philydor erythropterus 6¼" (16cm)
Above olive brown. Narrow buff eyebrow. *Wings and tail contrastingly rufous.* Throat yellowish ochre. Below dull ochraceous.

7. Rufous-tailed Foliage-gleaner
L-F

Philydor ruficaudatus 6¼" (16cm)
Upperparts olive-brown, wing coverts with pale edges. *Rump olive-brown like rest of back.* Below yellowish buff indistinctly pale-streaked. Tail rufous.

8. Crested Foliage-gleaner
L-F

Automolus dorsalis   6½" (17cm)
Like Olive-backed Foliage-gleaner (62-6) but *upperparts reddish brown* and has *buff streak* behind eye.

9. White-throated Foliage-gleaner
M-F

Automolus roraimae   6½" (17cm)
Rather like Olive-backed Foliage-gleaner (62-6) but has narrow eyering and *streak behind* eye white. White throat sharply contrasting with brown underparts.

10. Rufous-necked Foliage-gleaner
M-F

Automolus ruficollis   6½" (17cm)
Above bright rufescent brown. *Eyebrow and sides of neck rufous.* Throat cinnamon buff. Below brownish, breast streaked buffy whitish. Tail rufous.

11. Brown-rumped Foliage-gleaner
L-F

Automolus melanopezus
7" (18cm)
Above reddish brown. *Throat cinnamon,* below buffy brownish. Tail *(but not rump)* rufous.

12. Henna-hooded Foliage-gleaner
LM-F

Hylocryptus erythrocephalus
8" (20cm)
Head, neck, throat, wings and tail bright cinnamon-rufous. Back contrasting olive-brown. Breast contrasting grayish olive, belly buffy.

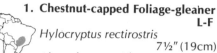

1. Chestnut-capped Foliage-gleaner
L-F
Hylocryptus rectirostris
7½" (19cm)
Above brown with *contrasting rufous crown, wings and tail. Below uniform light buffy brown.*

2. Pale-browed Treehunter **LM-F**
Cichlocolaptes leucophrys
8" (20cm)
Above rufous-brown, crown and back streaked whitish. *Long eyebrow and throat white.* Below whitish streaked brown. Tail cinnamon brown.

3. Flammulated Treehunter **MH-F**
Thripadectes flammulatus
8½" (21cm)
Very like Striped Treehunter (60-3) but underparts much more boldly streaked. Throat virtually unstreaked in some races. Wings rufous brown. Rump and tail chestnut.

4. Black-billed Treehunter **M-F**
Thripadectes melanorhynchus
7½" (19cm)
Above like Striped Treehunter (60-3). *Throat tawny, feathers edged dusky giving scaly appearance.* Underparts unstreaked. Breast tawny ochraceous, belly brown. Tail rufous.

5. Buff-throated Treehunter **H-F**
Thripadectes scrutator 9" (23cm)
Above brown. Throat buff, feathers edged blackish. Below pale olive brown.

6. Rufous-tailed Xenops **L-FT**
Xenops milleri 4" (10cm)
Like Streaked Xenops (68-10) but bill not noticeably upturned and no white streak below cheeks. Back streaked. *Tail all rufous.*

7. Slender-billed Xenops **L-FT**

Xenops tenuirostris 4" (10cm)
Like Plain Xenops (68-11) but bill more slender and *only slightly upturned.* Back streaked.

8. Great Xenops **L-TS**
Megaxenops parnaguae
5½" (14cm)
Bill very heavy, lower sharply upturned. Mostly bright cinnamon rufous, somewhat paler below. *Throat and sides of neck white.*

9. White-throated Treerunner
LM-FT
Pygarrhichas albogularis 5" (13cm)
Bill long, slender, *slightly upturned.* Above dark brown. *Below white,* scaled with black on sides. Tail rufous, spines protruding.

10. Rufous-breasted Leaftosser
(Leafscraper) **LM-F**
Sclerurus scansor 6½" (17cm)
Crown and rump rufous, contrasting with dark brown back and wings. *Throat white, contrasting with rufous breast.* Belly dark brown. Tail blackish.

11. Gray-throated Leaftosser
(Leafscraper) **LM-F**
Sclerurus albigularis 6¼" (16cm)
Above dark brown. Rump chestnut. Throat pale gray. Breast rufous. Below brown. Tail black.

12. Short-billed Leaftosser
(Leafscraper) **L-F**
Sclerurus rufigularis 6" (15cm)
Like Tawny-throated Leaftosser (68-3) but bill noticeably shorter. Chin white. Below dull brown, tinged chestnut on breast. Tail black.

1. Black-tailed Leaftosser (Leafscraper) **L-F**
Sclerurus caudacutus 6" (15cm)
Bill thin, nearly as long as head. Like Scaly-throated Leaftosser (68-4) but rump somewhat rufous. Throat whitish, spotted dusky. Breast and belly dark brown. Tail black.

2. Spot-backed Antshrike **LM-F**
Hypoedaleus guttatus 7½" (19cm)
Above black spotted white. Below white becoming buff on vent. ♀: Spots above tinged buff. Below becoming light ochraceous on vent.

3. Tufted Antshrike **LM-T**
Mackenziaena severa 9" (22cm)
Crested. Dark gray. Crown, cheeks and throat black. ♀: Crown rufous. Above black banded rufous. *Below buff banded black.*

4. Black-throated Antshrike **L-F**
Frederickena viridis 8" (21cm)
Crested. Slaty gray. *Crown, cheeks and breast black. Tail barred.* ♀: Above rufous. Cheeks and *underparts banded black and pale gray.*

5. Undulated Antshrike **L-F**
Frederickena unduligera 8" (21cm)
Crested. Black *with wavy white lines.* Throat all black. ♀: Brown barred black. Rump and tail black barred gray.

6. Silvery-cheeked Antshrike **L-SA**
Sakesphorus cristatus 6" (15cm)
Much like Black-crested Antshrike (72-11) but *tail barred black and white.* ♀: Like ♀ Black-crested Antshrike (72-12) but tail dark brown with buff barring.

7. Collared Antshrike **L-SA**
Sakesphorus bernardi 6½" (17cm)
Much like Black-crested Antshrike (72-11) but bill larger and white patch on middle of back semi-concealed. ♀: Tail rufous.

8. Black-backed Antshrike **L-SA**
Sakesphorus melanonotus
5½" (14cm)
Rather like Black-crested Antshrike (72-11) but *back black* (not brown). Sides white (not grayish). ♀: Like ♀ Black-crested Antshrike (72-12) but *crest blackish,* unstreaked buffy below, chestnut (not black) tail.

9. Band-tailed Antshrike **L-F**
Sakesphorus melanothorax
6¼" (16cm)
No crest. Deep black. Wing coverts and *tail broadly tipped white.* ♀: Rufous. Sides of head, throat and breast black. Belly brownish.

10. White-bearded Antshrike **LM-FT**
Biatas nigropectus 6¼" (16cm)
Crown and breast black. Collar and throat white. Above rufous brown. Below brown. ♀: Crown chestnut brown. Below all light brownish.

11. Cocha Antshrike **M-F**
Thamnophilus praecox 6" (15cm)
♂ unknown. ♀: Head, throat and upper breast black, front of head finely streaked white. Rest of plumage tawny ochraceous.

12. Blackish-gray Antshrike **L-F**
Thamnophilus nigrocinereus
6" (15cm)
Above black (back gray in some races). Wing coverts narrowly edged white. Below gray. Tail black. ♀: Mostly rufous brown, except for *contrasting dark gray crown and cheeks.*

1. **White-shouldered Antshrike L-F**
Thamnophilus aethiops
                 5½" (14cm)
Dark gray with black cap. Wings black, coverts with numerous small white spots. Tail all black. ♀: Above uniform chestnut without wing spots. Below paler chestnut. Tail chestnut brown.

2. **Upland Antshrike   LM-F**
Thamnophilus aroyae   5" (13cm)
Above dark gray, below lighter. Wing coverts black with large white spots. Tail black, tipped white. ♀: Crown rufous. Above reddish brown, *sides of head gray.* Below olive brown.

3. **Streak-backed Antshrike   LM-F**
Thamnophilus insignis 5½" (14cm)
Like Slaty Antshrike (74-7) but back streaked whitish. ♀: Like ♂ except forehead black dotted white *crown and nape chestnut.*

4. **Rufous-winged Antshrike   L-S**
Thamnophilus torquatus 5" (13cm)
Crown black, back grayish, *wings rufous.* Below whitish, breast barred black. Tail black barred white. ♀: Like ♂ but crown and tail rufous, unbarred below.

5. **Spot-winged Antshrike   L-F**
Pygiptila stellaris   4½" (12cm)
Bill notably heavy. Crown black. Above gray. *Wing coverts with small but conspicuous white dots.* Below pale gray. Tail *very short.* ♀: Above gray. Wings unspotted but edged rufous. Forehead and underparts ochraceous.

6. **Pearly Antshrike   L-F**
Megastictus margaritatus
                 4½" (12cm)
Bluish gray, paler below. Wing coverts and rump with large round white spots. Tail black with *large, conspicuous round white tips.* ♀: Gray and white replaced by brown and buff.

7. **Recurve-billed Bushbird   L-F**
Clytoctantes alixi   6¼" (16cm)
Like Black Bushbird (80-3) but above and below dark gray, only throat and breast black. Bill larger and more upturned. ♀: Brown. Face and most of underparts chestnut. Wings and tail blackish.

8. **Speckled (Speckle-breasted)**
   Antshrike   L-F
Xenornis setifrons   6" (15cm)
Above dark brown with short tawny streaks and two wing-bars. *Sides of head and underparts dark gray.* ♀: Lacks gray on head. Below light brown mottled whitish.

9. **Rufous-backed Antvireo   LM-F**
Dysithamnus xanthopterus
                 4½" (12cm)
Head gray speckled white on sides. *Lower back and wings rufous.* Below grayish. Tail black edged rufous. ♀: Above rufous, below pale olivaceous.

10. **Saturnine Antshrike   L-F**
Thamnomanes saturninus
                 4½" (12cm)
Much like Dusky-throated Antshrike (76-4) *but black throat patch much larger.* ♀: Like ♀ Dusky-throated Antshrike (76-5) but more olive on breast. Both sexes have obvious white patch on back.

11. **Western Antshrike   L-F**
Thamnomanes occidentalis
                 6" (15cm)
Slaty black. *Very small white dots on coverts* forming two wing-bars. ♀: *Crown chestnut.* Above dark rufous brown, wings marked as in ♂ but with buffy whitish. *Eyebrow, sides of head and underparts slaty gray.*

12. **Plumbeous Antshrike   LM-F**
Thamnomanes plumbeus
                 5" (13cm)
Dark gray, *throat and breast blackish.* Shoulders and spots on wing coverts white. ♀: Above brownish, tinged rufous on crown. *Below gray streaked white.* (In Brazil, underparts uniform brownish).

1. Bluish-slate Antshrike   **L-F**
Thamnomanes schistogynus
                         5½"(14cm)
Like Cinereous Antshrike (76-2) but
more bluish gray. ♀: Belly contrasting rufous.

2. Pygmy Antwren   **L-FT**
Myrmotherula brachyura 3" (8cm)
Above black, streaked white.
Wing-bars white. Rump gray. *Below*
Throat white, whisker black. *Below*
pale yellow. Tail very short. ♀:
Head streaked ochraceous.

3. Short-billed Antwren   **LM-F**
Myrmotherula obscura   3" (8cm)
Above black sparsely streaked
white. Wing bars white. Rump
blackish. Throat white, whisker
black. Below pale yellow. ♀:
Throat and breast ochraceous.

4. Sclater's Antwren   **L-F**
Myrmotherula sclateri   3" (8cm)
Above black streaked yellow.
Wing-bars white. Rump gray. Un-
derparts yellow. ♀: Below pale
yellow narrowly streaked black.

5. Yellow-throated Antwren   L-FT
Myrmotherula ambigua   3" (8cm)
Top and sides of head black,
streaked white. Back black,
streaked yellow. Whisker black.
All pale yellow below, not
streaked. ♀: Head streaks are
tawny.

6. Klages' Antwren   **L-FT**
Myrmotherula klagesi   3" (8cm)
Very like Streaked Antwren (90-4)
but has no white concealed patch
on back. ♀: Above black streaked
buff. Below buff, streaked black
on breast.

7. Stripe-chested Antwren   LM-T
Myrmotherula longicauda
                          4"(10cm)
Very like Streaked Antwren (90-4)
but tail much longer and underparts *much less streaked.* ♀: Like
♀ Streaked Antwren (90-5) but
mantle as well as head streaked
buff and underparts practically
unstreaked.

8. Cherrie's Antwren   **L-T**
Myrmotherula cherriei   4" (10cm)
Like Streaked Antwren (90-4) but
breast and belly heavily streaked
black. ♀: Like ♀ Streaked Antwren (90-5) but broadly streaked
black on breast and belly.

9. Rufous-bellied Antwren   **L-F**
Myrmotherula guttata   3" (8cm)
Above gray, wing coverts and tail
black *conspicuously tipped cinnamon.* Throat and breast gray.
Belly rufous. ♀: Above and below
mostly brown.

10. Plain-throated Antwren   **L-F**
Myrmotherula hauxwelli 3" (8cm)
Gray, paler below. Wing and tail
coverts black tipped white. ♀:
Above olive brown. *Below cinnamon-rufous.* Wing and tail coverts
tipped buff.

11. Star-throated Antwren   LM-F
Myrmotherula gularis   3½" (9cm)
Above reddish brown, shoulders
white. Wing coverts black dotted
white. *Throat and upper breast
black spotted white.* Below gray.

12. Brown-bellied Antwren   **L-F**
Myrmotherula gutturalis 4" (10cm)
Above reddish brown, wing coverts spotted white. *Throat checkered black and white.* Breast grayish. Belly brown. ♀: Dull brown
above, buffy below. Wing coverts
tipped buff.

1. White-eyed Antwren   **L-F**
Myrmotherula leucophthalma
             4″(10cm)
Very like Checker-throated Antwren (90-6) but breast purer gray and tail slightly longer.

2. Stipple-throated Antwren   **L-F**
Myrmotherula haematonota
             3½″(9cm)
Head brown. Back chestnut (or above all slaty gray). Wing coverts black tipped white. *Throat black checkered white.* Breast gray, belly rufous. ♀: Mostly brown.

3. Rufous-tailed Antwren   **L-F**
Myrmotherula erythrura 4″ (10cm)
Above olive brown, lower back and rump chestnut. Below gray. Wing coverts spotted pale buff. *Tail rufous.* ♀: Below dull buffy. Throat more yellowish.

4. Black-hooded Antwren   **LM-F**
Myrmotherula erythronotos
             4″(10cm)
Mostly black. *Back chestnut.* Sides white, belly dark gray. Wing coverts spotted white. ♀: Mostly olive brown above, *back chestnut.* Below light buffy brown, sides white.

5. Long-winged Antwren   **L-F**
Myrmotherula longipennis
             3½″(9cm)
Like Slaty Antwren (90-10) but paler gray. Wing-bars more conspicuous, also usually shows white tuft on shoulders. ♀: Brown above. *Eye-ring,* throat and breast *buff.*

6. Rio Suno Antwren   **L-F**
Myrmotherula sunensis 3″ (8cm)
Like Slaty Antwren (90-10) but tail shorter. Wing-spots very small. *Tail not tipped white.* ♀: Above grayish olive. Below olivaceous, paler on throat.

7. Salvadori's Antwren   **L-F**
Myrmotherula minor   3½″ (9cm)
Like Slaty Antwren (90-10) but tail with black bar near end and white tips. ♀: Above pale olive, *crown gray.* Throat whitish, below buff.

8. Ihering's Antwren   **L-F**
Myrmotherula iheringi   4″ (10cm)
Rather like Slaty Antwren (90-10) but bill larger and tail lacks white tips. ♀: Above pale gray. Wing coverts black with large buff spots. Below pale buff.

9. Ashy Antwren   **LM-F**
Myrmotherula grisea   4″ (10cm)
Uniform slaty gray, *wing coverts unmarked.* ♀: Above olive brown. Below bright rufous. Tail reddish brown. Wings unmarked.

10. Unicolored Antwren   **LM-F**
Myrmotherula unicolor 3½″ (9cm)
Dark gray. Throat black. *Wing coverts unmarked.* ♀: Above brown. Throat whitish. Below pale olive buff. Wings unmarked.

11. Plain-winged Antwren   **M-F**
Myrmotherula behni   4″ (10cm)
Dark gray. Black throat patch extending *only to breast.* Wings plain. Tail *not* tipped. ♀: Above brown. Throat whitish, below olive. *Wings and tail unmarked.*

12. Band-tailed Antwren   **L-F**
Myrmotherula urosticta 3½″ (9cm)
Gray, throat black. Wing coverts black with large white tips. Tail *very broadly tipped white.* ♀: Above light gray. Throat whitish, below buff.

13. Gray Antwren   **L-FT**
Myrmotherula menetriesii
             3½″(9cm)
Light gray (throat black in some races). *Wing coverts have black bar and white tip.* Tail short. ♀: Above gray. Eye dark. Faint wing-bars. Below light rufous. Tail gray.

1. Leaden Antwren   **L-F**
Myrmotherula assimillis 4" (10cm)
Light gray, paler below. Wing coverts tipped white. ♀: Throat white. Wing coverts tipped buff. Below buffy.

2. Stripe-backed Antbird   **L-TS**
Myrmorchilus strigilatus 6" (15cm)
Above rufous broadly streaked black. Eyebrow and whisker white. Throat and breast black. Belly white. ♀: Throat white, *breast buff streaked black.*

3. Black-capped Antwren   **L-TS**
Herpsilochmus pileatus
4½" (12cm)
Like Large-billed Antwren (84-11) but breast clear ashy gray. ♀: Forehead buffy brown, crown streaked white. Back olive gray. Underparts whitish.

4. Spot-tailed Antwren   **L-F**
Herpsilochmus sticturus
3½" (9cm)
Like Large-billed Antwren (84-11) but underparts clear pale gray and tail with large white oval spots on central feathers. Tail-tipped white. ♀: Crown streaked rufous and whitish.

5. Todd's Antwren   **L-F**
Herpsilochmus stictocephalus
4" (10cm)
Probably not separable from Spot-tailed Antwren (preceding) in field. Spots on tail somewhat smaller. ♀: Like ♂ but *entire crown black with white spots.*

6. Spot-backed Antwren   **L-F**
Herpsilochmus dorsimaculatus
4" (10cm)
Rather like Large-billed Antwren (84-11) but back broadly striped black and white. ♀: Forehead *spotted buff.* Crown has large white spots.

7. Roraiman Antwren   **M-F**
Herpsilochmus roraimae
4½" (12cm)
Like Large-billed Antwren (84-11) but occurs at higher elevations, and tail is much longer and with more white spots. ♀: Crown black spotted white.

8. Pectoral Antwren   **L-SA**
Herpsilochmus pectoralis
4½" (12cm)
Very like Large-billed Antwren (84-11) but has *black crescent on breast.* ♀: Head tawny. Above brownish, rump tipped white. Below ochraceous.

9. Yellow-breasted Antwren   **M-FT**
Herpsilochmus axillaris
4¼" (11cm)
Crown, nape and eyebrow black, spotted white. Back olive gray. Wing coverts black, margined white. Below pale yellow (with white throat w of Andes). Tail black, broadly tipped white. ♀: Crown rufous.

10. Rufous-winged Antwren   **LM-FT**
Herpsilochmus rufimarginatus
4" (10cm)
Like Large-billed Antwren (84-11) but *much rufous showing in wings.* Underparts pale yellow. ♀: Crown chestnut.

11. Narrow-billed Antwren   **LM-F**
Formicivora iheringi 4" (10cm)
Very like White-flanked Antwren (90-8) but feathers of throat edged white, of breast edged gray. ♀: Like ♀ White-flanked Antwren (90-9) but rump rufous.

12. Serra (Antbird) Antwren   **LM-F**
Formicivora serrana 5" (13cm)
Crown and back dark reddish brown. Long eyebrow white. Below black. Tail black edged and tipped white. ♀: Below white.

13. Rusty-backed Antwren   **L-TS**
Formicivora rufa 5" (13cm)
Above light brown. Long eyebrow white. Below black, sides of breast white. Wing coverts and tail brownish black, both tipped white.

1. **Rufous-tailed Antbird**   **LM-FT**
Drymophila genei   5" (13cm)
Crown black. Eyebrow white. Back grayish, finely streaked white. *Rump and tail rufous.* Below white, spotted black. Belly brown. ♀: Above rufous. Below buffy.

2. **Ochre-rumped Antbird**   **LM-FT**
Drymophila ochropyga
4½" (12cm)
Crown black. Eyebrow white. Back mixed gray and black. Throat and breast white, streaked black. *Belly rufous.* Tail broadly tipped white.

3. **Striated Antbird**   **L-F**
Drymophila devillei   4½" (12cm)
Rather like Long-tailed Antbird (82-10) but tail shorter. Crown and mantle black streaked white. Rump rufous. *Belly white.* Tail blackish, tipped white. ♀: Upperparts streaked buff.

4. **Streak-capped Antwren**   **L-F**
Terenura maculata   4" (10cm)
Like Rufous-rumped Antwren (90-2) but crown and sides of head black streaked white and breast white lightly streaked dusky.

5. **Chestnut-shouldered Antwren**
L-F
Terenura humeralis   4" (10cm)
Like Rufous-rumped Antwren (90-2) but *shoulders chestnut* (not yellow) and belly gray, (not yellow).

6. **Yellow-rumped Antwren**   **M-F**
Terenura sharpei   4" (10cm)
Like Rufous-rumped Antwren (90-2) but center of lower back and *rump yellow* (not rufous).

7. **Ash-winged Antwren**   **L-F**
Terenura spodioptila   4" (10cm)
Crown black. Narrow white eyestripe. *Back and rump bright chestnut.* Otherwise gray above, wings with two bold white bars. Below whitish. ♀: Crown, throat and breast brownish.

8. **Gray Antbird**   **L-FT**
Cercomacra cinerascens
5½" (14cm)
Like Dusky Antbird (80-7) but white tips of wing coverts very small or lacking entirely. Tail blackish broadly tipped white. ♀: Olive brown, *dull ochraceous below.* Wing coverts plain (or tipped white s of the Amazon).

9. **Rio de Janeiro Antbird**   **L-TS**
Cercomacra brasiliana   6" (15cm)
Like Dusky Antbird (80-7) but much paler gray. Tail longer. ♀: Very like ♀ Dusky Antbird (80-8) but wing coverts not tipped buff.

10. **Bananal Antbird**   **L-T**
Cercomacra ferdinandi   6" (15cm)
Black. Wing coverts edged white. Tail black narrowly tipped white. ♀: More distinctive. Grayer, not as deep black. *Throat and breast with distinct but narrow white streaking.*

11. **Black Antbird**   **L-F**
Cercomacra serva   5" (13cm)
Blackish. Wing coverts edged white. ♀: Above olive brown. Eyebrow and facial area pale buff. Below orange rufous.

12. **Rio Branco Antbird**   **L-FT**
Cercomacra carbonaria   6" (15cm)
Like Jet Antbird (80-9) but tail longer. ♀: Above dark gray. Throat white speckled gray. *Below fulvous.*

13. **Stub-tailed Antbird**   **L-F**
Sipia berlepschi   4½" (12cm)
Black. Bill heavy. Eye dark red. No white spots on wing. *Tail very short.* ♀: Blackish. Wing coverts, *throat and breast dotted white.*

1. Fringe-backed Fire-eye   **L-F**
Pyriglena atra   6½" (17cm)
Like White-shouldered Fire-eye
(78-3). Glossy black with *mantle
feathers fringed white,* always visible, usually conspicuous. ♀: Like
♀ White-backed Fire-eye (78-2)
with large white patch on back.

2. Slender Antbird   **LM-F**
Rhopornis ardesiaca   6¼" (16cm)
Eye red. Above dark gray, wing
coverts edged white. Tail long,
slender, black. *Throat and upper
breast black. Below gray.* ♀: *Crown
and nape buffy brown.* Throat
white. Below light gray.

3. Yellow-browed Antbird   **L-FT**
Hypocnemis hypoxantha
                          4" (10cm)
Much like Warbling Antbird (90-3)
but back uniform olive (not
streaked), long eyebrow yellow
(not white) and sides olive (not rufous).

4. Black-chinned Antbird   **L-FT**
Hypocnemoides melanopogon
                       4¼" (11cm)
Mostly gray, somewhat paler on
belly. *Throat patch black.* Wing
coverts black, conspicuously margined white. *Tail narrowly tipped
white.* ♀: Whitish below, *mottled
gray on throat and breast.*

5. Band-tailed Antbird   **L-FT**
Hypocnemoides maculicauda
                       4¼" (11cm)
Gray, paler on belly. *Throat patch
black.* Wing coverts black broadly
margined white. *Tail very broadly
tipped white.* ♀: Below whitish,
mottled gray.

6. White-lined Antbird   **L-FT**
Percnostola lophotes 5½" (14cm)
Like Black-headed Antbird (84-2)
but much darker. Throat and center of underparts black. ♀: *Crown
bright cinnamon rufous.* Above
brown, wing coverts with cinnamon spots. *Underparts gray, white
in center.* Includes Rufous-crested
Antbird, *Percnostola macrolopha,*
considered to be a separate species in BSA.

7. Slate-colored Antbird   **L-F**
Percnostola schistacea 5" (13cm)
Uniform gray. Wing coverts with
small white terminal *dots.* ♀:
Above reddish brown, wing coverts with cinnamon dots. *Sides of
head and underparts bright rufous.*

8. Spot-winged Antbird   **L-FT**
Percnostola leucostigma 5" (13cm)
Eye red. Above dark gray, paler
below. Black wing coverts with
large white spots. ♀: *Head gray,*
back brown. Wings with *prominent* cinnamon spots. Below bright
rufous.

9. Caura Antbird   **L-F**
Percnostola caurensis 6½" (17cm)
Dark gray above. Below lighter
gray. Wing coverts black with large
white spots. ♀: Head gray. Back
brown. Wings with *prominent* cinnamon spots. Below bright rufous.

10. Scalloped Antbird   **L-FT**
Myrmeciza ruficauda   5" (13cm)
Like Squamate Antbird (82-1) but
no white eyebrow. Feathers on
back broadly edged buff. Belly
reddish brown. Tail much shorter.
♀: Throat and breast pale buff.

11. Dull-mantled Antbird   **LM-F**
Myrmeciza laemosticta
                       4½" (12cm)
Eye red. No bare skin around eye.
Head and neck dark gray. Above
brown with small white spots on
wing coverts. Throat black. Below
dark gray. ♀: *Throat sharply
checkered black and white.*

12. Gray-bellied Antbird   **L-F**
Myrmeciza pelzelni 4½" (12cm)
*Lores and sides of head mixed gray
and white.* Above rufous brown
with *large buff spots on wing coverts.* Throat and breast black. Belly
gray. ♀: Below mostly whitish,
breast scaled dusky. Flanks chestnut.

1. Chestnut-tailed Antbird **L-F**
Myrmeciza hemimelaena
4½" (12cm)
Crown dark gray. Above brown with white spots on wing coverts. Throat and breast black. Belly rufous on sides, white in center. *Tail chestnut.* ♀: Wing coverts spotted buff and *eyebrow whitish. Throat and breast ochraceous orange, belly buffy whitish.*

2. Goeldi's Antbird **L-FT**
Myrmeciza goeldii 7" (18cm)
Uniform deep black. Like Immaculate Antbird (78-9) but has white patch on back usually partly visible. ♀: *Above bright rufous,* wings and tail browner. Cheeks and throat white. *Below bright ochraceous-cinnamon.*

3. White-shouldered Antbird **L-T**
Myrmeciza melanoceps
6½" (17cm)
Black. Skin around eye blue. White at shoulder often concealed. Like Immaculate Antbird (78-9) but tail extends only about 2.5 cm beyond wings. ♀: Rufous except head, throat and upper breast black.

4. Sooty Antbird **L-F**
Myrmeciza fortis 6" (15cm)
Black. Bend of wing white. *Bare skin around eye blue.* Like Immaculate Antbird (78-9). ♀: Crown chestnut. Back, wings and tail brown. Below light gray.

5. Gray-headed Antbird **M-F**
Myrmeciza griseiceps 5" (13cm)
Head and neck gray. Back brown. Wing coverts black, spotted white. Throat and breast black. Belly gray. Tail dark gray, tipped white. ♀: Throat and breast gray.

6. Black-throated Antbird **L-FT**
Myrmeciza atrothorax 5" (13cm)
Above dark brown (slaty gray in Ecuador and Peru) cheeks gray. Wing coverts blackish, dotted white. *Throat and breast black. Belly gray.* ♀: Wing coverts dotted buff. *Throat white. Breast rufous.* Belly whitish.

7. Spot-breasted Antbird **L-F**
Myrmeciza stictothorax 5" (13cm)
Above dark brown. Wing coverts blackish, dotted white. Throat black. Breast black streaked white. Belly gray. ♀: Wing coverts dotted buff. Throat white. Breast rufous. Belly whitish.

8. Yapacana Antbird **L-F**
Myrmeciza disjuncta 5" (13cm)
Blackish gray above. Wing coverts spotted white. Sides of head gray. *Below white, strongly washed with tawny on breast and sides.* ♀: Wing spots buff.

9. White-masked Antbird **L-F**
Pithys castanea 5½" (14cm)
Sides of head and chin white. Crown, cheeks and throat black. Otherwise entirely chestnut.

10. White-throated Antbird **L-F**
Gymnopithys salvini 5½" (14cm)
Gray. *Eyebrow and throat white.* Tail black, *barred white.* ♀: *Mostly chestnut brown.* Crown blackish. *Tail chestnut barred black.*

11. Lunulated Antbird **L-F**
Gymnopithys lunulata 5½" (14cm)
Gray. Eyebrow and throat white. Tail *all black.* ♀: Brown, feathers of back showing buffy fringe. Below more olive brown. Tail with some *white* barring.

12. Bare-eyed Antbird **L-F**
Rhegmatorhina gymnops
5½" (14cm)
Crested. *Large bare area around eye pale blue-green. Head black.* Above brown. *Below black.* ♀: No crest.

1. **Harlequin Antbird**   L-F
Rhegmatorhina berlepschi
5½" (14cm)
Like Chestnut-crested Antbird (80-11) but some black in crest and belly light gray. Tail brown. ♀: *Mostly buffy brown barred black.* Crown and breast chestnut, sides of head black.

2. **White-breasted Antbird**   L-F
Rhegmatorhina hoffmannsi
5½" (14cm)
Lores, crown and crest deep black. Bare area around eye pale green. Above olive brown. *Cheeks, throat and breast white.* Belly gray. ♀: Mostly buffy brown barred black. Crown chestnut.

3. **Hairy-crested Antbird**   L-F
Rhegmatorhina melanosticta
5½" (14cm)
Crown and crest whitish. Bare area around eye light blue. Lores and sides of head black. Above brown. Below olive brown. ♀: Spotted with black above.

4. **Pale-faced Bare-eye**   L-F
Skutchia borbae   6½" (17cm)
Yellowish bare patch around eye. Lores whitish. Black above eye. Back chestnut with scattered black bars. Head, throat and breast rufous. Belly brown. Tail blackish.

5. **Argus Bare-eye**   L-F
Phlegopsis barringeri   7" (18cm)
Bare area around eye red. Head, neck and most of underparts glossy black. Above brown. Back and wing coverts with *buff black-encircled spots.* Tail chestnut, outer half black.

6. **Reddish-winged Bare-eye**   L-F
Phlegopsis erythroptera
6¼" (16cm)
Bare area around eye red. Mostly black, *feathers of back and rump conspicuously fringed white. Much bright rufous on wings.* ♀: Rufous brown above. Wings with double bar and patch on primaries buff. Below orange rufous.

7. **Striated Antthrush**   L-F
Chamaeza nobilis   9" (22cm)
Like Short-tailed Antthrush (70-2) but crown blackish, streak back of eye smaller and less distinct. More heavily streaked on breast.

8. **Rufous-tailed Antthrush**   LM-F
Chamaeza ruficauda 7½" (19cm)
Like Short-tailed Antthrush (70-2) but tail has no black and is *not pale-tipped.* More rufescent above. *More heavily marked with black below.*

9. **Rufous-fronted Antthrush**   L-F
Formicarius rufifrons 6½" (17cm)
Resembles Black-faced Antthrush (70-5) but with *bright orange-rufous forehead.*

10. **Rufous-breasted Antthrush** LM-F
Formicarius rufipectus   7" (18cm)
Like Black-faced Antthrush (70-5) but *breast bright rufous* (contrasting with black throat).

11. **Wing-banded Antbird**   L-F
Myrmornis torquata   5½" (14cm)
Above chestnut. *Wings blackish crossed by three buff bars.* Cheeks speckled black and white. Throat and breast black (outlined in white e of Andes). Below gray. *Tail short, rufous.* ♀: *Throat and breast rufous.*

12. **Black-crowned Antpitta**   L-F
Pittasoma michleri   7" (18cm)
Crown and nape black. Back brown. Cheeks chestnut. *Below scalloped black and white* (♀ black and buff).

1. **Undulated Antpitta**　　**MH-F**
Grallaria squamigera　8½"(21cm)
Above grayish olive. Throat white
margined black. Below ochraceous, with coarse wavy black
barring.

2. **Giant Antpitta**　　**MH-F**
Grallaria gigantea　9½" (24cm)
Above olivaceous brown with
tawny forehead. Throat white (not
margined black). Underparts *deep
orange rufous* with *narrow* wavy
black barring.

3. **Great Antpitta**　　**M-F**
Grallaria excelsa　10" (25cm)
Crown and nape gray. Back
brownish olive. Throat white (not
margined with black). Below
tawny with bold wavy black barring.

4. **Variegated Antpitta**　　**L-F**
Grallaria varia　7½" (19cm)
Above brown, gray on hindcrown
and nape, feathers edged black,
giving scaled effect. Throat brown
with white whisker and small
white patch below. Breast brown
vaguely streaked whitish. Belly
buff.

5. **Moustached Antpitta**　　**M-F**
Grallaria alleni　7½" (19cm)
Crown and nape gray. Above
brown. Throat brown *broadly bordered white at sides and below*.
Breast brown lightly streaked
white. Belly whitish. Tail orange.

6. **Scaled Antpitta**　　**LM-F**
Grallaria guatimalensis
　　　　6½"(17cm)
*Grayish crown and olive brown
back scaled with black*. Throat
brown. White bar on lower throat.
Whisker buffy whitish. Below
brown faintly streaked white on
breast. Tail brown.

7. **Tachira Antpitta**　　**M-F**
Grallaria chthonia　6½" (17cm)
Crown and nape gray. Back olive
brown scaled with black. Throat
brown. Whisker whitish. Lower
breast and sides whitish lightly
barred gray.

8. **Plain-backed Antpitta**　　**M-F**
Grallaria haplonota　7" (18cm)
Above plain brown. Throat white.
Whisker blackish. Below buffy
ochraceous (or crown rufous and
all of underparts buffy in Ecuador).

9. **Ochre-striped Antpitta**　　**L-F**
Grallaria dignissima　6½" (17cm)
Above reddish brown. *Throat and
breast rufous. Belly white*, streaked
black on sides. Tail very short.

10. **Elusive Antpitta**　　**L-F**
Grallaria eludens　6½" (17cm)
Above brown. Throat white. Breast
pinkish buff. Belly white, streaked
black on sides.

11. **Santa Marta Antpitta**　　**M-F**
Grallaria bangsi　6½" (17cm)
Above olive brown. Throat ochraceous, *below white heavily
streaked olive on breast*.

12. **Stripe-headed Antpitta**　　**H-T**
Grallaria andicola　6½" (17cm)
Above brown (streaked buffy in
Bolivia). *Eye-ring white*. Below
whitish, feathers edged black giv-
ing *streaked look*.

1. Bicolored Antpitta MH-F
Grallaria rufocinerea 6½" (17cm)
*Above dark reddish brown. Below
uniform dark gray*, tinged rufous
on throat.

2. Chestnut-naped Antpitta MH-F
Grallaria nuchalis 7½" (19cm)
Head chestnut. Above dark brown.
Below dark gray.

3. White-throated Antpitta M-F
Grallaria albigula 7½" (19cm)
Head and wings chestnut. Back
olive. Below mostly white, except
breast and sides of body pale gray.

4. Bay-backed Antpitta M-FT
Grallaria hypoleuca 6½" (17cm)
Above chestnut brown. Underparts vary greatly—mostly pale
gray in central Colombia, pale yellow in w Colombia and Ecuador,
gray in n Peru, rufous in central
Peru, mostly brown in s Peru. Sides
chestnut brown in all races.

5. Gray-naped Antpitta M-F
Grallaria griseonucha 6" (15cm)
Like Rufous Antpitta (70-8) but
nape grayish.

6. Rufous-faced Antpitta M-F
Grallaria erythrotis 7" (18cm)
Above olive brown. *Sides of head
rufous.* Underparts white, *streaked
rufous on breast.*

7. Tawny Antpitta MH-TS
Grallaria quitensis 6" (15cm)
Above brownish olive. *Eye-ring and
short eyebrow buffy white.* Below
buffy ochraceous more or less
mixed with whitish.

8. Brown-banded Antpitta H-F
Grallaria milleri 5" (13cm)
All uniform dark brown except
lores, chin and center of belly
white. Very rare.

9. Spotted Antpitta L-F
Hylopezus macularius 5½" (14cm)
Like Streak-chested Antpitta (70-
9) but back unstreaked and flanks
plain ochraceous.

10. Fulvous-bellied Antpitta L-FT
Hylopezus fulviventris 5" (13cm)
Rather like Streak-chested Antpitta (70-9) but crown black, back
olive-gray with wings unspotted
and has no eye-ring. Less heavily
streaked below.

11. Amazonian Antpitta L-F
Hylopezus berlepschi 5" (13cm)
Above olive. *No eye-ring. Whisker
black.* Throat white. Below buff
streaked black.

12. Thrush-like Antpitta L-F
Myrmothera campanisona
5" (13cm)
Above reddish to olive brown.
Lores buffy whitish. No eye-ring or
obvious whisker. Below white,
streaked brownish on breast.

1. Brown-breasted Antpitta   **M-F**
Myrmothera simplex   5"(13cm)
Above chestnut brown. Throat
white, *sharply outlined.* Breast gray
(or brown in some races), unstreaked. Belly white.

2. Ochre-breasted Antpitta   **M-F**
Grallaricula flavirostris
                              4¼"(11cm)
Above brown. Bill yellow. *Eye-ring
buff.* Breast ochraceous lightly
streaked dusky (or buffy scalloped
black in Peru and Bolivia). Belly
white.

3. Scallop-breasted Antpitta   **M-F**
Grallaricula loricata   4"(10cm)
Crown and nape rufous. *Eye-ring
and lores yellow.* Back, wings and
tail brown. Whisker black. Throat
buff. Below white, *boldly scalloped black.*

4. Peruvian Antpitta   **M-F**
Grallaricula peruviana 4"(10cm)
Lores, eye-ring and throat buffy
yellow. Crown and nape rufous.
Above brown, not tinged rufescent. Whisker black. Below white,
boldly scalloped black.

5. Crescent-faced Antpitta   **H-F**
Grallaricula lineifrons 4½"(12cm)
Bill black. Head black with *prominent white crescent in front of
eye.* Above golden olive. Below
whitish, broadly streaked brown.

6. Hooded Antpitta   **M-F**
Grallaricula cucullata 4¼"(11cm)
Bill orange-yellow. Head, nape and
throat   orange-rufous.   Above
brown. Below gray with white
patch at base of throat and on center of belly.

7. Black-bellied Gnateater   **L-F**
Conopophaga melanogaster
                              5"(13cm)
Head black. Long white tuft back
of eye. Back, wings and tail chest-
nut. *Below black.* ♀: Above brown.
Below whitish.

8. Hooded Gnateater   **L-F**
Conopophaga roberti 4½"(12cm)
Head, throat and breast black.
Long white tuft back of eye. Above
rufous. Below gray. White in cen-
ter of belly. ♀: Crown rufous.
Below pale gray.

9. Ash-throated Gnateater   **L-F**
Conopophaga peruviana
                              4½"(12cm)
Crown brown, long white tuft back
of eye. Back gray. Wings and tail
dark brown, wing coverts spotted
white. Throat whitish, *breast gray*
(♀ dark rufous), belly white.

10. Slaty Gnateater   **LM-F**
Conopophaga ardesiaca
                              4½"(12cm)
Above brown, forehead gray. Long
white tuft back of eye. *Below uniform gray.* ♀: Above reddish
brown, forehead rufous. No tuft.

11. Chestnut-crowned Gnateater
                                    LM-F
Conopophaga castaneiceps
                              4½"(12cm)
*Forecrown bright orange-rufous.
Hindcrown chestnut.* Long white
tuft back of eye. Above dark olive
brown. Below gray. ♀: Above
browner. *Below rufous, grayish on
belly.*

12. Chestnut-belted Gnateater   **L-F**
Conopophaga aurita 4½"(12cm)
Crown brown. Long white tuft
back of eye. Above brown. Throat
and sides of head black. Breast ru-
fous (black in one race in Brazil).
Belly brown, white in center. ♀:
Throat whitish. Has tuft.

1. Chestnut-throated Huet-huet
M-F
Pteroptochos castaneus 9″ (23cm)
Above blackish, rump barred black
and buff, wing coverts tipped buff.
Forecrown, *eyebrow and under-
parts rufous,* barred black on belly.

2. Black-throated Huet-huet LM-F
Pteroptochos tarnii 9″ (23cm)
Forecrown chestnut. *Head, neck,
throat and breast blackish.* Rump
and lower underparts rufous,
barred black on belly.

3. Moustached Turca LM-S
Pteroptochos megapodius
8½″ (21cm)
Above smoky brown. Narrow eyebrow and broad whiskers white.
Breast rufous brown. Belly whitish
banded dusky and rufous.

4. White-throated Tapaculo LM-S
Scelorchilus albicollis 7″ (18cm)
Above rufous brown, wings and
tail rufous. Eyebrow and throat
whitish. Below buffy white with irregular dark brown bars.

5. Chucao Tapaculo L-F
Scelorchilus rubecula 6½″ (17cm)
Above dark brown, rump and tail
rufous. Cheeks gray. *Throat and
breast rufous.* Below gray irregularly barred black and white.

6. Crested Gallito L-SA
Rhinocrypta lanceolata
8½″ (21cm)
*Crest and head rufous streaked
white.* Above gray. Tail blackish.
Throat and breast pale gray, *bright
chestnut on sides.* Belly white.

7. Sandy Gallito LM-SO
Teledromas fuscus 6¼″ (16cm)
Above pale brown. Eyebrow whitish. Below whitish tinged cinnamon. Tail blackish, outermost
feathers *tipped white.*

8. Rusty-belted Tapaculo L-F
Liosceles thoracicus 7″ (18cm)
Above rufous brown. Narrow eyebrow white. *Sides of neck and of
breast gray.* Throat and breast
white, *breast crossed by rufous
band.* Belly black barred white and
rufous.

9. Collared Crescent-chest L-S
Melanopareia torquata 4½″ (12cm)
Above rufous brown, *collar rufous.* Eyebrow white. Sides of head
black. Below buffy with *black band
across breast.* Tail long, pointed.

10. Olive-crowned Crescent-chest
L-S
Melanopareia maximiliani
5½″ (14cm)
Above olive brown. Eyebrow and
throat buff. Sides of head and
breast band black. Below chestnut. Tail long, pointed.

11. Marañon Crescent-chest L-SA
Melanopareia maranonica
5½″ (14cm)
Head all black with long buffy
eyebrow. Back brown. Wing feath-
ers edged white. Throat white.
Breast and tail black. Belly rufous.
Tail long, pointed.

12. Elegant Crescent-chest L-SA
Melanopareia elegans 4½″ (12cm)
Head all black, except eyebrow
buff. Above olive. Wing coverts
edged chestnut. Throat buff. Black
band across breast. Belly buff. Tail
black, long, pointed.

13. Spotted Bamboo-Wren LM-FT
Psilorhamphus guttatus
4½″ (12cm)
Wren-like. Above mostly gray, *dotted white.* Rump and belly rufous.
Below whitish *dotted black.* Tail
long, brown, tipped white.

1. Slaty Bristlefront   **M-F**
Merulaxis ater   7" (18 cm)
Blackish. Long, pointed, bushy plumes in front of eyes. Lower back, flanks and belly dark olive brown. ♀: Brown above. Cinnamon brown below.

2. Stresemann's Bristlefront   **L-F**
Merulaxis stresemanni 8½" (21 cm)
Blackish. Long, pointed, bushy plumes in front of eyes. Lower back, flanks and belly dark olive brown. ♀: Dark brown above, *bright rufous below.*

3. Ochre-flanked Tapaculo   **LM-F**
Eugralla paradoxa   4½" (12 cm)
Slaty gray, paler below. *Rump and flanks rufous.*

4. Ash-colored Tapaculo   **H-F**
Myornis senilis   5" (13 cm)
Uniform ashy gray. Tail rather long. ♀: Has rearparts edged brown.

5. Unicolored Tapaculo   **MH-F**
Scytalopus unicolor   4½" (12 cm)
Uniform blackish. Rather like Pale-throated Tapaculo (132-11) but flanks usually dark brown with little or no barring. Imm: Dark brown above, buffy below.

6. Mouse-colored Tapaculo   **LM-F**
Scytalopus speluncae   4" (10 cm)
Much like Pale-throated Tapaculo (132-11). Blackish gray. ♀: Dark brown, barred dusky below.

7. Large-footed Tapaculo   **M-F**
Scytalopus macropus   5½" (14 cm)
Rather like Pale-throated Tapaculo (132-11). Tail relatively long. Feet very large.

8. Rufous-vented Tapaculo   **LM-F**
Scytalopus femoralis   4½" (12 cm)
Like Pale-throated Tapaculo (132-11) but crown-spot white in n part of range. Below gray, belly and flanks brown, barred black. Lower back and rump dark brown, *not barred.* Tail fairly long.

9. Brown-rumped Tapaculo MH-FT
Scytalopus latebricola 4¼" (11 cm)
Like Pale-throated Tapaculo (132-11). Slaty gray or grayish brown. Rump and flanks rusty barred dusky. Tail quite short. Imm: Rufous brown barred dusky.

10. Brasilia Tapaculo   **L-T**
Scytalopus novacapitalis
    4½" (12 cm)
Above slaty blue gray. Throat and breast pale gray. Rump and flanks rusty, barred dusky.

11. White-breasted Tapaculo   **L-F**
Scytalopus indigoticus 4½" (12 cm)
Above slaty blue black. *Throat and center of underparts white.* Flanks brown barred dusky. ♀: Above dark brown.

12. Andean Tapaculo   **MH-FT**
Scytalopus magellanicus
    4" (10 cm)
Like Pale-throated Tapaculo (132-11) but upperparts vary from dark gray in s to pale gray in n. Rump and flanks rufous in northern races.

13. White-browed Tapaculo   **H-F**
Scytalopus superciliaris
    4½" (12 cm)
Mostly slaty. *Eyebrow and throat white or pale grayish.* Vent and flanks barred brown and black.

14. Ocellated Tapaculo   **H-F**
Acropternis orthonyx 7½" (19 cm)
Face and throat bright rufous. Back, wings and underparts blackish *profusely spotted white.* Rump and vent plain rufous. Tail blackish.

1. Shrike-like Cotinga   L-F
Laniisoma elegans   6½" (17cm)
Crown, nape and lores black.
Above olive green. *Below bright
yellow,* lightly *barred black on
sides.* ♀: Has crown like back,
more barring below. Imm: Has
cinnamon spotting on wing coverts forming two bars.

2. Swallow-tailed Cotinga   LM-FT
Phibalura flavirostris 8½" (21cm)
Crown black. *Back olive, barred
black. Throat yellow.* Breast white,
barred black. Below light yellow.
spotted black. *Tail long, black,
deeply forked.* ♀: Crown dull
olive.

3. Black-and-gold Cotinga   M-F
Tijuca atra   10½" (26cm)
Black. Bill orange. *Yellow patch
on wings.* ♀: Dull green, yellowish on belly.

4. Hooded Berryeater   LM-F
Carpornis cucullatus 8½" (21cm)
*Whole head, neck and upper
breast black* (♀ greenish). *Collar
yellow.* Back brown. Wing coverts
black edged yellow. Lower breast
and *belly bright yellow.* Tail black,
edged olive.

5. Black-headed Berryeater   L-F
Carpornis melanocephalus
7" (18cm)
Head and neck black. Back and
breast olive. Below yellow *lightly
banded dusky.* Wings and tail
blackish, edged olive.

6. Purple-throated Cotinga   L-F
Porphyrolaema porphyrolaema
6" (15cm)
Above black, wing coverts broadly
edged white. *Throat purple. Below
white.* ♀: Brown above scaled
whitish. *Throat cinnamon rufous.*
Below buff narrowly barred black.

7. Blue Cotinga   L-FT
Cotinga nattererii   6½" (17cm)
*Shining blue. Throat and belly
purple.* Wings and tail black,
edged blue. ♀: Rather like ♀
Plum-throated Cotinga (92-3) but
darker, looking scaled (not spotted) below, with *buff throat.*

8. Spangled Cotinga   L-FT
Cotinga cayana   7½" (19cm)
Shining turquoise blue, spotted
with black above. Wings and tail
black. Throat purple. ♀: Rather
like ♀ Plum-throated Cotinga (92-
3) but much darker above.

9. Purple-breasted Cotinga   L-F
Cotinga cotinga   7" (18cm)
Above shining purplish blue.
Wings and tail black. *Throat and
breast reddish purple.* Belly shining purplish blue. ♀: Rather like
♀ Plum-throated Cotinga (92-3)
but more conspicuously scaled
above and below.

10. Banded Cotinga   L-F
Cotinga maculata   7½" (19cm)
Above shining purplish blue.
Wings and tail black. Below reddish purple with *blue band across
breast.* ♀: Rather like ♀ Plum-
throated Cotinga (92-3) but blacker
above and below.

11. Pompadour Cotinga   L-F
Xipholena punicea   7" (18cm)
Shining reddish purple, including
tail. Eye white. Wings white, wing
coverts purple, fringed. ♀: Gray.
Wings broadly edged white. Tail
blackish.

12. White-tailed Cotinga   L-FT
Xipholena lamellipennis
7½" (19cm)
Deep blackish purple. Eye whit-
ish. *Wings and tail white.* ♀:
Brownish gray, wings edged white.
Eye bluish gray.

1. White-winged Cotinga   **L-F**
Xipholena atropurpurea
7½" (19 cm)
Dark purple. Eye whitish. *Wings white.* Tail brownish purple. ♀: Brownish gray. Wings edged white.

2. White Cotinga   **L-F**
Carpodectes hopkei   9" (22 cm)
Bill black. Body all white except small black spot at end of wing. Central tail feathers black. ♀: *Dark grayish brown above,* wings blackish, edged white. Tail blackish. *Breast pale gray.*

3. Black-faced Cotinga   **L-F**
Conioptilon mcilhennyi
7½" (19 cm)
Head black. Back gray. Wings and tail black. Below pale gray.

4. Red-crested Cotinga   **MH-T**
Ampelion rubrocristatus
7½" (19 cm)
Dark gray. *Crest dark red.* Lower back white streaked black. Belly mixed with white. Tail gray with broad *white band near end.*

5. Chestnut-crested Cotinga   **M-F**
Ampelion rufaxilla   8½" (21 cm)
Forecrown black with *crest dark reddish.* Above olive gray. *Throat and collar rufous.* Breast olive gray. Below pale yellow broadly striped dusky.

6. White-cheeked Cotinga   **H-T**
Zaratornis stresemanni
7½" (19 cm)
Crown black. Cheeks white. Back streaked black and buff. Throat and breast grayish brown, below streaked cinnamon and black.

7. Bay-vented Cotinga   **H-FT**
Doliornis sclateri   7½" (19 cm)
Crown and nape black. Throat, sides of head and upper back gray. Breast and belly mouse brown. Vent pale brownish red.

8. Band-tailed Fruiteater   **M-F**
Pipreola intermedia   8" (20 cm)
Very like Green-and-black Fruiteater (92-7) but head and throat glossy black without greenish tint. Tail black, tipped white. ♀: Like ♀ Green-and-black Fruiteater (92-8) but upperparts bluer and *tail tipped white.*

9. Black-chested Fruiteater   **M-F**
Pipreola lubomirskii   6¼" (16 cm)
Like Green-and-black Fruiteater (92-7) but lacks yellow semi-collar and white tips on inner wing feathers. *Belly clear yellow.* ♀: Like ♀ Green-and-black Fruiteater (92-8) but *lacks white tips to wing feathers.*

10. Orange-breasted Fruiteater   **M-F**
Pipreola jucunda   6½" (17 cm)
Like Green-and-black Fruiteater (92-7) but lacks yellow semi-collar and white tips on inner wing feathers. *Belly clear yellow.* ♀: Like ♀ Green-and-black Fruiteater (92-8) but *lacks white tips to wing feathers.*

11. Masked Fruiteater   **M-F**
Pipreola pulchra   6½" (17 cm)
Bill and legs red. *Head and throat dark green.* Above bright green. Breast orange surrounded narrowly by black. Center of belly light yellow, sides green. ♀: Like ♀ Golden-breasted Fruiteater (92-10) but breast greener.

12. Scarlet-breasted Fruiteater   **LM-F**
Pipreola frontalis   6" (15 cm)
Like Golden-breasted Fruiteater (92-9) but *bill black* and *forehead blackish.* Throat yellow mixed with red. Breast patch all red. ♀: Mostly green. Forehead and throat yellow. Belly green mixed with yellow.

1. Handsome Fruiteater LM-F
Pipreola formosa 6" (15 cm)
Bill red. Head and throat glossy
black. Back, wings and tail green.
Large white tips on inner wing
feathers. Below yellow with *bright
orange band across breast*. Legs
dusky. ♀: All green above. Throat
green. Patch on upper breast yellow. Below barred green and yellow.

2. Fiery-throated Fruiteater L-F
Pipreola chlorolepidota
4¼" (11 cm)
Green. Bill and legs red. *Throat
and breast scarlet*. Belly yellowish.
♀: Below, including throat, barred
green and yellow.

3. Red-banded Fruiteater M-F
Pipreola whitelyi 6½" (17 cm)
Bill and legs red. Above dull grayish green. *Forecrown, semi-collar
and eyebrow dull orange. Below
gray with red band across breast.*
♀: *Below white, streaked black.*

4. Scaled Fruiteater LM-F
Ampelioides tschudii 7½" (19 cm)
Head and nape glossy black. Lores
white. Back black *scaled green*.
Throat and collar whitish, spotted
black. Below yellow *scaled olive*.
♀: Head green.

5. Buff-throated Purpletuft L-FT
Iodopleura pipra 3" (8 cm)
Above gray. *Throat and upper
breast buff*. Belly white barred gray.
Purple on sides. ♀: Sides white.

6. Dusky Purpletuft L-FT
Iodopleura fusca 3½" (9 cm)
Above black, rump white. Below
brown, center of belly white, purple patch on sides. ♀: Patch on
sides white instead of purple.

7. White-browed Purpletuft L-FT
Iodopleura isabellae 4" (10 cm)
Above dark brown. *Crescent in
front of eye and line behind eye
white*. Rump white. Underparts
white, sides barred dusky with
purple patch. ♀: Lacks purple.

8. Kinglet Calyptura LM-F
Calyptura cristata 2¾" (7 cm)
Crown scarlet *bordered by broad
black stripes*. Greenish above,
rump yellow. Wing coverts tipped
white forming two bars. Below
yellow. *Tail very short.*

9. Dusky Piha MH-F
Lipaugus fuscocinereus
10½" (26 cm)
All ashy gray. Lighter gray on
throat. Breast and belly tinged
brownish. *Tail long.*

10. Screaming Piha L-F
Lipaugus vociferans 8½" (21 cm)
Gray, *lighter below*. Wings and
tail brownish. Tail not conspicuously long. Has loud, explosive
call "pee-pe-yo".

11. Cinnamon-vented Piha LM-F
Lipaugus lanioides 9½" (24 cm)
Above gray, more brownish on
back. Rump, wings and tail tinged
brown. Throat and breast grayish
with white streaks.

12. Rose-collared Piha LM-F
Lipaugus streptophorus
7½" (19 cm)
Above dark gray. Below pale gray
with *broad pink band across lower
throat, forming collar on hindneck*. Vent pink. ♀: Lacks pink
collar. Vent rufous.

1. Gray-tailed Piha   **L-F**
Lipaugus subalaris   8″ (20cm)
Above bright olive green. Semi-concealed black crest (lacking in ♀), shoulder yellow. Throat and breast grayish green becoming *pale gray on belly*. Tail gray.

2. Olivaceous Piha   **M-F**
Lipaugus cryptolophus
         8½″ (21cm)
Above dark olive green with semi-concealed black crest. Shoulder yellow. Tail dark olive. Below yellowish olive, brightest on belly.

3. Scimitar-winged Piha   **M-F**
Chirocylla uropygialis 9½″ (24cm)
Above dark gray, below paler gray. *Rump and sides of body chestnut.*

4. White-naped Xenopsaris **L-S**
Xenopsaris albinucha 4½″ (12cm)
Crown glossy blue black. Forehead, lores, cheeks, nape and underparts white. Back gray, wing coverts margined white. Tail blackish, edged and tipped white. ♀: Crown brown. Belly buffy.

5. Glossy-backed Becard   **L-F**
Pachyramphus surinamus
         5″ (13 cm)
Above black. Below white. Tail black, outers tipped white. ♀: *Crown dark brown.* Back gray. Wings black; coverts broadly edged chestnut. *Rump and underparts white.*

6. Slaty Becard   **L-FT**
Pachyramphus spodiurus
         4½″ (12cm)
Above blackish with narrow white edging on wing coverts and flight feathers. Below gray. Tail dark gray. ♀: Like Cinnamon Becard (94-8).

7. Black-capped Becard   **L-TS**
Pachyramphus marginatus
         4½″ (12cm)
Very like gray-collared form of White-winged Becard (94-5) but *narrow forehead and lores white.* Back gray striped black. Underparts pale gray. ♀: Very like ♀ White-winged Becard (94-6) but *crown rufous* instead of brownish.

8. Masked Tityra   **LM-FT**
Tityra semifasciata   8″ (20cm)
Bill red, tipped black. Like Black-tailed Tityra (92-4) but only *forecrown black and tail tipped white.* Hindcrown white. Back and underparts whitish. Wings black. Bare skin around eye red. ♀: Above brownish. Throat and belly whitish. Breast gray. Tail black.

9. Black-crowned Tityra   **L-FT**
Tityra inquisitor   6½″ (17cm)
Rather like Black-tailed Tityra (92-4) but *bill all black* and *no bare red skin around eye.* In some races tail white with black band. ♀: Has *chestnut face.* Back and underparts streaked dusky.

10. Crimson Fruitcrow   **L-F**
Haematoderus militaris
         12½″ (32cm)
All red (including bill) except wings and tail blackish brown. ♀: Head red. Above dark brown. *Below pinkish red.*

11. Purple-throated Fruitcrow **L-F**
Querula purpurata   9″ (23cm)
Glossy black. *Throat patch red* (♀ lacking). Bill slate blue.

12. Red-ruffed Fruitcrow   **LM-F**
Pyroderus scutatus   14″ (35cm)
Above black. *Throat and breast orange reddish,* feathers stiff and crinkled. Lower breast and belly spotted chestnut (solid chestnut in w Colombia and Ecuador).

1. **Amazonian Umbrellabird**   **LM-F**
Cephalopterus ornatus 17"(43cm)
Black. Tall, upstanding *umbrella-shaped crest*. Short, flat hanging wattle at base of neck. ♀: Has smaller crest and wattle.

2. **Long-wattled Umbrellabird LM-F**
Cephalopterus penduliger
17"(43cm)
Black. Upstanding *umbrella-shaped crest*. Hanging *wattle cylindrical, up to 18" long*, hanging from lower throat, feathered all around. ♀: Has smaller crest, much shorter wattle.

3. **Capuchinbird**   **L-F**
Perissocephalus tricolor
13"(33cm)
Above cinnamon brown, *head bare, gray*. Wings dark brown. *Below chestnut rufous*. Tail black.

4. **Bare-necked Fruitcrow**   **L-FT**
Gymnoderus foetidus 14"(35cm)
Black. *Neck sparsely feathered, skin blue to whitish*. Wings silvery gray. ♀: Grayish. Wings slaty like back.

5. **White Bellbird**   **L-F**
Procnias alba 10"(25cm)
White. *Long thin wattle hanging from forehead*. ♀: Above olive green. Below yellowish, heavily streaked olive.

6. **Bare-throated Bellbird**   **LM-F**
Procnias nudicollis 9½"(24cm)
White. *Bare skin around eye and on throat*, greenish with black bristles. ♀: Head black. Above olive green. Below yellowish.

7. **Bearded Bellbird**   **LM-F**
Procnias averano 9"(23cm)
Head and nape brown. Back, rump, underparts and tail whitish. Wings black. *Throat thickly covered with black wattles*. ♀: Head grayish olive. Above olive green. *Below olive streaked yellowish*.

8. **Guianan Red-Cotinga**   **L-F**
Phoenicircus carnifex 7½"(19cm)
Crown and rump crimson. Face, back and wings blackish. Throat and breast reddish black. *Belly red*. Tail red tipped blackish. ♀: Mostly olive brown. *Crown, tail and belly dull red*.

9. **Black-necked Red-Cotinga**   **L-F**
Phoenicircus nigricollis
8½"(21cm)
Bright red. Back, sides of head, throat, breast and tip of tail black. ♀: Back olive. Throat brown. Belly dull red.

10. **Guianan Cock-of-the-Rock LM-F**
Rupicola rupicola 10½"(26cm)
Like Andean Cock-of-the-Rock (92-1) but wings and tail brownish, edged and tipped pale orange and *lacking gray wing feathers*. ♀: Olive brown. Crest very small.

11. **Round-tailed Manakin**   **LM-F**
Pipra chloromeros 4"(10cm)
Very like Red-capped Manakin (96-4) but tail shorter, rounded instead of square. Underwing coverts black (not yellow). Thighs yellow. ♀: Almost exactly like ♀ Red-capped Manakin (102-5).

12. **Scarlet-horned Manakin**   **LM-F**
Pipra cornuta 4¼"(11cm)
Glossy blue black. *Entire head and long two-pronged crest red*. Thighs red. ♀: Dull olive above, paler grayish olive below. Thighs yellowish. Tail comparatively long.

1. Blue-rumped Manakin L-F
Pipra isidorei 3" (8 cm)
Black. *Top of head white. Rump blue.* ♀: Crown yellowish olive. Above *bluish green, emerald green on rump.* Below dull green, center of belly yellow.

2. Cerulean-capped Manakin L-F
Pipra coeruleocapilla 3" (8 cm)
Black. *Crown light blue. Rump darker blue.* ♀: Above bright green. *Rump bluish green.* Below dull green, center of belly yellow.

3. Opal-crowned Manakin L-F
Pipra iris 3½" (9 cm)
Bill whitish in both sexes. Crown silvery. Above bright green. Below darker green. Belly yellow. ♀: Crown green.

4. Golden-crowned Manakin L-S
Pipra vilasboasi 3½" (9 cm)
Crown and nape glistening golden yellow. Above grass green. Throat and breast darker green. Belly yellow.

5. Snow-capped Manakin L-F
Pipra nattereri 3" (8 cm)
Crown and rump white. Back, throat and breast green. Belly yellow. ♀: Crown bluish green. No white on rump.

6. White-throated Manakin L-F
Corapipo gutturalis 3" (8 cm)
Like White-ruffed Manakin (98-10) but white throat feathers extend down in point to upper breast. ♀: Above bright olive. Below whitish with olive band across breast.

7. Fiery-capped Manakin L-F
Machaeropterus pyrocephalus 3"(8 cm)
Crown and nape yellow, central stripe red. Eye reddish. Black pinkish chestnut. Wings olive. *Below whitish lightly streaked pink.* ♀: Above bright olive. Below whitish with olive band across breast.

8. Jet Manakin LM-F
Chloropipo unicolor 4½"(12 cm)
Black. Feathers at sides of breast white. ♀: Very like ♀ Striped Manakin (100-10) but eye more reddish.

9. Olive Manakin M-F
Chloropipo uniformis 5" (13 cm)
Uniform olive except paler and grayer on belly. Throat tinged grayish.

10. Cinnamon Manakin L-F
Neopipo cinnamomea 3" (8 cm)
Head and back gray, *semi-concealed crown stripe yellow* (rufous in ♀). Rump, wings and tail mostly rufous. *Cinnamon buffy below.*

11. Flame-crowned Manakin L-FT
Heterocercus linteatus 5" (13 cm)
Head black with red spot on crown. Back dark gray. *Throat white,* feathers lengthened on sides. *Breast chestnut.* Belly cinnamon. ♀: Head olive, (no crown spot). Throat grayish white.

1. Yellow-crowned Manakin L-FT
Heterocercus flavivertex
5" (13 cm)
Crown green with *central yellow stripe. Back bright green.* Throat and sides of neck white. Breast chestnut. Belly cinnamon. ♀: Head olive, (no crown stripe). Cheeks gray, throat grayish.

2. Orange-crowned Manakin L-F
Heterocercus aurantiivertex
5" (13 cm)
Crown green, *central stripe orange.* Above bright green. Throat and sides of neck white. *Below all cinnamon.* ♀: Head olive, (no crown stripe). Throat grayish.

3. Sulphur-bellied Tyrant-Manakin L-F
Neopelma sulphureiventer
4½" (12 cm)
Very like Wied's Tyrant-Manakin (100-7) but bill larger and belly brighter yellow.

4. Saffron-crested Tyrant-Manakin L-F
Neopelma chrysocephalum
4½" (12 cm)
Crest and center of nape yellow. Above uniform olive green. Below grayish, belly pale yellow. Quite like Wied's Tyrant-Manakin, (100-7) but yellow crown reaching nape.

5. Pale-bellied Tyrant-Manakin L-TS
Neopelma pallescens   5" (13 cm)
Crown patch yellow. Above uniform olive. Throat whitish, streaked gray. Breast gray. Belly white.

6. Tiny Tyrant-Manakin L-F
Tyranneutes virescens   2¾" (7 cm)
Very small. Above olive. Eye pale gray. Semi-concealed yellow crown patch (small in ♀). Throat whitish. Breast and sides grayish olive. Center of belly light yellow. Quite like Wied's Tyrant-Manakin (100-7) but much smaller and with shorter tail.

7. Dwarf Tyrant-Manakin L-F
Tyranneutes stolzmanni   3" (8 cm)
Small. Eye pale. Above uniform olive. *No crown patch.* Throat and breast grayish, faintly streaked white. Belly pale yellow.

8. Black-capped Manakin LM-F
Piprites pileatus   4¼" (11 cm)
Cap black. Back maroon chestnut. Wings black edged white. Throat, breast and sides light cinnamon. Center of belly pale yellow. Outer tail feathers rufous.

9. Broad-billed Manakin L-F
Sapayoa aenigma   5½" (14 cm)
Bill flat. Olive green with semi-concealed yellow crown stripe (lacking in ♀). Paler and yellower olive green below. Rather similar to Olivaceous Flatbill (108-11) but lacks white eye-ring and edging on wings.

10. Great Shrike-Tyrant LM-SO
Agriornis livida   10¼" (26 cm)
Above *dark* brown. Throat white streaked black. Below light brown, *belly tinged cinnamon. Tail blackish,* edged white.

11. Gray-bellied Shrike-Tyrant LM-SO
Agriornis microptera 9½" (24 cm)
Above brown. *Narrow eyebrow white.* Throat white streaked black. Below light grayish. *Tail blackish,* edged white.

12. Black-billed Shrike-Tyrant MH-O
Agriornis montana   9" (22 cm)
Bill black. Above dark brown. Narrow eyebrow buff. Throat whitish streaked dusky. Below dull brown. *Outer tail feathers all white or half white.*

1. White-tailed Shrike-Tyrant H-SO
Agriornis albicauda 10" (25 cm)
Lower bill pale. Above dark brown.
Narrow eyebrow buff. *Throat white
sharply streaked blackish.* Below
brown. *Tail all white.*

2. Chocolate-vented Tyrant LM-O
Neoxolmis rufiventris 8½" (21 cm)
Above gray, face blackish. *Wing
coverts mostly white, flight feathers cinnamon;* both conspicuous
in flight. Throat and breast pale
gray, contrasting with *rufous belly
and vent.* Tail black edged white.
Imm: Grayish brown above, *below
cinnamon buff broadly streaked
dusky.*

3. Gray Monjita L-SO
Xolmis cinerea 8½" (21 cm)
Above gray. Forehead and short
eyebrow white. Wings black with
*large white wing patch conspicu-
ous in flight.* Whisker black. Throat
and belly white. *Breast gray.* Tail
black, tipped whitish.

4. White-rumped Monjita L-S
Xolmis velata 7½" (19 cm)
Above gray. Forehead and eyebrow white. Wings black with
white patch obvious in flight.
Rump and underparts white. Tail
black, white near base.

**5. Black-crowned Monjita
L-SO**
Xolmis coronata 7½" (19 cm)
Forehead white. *Crown black sur-
rounded by white.* Back gray.
Wings blackish with white stripe
conspicuous in flight. Below white.
Tail black, tipped white.

6. Mouse-brown Monjita L-SO
Xolmis murina 7" (18 cm)
Above grayish brown. Wings
blackish, feathers edged white.
Below whitish, throat streaked
dusky, breast washed with grayish
brown. Tail black, tipped and
edged white.

7. Rusty-backed Monjita L-SO
Xolmis rubetra 7" (18 cm)
Above rufous brown. *Broad eyebrow white.* Wings blackish, coverts edged white (cinnamon band
shows when wings spread). Below
white, *streaked black on breast
and sides of neck.* Tail black,
tipped and edged white.

8. Rufous-webbed Tyrant MH-SO
Xolmis rufipennis 8" (20 cm)
Mostly dark gray, paler on throat,
white on belly. *Wings with rufous
showing in flight.*

9. Fire-eyed Diucon LM-TS
Pyrope pyrope 8" (20 cm)
Eye red. Above gray, wings black-
ish. Throat and belly whitish.
Breast and tail gray.

**10. Rufous-naped Ground-Tyrant
H-O**
Muscisaxicola rufivertex
6" (15 cm)
Crown chestnut. Above pale gray.
Short, narrow eyebrow white.
Below whitish. Tail black edged
white.

**11. White-browed Ground-Tyrant
H-TO**
Muscisaxicola albilora
6¼" (16 cm)
Above brownish gray. Patch on
hindcrown rufous, usually not
prominent. Long narrow eyebrow
white. Below whitish. Tail black
edged white.

12. Puna Ground-Tyrant H-O
Muscisaxicola juninensis
6" (15 cm)
Above dark brownish. Long, narrow eyebrow white. Patch on
hindcrown dull rufous. Tail black
edged white.

Ground-Tyrants are terrestrial, usually on rocky hillsides.

1. Ochre-naped Ground-Tyrant
MH-O

Muscisaxicola flavinucha
　　　　　7½" (19 cm)
Forehead white. Prominent eyebrow and area below eye white. Dull mouse gray above. *Conspicuous buffy yellow patch on hindcrown.* Below whitish. Tail black, edged white.

2. Cinnamon-bellied Ground-Tyrant
H-O

Muscisaxicola capistrata
　　　　　6½" (17 cm)
Above gray brown. *Forehead and area around eye black. Crown and nape chestnut.* Throat whitish, breast grayer, belly *cinnamon.* Tail black, edged white.

3. Black-fronted Ground-Tyrant
H-O

Muscisaxicola frontalis
　　　　　6½" (17 cm)
Forehead and center of crown black. Lores white. Above gray brown. Below whitish. Tail black, edged white.

4. White-fronted Ground-Tyrant
H-O

Muscisaxicola albifrons
　　　　　8½" (21 cm)
Above gray brown. *Forehead and streak before eye white.* Lores dusky. Below whitish. Tail black, edged white.

5. Plain-capped Ground-Tyrant
H-O

Muscisaxicola alpina 6½" (17 cm)
Above gray (grayish brown in Colombia and Ecuador). Short eyebrow white. Lores dusky. Below light gray. Tail black, edged white.

6. Dark-faced Ground-Tyrant
LMH-O

Muscisaxicola macloviana
　　　　　5½" (14 cm)
Crown dark reddish brown. Above brownish gray. *Face blackish.* Below whitish. Tail black, edged white.

7. Spot-billed Ground-Tyrant
LMH-O

Muscisaxicola maculirostris
　　　　　5" (13 cm)
Above light brown, wing coverts edged whitish. *Lower bill yellow,* black at base. Indistinct eyebrow whitish. Below whitish (buffy in n part of range). Tail black, edged white.

8. Little Ground-Tyrant　　**L-OW**

Muscisaxicola fluviatilis
　　　　　4½" (12 cm)
Above grayish brown. Throat and breast pale buff. Belly white. Tail black, edged white.

9. Short-tailed Field-Tyrant　**L-SO**

Muscigralla brevicauda 4" (10 cm)
Above brownish gray, rump chestnut. Crown stripe yellow. Two whitish wing-bars. Below whitish, grayer on breast. Legs long. *Tail very short,* black, tipped white. Terrestrial. Flicks tail.

10. Rufous-backed Negrito
LMH-OW

Lessonia rufa　　　4½" (12 cm)
Black. Back rufous. ♀: Crown and nape grayish, back brown (rufous in n Andes). Wings and tail black. Below grayish. Terrestrial.

11. Streak-throated Bush-Tyrant
H-TS

Myiotheretes striaticollis
　　　　　8½" (21 cm)
Above brown. Lores buffy. *Throat white streaked black.* Below cinnamon. *Flight feathers and outer tail feathers mostly cinnamon* (very conspicuous in flight).

12. Santa Marta Bush-Tyrant　**H-S**

Myiotheretes pernix 6½" (17 cm)
Above brown. Wings darker brown, feathers edged rufous. Throat white, streaked black. Breast and belly rufous. Tail dusky, edged rufous.

1. Rufous-bellied Bush-Tyrant   H-S

Myiotheretes fuscorufus
6½" (17cm)
Above brown. Wings dusky with *two rufous bars. Throat buffy white,* not streaked. Below cinnamon. Tail blackish, feathers edged cinnamon.

2. Red-rumped Bush-Tyrant   H-S
Myiotheretes erythropygius
8½" (21cm)
Above dark gray, *rump rufous.* Wings blackish with *white patch* showing when spread. *Forehead and throat whitish.* Breast gray. Belly rufous. Outer tail feathers rufous, tipped dusky.

3. D'Orbigny's Chat-Tyrant   H-TS
Ochthoeca oenanthoides
5½" (14cm)
Like Brown-backed Chat-Tyrant (112-8) but less brownish (more grayish) above. *Pure white eyebrow* and buff (not rufous) wing-bars (wings plain in Peru). Underparts cinnamon. Tail edged white.

4. White-browed Chat-Tyrant   LMH-TS

Ochthoeca leucophrys 5" (13cm)
Above grayish brown. Forehead and long broad eyebrow white. Two broad rufous wing-bars (lacking in Peru). *Throat and breast pale gray.* Belly white.

5. Piura Chat-Tyrant   M-S
Ochthoeca piurae 4¼" (11cm)
Above dark brown. Forehead and long broad eyebrow white. *Two bright rufous wing-bars.* Throat and breast light gray. Belly white.

6. Golden-browed Chat-Tyrant   MH-S

Ochthoeca pulchella 4¼" (11cm)
Very like Crowned Chat-Tyrant (112-11) with *prominent rufous*

wing-bars but back more reddish brown, rump rufous and belly whiter. Sides of head and breast brown, not gray.

7. Streamer-tailed Tyrant   L-TS

Gubernetes yetapa
7" (18cm) plus tail
Above pale gray. *Eyebrow and throat white. Chestnut band across breast.* Below pale gray, center of belly white. *Tail very long, deeply forked.*

8. Cock-tailed Tyrant   L-TS

Alectrurus tricolor 7½" (19cm)
Above black, rump gray. Wing coverts white. Eyebrow and underparts white, *partial band across breast* black. *Tail long, black, feathers wide, usually held cocked.* ♀: Brown above, whitish below with *incomplete breast band* brown. Tail normal.

9. Strange-tailed Tyrant   L-O
Yetapa risora 5½" (14cm) plus tail
Above black, rump gray. Wing coverts white. Below white with *broad black breast band. Throat unfeathered, reddish in breeding season.* Tail black, *outer feather greatly elongated and wide.* ♀: Above brown, rump buff. Below buff with *dark brown breast band. Tail like ♂ but shorter.*

10. Velvety (Black-Tyrant) Tyrant   LM-SO
Knipolegus nigerrimus 6½" (17cm)
Like Crested Tyrant (106-8) but *crest smaller and bill blue.* ♀: Throat dark cinnamon, streaked black.

11. White-winged (Black-Tyrant) Tyrant   MH-TS

Knipolegus aterrimus 6½" (17cm)
Like Crested Tyrant (106-8) but duller black plumage, crest smaller and bill whitish blue. ♀: Above grayish brown, *rump rufous. Two broad buff to whitish wing-bars.* Below dull buffy, throat and breast whiter. Tail mostly cinnamon buff, broadly tipped blackish.

1. Plumbeous Tyrant   **LM-FT**
Knipolegus cabanisi   6" (15cm)
Slaty gray, lighter below. Wings
and tail blackish. ♀: Above grayish brown, rump rufous. Wing-bars
and underparts whitish.

2. Amazonian Black-Tyrant   **L-FT**
Phaeotriccus poecilocercus
           4½" (12cm)
Glossy black. Bill black *(not blue).*
♀: Above olive brown, *rump and
tail mostly rufous.* Two prominent
buffy wing-bars. Below whitish
streaked dark brown on breast.

3. Hudson's Black-Tyrant   **L-S**
Phaeotriccus hudsoni 5½" (14cm)
Glossy black. Bill black. *Wings
with white band showing in flight.*
♀: Above grayish brown, *rump rufous.* Two whitish wing-bars. Below
light buffy. *Tail cinnamon buff.*

4. Cinereous Tyrant   **L-S**
Entotriccus striaticeps 4¼" (11cm)
Eye red. Dark gray, wing coverts
edged lighter gray. Tail black. ♀:
Olivaceous above, rump and
crown browner, *crown streaked
dusky.* Two wing-bars white. *Below
whitish streaked dusky.* Tail blackish, feathers edged rufous.

5. Shear-tailed Gray-Tyrant **LM-TS**
Muscipipra vetula   8" (20cm)
Dark gray. Wings and tail black.
Tail long, conspicuously forked.
♀: Below whitish.

6. Drab Water-Tyrant   **L-W**
Ochthornis littoralis 4½" (12cm)
Pale, sandy brown, paler below
and on rump. *Eyebrow white.*
Streak through eye dusky. Wings
and tail dusky.

7. Tumbes Tyrant   **L-SA**
Tumbezia salvini   4½" (12cm)
*Forehead, eyebrow and under-
parts yellow.* Above dark gray.
Wings blackish with two bold
white wing-bars. Tail blackish
edged and tipped white, often
fanned and cocked.

8. Eastern Kingbird   **L-O**
Tyrannus tyrannus*   7" (18cm)
Top and sides of head black. Concealed crest orange. Above dark
gray. Below white. Tail black with
white band on end.

9. Gray Kingbird   **L-O**
Tyrannus dominicensis* 7" (18cm)
Bill rather heavy. Concealed crest
orange. Gray above. White below,
shaded gray on breast. Tail slightly
forked.

10. Snowy-throated Kingbird **L-TS**
Tyrannus niveigularis 6½" (17cm)
Like Tropical Kingbird (104-5) but
above paler gray, *throat pure white.*
Breast pale gray (no olive tinge).
Belly bright yellow.

11. Dusky-chested Flycatcher **L-FT**
Tyrannopsis luteiventris
           5½" (14cm)
Rather like Sulphury Flycatcher
(104-8) but *dark brown above,*
throat streaked dusky and *bill
smaller.* Below bright yellow, *mottled olive and dusky on breast.*

12. Variegated Flycatcher   **L-T**
Empidonomus varius   7" (18cm)
Like Piratic Flycatcher (110-11) but
has primaries edged rufous and
tail longer *with prominent rufous
edges.* Wing feathers conspicuously margined whitish.

1. **Crowned Slaty-Flycatcher LM-ST**

Empidonomus aurantioatrocristatus 6½" (17cm)
Crown black. Semi-concealed crest yellow. Above brownish gray. *Below pure gray*, center of belly white. Perches conspicuously at forest edge.

2. **Three-striped Flycatcher L-FT**
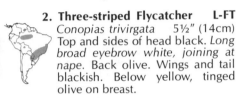
Conopias trivirgata 5½" (14cm)
Top and sides of head black. *Long broad eyebrow white, joining at nape*. Back olive. Wings and tail blackish. Below yellow, tinged olive on breast.

3. **Lemon-browed Flycatcher M-FT**
Conopias cinchoneti 6" (15cm)
Crown and cheeks olive. Forehead yellow. Above dark olive green, browner on wings and tail. *Long broad eyebrow yellow, meeting across nape*. Below all bright yellow.

4. **White-ringed Flycatcher L-F**
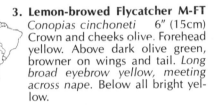
Conopias parva 5½" (14cm)
Crown (with semi-concealed yellow crest) and nape blackish. *Long broad white eyebrow meeting on nape*. Back, wings and tail dark olive brown. Below yellow (throat white w of Andes).

5. **Sulphur-bellied Flycatcher LM-T**
Myiodynastes luteiventris*
7" (18cm)
Very similar to Streaked Flycatcher (108-1) but bill almost all dark (lower not light colored). Eyebrow white (not dull yellowish). Underparts yellower.

6. **Baird's Flycatcher L-SA**

Myiodynastes bairdi 8½" (21cm)
Above pale brown, *rump and tail rufous. Wing feathers broadly edged rufous*. Concealed crest lemon-yellow. Eyebrow whitish, black stripe from forehead through eye. Throat white, streaked gray. Breast buff, below light yellow.

7. **Gray-capped Flycatcher L-TS**
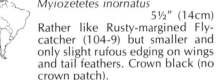
Myiozetetes granadensis
6¼" (16cm)
Much like Social Flycatcher (104-10) but white eyebrow short, only in front of eye. Forehead white. Head gray with usually concealed orange patch.

8. **White-bearded Flycatcher L-SO**

Myiozetetes inornatus
5½" (14cm)
Rather like Rusty-margined Flycatcher (104-9) but smaller and only slight rufous edging on wings and tail feathers. Crown black (no crown patch).

9. **Dull-capped Attila L-FT**

Attila bolivianus 7½" (19cm)
Crown dull grayish brown gradually becoming more rufous on back to *pale cinnamon on rump and tail*. No wing-bars. Below cinnamon rufous. Rather like Bright-rumped Attila (106-2) but more rufous.

10. **Citron-bellied Attila L-F**
Attila citriniventris 6½" (17cm)
Somewhat like rufous phase of Bright-rumped Attila (106-2) but no wing-bars. *Crown, nape and sides of head grayish*. Back brown, rump and tail rufous, yellower on rump. Below cinnamon rufous, yellowish in center of belly.

11. **Ochraceous Attila L-F**
Attila torridus 7½" (19cm)
Rather like Cinnamon Attila (106-3) but paler and wing coverts black with two cinnamon wing-bars. Center of belly yellowish.

12. **Rufous-tailed Attila LM-F**

Pseudattila phoenicurus
6½" (17cm)
Like Cinnamon Attila (106-3) but *top and sides of head gray*, contrasting with rufous back.

1. Rufous Casiornis   **L-TS**
Casiornis rufa   6½" (17cm)
Above chestnut rufous, darker and
redder on crown. Wing coverts
tipped black. *Throat and breast
cinnamon.* Belly yellowish white.

2. Ash-throated Casiornis   **L-TS**
Casiornis fusca   6½" (17cm)
Crown and rump rufous, contrast-
ing with brown back. *Throat gray.*
Breast cinnamon. Belly yellow.

3. Grayish Mourner   **L-FT**
Rhytipterna simplex   7½" (19cm)
Mostly uniform gray, paler below.
Back, breast and belly slightly
tinged greenish.

4. Pale-bellied Mourner   **L-S**
Rhytipterna immunda   8" (20cm)
Above grayish brown, browner on
rump and tail. Primaries and tail
feathers edged rufous. *Two narrow
whitish wing-bars.* Throat and
breast gray. Belly pale yellowish,
tinged rusty.

5. Rufous Flycatcher   **L-SA**
Myiarchus semirufus 6½" (17cm)
Upperparts and sides of head dark
brown. Wing edging and tail rufous. *Below uniform cinnamon.*

6. Apical Flycatcher   **LM-S**
Myiarchus apicalis   7½" (19cm)
Like Short-crested Flycatcher (106-
11) but throat and breast darker
gray and *tail broadly tipped whitish.*

7. Pale-edged Flycatcher   **M-FT**
Myiarchus cephalotes
        7½" (19cm)
Like Short-crested Flycatcher (106-
11) but wing-bars wider and more
conspicuous, whitish. Outer tail
feathers edged whitish.

8. Sooty-crowned Flycatcher
                  L-TS
Myiarchus phaeocephalus
        7½" (19cm)
Crown blackish. Above gray becoming olive on rump. Forehead
and lores ashy gray. Breast gray.
Belly yellow. Tail tipped pale grayish.

9. Great-crested Flycatcher LM-FT
Myiarchus crinitus*   7½" (19cm)
Like Brown-crested Flycatcher
(106-10) but throat not paler gray
than breast and tail appearing almost all rufous below.

10. Olive-sided Flycatcher   **LM-TS**
Contopus (Nuttallornis) borealis*
        6½" (17cm)
Above grayish olive. *Throat and
narrow line down center of breast
white.* Sides of breast olive. Tuft of
white usually shows on sides of
rump. Placed in genus *Nuttalornis*
in BSA.

11. White-throated Pewee   **L-FT**
Contopus albogularis 4¼" (11cm)
*Uniform dark gray with conspicu-
ous large white throat patch.*

12. Blackish Pewee   **L-FT**
Contopus nigrescens 4½" (12cm)
Very like Greater Pewee (108-4)
but much smaller. *Uniform dark
gray.* No wing-bars in adult but
immatures have two whitish bars.

1. Gray-breasted Flycatcher **L-T**
Empidonax griseipectus
4½" (12cm)
Above olive gray, grayer on crown. *Prominent incomplete white eye-ring.* Double wing-bars white. Throat whitish. Breast pale gray sharply contrasting with white belly.

2. Black-billed Flycatcher
L-FT
Aphanotriccus audax 4½" (12cm)
Bill black. Above olive green. *Eye-ring and line above lores white.* Wings brownish with two pale buffy bars. Throat whitish, contrasting with broad olive band across breast. Below pale yellow.

3. Olive-chested Flycatcher **L-T**
Myiophobus cryptoxanthus
4½" (12cm)
Semi-concealed crown patch yellow. *Above dark brown,* wings with double light buffy bars. Throat whitish. Breast grayish brown, streaked dusky. Belly pale yellow.

4. Unadorned Flycatcher **M-FT**
Myiophobus inornatus
4½" (12cm)
Semi-concealed crown patch yellow. Above brownish olive. Well-marked yellow eye-ring. Wing-bars faint or absent. *Breast olive streaked pale yellow.*

5. Orange-banded Flycatcher M-FT
Myiophobus lintoni 4¼" (11cm)
Rather like Handsome Flycatcher (122-10) but *below greenish yellow,* without orange tinge. Above dark olive brown. Semi-concealed orange crown patch (smaller or absent in ♀). Two prominent cinnamon wing bands.

6. Ochraceous-breasted Flycatcher
M-F
Myiophobus ochraceiventris
4½" (12cm)
Semi-concealed crown patch yellow (rufous in ♀). Above dark brownish olive. Two light buffy wing-bars. Throat and breast light ochraceous. Belly bright yellow.

7. Roraiman Flycatcher **LM-F**
Myiophobus roraimae
4¼" (11cm)
Semi-concealed crown patch orange rufous (lacking in ♀). Above olive to reddish brown. Two *conspicuous cinnamon wing-bars* and cinnamon edging to flight feathers. Below pale yellow, breast and sides tinged olive. Tail brown edged rufous.

8. Cliff Flycatcher **L-TO**
Hirundinea ferruginea 4½" (12cm)
Above black. Wings blackish with *chestnut patch, especially conspicuous in flight.* Sides of head and upper throat freckled black and white in n part of range. *Below chestnut.* Tail blackish (or chestnut ending in black s of the Amazon). Flies like a swallow.

9. White-crested Spadebill **L-F**
Platyrinchus platyrhynchos
4" (10cm)
Crown and sides of head gray, contrasting with otherwise brown upperparts. Semi-concealed white crown streak. Throat white. Below bright tawny ochraceous. Legs yellowish flesh.

10. Yellow-throated Spadebill LM-F
Platyrinchus flavigularis 3½" (9cm)
Head and nape rufous. Above olive brown. Crown stripe white. Below yellow, brightest on throat, washed with olive on breast.

11. Yellow-margined Flycatcher
LM-F
Tolmomyias assimilis 5" (13cm)
Very like Yellow-olive Flycatcher (112-1) but crown somewhat darker gray. A small, inconspicuous white speculum can sometimes be seen. No white on lores.

12. Rufous-tailed Flatbill **L-F**
Ramphotrigon ruficauda
5½" (14cm)
Wide flat bill. Above dark olive. Eye-ring and spot above lores white. *Wings and tail bright rufous.* Throat and breast whitish streaked olive. Belly yellow, lightly streaked olive.

Tody-Flycatchers have long, flat bills

1. Black-headed Tody-Flycatcher
L-FT
Todirostrum nigriceps 3½" (9cm)
Bill nearly as long as head. *Eye dark.* Head and nape black. Back olive yellow. Prominent wing-bars yellow. Throat white, below yellow.

2. Painted Tody-Flycatcher   L-FT
Todirostrum chrysocrotaphum
3½" (9cm)
Like Common Tody-Flycatcher (126-7) but head all black and back olive yellow. Yellow stripe back of eye in some races. Below with yellow or white throat and with or without *black spots across breast* or black whiskers.

3. Golden-winged Tody-Flycatcher
L-T
Todirostrum calopterum
3½" (9cm)
Head black. Back olive (black in Peru). *Shoulder chestnut, bordered below by single broad yellow band.* Throat white. Below bright yellow. Tail black.

4. Yellow-lored (Gray-headed)
Tody-Flycatcher   L-T
Todirostrum poliocephalum
3½" (9cm)
Crown gray. *Lores bright yellow.* Back yellowish green. Wings black with yellow bars. Below bright yellow.

5. Black-and-white Tody-Flycatcher
L-F
Todirostrum capitale 3½" (9cm)
Mostly black. Lores and eye-ring white. Bend of wing yellow. Center of throat, breast and entire belly white (with black breast band in w Brazil). ♀: Above olive. Eye-ring buffy. Crown chestnut. Sides of head and breast gray. Center of underparts and whole belly white.

6. White-cheeked Tody-Flycatcher
L-F
Todirostrum albifacies 3½" (9cm)
Crown chestnut, back olive. *Wide black collar on hindneck. Sides of head white* (not gray). Wing and tail feathers edged olive. Throat and belly white, breast gray.

7. Ruddy Tody-Flycatcher   M-F
Todirostrum russatum 3½" (9cm)
Crown and nape gray. Above dark olive. Wing coverts blackish with two rufous bars. *Face, throat and breast rufous.* Belly white, grayish on flanks.

8. Fork-tailed Pygmy-Tyrant   LM-F
Ceratotriccus furcatus 3½" (9cm)
Head and throat rufous. Above olive green. Breast and sides gray. Belly white. *Tail gray, forked, outer feathers curving outward.* ♀: Has less forked tail.

9. Hangnest Tody-Tyrant   LM-FT
Idioptilon nidipendulum
3½" (9cm)
Above uniform olive green, bend of wing yellow. Throat and breast pale gray lightly streaked whitish. Belly whitish.

10. Buff-throated Tody-Tyrant LM-FT
Idioptilon rufigulare 4" (10cm)
Above olive green. No wing-bars. *Eye-ring buff. Sides of neck, throat and breast buffy.* Belly white.

11. Yungas Tody-Tyrant   LM-FT
Idioptilon spodiops 3½" (9cm)
Above olive green. Lores grayish buff. Wings dusky with two narrow olive bars. *Throat and breast grayish olive streaked whitish.* Belly yellowish white.

12. Zimmer's Tody-Tyrant   L-F
Idioptilon aenigma 3½" (9cm)
Above dark olive green. *Two broad yellowish wing-bars.* Throat whitish, sharply streaked dusky. Breast and sides yellowish streaked dusky. Center of belly yellowish white.

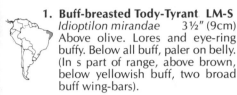

1. **Buff-breasted Tody-Tyrant LM-S**
Idioptilon mirandae 3½" (9cm)
Above olive. Lores and eye-ring buffy. Below all buff, paler on belly. (In s part of range, above brown, below yellowish buff, two broad buff wing-bars).

2. **Pearly-vented Tody-Tyrant L-TS**
Idioptilon margaritaceiventer
3½" (9cm)
Above olive (dull brown in nw part of range). Wings with two whitish bars and yellow shoulder. Lores and eye-ring white. Below white, *streaked gray on throat and breast.*

3. **White-eyed Tody-Tyrant L-F**
Idioptilon zosterops 4" (10cm)
Above olive green. Wings blackish with two narrow, yellowish bars. *Eye-ring and lores white.* Eye pale yellowish. Below whitish, streaked gray on throat and breast, tinged yellow on flanks.

4. **Boat-billed Tody-Tyrant L-F**
Microcochlearius josephinae
4" (10cm)
Above olive green, *no wing-bars.* Lores and chin grayish. *Throat and breast olive,* shading into pale yellow on belly. Vent buffy yellow.

5. **Snethlage's Tody-Tyrant L-F**
Snethlagea minor 3½" (9cm)
Above dull olive. Eye white. *No white eye-ring* or lores. Wing-bars whitish. Throat and breast pale yellowish lightly streaked olive. Belly yellowish.

6. **Black-chested Tyrant L-F**
Taeniotriccus andrei 4" (10cm)
Forehead, throat and sides of head chestnut. Above black except conspicuous yellow patch on wings. Breast black. Belly grayish. ♀: Back olive, breast gray, center of belly white.

7. **Long-crested Pygmy-Tyrant L-F**
Lophotriccus eulophotes
4" (10cm)
Like Double-banded Pygmy-Tyrant (124-6) but lacks wing-bars, has *conspicuous buffy eye-ring* and is *white* (not yellowish) be low with dark streaks.

8. **Hazel-fronted Pygmy-Tyrant M-F**
Pseudotriccus simplex 4" (10cm)
Like Bronze-olive Pygmy-Tyrant (120-4) but forehead, sides of head and edges of wing and tail feathers brown. *Center of belly bright yellow.*

9. **Drab-breasted Pygmy-Tyrant L-F**
Hemitriccus diops 4" (10cm)
Above uniform olive green. *Conspicuous spot in front of eye white.* Below gray. Lower throat and center of belly white.

10. **Flammulated Pygmy-Tyrant L-F**
Hemitriccus flammulatus
4" (10cm)
Above uniform olive green. *Conspicuous spot in front of eye light grayish.* Throat and breast whitish, streaked dusky.

11. **Southern Bristle-Tyrant LM-F**
Pogonotriccus eximius 4" (10cm)
Forehead, large eye-ring and streak behind eye white. Crown gray. *Black crescent behind ear coverts.* Otherwise bright olive green above, wings and tail edged yellow. Below greenish yellow, becoming bright yellow on belly.

12. **Ecuadorian Bristle-Tyrant M-F**
Pogonotriccus gualaquizae
4" (10cm)
Like Marble-faced Bristle-Tyrant (122-2) but *ear coverts mostly pale yellowish surrounded by a dark line.* Eye-ring and streak through eye white.

1. **Spectacled Bristle-Tyrant**   **M-F**
Pogonotriccus orbitalis
4″ (10cm)
Crown gray. *Conspicuous eye-ring white. Ear coverts yellowish.* Back dull olive. Wing-bars yellowish. Below yellow.

2. **Venezuelan Bristle-Tyrant**   **M-F**
Pogonotriccus venezuelanus
4″ (10cm)
Very like Marble-faced Bristle-Tyrant (122-2) but lower bill pale and wing-bars slightly broader.

3. **Yellow-bellied Bristle-Tyrant** **L-F**
Pogonotriccus flaviventris
4¼″ (11cm)
Crown gray. Back olive. *Lores, eyebrow and eye-ring rufous.* Ear coverts dull buff surrounded by black line. Wing-bars conspicuous, yellow. *Below bright clear yellow.*

4. **Bay-ringed Tyrannulet**   **LM-F**
Leptotriccus sylviolus   4″ (10cm)
Lores and eye-ring chestnut. Upperparts bright yellowish green. Wing and tail feathers edged olive. Below whitish, throat and sides washed with greenish yellow.

5. **Olive-green Tyrannulet**   **L-F**
Phylloscartes virescens
4¼″ (11cm)
Above dull olive. *Wing-bars yellow. Eye-ring yellow.* Lores and throat grayish. Below pale yellow mottled olive on breast.

6. **Chapman's Tyrannulet**   **M-F**
Phylloscartes chapmani
4¼″ (11cm)
Above olive green. Eye-ring and long eyebrow whitish. Face mottled pale yellow and grayish. *Two broad wing-bars and wing-edging ochraceous buff. Below pale greenish yellow,* clearest on belly.

7. **Black-fronted Tyrannulet**   **M-F**
Phylloscartes nigrifrons
4½″ (12cm)
Forehead black. Crown grayish, above drab olive. Short whitish eyebrow, face mottled light gray and blackish. Two broad yellowish wing-bars. *Below pale grayish,* whiter on belly.

8. **Yellow-eared (Oustalet's) Tyrannulet**   **LM-F**
Phylloscartes oustaleti
4¼″ (11cm)
Conspicuous eye-ring yellow. Cheeks black, bordered behind by *bright yellow ear patch.* Above olive green. No wing-bars. Below yellow tinged olive. Tail olive.

9. **São Paulo Tyrannulet**   **LM-F**
Phylloscartes paulistus   4″ (10cm)
Forehead and eyebrow yellowish. Above light olive green. Cheeks dusky. No wing-bars. Below uniform deep yellow.

10. **Rufous-browed Tyrannulet** **LM-F**
Phylloscartes superciliaris
4¼″ (11cm)
Crown grayish. *Forehead and eyebrow rufous.* Back olive green. No wing-bars. Cheeks white surrounded by dusky line. White below, tinged gray on breast and yellow on belly.

11 **Minas Gerais Tyrannulet**   **L-F**
Phylloscartes roquettei   4″ (10cm)
Forehead, lores and eye-ring rufous. Above bright olive green. Two pale yellow wing-bars. *Below bright yellow,* shaded with olive on breast.

12. **Yellow Tyrannulet**   **L-FTS**
Capsiempis flaveola   4″ (10cm)
Above yellowish olive. Eyebrow yellow (white in central Colombia). Wing-bars yellowish. Below bright yellow tinged olive on breast. Wing and tail feathers edged yellowish.

1. Tawny-crowned Pygmy-Tyrant
L-S
Euscarthmus meloryphus
4″ (10cm)
Above light brown, *crown patch orange rufous*. Wing-bars obscure (prominent buff w of Andes). Below whitish, sides gray.

2. Rufous-sided Pygmy-Tyrant   L-S
Euscarthmus rufomarginatus
4¼″ (11cm)
Above brown. Wings with two ochraceous bars. Throat white, below pale yellow, deep ochraceous on sides and vent.

3. Dinelli's Doradito   LM-S
Pseudocolopteryx dinellianus
3½″ (9cm)
Crown brown, feathers edged rusty. Above dull greenish. *Three pale yellowish wing-bars.* Below bright yellow.

4. Crested Doradito   L-SOW
Pseudocolopteryx sclateri
3½″ (9cm)
Prominent crest of black, yellow-edged feathers. Eye-stripe whitish. Above dull olive. Two wing-bars light buffy. Below uniform bright yellow.

5. Subtropical Doradito   M-S
Pseudocolopteryx acutipennis
4″ (10cm)
Above dark olive green. Wings with two grayish olive bars. Below bright yellow.

6. Warbling Doradito   L-SW
Pseudocolopteryx flaviventris
4¼″ (11cm)
Crown feathers edged reddish brown. Above dull brown. Below lemon yellow.

7. Bearded Tachuri   LMH-OW
Polystictus pectoralis   3½″ (9cm)
Crest gray streaked black. Line above lores white. Above brown, two wing-bars buffy. *Throat mottled gray and white.* Below white, cinnamon on breast and sides (all rufous in Colombia).   ♀: Has brown crown, buffy white throat.

8. Gray-backed Tachuri   LM-SO
Polystictus superciliaris
3½″ (9cm)
Head gray, eyebrow white. Back brownish gray. Faint pale gray wing-bars. *Underparts cinnamon,* center of belly white.

9. Tufted Tit-Tyrant   MH-SO
Anairetes parulus   4″ (10cm)
Long recurved crest black. Eye white. Eyebrow white. Sides of head black. Back gray. Wings black with two white bars. Below pale yellow or whitish, streaked black on throat and breast.

10. Yellow-billed Tit-Tyrant   H-S
Anairetes flavirostris   4″ (10cm)
Long recurved crest black. Eye dark. Base of lower bill yellow. Eyebrow white. Back gray. Wings black, well-marked bars white. Below whitish coarsely streaked black on throat and breast. Belly pale yellow.

11. Pied-crested Tit-Tyrant   H-S
Anairetes reguloides   4¼″ (11cm)
Very long recurved crest black, hindcrown white. Upper bill black, lower yellow. *Back black streaked white,* wing-bars white. Throat and breast white, heavily streaked black, (face and throat all black in some races). Belly pale yellow.

12. Ash-breasted Tit-tyrant   H-O
Anairetes alpinus   4½″ (12cm)
Above dark gray, unstreaked. Long crest black. Wing-bars, throat and breast dark gray. Belly white.

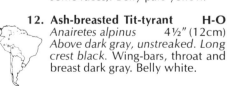

1. Unstreaked Tit-Tyrant   H-FT
Uromyias agraphia   4½" (12cm)
Like Agile Tit-Tyrant (118-3) but
back gray, unstreaked and underparts white, *unstreaked.*

2. Greater Wagtail-Tyrant   LM-S
Stigmatura budytoides 5½" (14cm)
Very like Lesser Wagtail-Tyrant
(114-11) but *back grayish olive
with no brownish tinge.*

3. White-bellied Tyrannulet   L-S
Serpophaga munda   4" (10cm)
Like White-crested Tyrannulet
(120-11) but *back pure gray* without greenish tinge and *belly white*
instead of pale yellow.

4. Gray-crowned Tyrannulet   M-S
Serpophaga griseiceps   3½" (9cm)
Crown and nape gray. *No white
crest.* Eyebrow and eye-ring white.
Back grayish. Wings with *two
ochraceous bars.* Below grayish
white, washed yellow on belly.

5. Sooty Tyrannulet   L-SW
Serpophaga nigricans 4¼" (11cm)
Semi-concealed   crown   patch
white. *Above dark gray, below
paler gray.* Wings blackish with
two pale gray wing-bars. *Tail black.*

6. Bananal Tyrannulet   L-TS
Serpophaga araguayae   4" (10cm)
Above gray, darker on crown. Sides
of head streaked white. Two wing-
bars white. Throat whitish, breast
and sides washed with gray. Belly
white. Tail dusky.

7. Slender-billed Tyrannulet   L-S
Inezia tenuirostris   3½" (9cm)
Very like Southern Beardless Tyrannulet (124-8) but has no crest
and *throat is white* instead of pale
gray.

8. Plain Tyrannulet   L-S
Inezia inornata   3½" (9cm)
Crown and nape ashy gray, back
olive gray. Wings brownish with
two white bars. Throat and breast
grayish, lower breast whitish. Belly
pale yellow.

9. White-tailed Tyrannulet   MH-F
Mecocerculus poecilocercus
                              4" (10cm)
Eyebrow white. Crown gray. Back
olive green, rump pale yellow. Two
wing-bars pale yellowish. Throat
and breast pale gray. Belly pale
yellowish. *Tail looks mostly white,*
especially obvious in flight.

10. Buff-banded Tyrannulet   M-F
Mecocerculus hellmayri 4" (10cm)
Above olive green. *Two wing-bars
buff.* Eyebrow white. Below pale
grayish becoming pale yellow on
belly. Tail brownish.

11. Rufous-winged Tyrannulet M-FT
Mecocerculus calopterus
                              4" (10cm)
Crown gray. *Broad eyebrow and
throat white.* Black mark through
eye. Back olive gray. Breast pale
gray. Belly pale yellow. *Conspicuous rufous patch on primaries.*

12. Sulphur-bellied Tyrannulet   M-F
Mecocerculus minor   4" (10cm)
Crown gray. Back olive. Wings gray
with *two broad cinnamon bars.*
Eyebrow white. *Below bright yellow,* paler on throat, shaded olive
on breast.

1. White-banded Tyrannulet MH-F

Mecocerculus stictopterus
4¼" (11cm)
Crown gray. Above olive to olive brown. *Long, broad eyebrow white. White wing-bars well marked.* Throat and breast pale grayish. Belly white.

2. Patagonian Tyrant LM-FT
Colorhamphus parvirostris
4½" (12cm)
Bill very small. Cheek patch black. Dark grayish brown above. Wing-bars cinnamon. *Below dark gray* becoming yellowish on belly.

3. Large Elaenia L-FTS

Elaenia spectabilis 6¼" (16cm)
Very like Yellow-bellied Elaenia (110-3) but larger. Has *three wide whitish wing-bars* (not two). Throat and breast darker gray, contrasting more with pale yellow belly. *Very little (if any) white shows in crest.*

4. Olivaceous Elaenia L-FT
Elaenia mesoleuca 5½" (14cm)
Above olive. No crown patch. Wing-bars narrow but distinct, usually a third bar visible. *Below rather dark olive grayish,* paler and yellower on belly.

5. Slaty Elaenia LM-F
Elaenia strepera 5½" (14cm)
Mostly slaty gray. Semi-concealed white crown patch. Center of belly white. Wings with two narrow, inconspicuous gray bars.

6. Mottle-backed Elaenia L-FT
Elaenia gigas 7" (18cm)
Large size. Above dark brown. Feathers of back edged paler, producing mottled effect. Quite conspicuous white crown patch. Two whitish wing-bars. Throat white, breast brownish. Belly pale yellow, sides faintly streaked olive.

7. Brownish Elaenia L-FT
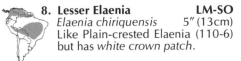
Elaenia pelzelni 7" (18cm)
Large size. Above dull dark brown. Semi-concealed white crown patch (♂ only). Three wing-bars narrow, whitish. Throat pale grayish. Breast and sides pale brown. Belly white.

8. Lesser Elaenia LM-SO
Elaenia chiriquensis 5" (13cm)
Like Plain-crested Elaenia (110-6) but has *white crown patch.*

9. Mountain Elaenia MH-TS

Elaenia frantzii 5" (13cm)
Like Plain-crested Elaenia (110-6) but wing-bars grayish, not pure white. Also upperparts are more olive, less grayish. Occurs only at higher elevations.

10. Great Elaenia M-F
Elaenia dayi 7" (18cm)
A *large, dark* Elaenia. Head blackish without white. Back dark brown. Wing-bars broad, conspicuous, whitish. Below light grayish becoming pale yellowish on belly. Tail blackish.

11. Sierran Elaenia M-T

Elaenia pallatangae 5½" (14cm)
Concealed crown patch white. Above olive. Two broad conspicuous wing-bars white. Throat and breast grayish yellow. Belly pale yellow. *Yellower below than most other Elaenias.*

12. Pacific Elaenia L-TS

Myiopagis subplacens
5½" (14cm)
Crown grayish brown with semi-concealed bright yellow patch. *Broad eyebrow grizzled whitish,* curling around darker ear coverts. Two yellowish wing-bars. Throat and breast pale gray streaked whitish. Belly pale yellow.

1. **Yellow-crowned Elaenia**   **L-FT**
Myiopagis flavivertex 4½" (12cm)
Above dull olive green. *Semi-concealed bright yellow crown patch.*
Wings and tail brownish. Wing-bars yellowish. Throat whitish. Breast pale grayish. Belly pale yellow.

2. **Suiriri Flycatcher**   **L-S**
Suiriri suiriri   5½" (14cm)
Above gray. Streak over lores white. Wings black with wide gray bars and edging. Throat white. Breast pale grayish. Belly pale yellow. Tail black, outer feather edged white. (In Brazil belly is white and tail gray at end and whitish at base).

3. **Scrub Flycatcher**   **L-TS**
Sublegatus modestus 5½" (14cm)
Short black bill. Above brownish. *Line through eye white.* Wings with two whitish bars and edging. Throat and breast gray contrasting with yellow belly. Tail dark brown.

4. **Gray-and-white Tyrannulet L-SA**
Phaeomyias leucospodia
4½" (12cm)
Semi-concealed crown patch white. Above dark brownish gray. Two whitish wing-bars. Throat whitish. Breast pale gray. Belly white in center. Flanks pale yellow.

5. **Greenish Tyrannulet**   **LM-F**
Xanthomyias virescens
4½" (12cm)
Olive green above. *Two bold wing-bars and wing-edging yellowish.* Narrow eyebrow and eye-ring white. Throat whitish. Breast olive mottled yellow. Belly yellow.

6. **Reiser's Tyrannulet**   **LM-F**
Xanthomyias reiseri 4¼" (11cm)
Above yellowish green. Wing-bars yellowish. Forehead grayish, lores and eye-ring white. Throat whitish. *Breast olive mottled yellow.* Belly yellow.

7. **Sclater's Tyrannulet**   **M-F**
Xanthomyias sclateri 4½" (12cm)
Olive green above. Bold wing-bars and edging yellowish. Forehead grayish, lores and eye-ring white. Throat and breast grayish white, mottled yellow. Belly whitish mottled yellow.

8. **Planalto Tyrannulet**   **LM-FT**
Phyllomyias fasciatus 4¼" (11cm)
Head gray. *Short white eye-stripe.* Above light olive, wing-bars whitish. Throat whitish. Breast yellowish tinged gray. Belly pale yellow.

9. **Sooty-headed Tyrannulet**   **L-T**
Phyllomyias griseiceps 4" (10cm)
Crown and nape dark brown with slight bushy-crested effect. Narrow eyebrow white. Back olive. Wings and tail dusky, indistinctly edged paler *(no wing-bars).* Throat whitish. Below pale yellow tinged olive on breast.

10. **Olrog's Tyrannulet**   **M-F**
Tyranniscus australis   4" (10cm)
Above pale olive gray, crown darker. Rump olive. Throat and breast pale gray. Belly pale yellowish.

11. **Bolivian Tyrannulet**   **M-F**
Tyranniscus bolivianus
4¼" (11cm)
Bill black. Above uniform dark olive green. Wings dusky, coverts edged yellow. Below pale yellow, tinged gray on breast, brightest on belly.

12. **Red-billed Tyrannulet**   **LM-F**
Tyranniscus cinereicapillus
4¼" (11cm)
Lower bill reddish. Crown grayish olive. Back olive green. Wings dusky, coverts edged yellow. Below bright yellow.

1. Slender-footed Tyrannulet LM-F

Tyranniscus gracilipes   4" (10cm)
Crown dull gray. Eye white. Back olive. Wings and tail dusky with two yellow wing-bars and edging. Below yellowish, clear pale yellow on belly.

2. Plumbeous-crowned Tyrannulet M-F

Oreotriccus plumbeiceps   4¼" (11cm)
Crown gray. Eyebrow white. *Spot on ear coverts black bordered with whitish.* Back olive green. Wings blackish with two yellow bars. Throat whitish, below yellow, washed olive on breast and sides.

3. Gray-capped Tyrannulet LM-FT

Oreotriccus griseocapillus   4" (10cm)
Head grayish brown. Eye-ring and lores pale gray. Back olive green. Two wing-bars and broad wing-edging yellow. *Below grayish white,* greenish yellow on sides.

4. Rough-legged Tryannulet LM-F

Acrochordopus burmeisteri   4¼" (11cm)
Lower bill pale reddish. Crown dark gray (olive in se part of range). *Forehead, eyebrow and around eye whitish.* Back olive. Wings blackish with two broad yellow wing-bars and edging. *Below yellow,* throat and breast tinged olive.

5. White-lored Tyrannulet L-FT

Ornithion inerme   3" (8cm)
Sharp, narrow eyebrow white. Back olive. *Two wing-bars of distinct white spots.* Throat whitish. Below greenish yellow, clear yellow on belly.

6. Yellow-bellied Tyrannulet L-FT

Ornithion semiflavum   3" (8cm)
Crown brown. Above brownish olive. No wing-bars. *Prominent eyebrow white.* Underparts bright yellow, tinged olive on breast.

7. Rufous-breasted Flycatcher M-F

Leptopogon rufipectus   4½" (12cm)
Crown gray. Lores and area around eye rufous. Back olive green. *Wings dusky with two buffy bars. Throat and breast rufous.* Belly pale yellow.

8. Inca Flycatcher M-F

Leptopogon taczanowskii   4½" (12 cm)
Crown olive. Lores and around eye gray. Back olive green. Wings dusky, bars ochraceous. Throat gray. *Breast pale rufous.* Belly yellow.

9. Southern Antpipit LM-F

Corythopis delalandi   5" (13cm)
Very like Ringed Antpipit (114-12) but back and sides of head lighter, tinged olive. Underwing coverts white (not gray).

10. White-tipped Plantcutter MH-TS

Phytotoma rutila   7" (18cm)
Slightly crested. Forecrown rufous. Back gray streaked black. Wings brownish with two prominent white bars. Below rufous. *Tail blackish tipped white.* ♀: Above brown streaked white. Below whitish, belly buffy, both *heavily streaked black.*

11. Rufous-tailed Plantcutter LM-TS

Phytotoma rara   7½" (19cm)
Crown chestnut. Sides of head black. Back olive brown heavily streaked black. Wings black, coverts edged white. Below rufous. *Tail mostly chestnut,* broadly tipped black. ♀: Below buffy streaked black.

12. Peruvian Plantcutter L-TS

Phytotoma raimondii 6½" (17cm)
Forehead rufous. Back gray spotted black. Wings black, broad bars white. *Below pale gray, belly rufous.* Tail blackish tipped white. ♀: Above dark brown streaked white. Below buffy whitish streaked dark brown.

1. Horned Lark   **H-O**
Eremophila alpestris* 5½" (14cm)
Prominent forehead and eyebrow white. Lores and stripe below eye black. Above brownish. Throat yellowish. *Breast band black.* Below white. Terrestrial. Walks.

2. Mangrove Swallow   **L-W**
Tachycineta albilinea 4¼" (11cm)
Above shiny green. Rump whitish. Wings and slightly forked tail blackish. Narrow white streak above lores. Below grayish white, darkest on breast.

3. White-winged Swallow   **L-TOW**
Tachycineta albiventer
     4½" (12cm)
Above shiny blue green. *Large white patch on closed wing. Rump and entire underparts white.*

4. Chilean Swallow   **LM-TO**
Tachycineta leucopyga
     4¼" (11cm)
Above shiny deep blue. No white in wings or tail. Rump and underparts white.

5. Purple Martin   **L-O**
Progne subis*   6½" (17cm)
Shiny purple. Wings and tail blackish. Tail forked. ♀: *Forehead usually gray.* Narrow collar whitish. Above brown glossed purple on head and wings. Below whitish, browner on breast, streaked brown on belly.

6. Gray-breasted Martin   **LM-TO**
Progne chalybea*   6½" (17cm)
Glossy dark blue above. Throat, breast and sides ashy brown. Belly white.

7. Southern Martin   **L-TO**
Progne modesta   6½" (17cm)
All glossy blue-black. Tail quite forked. ♀: Above blackish. Below entirely sooty brown or dusky, feathers often edged paler.

8. Pale-footed Swallow   **H-FT**
Notiochelidon flavipes
     4½" (12cm)
Like Blue-and-white Swallow (128-5) but *throat and breast buff* (not uniform white below). *Feet pink* (not black). Prefers forest instead of open country.

9. White-banded Swallow   **L-TW**
Atticora fasciata   5½" (14cm)
Glossy steely blue, band across breast white. Tail long, deeply forked.

10. Black-collared Swallow   **L-TW**
Atticora melanoleuca 5½" (14cm)
Upperparts, sides of head and undertail coverts steely blue. *Below white with dark blue band across breast.* Tail long, deeply forked.

11. Tawny-headed Swallow   **L-TSO**
Alopochelidon fucata 4¼" (11cm)
Forehead, eyebrow and collar on hindneck tawny rufous. Crown blackish brown. Back, wings and tail grayish brown. Throat and breast buff. Belly and undertail coverts white. Tail slightly forked.

12. Bank Swallow   **LM-O**
Riparia riparia*   4¼" (11cm)
Above smoky brown. Below white with *brown band across breast.* Wings and tail blackish brown. Tail forked.

1. Barn Swallow   **LMH-O**
Hirundo rustica*   5½" (14cm)
Upperparts shiny dark blue. *Forehead and throat chestnut.* Below buff to whitish. *Tail deeply forked,* black with white spot on middle of all feathers except central ones. Immature and molting adult lack lengthened outer tail feathers.

2. Andean Swallow   **H-O**
Petrochelidon andecola
                    5½" (14cm)
Glossy bluish above, rump brownish. Wings and tail dusky. Throat and breast grayish brown. *Belly white.* Tail only slightly forked.

3. Cliff Swallow   **LMH-O**
Petrochelidon pyrrhonota*
                    5" (13cm)
Forehead pale buff. Above blackish. Grayish collar on hindneck and white streaks on back. *Sides of head and throat chestnut.* Rump buffy brown. Breast black in center, buff at sides. Belly white. Tail square.

4. Cave Swallow   **L-SO**
Petrochelidon fulva   4½" (12cm)
Forehead chestnut. Above glossy blue black. Rump chestnut. *Entire sides of head, throat and breast pale cinnamon.* Below whitish.

5. Collared Jay   **MH-F**
Cyanolyca viridicyana
                    11½" (28cm)
Purplish blue. Forehead and mask black. Narrow band across breast black (white in Peru and Bolivia).

6. Turquoise Jay   **MH-F**
Cyanolyca turcosa   11" (27cm)
Blue. Crown and throat light blue. Forehead and mask black. Narrow breast band black.

7. Beautiful Jay   **LM-F**
Cyanolyca pulchra   9" (23cm)
Forehead and mask black. *Crown and nape bluish white.* Mantle brownish. Back, rump, wings and tail purplish blue. Underparts purplish blue tinged dusky on breast.

8. Azure Jay   **L-F**
Cyanocorax caeruleus 13" (33cm)
Bright blue. Head, throat and breast black.

9. Purplish Jay   **LM-T**
Cyanocorax cyanomelas
                    13" (33cm)
A very dark, uniform appearing jay. Forehead and lores black. Hindcrown and nape brownish. Above dull violet. Throat and breast blackish. Belly dull violet. Tail violet blue.

10. Violaceous Jay   **L-FT**
Cyanocorax violaceus 14" (35cm)
Head, throat and breast black. Hindcrown whitish. Rest of plumage violet blue, paler below and darker on wings and tail. No white tipping on tail.

11. Curl-crested Jay   **L-S**
Cyanocorax cristatellus
                    12½" (31cm)
Crest curling foreward on forehead. Head, throat and breast black. Mantle brownish. Back and wings purplish blue. Breast, belly and *outer half of tail white.*

12. Azure-naped Jay   **L-FTO**
Cyanocorax heilprini 13" (32cm)
Forecrown, sides of head, throat and breast black. Whisker white. Hindcrown whitish becoming *blue on nape.* Rest of plumage grayish blue. *Tail tipped white.*

1. Cayenne Jay   **L-FT**
Cyanocorax cayanus   12″ (30cm)
Forecrown, sides of head, throat
and breast black. Small spots above
and below eye whitish. Whisker
white. Back dull violet. *Nape,
rump and underparts white.* Wings
and tail violet blue. *Tail tipped
white.*

2. Black-chested Jay   **L-FT**
Cyanocorax affinis   12″ (30cm)
Head, throat and breast black.
Whisker and spots above and
below eye bright blue. Back drab
violet, wings bluer. Nape and rump
blue. *Lower breast and belly
creamy white. Tail broadly tipped
white.*

3. Plush-crested Jay   **L-TS**
Cyanocorax chrysops   13″ (32cm)
Head (*including plush-like crest*),
throat and breast black. Whisker
and spots above and below eye
bright blue. Nape bluish white.
Above dark violet blue, bluer on
wings and tail. Breast, belly and
broad tips on tail creamy white.

4. White-naped Jay   **L-TS**
Cyanocorax cyanopogon
               13″ (32cm)
Head black, *not crested. Nape and
upper back bluish white.* Wings
and tail black, tail broadly tipped
pure white. Throat black. Below
pure white.

5. White-tailed Jay   **L-SA**
Cyanocorax mystacalis 12″ (30cm)
Head, throat and breast black. Spot
above eye and broad whisker
whitish. Hindcrown, upper back
and lower underparts white. Wings
bright blue. *Tail mostly white, central feathers blue.*

6. Rufous-throated Dipper   **M-W**
Cinclus schultzi   5″ (13cm)
Dark leaden gray. *Throat and sides
of neck cinnamon.* Generally like
white-capped Dipper (132-12) in
shape and actions.

7. White-headed Wren   **L-F**
Campylorhynchus albobrunneus
               7″ (18cm)
Head and underparts white (mixed
dusky below in s Colombia). Back,
wings and tail dark brown.

8. Thrush-like Wren   **L-FT**
Campylorhynchus turdinus
               7″ (18cm)
Above dull grayish brown. Narrow
eyebrow and eye-ring white.
Throat white. *Below white heavily
spotted dark brown* (or virtually
unspotted in Bolivia and adjacent
Brazil).

9. Stripe-backed Wren   **L-TW**
Campylorhynchus nuchalis
              6¼″ (16cm)
Like Band-backed Wren (130-2)
but crown mottled black, nape and
*back boldly striped (not banded)
black and white. Below white
spotted black.* No cinnamon on
belly or rump.

10. Fasciated Wren   **LM-SA**
Campylorhynchus fasciatus
              6¼″ (16cm)
Like Band-backed Wren (130-2)
but *entire upperparts* (including
crown) *barred grayish brown and
white.* No cinnamon on belly,
rump or tail.

11. Tooth-billed Wren   **L-F**
Odontorchilus cinereus
              4½″ (12 cm)
Above mouse-gray, crown tinged
dark brown. Eyebrow buffy. Below
whitish. *Tail grayish, banded black.*

12. Gray-mantled Wren   **M-F**
Odontorchilus branickii
              4½″ (12cm)
Above bluish slaty gray. Crown
brown. Sides of head streaked
white. Below white. *Tail long,
barred black and gray.*

1. Paramo Wren   **H-O**
Cistothorus meridae   4" (10cm)
Very like Grass Wren (132-6) but
has broader, more conspicuous,
whiter eyebrow. Flanks barred
blackish. *Stripes on back reach to
tail.*

2. Apolinar's Marsh-Wren   **H-OW**
Cistothorus apolinari 4½" (12cm)
Like Grass Wren (132-6) but black
bands on tail are broader. *Eyebrow
gray* (not buffy white).

3. Sooty-headed Wren   **LM-FT**
Thryothorus spadix   5½" (14cm)
Crown dark gray. *Sides of head
and throat black.* Ear coverts
streaked white. *Body plumage
chestnut,* belly gray. Tail broadly
barred black.

4. Plain-tailed Wren   **MH-F**
Thryothorus euophrys   6" (15cm)
Forecrown blackish. Eyebrow
white. Above rufous, *wings and
tail unbarred.* Streak through eye
black. *Throat and breast white
prominently spotted black.* Below
dull buff (only lightly spotted in s
part of range).

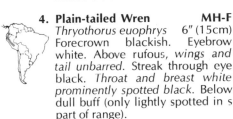

5. Niceforo's Wren   **L-T**
Thryothorus nicefori 5½" (14cm)
Like Rufous-and-white Wren (130-
6) but *crown and upper back olive
brown* contrasting with rufous
lower back and rump.

6. Fawn-breasted Wren   **L-TS**
Thryothorus guarayanus 5" (13cm)
Very like Buff-breasted Wren (130-
10) but darker, grayer, less reddish
back and more strongly streaked
cheeks.

7. Superciliated Wren   **L-SA**
Thryothorus superciliaris
    5½" (14cm)
Like Buff-breasted Wren (130-10)
but *white eyebrow broader, sides
of head white, unstreaked.* Underparts whiter.

8. Long-billed Wren   **L-TS**
Thryothorus longirostris
    5½" (14cm)
Very like Buff-breasted Wren (130-
10) in color but *bill much longer.*

9. Gray Wren   **L-TS**
Thryothorus griseus   4¼" (11cm)
Above light grayish brown. Eyebrow dull white. *Below smoky
gray,* darker on flanks. *Tail very
short, gray, barred black.*

10. Mountain Wren   **MH-FT**
Troglodytes solstitialis   3½" (9cm)
Like House Wren (132-5) but
smaller and has *conspicuous broad
whitish or buffy eyebrow.* Wings
and tail prominently barred.

11. Tepui Wren   **M-FT**
Troglodytes rufulus   4" (10cm)
Upperparts rufous brown, wings
and tail narrowly barred black.
Eyebrow pale chestnut. Below ru-
fescent or grayish white.

12. Flutist Wren   **M-F**
Microcerculus ustulatus 3½" (9cm)
Quite like Nightingale Wren (132-
9) but more chestnut brown with
no white on underparts. Tail very
short.

1. Wing-banded Wren   **L-F**
Microcerculus bambla   4" (10cm)
Above dark brown lightly scalloped black. *Broad white wing band* which no other wren has. Throat and breast pale gray, finely barred blackish. Belly dark brown, barred dusky. Tail blackish, very short.

2. Chilean Mockingbird   **LM-S**
Mimus thenca   10" (25cm)
Above dull brown. Wings dusky, wing-bars white. Broad eyebrow and throat white. Below brownish gray, streaked dusky on belly. *Tail dusky tipped white.*

3. Long-tailed Mockingbird   **L-SA**
Mimus longicaudatus 10" (25cm)
Above dusky brown. Sides of head mixed black and white. Broad eyebrow, throat and belly white. *Wing coverts mostly white. Breast gray scalloped white.* Tail broadly tipped white.

4. Patagonian Mockingbird   **LM-S**
Mimus patagonicus   8½" (21cm)
Above plain brownish gray. Wings black with two white bars. Eyebrow and throat white. Breast brownish. Belly whitish. Tail tipped white.

5. White-banded Mockingbird   **L-S**
Mimus triurus   8½" (21cm)
Above grayish brown, becoming *rufous brown on rump.* Wings black with *broad white stripe.* Narrow eyebrow white. Underparts whitish. Central tail feathers black, rest white.

6. Brown-backed Mockingbird H-S
Mimus dorsalis   10" (25cm)
Above brown, becoming rufous on rump. Wings black, conspicuous wing patch white. Eyebrow and underparts whitish. Central tail feathers black, rest white.

7. White-eared Solitaire   **M-F**
Entomodestes leucotis   8" (20cm)
Crown and nape black (dark brown in ♀). *Broad streak below eye white.* Back rufous chestnut. Wings black with white patch visible in flight. *Below glossy black.* Tail black, outer feathers broadly tipped white.

8. Chiguanco Thrush   **LMH-TS**
Turdus chiguanco   9" (23cm)
Bill and legs yellow. Grayish brown, somewhat paler below. Throat vaguely streaked whitish.

9. Plumbeous-backed Thrush   **L-T**
Turdus reevei   8" (20cm)
Eye bluish white. Bill dusky, tipped yellow. *Upperparts blue gray.* Throat white, sharply streaked black. Below grayish white, buff on sides. Legs pale brown.

10. Marañon Thrush   **M-T**
Turdus maranonicus   7" (18cm)
Bill blackish. Above olive brown. Underparts white *profusely spotted dark brown.* Legs leaden horn color.

11. Chestnut-bellied Thrush   **M-FT**
Turdus fulviventris   8½" (21cm)
Bill yellow. *Whole head black.* Eyering orange. Above dark gray. Breast paler gray. *Belly rufous.* Legs yellowish. ♀: Head brownish.

12. Austral Thrush   **LM-TO**
Turdus falcklandii   9" (23cm)
Bill and legs yellow. *Head blackish.* Back and wings olive brown. *Throat white streaked black.* Breast and belly buff. Tail blackish.

Pipits are terrestrial. They run and walk in grassy areas.

1. Lawrence's Thrush   **L-F**
Turdus lawrencii   8½" (21cm)
Bill yellow with black tip. Above dark smoky brown. Wings and tail darker. Below light smoky brown, throat streaked black. Vent and center of belly white.

2. Unicolored Thrush   **L-FT**
Turdus haplochrous   9" (22cm)
Like Bare-eyed Thrush (136-6) but browner above and below and with vent brownish olive instead of white.

3. Collared Gnatwren   **L-F**
Microbates collaris   4" (10cm)
Bill long. Above brown.*Long eyebrow white.* Line behind eye black. Cheeks white. Broad whisker black. Below white with *conspicuous black band across breast.* Tail short, usually cocked. Like Long-billed Gnatwren (128-8) in shape.

4. Cream-bellied Gnatcatcher   **L-F**
Polioptila lactea   4" (10cm)
Crown black. Above dark gray. Lores and eyebrow white. Sides of head and all underparts creamy white. Central tail feathers black, outer feathers white. ♀: No black crown.

5. Guianan Gnatcatcher   **L-F**
Polioptila guianensis   4" (10cm)
Above, throat and breast uniform bluish gray (no black). Narrow eyering and belly white. Tail black edged white. ♀: Paler than ♂, with whitish throat and eye-stripe.

6. Slate-throated Gnatcatcher   **L-F**
Polioptila schistaceigula 4" (10cm)
Upperparts, throat and breast dark gray. Narrow eye-ring and belly white. Tail black, outer feather tipped white.

7. Cedar Waxwing   **MH-FT**
Bombycilla cedrorum*
    6¼" (16cm)
Brown. Head crested. Mask black, bordered by narrow white line. Throat blackish. Belly white. Tail with broad black band near end and yellow tip.

8. Short-billed Pipit   **H-O**
Anthus furcatus   6" (15cm)
Like Yellowish Pipit (128-12) but *breast buff heavily streaked dusky,* sharply demarcated from white belly.

9. Hellmayr's Pipit   **MH-O**
Anthus hellmayri   5½" (14cm)
Like Yellowish Pipit (128-12) but *outer tail feathers buffy.* Below buffy. *Legs pinkish.*

10. Chaco Pipit   **L-O**
Anthus chacoensis   4¼" (11cm)
Much like Yellowish Pipit (128-12) but streaks on back whiter and underparts more buffy instead of yellowish.

11. Correndera Pipit   **LMH-O**
Anthus correndera   5" (13cm)
Like Yellowish Pipit (128-12) but is most richly colored Pipit with *back boldly striped black and rufous.*

12. Ochre-breasted Pipit   **L-O**
Anthus nattereri   5" (13cm)
Rather like Yellowish Pipit (128-12) but *very yellow appearance,* especially on face and breast.

13. Paramo Pipit   **H-O**
Anthus bogotensis   5½" (14cm)
Rather like Yellowish Pipit (128-12) but has rufous brown shoulders and buffy brown underparts. *Little streaking below.*

1. Green Shrike-Vireo   **L-F**
Smaragdolanius pulchellus
5" (13cm)
Rather like Slaty-capped Shrike-Vireo (140-1) but *crown blue* (not gray). *Above bright emerald green.* Long narrow eyebrow and spot below eye yellow. *Throat yellow* becoming bright greenish yellow on belly.

2. Tepui Greenlet   **LM-F**
Hylophilus sclateri   4¼" (11cm)
Like Ashy-headed Greenlet (140-9) but *crown and wings gray*, contrasting strongly with olive green back. Breast and sides yellowish.

3. Buff-cheeked (chested) Greenlet
L-F
Hylophilus muscicapinus
4¼" (11cm)
Eye dark. *Forehead and face pinkish buff contrasting with gray crown.* Above olive green. Below whitish, strongly tinged buff on throat and breast.

4. Brown-headed Greenlet   **L-F**
Hylophilus brunneiceps
4¼" (11cm)
Crown and nape dull brown. Brownish olive above. Dull grayish below, tinged buff on breast. (Belly yellowish s of the Amazon.)

5. Dusky-capped Greenlet   **L-F**
Hylophilus hypoxanthus 4" (10cm)
Crown grayish brown. Back olive brown becoming olive green on rump and tail. Throat whitish. *Below bright olive yellow*, tinged buff on breast.

6. Olivaceous Greenlet   **M-F**
Hylophilus olivaceus 4½" (12cm)
Above dull olive, more yellowish on forehead. *Below yellowish olive,* yellower on belly.

7. Scrub Greenlet   **L-TS**
Hylophilus flavipes 4¼" (11cm)
Bill pale pinkish. Above olive green, darker and browner on crown. *Eye pale* in adults, dark in juveniles. Throat whitish. Below pale yellow.

8. Lesser Greenlet   **L-FT**
Hylophilus minor 3½" (9cm)
Upperparts bright yellowish olive green. Eye dark. Below white. Sides of body and undertail coverts lemon yellow.

9. Screaming Cowbird   **LM-SO**
Molothrus rufoaxillaris
6½" (17cm)
Like Shiny Cowbird (142-10) but more uniform silky black.

10. Bronze-brown Cowbird   **L-SO**
Molothrus armenti 8" (20cm)
Mostly shining bronzy brown. Eye reddish brown. Small ruff on hindneck. Wings and tail blackish.

11. Giant Cowbird   **LM-TSO**
Scaphidura oryzivora
13" (33cm)
Shiny purple. Eye red. Wings and tail blackish. Feathers at sides of neck elongated forming a ruff, giving the bird a small-headed appearance. ♀: Much smaller. Less glossy, lacks ruff.

12. Band-tailed Oropendola   **L-FT**
Ocyalus latirostris 12" (29cm)
Rounded frontal shield and upper bill blackish, lower bill yellowish. *Crown and upper back chestnut.* Eye blue. Back, wings and underparts black. *Outer tail feathers bright yellow, broadly tipped black.* ♀: Similar but smaller.

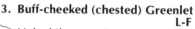

Oropendolas and Caciques have long, sharp bills.

1. Chestnut-headed Oropendola
L-FT
Zarhynchus wagleri 12" (30 cm)
Bill whitish to pale greenish yellow. Eye blue. *Head and neck chestnut.* Back, wings and belly black. Rump and sides of body chestnut. Outer tail feathers bright yellow.

2. Casqued Oropendola **L-FT**
Clypicterus oseryi 13" (33cm)
Mainly chestnut. Rounded frontal shield and bill whitish. Eye blue. *Throat and breast bright olive yellow.* Outer tail feathers bright yellow.

3. Green Oropendola **L-FT**
Psarocolius viridis 15" (38cm)
Mostly olive green. Bill pale greenish or yellowish with orange-red tip. Eye blue. Rump and belly chestnut. Outer tail feathers bright yellow.

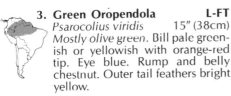

4. Dusky-green Oropendola **M-FT**
Psarocolius atrovirens
14½" (37cm)
Mostly dark olive green. Bill pale greenish yellow. Rump and belly chestnut. Central tail feathers olive, outers bright yellow.

5. Black Oropendola **L-FT**
Gymnostinops guatimozinus
17" (42cm)
Bill black, tipped yellow. Eye brown. *Bare cheeks blue edged pink below.* Head, mantle and underparts black. Back, rump and undertail coverts dark chestnut. Outer tail feathers bright yellow.

6. Chestnut-mantled Oropendola
L-FT
Gymnostinops cassini 17" (42cm)
Eye brown. Bill black, tipped whitish. *Entire back and wings bright chestnut.* Bare cheeks blue, edged pink below. Underparts black, flanks chestnut. Outer tail feathers bright yellow.

7. Para Oropendola **L-FT**
Gymnostinops bifasciatus
16" (40cm)
Bill black tipped orange-red. Eye brown. *Bare cheeks pink.* Head, neck and upper breast brownish black. *Back, wings, lower breast and belly chestnut.* Outer tail feathers yellow.

8. Olive Oropendola **L-FT**
Gymnostinops yuracares
18" (45cm)
Bright olive yellow. Bill black tipped orange. Eye brown. Bare cheeks pink. Back, wings and belly chestnut. Outer tail feathers yellow.

9. Selva Cacique **L-F**
Cacicus koepckeae 8½" (21cm)
Rather like Yellow-rumped Cacique (142-3) but *all black, only rump yellow.* Bill bluish gray.

10. Golden-winged Cacique **LM-FT**
Cacicus chrysopterus 9" (22cm)
Very like Yellow-rumped Cacique (142-3) but bill bluish gray with pale tip, and large yellow patch on wings. *Eye yellowish white.*

11. Mountain Cacique **MH-F**
Cacicus leucorhamphus
10½" (26cm)
Very like Yellow-rumped Cacique (142-3) but *tail all black, only rump and wing coverts yellow.* (No yellow on wings in s Peru and Bolivia.) Eye blue.

12. Ecuadorian (Black) Cacique
L-FT
Cacicus sclateri 9" (23cm)
Resembles Solitary Cacique (142-7) but *eye blue* (not brown). Bill bluish-horn, tipped whitish. Arboreal, not foraging in undergrowth as the Solitary Cacique does.

1. Scrub Blackbird   **L-SA**
Dives warszewiczi   8½" (21cm)
      (27 cm in central Peru).
Eye dark. All glossy black, including bill.

2. Carib Grackle   **L-OW**
Quiscalus lugubris   9" (22cm)
Bill black. *Eye white* (dark in young birds). Glossy black tinged purple. Wings and *wedge-shaped tail* glossy bluish green. ♀: Dark brown, somewhat paler below, especially on throat.

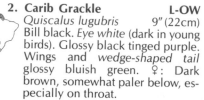

3. Great-tailed Grackle   **L-OW**
Quiscalus (Cassidix) mexicanus
      14" (36cm)
Shiny black, tinged violet. Eye yellow. Wings and tail greenish black. *Tail very long,* wedge-shaped. ♀: Above brownish. Eyebrow and underparts lighter buffy brown.

4. Austral Blackbird   **LM-SO**
Curaeus curaeus   10" (25cm)
Glossy black. Eye dark. Bill long, black, very pointed. ♀: Brownish black.

5. Forbes' Blackbird   **L-O**
Curaeus forbesi   9" (22m)
Glossy black. Bill black, narrow and pointed, flat on top.

6. Bolivian Blackbird   **H-S**
Oreopsar bolivianus   9" (22cm)
Dull brownish black. Wings browner. Bill short, black. Eye dark.

7. Red-bellied Grackle   **M-FT**
Hypopyrrhus pyrohypogaster
      11" (27cm)
Black. *Belly and undertail coverts red.*

8. Golden-tufted Grackle   **LM-F**
Macroagelaius imthurni
      10" (25cm)
Blue black. Rather long pointed black bill. *Semi-concealed yellow tufts on sides under wings.* Tail rather long, rounded.

9. Mountain Grackle   **MH-F**
Macroagelaius subalaris
      10½" (26cm)
Silky blue black. Rather long pointed black bill. *Semi-concealed chestnut tufts under wing.* Tail rounded, rather long.

10. Chopi Blackbird   **L-SO**
Gnorimopsar chopi   9" (22cm)
Glossy blue black. Bill stout, pointed, with *distinctive ridge on upper bill.*

11. Unicolored Blackbird   **L-OW**
Agelaius cyanopus   8" (20cm)
Glossy black. ♀: Crown light brown and streaked black. *Back streaked chestnut and black.* Wings and tail black. *Below yellow* streaked gray, most heavily on flanks.

12. Pale-eyed Blackbird   **L-OW**
Agelaius xanthophthalmus
      7½" (19cm)
Black. *Eye pale orange.*

1. Epaulet Oriole   **L-FT**
Icterus cayanensis   7" (18cm)
Like Moriche Oriole (144-5) but *only shoulder yellow* (chestnut in s part of range), otherwise all black.

2. Orchard Oriole   **L-TS**
Icterus spurius*   6" (15cm)
Mostly black. *Shoulder, rump, breast and belly chestnut.* ♀: Yellowish olive above, wings dusky with two white bars. *Below greenish yellow.* Immature ♂ like ♀ but with black throat.

3. Orange-crowned Oriole   **L-T**
Icterus auricapillus   6½" (17cm)
Crown and sides of head orange. Face, throat, breast, back, wings and tail black. Shoulders, rump, lower breast and belly yellow.

4. White-edged Oriole   **L-SA**
Icterus graceannae   7½" (19cm)
Resembles Yellow-tailed Oriole (144-3) but somewhat smaller. *Inner flight feathers broadly edged white.* Outer tail feathers tipped white.

5. Scarlet-headed Blackbird L-OW
Amblyramphus holosericeus
           9" (22cm)
Black. *Head, breast and thighs scarlet.*

6. Yellow-rumped Marshbird
                 L-OW

Pseudoleistes guirahuro 9" (22cm)
Much like Brown-and-yellow Marshbird (142-8) but *rump and flanks yellow* and yellow wing coverts more extensive. Wings and tail dark brown.

7. Red-breasted Blackbird   **L-O**
Leistes militaris   6½" (17cm)
Black (feathers edged brown in non-breeding plumage). *Throat, breast and wing coverts red.* ♀: Above brown streaked buff. *Crown streak and eyebrow buff.* Below buff usually tinged pink on breast.

8. White-browed Blackbird   **L-O**
Leistes superciliaris   6½" (17cm)
Black. *Long streak back of eye white. Throat, breast and wing coverts red.* ♀: Above dark brown streaked buff. Crown streak and eyebrow buff. Below buffy, reddish on breast.

9. Peruvian Red-breasted
  Meadowlark   **L-O**
Sturnella bellicosa   7½" (19cm)
Upperparts and belly blackish, feathers edged brown. *Eyebrow red before eye, white behind it. Throat and breast bright red. Thighs white.* ♀: Above streaked blackish and brown. Below whitish, speckled black on breast, tinged pink on belly.

10. Lesser Red-breasted
    Meadowlark   **L-O**

Sturnella defilippi   7½" (19cm)
Upperparts and belly blackish, feathers edged brown. *Eyebrow red before eye, white behind it. Throat and breast red. Thighs black.* ♀: Above streaked brown and blackish. Below whitish, speckled black on breast, tinged pink on belly.

11. Long-tailed Meadowlark   **L-O**
Sturnella loyca   9" (23cm)
Upperparts and belly blackish. Throat and breast red. Eyebrow red and white. ♀: Throat white bordered by black at sides.

12. Eastern Meadowlark   **LMH-O**
Sturnella magna   9" (22cm)
Chunky with slender bill and short tail. *Above brown streaked black and buff. Below yellow with broad, U shaped black band on breast. Outer tail feathers conspicuously white in flight.*

1. Bobolink   **L-SO**
Dolichonyx oryzivorus*
5½" (14cm)
♀ and winter ♂ rather sparrow-like. Above streaked brown, buff and black. *Eyebrow, crown stripe and underparts buff.* Brown streaks on sides. ♂ in breeding plumage: Black, nape buff. Rump and shoulders white.

2. Blackpoll Warbler   **LM-T**
Dendroica striata*   4½" (12cm)
Non-breeding plumage: Much like non-breeding Bay-breasted Warbler (148-4). Back olive streaked black. White wing-bars prominent.

3. Louisiana Waterthrush **LM-TW**
Seiurus motacilla*   5" (13cm)
Very like Northern Waterthrush (146-1) and difficult to separate. Look for *unstreaked throat, broader and purer white eye-stripe.* Teeters.

4. Connecticut Warbler   **L-TS**
Oporornis agilis*   4½" (12cm)
Head and breast gray. Above olive. Below yellow. *Conspicuous white eye-ring* in all plumages. ♀: Closely resembles ♀ Mourning Warbler (146-12) but has complete (not partial) whitish eye-ring.

5. Common Yellowthroat **LM-FTW**
Geothlypis trichas   4½" (12cm)
Above dull olive. Mask, cheeks and sides of neck black bordered above by white line. Below yellow, belly whitish in center. ♀: Lacks black and white on head and neck.

6. Rose-breasted Chat   **L-FT**
Granatellus pelzelni   4¼" (11cm)
Head blackish, *streak back of eye white.* Above bluish slate. *Throat white* surrounded by black line. Below rosy red: ♀: Above slaty gray. Face and throat buff. *Below dull rosy pink.*

7. Spectacled Whitestart (Redstart)
Myioborus   **MH-FT**
melanocephalus   5" (13cm)
Head black with chestnut crown patch and bright yellow eye-ring (or crown all black from central Peru to Bolivia). Back blackish. *Underparts bright yellow.* Tail black, outer feathers white.

8. White-fronted Whitestart (Redstart)   **MH-FT**
Myioborus albifrons 4½" (12cm)
Forehead and around eye pure white. Crown black with rufous patch in center. Back dark gray. *Below bright yellow.* Tail black, outer feathers white.

9. White-faced Whitestart (Redstart)   **MH-FT**
Myioborus albifacies 4½" (12cm)
Crown black. *Lores, facial area and cheeks white.* Back brownish gray. *Underparts bright orange.* Tail black, outer feathers white.

10. Brown-capped Whitestart (Redstart)   **M-FT**
Myioborus brunniceps 4½" (12cm)
Crown rufous chestnut. Narrow eyebrow and eye-ring white. Sides of head, back and wings gray. *Below bright yellow.* Tail black, outer feathers white.

11. Yellow-faced Whitestart (Redstart)   **M-FT**
Myioborus pariae   4½" (12cm)
Crown rufous chestnut. Eyebrow, eye-ring and narrow forehead yellow. Back, wings and sides of head grayish. *Below bright yellow.* Tail black, outer feathers white.

12. Saffron-breasted Whitestart (Redstart)   **M-FT**
Myioborus cardonai 4½" (12cm)
Crown, lores and below eye black. *Eye-ring and chin white.* Back dark gray. Underparts orange yellow.

13. Pale-legged Warbler **MH-FT**
Basileuterus signatus 4½" (12cm)
Very like Citrine Warbler (150-2) but with incomplete yellow eye-ring and black streak through eye. Somewhat paler yellow below. Legs pale.

1. Two-banded Warbler   LM-F
Basileuterus bivittatus   5" (13cm)
Very like Golden-bellied Warbler (150-5) but eyebrow yellowish instead of grayish-white.

2. Santa Marta Warbler   H-FT
Basileuterus basilicus 5½" (14cm)
Like Three-striped Warbler (150-10) but *head stripes whiter, center of throat white* (not buffy yellowish). Back, wings and tail olive green.

3. Three-banded Warbler   M-FT
Basileuterus trifasciatus
                              4½" (12cm)
Top and sides of head gray. Stripe through eye and two broad stripes at sides of crown black. *Above grayish olive. Throat and breast grayish white.* Below bright yellow.

4. Gray-throated Warbler   M-FT
Basileuterus cinereicollis
                              5" (13cm)
Crown yellow (partly concealed) bordered by black. Back, wings and tail dark olive. *Head, throat and breast gray.* Belly yellow.

5. Gray-and-gold Warbler   L-TS
Basileuterus fraseri   5" (13cm)
Crown yellow or orange, bordered by black stripes. Above gray. Underparts bright yellow.

6. Gray-headed Warbler   M-FT
Basileuterus griseiceps
                              4½" (12cm)
Top and sides of head gray. Lores white. Back and wings yellowish olive. Underparts all bright yellow.

7. White-striped Warbler   L-TS
Basileuterus leucophrys
                              5½" (14cm)
Like White-browed Warbler (150-8) but black crown stripes fainter and *white eyebrow broad.* Back olive. *Underparts white.*

8. Chestnut-vented Conebill   L-TS
Conirostrum speciosum 4" (10cm)
Dark blue gray above (wings with speculum in one race). *Paler gray below. Vent chestnut.* ♀: Head bluish green, otherwise yellowish green above. Below buffy whitish, paler on belly. Vent buff.

9. White-eared Conebill   L-TS
Conirostrum leucogenys
                              3½" (9cm)
Crown and nape black. *Cheeks white.* Back dark blue gray, *rump white.* Underparts light blue gray. ♀: Above blue-gray, rump whitish. Cheeks and underparts buffy, flanks grayish.

10. Pearly-breasted Conebill   L-FT
Conirostrum margaritae 4" (10cm)
Very like Bicolored Conebill (154-3) but upperparts lighter blue gray and below paler gray.

11. Cinereous Conebill   H-TS
Conirostrum cinereum
                              4¼" (11cm)
Crown blackish. Back grayish. *Forehead and broad eyebrow white.* Wings blackish, *broad wingbar and speculum white.* Below pale gray. Tail black.

12. White-browed Conebill   H-FT
Conirostrum ferrugineiventre
                              4½" (12cm)
Crown black. *Broad eyebrow and patch on shoulder white.* Back and sides of head gray. Chin white, rest of *underparts bright rufous.*

1. **Capped Conebill   MH-FT**
Conirostrum albifrons   5″ (13cm)
Dark blue to blackish (with *crown
white* in some races). Rump lighter
blue. ♀: Crown dull blue, otherwise yellowish green above. Throat
and breast bluish gray. Below pale
greenish yellow.

2. **Giant Conebill   H-T**
Oreomanes fraseri   6¼″ (16cm)
Above light gray. *Eyebrow and underparts chestnut. Broad streak
from below eye to ear coverts
white.*

3. **Carbonated Flower-Piercer**
                             H-TS
Diglossa carbonaria   4½″ (12cm)
Mostly black. Short eyebrow and
shoulders blue gray. Rump slaty.
Amount of chestnut on underparts
varies from only vent (in Bolivia)
to all underparts except throat (in
Peru).

4. **Venezuelan Flower-Piercer**
                             M-TS
Diglossa venezuelensis 5″ (13cm)
Resembles White-sided Flower-
piercer (154-7) but larger and
blacker with much smaller white
patch on sides. ♀: Head olive.
Above brownish. Below dull grayish.

5. **Scaled Flower-Piercer   M-FT**
Diglossa duidae   5″ (13cm)
Above slaty gray, head blackish.
Underparts with feathers pale gray
in centers giving slightly *scaled
look.* Undertail coverts gray.

6. **Greater Flower-Piercer   M-FT**
Diglossa major   7½″ (17cm)
Forehead, lores and cheeks black.
Above slaty blue with fine whitish
shaft streaks. Chin black. Vent
chestnut.

7. **Deep-blue Flower-Piercer   M-F**
Diglossa glauca   4¼″ (11cm)
Very like Indigo Flower-piercer
(154-11) but dull, dark, indigo blue
instead of shining indigo blue.
Lores and forehead black. *Eye orange to yellow* (not bright red).

8. **Short-billed Honeycreeper   L-F**
Cyanerpes nitidus   4¼″ (11cm)
Very like Purple Honeycreeper
(152-4) but *bill short,* black throat
patch larger and legs pinkish (not
yellow). ♀: Closely resembles ♀
Purple Honeycreeper (152-5) but
bill shorter and sides of head green
(not rufous streaked white).

9. **Shining Honeycreeper   L-FT**
Cyanerpes lucidus   4¼″ (11cm)
Very like Purple Honeycreeper
(152-4) but bluer (not so purple)
with smaller black throat patch.
♀: Like ♀ Purple Honeycreeper
(152-5) but dusky (not buffy) lores,
lighter buffy throat, and *breast
streaked blue* (not green).

10. **Golden-collared Honeycreeper**
                             LM-FT
Iridophanes pulcherrima
                      4½″ (12cm)
Head, back and throat black. *Collar on hindneck golden yellow.*
Lower back, rump and underparts
shining light greenish yellow.
Shoulders bright blue. ♀: Olive
green above. Wing feathers edged
bluish green. Below buffy yellowish, greener on breast and sides.

11. **Black-legged Dacnis   L-FT**
Dacnis nigripes   4″ (10cm)
Very like Blue Dacnis (152-10) but
with less black on back and throat.
♀: Rather like ♀ Scarlet-thighed
Dacnis (152-9) but brownish olive
above, tinged blue on crown and
rump. Pale buffy below.

12. **Viridian Dacnis   L-FT**
Dacnis viguieri   4″ (10cm)
Eye pale. *Shining blue green,* rump
more bluish. Wing coverts bright
green. Lores, upper back, primaries and tail black. ♀: Lacks black
on back. Below yellowish green.

1. Scarlet-breasted Dacnis   L-F
Dacnis berlepschi   4¼" (11cm)
Head, throat and upper breast dark
blue. Back and wing coverts dark
blue, *broadly streaked with silvery
blue.* Breast red. Belly yellow. ♀:
Above brown. Below light brown.
Breast orange-red.

2. White-bellied Dacnis   L-F
Dacnis albiventris   4" (10cm)
Mostly bright purplish blue. *Mask
through eyes and over ear coverts
black. Center of breast and belly
white.* Wings and tail blackish.
♀: Above olive green. Throat
whitish, below greenish yellow,
center of belly all yellow.

3. Tit-like Dacnis   H-TS
Xenodacnis parina   4½" (12cm)
Bright purplish blue (streaked with
paler blue in n Peru). Bill small.
♀: Head light blue (only fore-
crown and face light blue in n
Peru). Back brown, wing coverts
and rump blue. Below dull rufous.

**4. Blue-naped Chlorophonia
LMH-FT**
Chlorophonia cyanea 4¼" (11cm)
*Head, throat and breast bright grass
green.* Narrow eye-ring, upper
back and rump bright blue. Belly
golden yellow. ♀: No blue on
rump. Underparts duller yellow.

**5. Chestnut-breasted Chlorophonia
MH-F**
Chlorophonia pyrrhophrys
4¼" (11cm)
Crown and nape blue. Eyebrow
black. Above grass green, *rump
yellow.* Throat and breast bright
green, below yellow with *broad
chestnut stripe down center of
breast and belly.* ♀: Lacks yellow
rump and chestnut median stripe.

6. Tawny-capped Euphonia   L-T
Euphonia anneae   4¼" (11cm)
Like Orange-bellied Euphonia
(174-9) but crown and nape rufous, back purplish, undertail coverts white instead of yellow.

7. Fulvous-vented Euphonia   L-T
Euphonia fulvicrissa   3½" (9cm)
Above glossy blue black. Yellow
forecrown *reaches past eye.* Throat
black. Below deep yellow tinged
rufous on vent. ♀: Above olive, forecrown rufous. Below yellowish
olive, vent tinged rufous.

8. Trinidad Euphonia   L-FTS
Euphonia trinitatis   3½" (9cm)
Like White-vented Euphonia (174-
11) but *yellow crown patch* extends beyond eye, and vent yellow
(not white). ♀: Yellowish green
above. Below yellowish, whitish in
center of breast and belly.

9. Finsch's Euphonia   LM-TS
Euphonia finschi   3½" (9cm)
Rather like White-vented Euphonia (174-11) but *belly and vent
fulvous* and no white in tail. ♀:
Yellowish olive green above. Sides
of head and underparts greenish
yellow.

10. Velvet-fronted Euphonia   L-TS
Euphonia concinna   3½" (9cm)
Like White-vented Euphonia (174-
11) but forehead black with round
yellow spot on forecrown. ♀:
Above dull olive with *narrow yellow forehead.* Below dull yellow,
brightest on center of belly.

**11. Orange-crowned Euphonia
LM-TS**
Euphonia saturata   4" (10cm)
Upperparts and throat glossy purplish black. *Entire crown and nape
deep yellow.* Below deep orange
ochraceous. ♀: Above bright yellowish olive. Below ochraceous
yellow, brightest on center of belly.

12. Golden-sided Euphonia   L-FT
Euphonia cayennensis
4¼" (11cm)
*All steel blue except patch at sides
of breast orange yellow.* ♀: Above
olive. Below gray in center, olive
yellow on sides. Vent gray.

1. Bronze-green Euphonia   M-FT
Euphonia mesochrysa   3½" (9cm)
Forehead yellow. Above bronzy olive, nape bluish gray. Below olive yellow except center of belly ochraceous yellow. ♀: Forehead olive. Breast and belly gray.

2. Plumbeous Euphonia   L-FT
Euphonia plumbea   3½" (9cm)
Upperparts, sides of head, *throat and breast glossy grayish blue.* Belly rich yellow. ♀: Crown and nape gray. Above olive. Throat pale gray. Below yellow.

3. Green-throated Euphonia   L-FT
Euphonia chalybea   4½" (12cm)
Upperparts and throat glossy bronze green. Forehead and underparts bright yellow. ♀: Upperparts and throat dull olive green. Below gray, yellowish olive on sides.

4. Turquoise Dacnis-Tanager   M-F
Pseudodacnis hartlaubi
   4¼" (11cm)
Crown, eye-ring, rump, shoulders, breast and belly turquoise blue. Otherwise black. ♀: Above dull brown, wing coverts and back feathers edged paler. Below buffy grayish, yellowish white along center of belly.

5. Orange-eared Tanager   M-F
Chlorochrysa calliparaea
   4½" (12cm)
Upperparts shining green with yellow spot on crown. Rump orange. *Orange tufts on ear coverts.* Throat black. Breast and belly shining blue.

6. Opal-rumped Tanager   L-FT
Tangara velia   5½" (14cm)
Crown and back black. Forehead, sides of head and underparts dark blue. *Rump silvery.* Wings and tail black edged blue. *Center of belly and vent chestnut.*

7. Seven-colored Tanager   L-FT
Tangara fastuosa   5½" (14cm)
Head shining greenish blue, forehead black. Upperparts black, wing coverts blue, *rump orange yellow.* Throat and breast black, below blue, deeper on belly. Tail black.

8. Brassy-breasted Tanager   LM-F
Tangara desmaresti   5½" (14cm)
Forehead black, crown and eyering blue. Above black streaked gold or emerald green. Sides of head green. *Throat and breast yellowish brown, small black patch on center of throat.* Belly and vent dull yellow, sides green.

9. Blue-whiskered Tanager   L-T
Tangara johannae   5"(13cm)
Crown green. Forehead, sides of head and throat black. Short blue streak behind eye and *short blue whisker.* Throat edged below with blue. Breast greenish yellow, belly green.

10. Spotted Tanager   LM-FT
Tangara punctata   4¼" (11cm)
Like Speckled Tanager (170-9) but *no yellow on face.* Wing edging pure green (no blue). Above green, spotted black. Below white, spotted black.

11. Dotted Tanager   L-FT
Tangara varia   4" (10cm)
Body all green, very *sparsely spotted black.* Wings and tail light blue.

12. Golden-eared Tanager   M-FT
Tangara chrysotis   5½" (14cm)
Forehead and eyebrow shining yellow. Crown, lores and band below cheeks *black. Patch from eye to ear coverts coppery gold* bordered below by black streak. Back black streaked with yellowish green. Rump and underparts shining bluish green. Center of belly and vent chestnut.

1. Flame-faced Tanager   M-FT
Tangara parzudakii   5½" (14cm)
Forehead and cheeks red. Crown and nape yellow. Lores, throat and band under cheeks black. Mantle black. Rump, wing coverts and underparts shining golden green. Vent cinnamon.

2. Rufous-cheeked Tanager   M-F
Tangara rufigenis   5½" (14cm)
Crown and rump glistening blue green. Back dark green. Wings and tail black. *Cheeks and throat rufous.* Breast silvery green to blue. Center of belly and vent cinnamon buff.

3. Blue-browed Tanager   M-FT
Tangara cyanotis   4½" (12cm)
Above mostly black. (In Bolivia cheeks dark blue and back dusky blue). *Long broad eyebrow,* wing coverts, rump, throat and breast *sky blue.* Belly and vent buff.

4. Black-backed Tanager   L-FT
Tangara peruviana   5½" (14cm)
Top and sides of head, nape and mantle chestnut. *Back black.* Underparts silvery bluish green. ♀: Like ♀ Chestnut-backed Tanager (168-3).

5. Silvery Tanager   M-FT
Tangara viridicollis   5" (13cm)
Crown and nape black. *Back shining silvery greenish or yellowish.* Wings and tail black, edged blue. *Throat and belly black.* Breast dark bluish. ♀: Crown brown. Breast dull silvery green. Belly gray.

6. Green-throated Tanager   M-FT
Tangara argyrofenges   4½" (12cm)
Crown, wings and tail black. *Back silvery straw color.* Cheeks and throat silvery green. *Below black.* ♀: Crown dull brown, feathers edged green. Back shining yellowish green, wings and tail green. *Below pale silvery green,* belly gray.

7. Yellow-throated Tanager   M-F
Iridosornis analis   5½" (14cm)
Like Purplish-mantled Tanager (164-2) but *yellow of throat reaches upper breast.* Lower breast and below *all tawny buff.*

8. Golden-collared Tanager   H-FT
Iridosornis jelskii   5½" (14cm)
Forehead, face and throat black. *Crown and broad collar golden yellow.* Above blue. Breast and belly dull chestnut.

9. Yellow-scarfed Tanager   MH-FT
Iridosornis reinhardti   6" (15cm)
Like Golden-crowned Tanager (164-1) but head all black and *broad golden yellow band extends across nape to ear coverts.*

10. Black-chinned Mountain-Tanager
LM-FT
Anisognathus notabilis   7" (18cm)
Like Blue-winged Mountain-Tanager (156-7) but *wings inconspicuously edged blue.* Head, neck and *chin black.* Back contrastingly yellowish olive. Narrow stripe on hindcrown yellow. Below bright orange yellow.

11. Masked Mountain-Tanager   H-T
Buthraupis wetmorei   7½" (19cm)
Above mostly yellowish green, rump bright yellow. Mask and throat black bordered on crown and neck with yellow. Wings and tail black, wing coverts blue. Below bright yellow, sides mottled black.

12. Black-chested Mountain-Tanager
H-FT
Buthraupis eximia   8" (20cm)
Crown and nape blue. *Face, throat and breast black.* Above greenish. (Rump blue in w Venezuela and ne Colombia). Wings black, *shoulders blue.* Belly yellow. Tail black.

1. Orange-throated Tanager   L-F
Wetmorethraupis sterrhopteron
                            6½"(17cm)
Above velvety black. Wing coverts
shining blue. *Throat and breast
bright orange.* Below bright yellow.

2. Black-and-gold Tanager   M-F
Bangsia melanochlamys 6"(15 cm)
Mainly black. Shoulders and rump
blue. *Breast orange with yellow
stripe down center to the vent.*

3. Gold-ringed Tanager   LM-F
Bangsia aureocincta   6"(15cm)
Like Moss-backed Tanager (164-3)
but has *golden yellow ring* back
from eye, encircling ear coverts
and curving forward to base of
bill. ♀: Head, throat and sides of
breast green.

**4. Chestnut-bellied Mountain-
Tanager   H-FT**
Dubusia castaneoventris 6"(15cm)
Above blue, silvery on crown.
Sides of head and *whisker black.
Below chestnut.*

**5. Golden-chevroned Tanager
                            LM-FT**
Thraupis ornata   6½"(17cm)
Head and underparts violet blue,
bluer on crown. Mantle dull dark
blue becoming dull dark olive on
rump. *Wing coverts edged bright
yellow.* ♀: Duller and grayer.

6. Black-bellied Tanager   L-TS
Ramphocelus melanogaster
                            6½"(17cm)
Like Silver-beaked Tanager (158-
7) but has *black line down center*
of lower breast and belly. ♀: Like
♀ Silver-beaked Tanager (158-8)
but has *bright rosy red forehead
and upper throat.*

7. Vermilion Tanager   LM-FT
Calochaetes coccineus 6¼"(16cm)
Like Brazilian Tanager (158-4) but
mask and throat black. Shining
bright red with black wings and
tail.

8. Scarlet Tanager   LM-FT
*Piranga olivacea**   6½"(17cm)
Scarlet. Wings and tail black. In
non-breeding plumage: Olive
above. Yellow below. Wings and
tail black. ♀: Olive above. Yellow
below. Wings and tail dark brown.

9. White-winged Tanager   LM-FT
Piranga leucoptera   5"(13cm)
Scarlet. Lores, wings and tail black,
wings with *bold white wing-bars.*
♀: Olive above. Yellow below.
Wings grayish black with two bold
white bars. Tail grayish black.

10. Red-hooded Tanager   MH-F
Piranga rubriceps   7"(18cm)
Whole head, throat and breast
scarlet. Back olive yellow. Rump
yellow. Wings black, coverts bright
yellow. Below bright yellow.

11. Blue-backed Tanager   L-F
Cyanicterus cyanicterus 6"(15cm)
Bill large. *Upperparts, throat, wings
and tail purplish blue.* Breast and
belly bright yellow. Thighs black.
♀: Above greenish blue, wings
and tail blue. Below yellow.

12. Olive-green Tanager   L-FT
Orthogonys chloricterus 7"(18cm)
Bill rather slender. Upperparts,
wings and tail dark olive green.
Underparts olive yellow.

1. Carmiol's Tanager   **L-F**
Chlorothraupis carmioli 6" (15cm)
Like Lemon-browed Tanager (160-9) but eye-ring and lores yellowish olive (not bright yellow). Upperparts, wings and tail olive. Underparts yellowish olive, throat somewhat yellower.

2. Red-throated Ant-Tanager   **L-T**
Habia fuscicauda 6½" (17cm)
Very like Red-crowned Ant-Tanager (158-11) but chin blackish, throat rosy-red and tail dusky red. ♀: Like ♀ Red-crowned Ant-Tanager (158-12) but lacks crown stripe and has buffy white throat.

3. Sooty Ant-Tanager   **L-FT**
Habia gutturalis 7" (18cm)
Mostly slaty gray. Throat and conspicuous bushy crest scarlet. Sides of head black. ♀: Throat pinkish white.

4. Crested Ant-Tanager   **M-FT**
Habia cristata 6½" (17cm)
Long pointed crest scarlet. Above brick red, browner on wings. Head, neck, throat and breast scarlet, brightest on throat. Lower underparts grayish tinged crimson.

5. Fulvous Shrike-Tanager   **L-F**
Lanio fulvus 6¼" (16cm)
Head, throat, wings and tail black. Otherwise mostly ochraceous yellow, deepest on rump and vent. *Center of breast chestnut.* ♀: Above rufous brown, more rufous on rump and tail. Below deep buffy ochraceous.

6. White-winged Shrike-Tanager   **L-F**
Lanio versicolor 6½" (17cm)
Forehead yellow, head black. Back ochraceous, rump yellow. Wings black, *wing coverts extensively white. Throat olive, below bright yellow.* Tail black. ♀: Rufous brown above, becoming more rufous on rump and tail. Below ochraceous, center of belly yellow.

7. Natterer's Tanager   **L-FT**
Tachyphonus nattereri
5½" (14cm)
Like Fulvous-crested Tanager (162-9) but crest and rump orange rufous.

8. Yellow-crested Tanager   **L-FT**
Tachyphonus rufiventer
5½" (14cm)
Crest yellow. Above black. *Throat and rump buff.* Sides of head and *narrow breast band black.* Lower underparts chestnut. ♀: Dull yellowish above. Sides of head grayish. Throat white. Below ochraceous yellow.

9. Scarlet-browed Tanager   **L-F**
Heterospingus xanthopygius
6" (15cm)
Black. Narrow eyebrow white *becoming prominent scarlet stripe behind eye. Shoulders and rump yellow.* White tufts at sides of breast. ♀: Above grayish black, below gray. No eyebrow. Rump yellow. Has breast tufts like ♂.

10. Rufous-crested Tanager   **M-F**
Creurgops verticalis 6" (15cm)
Above bluish gray. Crown patch and entire underparts cinnamon rufous. ♀: Lacks crown patch.

11. Slaty Tanager   **M-F**
Creurgops dentata 5½" (14cm)
Slaty gray. Crown chestnut bordered at sides with black. ♀: Above slaty gray, crown blackish. Eyebrow, eye-ring and throat whitish. *Cheeks, sides of neck and underparts orange rufous.* Center of belly white.

12. Olive-backed Tanager   **LM-F**
Mitrospingus oleagineus
7" (18cm)
Like Dusky-faced Tanager (160-7) but upperparts (including crown) mostly dull olive, face and throat gray and underparts olive yellow (or bright yellow in Guyana and Venezuela).

1. White-rumped Tanager   **L-S**
Cypsnagra hirundinacea
5½"(14cm)
Above black, wing coverts and
large area on rump white. Throat
deep buff becoming paler on
breast and white on belly.

2. Hooded Tanager   **L-TS**
Nemosia pileata   4½"(12cm)
Above blue gray. Head black.
Forehead and lores prominently
white. Eye yellow. Below all white.
Legs yellow. ♀: Lacks black hood
and is buffier below.

3. Rufous-headed Tanager   **LM-FT**
Hemithraupis ruficapilla
4½"(12cm)
*Head orange rufous. Patch behind
cheeks yellow.* Back, wings and
tail olive green. Rump ochraceous. Breast rufous. Belly gray,
yellowish in center. ♀: Olive green
above. Below whitish, vent yellow.

4. Guira Tanager   **LM-FT**
Hemithraupis guira   4½"(12cm)
Throat and cheeks black, surrounded by *long yellow eyebrow,*
curving around cheeks. Above
bright olive green, rump and *breast
orange rufous.* Below yellowish.
♀: Bill yellow, ridge black. Upperparts yellowish olive, yellower on
rump. Below yellow, sides of body
light gray. Legs leaden blue.

5. Fulvous-headed Tanager   **M-FTS**
Thlypopsis fluviceps   4½"(12cm)
Very like Orange-headed Tanager
(168-6) but generally darker, head
and throat chestnut rufous in some
races. ♀: Throat whitish.

6. Buff-bellied Tanager   **M-TS**
Thlypopsis inornata   5"(13cm)
Crown orange rufous. Back, wings
and tail gray. Sides of head and
entire underparts cinnamon buff.

7. Rufous-chested Tanager   **M-FT**
Thlypopsis ornata   4½"(12cm)
Entire head and neck tawny rufous. Rest of upperparts greenish
gray. Breast and flanks tawny rufous. Center of belly pure white.

8. Brown-flanked Tanager   **H-S**
Thlypopsis pectoralis 4½"(12cm)
Head, throat and breast orange ru-
fous. Back, wings and tail gray.
Center of belly white, *flanks gray-
ish brown.*

9. Rust-and-yellow Tanager   **MH-TS**
Thlypopsis ruficeps   4½"(12cm)
Head orange rufous. Back, wings
and tail olive green. *Below bright
yellow,* olive at sides.

10. Scarlet-throated Tanager   **L-TS**
Sericossypha loricata   8"(20cm)
Glossy blue black. Throat and
breast scarlet. ♀: All glossy blue
black.

11. White-capped Tanager   **MH-F**
Sericossypha albocristata
8½"(21cm)
Glossy blue black. *Crown and lores
snow white.* Throat and breast
scarlet.

12. Yellow-green Bush-Tanager
   LM-FT
Chlorospingus flavovirens
4½"(12cm)
Above olive green, more dusky on
ear coverts. *Below olive yellow,*
brightest on throat. Center of belly
dull yellow.

1. **Short-billed Bush-Tanager** M-F
Chlorospingus parvirostris
5½" (14cm)
Very like form of Yellow-throated Bush-Tanager (166-2) w of the Andes with *yellow only at sides of throat*. Darker olive above. Sides of throat deeper yellow extending back like a streak below ear coverts.

2. **Gray-capped Hemispingus**
MH-FT
Hemispingus reyi 5½" (14cm)
Cap gray. Above olive. Below yellow, more olive on sides and vent.

3. **Oleaginous Hemispingus** MH-F
Hemispingus frontalis 5½" (14cm)
Above olive with long narrow yellowish eyebrow. Below dull yellowish olive. Eyebrow and underparts more buffy in Venezuela.

4. **Black-eared Hemispingus** M-FT
Hemispingus melanotis
5½" (14cm)
Variable. Above gray, becoming olive on rump and browner on wings and tail. *Sides of head black* (dusky in sw Colombia and nw Ecuador). Long grayish-white to white eyebrow (eyebrow lacking in Venezuela, sw Colombia and nw Ecuador). Below cinnamon buff (Venezuela to Ecuador) or orange rufous (Peru and Bolivia).

5. **Slaty-backed Hemispingus** H-FT
Hemispingus goeringi 5½" (14cm)
Head black, *long eyebrow white*. *Above slaty gray. Below rufous*, flanks grayish brown.

6. **Black-headed Hemispingus** H-FT
Hemispingus verticalis 5" (13cm)
Head black with *pale crown stripe*. *Eye pale. Throat black*. Back gray, wings and tail blackish. Below gray, center of breast and belly white.

7. **Drab Hemispingus** H-F
Hemispingus xanthophthalmus
5½" (14cm)
Like gray backed form of Superciliaried Hemispingus (164-10) but *no eyebrow*. Eye yellow (not brown). Below grayish white.

8. **Three-striped Hemispingus** H-F
Hemispingus trifasciatus 5" (13cm)
Upperparts, wings and tail olive brown. *Crown stripe and long eyebrow buffy white*. Sides of head black. Underparts ochraceous tawny, paler in center.

9. **White-banded Tanager** L-S
Neothraupis fasciata 5½" (14cm)
Upperparts bluish gray. *Wing coverts black with single broad white bar*. Lores and sides of head black. Below whitish, washed gray on breast.

10. **Cone-billed Tanager** L-T
Conothraupis mesoleuca
5" (13cm)
Mostly black. Breast and belly white in center. Thighs white.

11. **Black-and-white Tanager** L-SO
Conothraupis speculigera
6½" (17cm)
Glossy blue black. Rump gray. Wing speculum and belly white.
♀: Above olive. Below light yellow tinged olive on breast.

12. **Brown Tanager** LM-F
Orchesticus abeillei 6½" (17cm)
Above brown, *forehead and eyebrow rufous*. Hindcrown and line through eye gray. Wings and tail more rufous brown. Below ochraceous.

13. **Red-billed Pied Tanager** L-FT
Lamprospiza melanoleuca
6" (15cm)
Bill red. Above glossy blue black. Throat and center of breast black, below white with two diagonal bands on sides. ♀: Blue gray nape and back.

1. **Orinocan Saltator**   **L-S**
Saltator orenocensis   6½" (17cm)
Above gray. Long eyebrow white.
Cheeks and sides of neck black. A
white spot at base of lower bill.
Throat white. Below cinnamon
buff, deepest on flanks.

2. **Thick-billed Saltator**   **LM-TS**
Saltator maxillosus   7½" (19cm)
Much like Grayish Saltator (176-
1) but *bill much thicker, more
curved and shorter,* black with
yellow at base of lower bill. *Throat
deep buff* (not white). ♀: Has
bright green upperparts.

3. **Black-cowled Saltator**   **LM-TS**
Saltator nigriceps   8" (20cm)
Gray. Bill red. Head black. Center
of belly buff. Outer tail feathers
tipped white.

4. **Masked Saltator**   **MH-F**
Saltator cinctus   7½" (19cm)
Bill dusky usually with some red.
Above dark bluish gray. *Mask and
upper throat black,* lower throat
and *breast white, bordered below
by black band.* Vent and center of
belly white, sides contrasting gray.
Tail blackish, outer feathers broadly
tipped white.

5. **Black-throated Saltator**   **L-S**
Saltator atricollis   7½" (19cm)
Bill orange. Above brown. *Lores,
cheeks and throat black.* Ear coverts and sides of neck gray. Breast
and belly white, flanks buffy. Tail
dusky.

6. **Rufous-bellied Saltator**   **H-TS**
Saltator rufiventris   8" (20cm)
Upperparts, throat and breast gray.
Wings and tail dusky. Broad eye-
brow white. *Belly rufous.*

7. **Yellow-shouldered Grosbeak**
     L-FT
Caryothraustes humeralis
    5½" (14cm)
Above bright yellowish olive green,
crown and nape gray. *Broad mask
black. Whisker white,* scaled
dusky. Center of throat white.
Below gray, vent yellow.

8. **Red-and-black Grosbeak**   **L-F**
Periporphyrus erythromelas
    7½" (19cm)
*Head and throat black. Above
crimson.* Below rosy red. ♀: Above
olive. Below dull yellow.

9. **Yellow Cardinal**   **L-S**
Gubernatrix cristata   7½" (19cm)
*Long pointed crest and throat
black. Broad eyebrow and whisker
bright yellow.* Back olive streaked
black. Wings brown, coverts bright
yellow. Below olive yellow, bright
yellow on center of belly. ♀: Eyebrow and whisker white.

10. **Red-cowled Cardinal**   **L-S**
Paroaria dominicana   6½" (17cm)
Like Red-crested Cardinal (180-3)
but *lacks crest.* Upper back black
spotted white. Flight feathers
edged white.

11. **Crimson-fronted Cardinal L-SW**
Paroaria baeri   6½" (17cm)
Very like race of Red-capped Cardinal (180-4) which has black line
through eye. Forehead and throat
deeper red. *Bill all black.*

12. **Yellow-billed Cardinal**   **L-SW**
Paroaria capitata   6½" (17cm)
Much like Red-capped Cardinal
(180-4) but *bill all brownish pink*
(not black on upper bill). Narrow
white collar on nape. Legs flesh
color (not blackish).

1. Vermilion Cardinal   L-SA
Cardinalis phoeniceus   7" (18cm)
*Long crest, head and underparts
scarlet.* Back, wings and tail red.
♀: *Long red crest as in ♂.* Head
mostly gray. Above light sandy gray,
tail tinged red. Chin black. Below
ochraceous buff.

2. Yellow Grosbeak   LMH-TSA
Pheucticus chrysopeplus
7" (18cm)
*Golden yellow, back more or less
streaked black in some races.*
Wings black, speculum and spots
on inner feathers white. Tail black
tipped white. ♀: Head and back
streaked black.

3. Ultramarine Grosbeak   LM-S
Cyanocompsa cyanea   6" (15cm)
Like Blue-black Grosbeak (182-2
but bill more curved and shorter,
rump brighter and paler blue. ♀:
Like ♀ Blue-black Grosbeak (182-
3) but much paler below, (cinnamon buff not reddish brown).

4. Dickcissel   L-O
Spiza americana   6" (15cm)
Head pale gray, *eyebrow yellow.*
Above brown, streaked black on
back. *Prominent chestnut area on
shoulders.* Chin white. Throat
black. Breast yellow to whitish on
belly. ♀ and non-breeding ♂:
Lacks black, but eyebrow and
shoulders as in breeding ♂.

5. Sooty Grassquit   LM-O
Tiaris fuliginosa   4" (10cm)
Uniform sooty black. Bill black.
♀: Above dull olive brown. Below
olive brown, *center of belly creamy
whitish.*

6. Cinereous Finch   L-SA
Piezorhina cinerea   6" (15cm)
Bill heavy, yellow. Lores black.
Above pale gray, sides of rump
white. *Below whitish* tinged gray
on breast.

7. White-naped Seedeater   L-O
Dolospingus fringilloides
5½" (14cm)
Bill horn color. *Above black, rump
and spot on hindneck white.* Wing
coverts and small wing speculum
white. Below white. ♀: Cinnamon
brown, throat and center of belly
whitish.

8. Buffy-fronted Seedeater   LM-T
Sporophila frontalis   4½" (12cm)
Bill thick, dull yellow. Above
brown. Wing coverts tipped white.
Forecrown and narrow stripe behind eye white. Below whitish with
grayish brown band across breast.

9. Temminck's Seedeater   L-FT
Sporophila falcirostris 4¼" (11cm)
Like Slate-colored Seedeater (188-
7) but above lighter gray. Bill yellow. Center of belly white. Vent
brownish (not white).

10. Dubois' Seedeater   L-S
Sporophila ardesiaca   4" (10cm)
Like Yellow-bellied Seedeater
(188-4) but above gray (not olive)
and belly white (not yellow).

11. Dull-colored Seedeater   LM-SO
Sporophila obscura   4" (10cm)
Above light reddish brown. Throat,
breast and flanks brownish gray,
belly whitish (or below uniform
grayish brown in Venezuela and
ne Colombia). ♀ like ♂.

12. White-throated Seedeater   L-S
Sporophila albogularis   4" (10cm)
Like Double-collared Seedeater
(188-9) but *entire throat white,*
wings and tail black, feathers
edged gray.

1. White-bellied Seedeater **L-S**
Sporophila leucoptera
4½" (12 cm)
Bill dull yellow. Above gray (or glossy black in Bolivia). White wing speculum. Underparts white.

2. Parrot-billed Seedeater **L-SO**
Sporophila peruviana 4½" (12cm)
Bill very thick, very curved, dusky yellow. Above grayish brown, blacker on head. Wing-bars and speculum white. *White whisker streak. Throat and upper breast black.* Below white. ♀: Can be recognized by very large bill.

3. Drab Seedeater **LM-S**
Sporophila simplex 4¼" (11cm)
Grayish brown, rump and belly paler. *Two wing-bars and speculum whitish.* Throat white. Breast grayish. ♀: Has conspicuous buffy double wing-bars.

4. Black-and-tawny Seedeater L-O
Sporophila nigrorufa 4" (10cm)
Cap, hindneck and upperparts black. *Sides of head and underparts cinnamon rufous.* Speculum and edging on inner wing feathers white.

5. Capped Seedeater **L-SO**
Sporophila bouvreuil 4" (10cm)
Cap, wings and tail black, wing speculum white. Rest of plumage cinnamon rufous. In s part of range, cinnamon buff below with pale grayish brown back.

6. Tumaco Seedeater **L-TSO**
Sporophila insulata 3½" (9cm)
Like Ruddy-breasted Seedeater (190-4) but only narrow band of rufous on rump. Some white at base of tail (lacking in (190-4). ♀: Has vague dusky streaks on back.

7. Tawny-bellied Seedeater
LM-TSO
Sporophila hypoxantha 3½" (9cm)
Very like Ruddy-breasted Seedeater (190-4) but *cheeks and ear coverts tawny rufous.* Some forms have cheeks, throat and upper breast black (Dark-throated Seedeater, *S. ruficollis* in BSA). Others have cheeks, throat and upper breast white (Marsh Seedeater, *S. palustris* in BSA). Both are here considered to be races of *Sporophila hypoxantha,* which was part of Ruddy-breasted Seedeater, *S. minuta,* in BSA.

8. Rufous-rumped Seedeater **L-O**
Sporophila hypochroma 4" (10cm)
Like Ruddy-breasted Seedeater (190-4) but rump and entire underparts deeper chestnut.

9. Chestnut Seedeater **L-O**
Sporophila cinnamomea
4" (10cm)
Cap gray. *Otherwise rufous chestnut.* Wings and tail blackish with white on inner flight feathers. Speculum white.

10. Black-bellied Seedeater **L-O**
Sporophila melanogaster
4" (10cm)
Like Chestnut-bellied Seedeater (190-5) but paler gray above and on sides and belly. *Throat and central underparts black* instead of chestnut.

11. Chestnut-throated Seedeater
L-SO
Sporophila telasco 4" (10cm)
Above gray, streaked blackish. White patch at base of black tail. Wings black, speculum white. *Upper throat chestnut. Below white.*

12. Large-billed Seed-Finch **L-TS**
Oryzoborus crassirostris 5" (13cm)
Differs from Great-billed Seed-Finch (182-1) only in size and bill somewhat less massive. Also tail is somewhat shorter.

1. Blue Seedeater **LM-FT**
Amaurospiza concolor
4¼" (11cm)
Uniform dark blue, slightly brighter on forehead and above eye. Lores and ear coverts black. ♀: Bright cinnamon brown, paler below.

2. Blackish-blue Seedeater **LM-FT**
Amaurospiza moesta 4¼" (11cm)
Dark slaty blue gray, blackish on lores and throat. Underparts blue speckled black. Wings and tail black. ♀: Above reddish brown. Wings and tail dusky. Below light brown.

3. Plain-colored Seedeater **H-SO**
Catamenia inornata 4½" (12cm)
Bill light reddish brown, light gray, back streaked black. Undertail coverts rufous. ♀: Above brownish buff streaked dusky, below bright yellowish buff, *unstreaked.*

4. Sulphur-throated Finch **L-SO**
Gnathospiza taczanowskii
4¼" (11cm)
Very heavy bill. Upperparts light grayish brown, streaked brown on back. Wings edged pale yellow. Around eye white. Eyebrow and throat yellow. Below white.

5. Stripe-tailed Yellow-Finch
LMH-O
Sicalis citrina 4" (10cm)
Above olive green, back indistinctly streaked dusky. *Forecrown and rump yellowish.* Below yellow, tinged olive on breast. White patch on underside of tail. ♀: Above brownish streaked dusky. Below dull yellow, streaked dusky on throat and breast, belly brighter yellow.

6. Puna Yellow-Finch **H-SO**
Sicalis lutea 5" (13cm)
Above bright olive yellow, rump yellow. Underparts and sides of head bright yellow. Wings and tail brownish, feathers edged yellowish. ♀: Sides of head grayish.

7. Bright-rumped Yellow-Finch
H-O
Sicalis uropygialis 5" (13cm)
Head, neck and rump bright olive yellow. Lores and cheeks pale gray. *Back slaty gray indistinctly streaked black.* Below bright yellow. Wings and tail black, edged gray. ♀: Crown streaked.

8. Citron-headed Yellow-Finch
H-O
Sicalis luteocephala 5½" (14cm)
Head bright olive yellow. Above grayish. Throat, breast and vent bright yellow, *sides gray.* Belly white. ♀: Browner.

9. Greater Yellow-Finch **MH-O**
Sicalis auriventris 6" (15cm)
Head, neck and rump bright olive yellow. Back greenish gray. Below bright yellow, sides pale gray. Wings and tail blackish, wing coverts edged gray.

10. Greenish Yellow-Finch **MH-O**
Sicalis olivascens 5" (13cm)
Crown and nape yellowish olive, back olive brown, *all streaked gray.* Rump and underparts olive yellow *(no gray on sides),* brightest on belly. Wings and tail blackish, feathers edged yellow.

11. Patagonian Yellow-Finch **LM-O**
Sicalis lebruni 5" (13cm)
Above yellowish olive broadly streaked grayish. Wings and tail dusky edged whitish. Below yellow, sides pale gray. Vent white.

12. Orange-fronted Yellow-Finch
L-O
Sicalis columbiana 4" (10cm)
Like Saffron Yellow-Finch (184-10) but *only forecrown reddish orange.* Upperparts darker yellowish olive. ♀: Like ♀ Saffron Yellow-Finch (184-11).

1. Raimondi's Yellow-Finch LM-OA
Sicalis raimondii   4¼" (11cm)
Like Grassland Yellow-Finch (184-
12) but lacks yellow eye-ring, is
grayer and less broadly streaked
on back. Crown and nape yellowish on front and sides.

2. White-winged Diuca-Finch H-O
Diuca speculifera   6½" (17cm)
Ashy gray. White spot below eye.
Conspicuous white wing patch.
Throat, belly, vent and outer tail
feathers white.

3. Common Diuca-Finch   LM-SO
Diuca diuca   6¼" (16cm)
Ashy gray. Wings and tail blackish, tail showing white on underside. *Throat and center of belly
white.*

4. Short-tailed Finch   H-O
Idiopsar brachyurus 6¼" (16cm)
Bill long, slender. Leaden gray,
paler below, whitish on lower
belly. Cheeks and below eye
speckled gray and white. Wings
and tail blackish. Tail rather short.

5. Patagonian Sierra-Finch   H-T
Phrygilus patagonicus 5½" (14cm)
Head, neck, throat, wings and tail
gray. *Back cinnamon rufous, rump
yellowish.* Below greenish yellow,
brightest on center of belly. ♀:
Back dark olive green.

**6. Gray-hooded Sierra-Finch
MH-O**
Phrygilus gayi   6" (15cm)
*Head, neck, throat, wings and tail
bluish gray.* Above yellowish green,
rump yellower. Below bright
greenish yellow.

**7. Black-hooded Sierra-Finch
H-SO**
Phrygilus atriceps   6" (15cm)
*Head, neck, throat, wings and tail
deep black. Back bright rufous
brown,* shading into yellow on
rump. Breast ochraceous, belly
yellow. ♀: Has gray hood with
blacker throat and cheeks. Breast
dull orange yellow, belly whitish.

8. Red-backed Sierra-Finch   H-O
Phrygilus dorsalis   6" (15cm)
Back reddish brown. Rest of plumage ashy gray except throat and
belly white.

**9. White-throated Sierra-Finch
H-O**
Phrygilus erythronotus 6" (15cm)
Gray. *Throat, belly* and *vent white.*
No white wing markings. Tail gray.

10. Ash-breasted Sierra-Finch H-SO
Phrygilus plebejus   5" (13cm)
Above grayish streaked black.
Rump gray. Below light gray, be-
coming *white on belly and vent.*
♀: Above browner. Throat and
breast streaked dusky.

11. Band-tailed Sierra-Finch   LH-S
Phrygilus alaudinus 5½" (14cm)
Quite like Band-tailed Seedeater
(184-7) but bill longer and conical, legs yellow and belly white.
Head, throat and breast gray.
Above brown streaked black. *Tail
black with conspicuous white
band.* ♀: Below whitish, streaked
dusky except on belly.

12. Carbonated Sierra-Finch LM-SO
Phrygilus carbonarius 5½" (14cm)
Bill and legs yellow. Above gray,
streaked black. Rump brown. Face
and most of underparts black, sides
gray. Tail black. ♀: Below whitish
narrowly streaked dusky on breast.

1. Black-throated Finch   LM-SO
Melanodera melanodera
5½" (14cm)
Above gray, eyebrow white. Lores black. *Throat black bordered all around by white.* Wing coverts bright yellow. Breast and belly yellowish, sides gray. ♀: Brown. Throat white.

2. Yellow-bridled Finch   LMH-SO
Melanodera xanthogramma
6" (15cm)
Above bluish gray. Eyebrow yellow. Lores and *throat black bordered all around by yellow.* Wing coverts bright yellow. Breast and belly olive yellow, sides gray. ♀: Grayish brown above streaked blackish. Whitish below streaked dusky on breast and sides.

3. Black-crested Finch   L-SO
Lophospingus pusillus 4½" (12cm)
Gray. Long crest, cheeks and *throat black. Broad eyebrow and broad whisker white.* Tail black, outer feathers broadly tipped white. ♀: Throat white.

4. Gray-crested Finch   M-S
Lophospingus griseocristatus
5" (13cm)
Gray, paler below. *Long crest black.* Center of belly white. Tail black, outer feathers broadly tipped white. ♀: Throat white.

5. Moustached Brush-Finch   M-F
Atlapetes albofrenatus 6¼" (16cm)
Above olive, crown and nape chestnut. Cheeks black. *Whisker white.* Below bright yellow, sides and vent olive.

6. Tricolored Brush-Finch   LM-FT
Atlapetes tricolor   6¼" (16cm)
Above dark olive. *Crown and nape bronzy yellow to olive yellow.* Sides of head black. Underparts yellow, olive on sides.

7. Fulvous-headed Brush-Finch
M-T
Atlapetes fulviceps   6" (15cm)
Top and sides of head and whisker rufous. Above and sides of body olive. Lores and underparts yellow.

8. Tepui Brush-Finch   M-F
Atlapetes personatus 6¼" (16cm)
Head and nape (also throat and breast in some races) *rufous.* Rest of underparts yellow, sides olive. Above dark gray to black.

9. Yellow-striped Brush-Finch
M-TS
Atlapetes citrinellus   6" (15cm)
Above brownish olive. *Conspicuous eyebrow and throat bright yellow.* Whisker and sides of face black. Breast yellow. Belly bright yellow.

10. Rufous-eared Brush-Finch MH-T
Atlapetes rufigenis   6½" (17cm)
Crown, nape and sides of head bright rufous. Above gray. *Lores, throat and sides of neck white.* Whisker black. Below white, tinged gray on breast. Sides brownish gray.

11. Bay-crowned Brush-Finch M-TS
Atlapetes seebohmi   6¼" (16cm)
Like Slaty Brush-Finch (178-8) but without white wing speculum or white lores. Race in Peru is smaller (15cm) and has brownish gray back, sides of neck white and ear coverts gray.

12. Rusty-bellied Brush-Finch MH-T
Atlapetes nationi   6¼" (16cm)
Crown and sides of head blackish. Eye-ring whitish. Back, wings and tail grayish brown. Throat white with short black whisker. Breast gray. *Belly cinnamon.*

1. White-headed Brush-Finch
LM-TS
Atlapetes albiceps   6" (15cm)
Forecrown, throat, sides of head and neck white. Hindcrown and nape dark brown. Above grayish brown. *Large white wing speculum.* Breast pale gray. Belly light brown.

2. Pale-headed Brush-Finch LM-SA
Atlapetes pallidiceps   6" (15cm)
Head whitish, stripe through eye pale brown. Above light brownish, *white wing speculum conspicuous.* *Below white,* sides gray.

3. Black-capped Sparrow   L-TSA
Arremon abeillei   5½" (14cm)
Bill black. *Top and sides of head black. Long eyebrow white.* Upperparts and sides gray. No yellow at bend of wing. Below white, narrow breast band black. ♀: Has brownish gray sides.

4. Tocuyo Sparrow   L-SA
Arremonops tocuyensis
                            4½" (12cm)
Very like Black-striped Sparrow (180-6) but somewhat paler overall.

5. Grasshopper Sparrow   LMH-O
Ammodramus savannarum
                            4" (10cm)
Above blackish brown streaked buffyish. *Crown black, center stripe buff.* Bend of wing yellow. Eyering and eyebrow buff. *Throat and breast buff.* Belly white.

6. Tumbes Sparrow   L-SA
Rhynchospiza stolzmanni
                            5½" (14cm)
Crown chestnut with broad gray center stripe and eyebrow. Above brown streaked dusky. *Whisker black.* Bend of wing yellow. *Shoulder chestnut.* Below whitish.

7. Stripe-capped Sparrow   L-O
Aimophila strigiceps   6" (15cm)
Crown brown with gray center stripe. Eyebrow gray. Above reddish brown streaked black. Lores and cheeks black. Whisker dusky. Below white tinged gray on breast.

8. Great Inca-Finch   M-SA
Incaspiza pulchra   6" (15cm)
Bill and legs yellow. Above reddish brown, wing coverts gray. *Eyebrow, sides of head and neck gray.* Lores, around eye and throat black. Breast gray. Belly buff. Tail black, *broadly edged white.*

9. Rufous-backed Inca-Finch
MH-SA
Incaspiza personata   6" (15cm)
Bill and legs yellow. Above reddish brown, *back bright chestnut.* Wing coverts gray. No eyebrow. Forehead, face and upper throat black. Sides of head and neck gray. Breast gray. Belly whitish. Tail black, outer feathers white.

10. Buff-bridled Inca-Finch MH-SA
Incaspiza laeta   5" (13cm)
Bill orange. Forehead and face black. Throat black with *white patch at sides.* Crown and nape gray, back chestnut, rump dark gray. Below gray, tinged buff on belly. Tail black, outer feathers white. Legs yellow.

11. Little Inca-Finch   L-SA
Incaspiza watkinsi   4½" (12cm)
Bill and legs yellow. Crown and nape grayish brown. Eyebrow and sides of head blue gray. Back reddish streaked black. Wing coverts gray. Chin and area around eye black. Throat white. Lower throat, sides of neck and breast gray. Belly white. *Tail black, outer feathers white.*

12. Black-masked Finch   L-O
Coryphaspiza melanotis 5" (13cm)
Crown and sides of head black, long eyebrow white. Back olive brown broadly streaked black. Shoulders olive. Below white.

1. Slender-billed Finch   **L-SO**
Xenospingus concolor   6" (15cm)
Uniform bluish gray. Slender bill
and legs yellow. Forehead and
lores black. Below pale bluish gray,
whitish on center of belly.

2 Bay-chested Warbling-Finch
                   LM-T
Poospiza thoracica   4½" (12cm)
Above gray, wing with conspicuous white speculum. Cheeks gray,
line below eye white. Below white.
Band across breast chestnut. Flanks
broadly chestnut.

3. Bolivian Warbling-Finch   **H-TS**
Poospiza boliviana   5½" (14cm)
Above pale reddish brown, wings
blackish. *Long, broad eyebrow
white.* Below white. Breast band,
sides and flanks cinnamon. Tail
black, broadly tipped white.

4. Plain-tailed Warbling-Finch H-S
Poospiza alticola   6" (15cm)
Above dark brown, wings blackish, edged whitish. Long broad
eyebrow white. *Narrow black
whisker.* Below whitish, sides of
breast orange rufous, becoming
pale cinnamon buff on sides of
belly. *Tail blackish with no white.*

5. Rufous-sided Warbling-Finch
                    H-S
Poospiza hypochondria 6" (15cm)
Above brownish, wings blackish.
Crown black, eyebrow white. *Spot
below eye white.* Throat buff, *narrow whisker black.* Breast band
pale gray. Below whitish with
chestnut flanks. Tail black, outer
feathers broadly tipped white.

6. Collared Warbling-Finch LM-SA
Poospiza hispaniolensis
                    4½" (12cm)
Above gray, wings black, coverts
edged buffy. *Crown and sides of
head black.* Long eyebrow white.
Below white, *breast band black,*
sides gray. Tail black, outer feathers partly white. ♀: Brown above
except for gray rump. Breast
streaked grayish.

7. Ringed Warbling-Finch   **LM-S**
Poospiza torquata   4¼" (11cm)
Above gray, wings black, speculum and edges of coverts pure
white. *Breast band all black* (no
gray on sides). Belly white. Vent
chestnut.

8. Black-capped Warbling-Finch
                    LM-S
Poospiza melanoleuca
                    4½" (12cm)
Head black. Back gray. Wings
black, feathers edged gray. Below
white. Tail black, outer feathers
broadly tipped white.

9. Cinereous Warbling-Finch   **L-S**
Poospiza cinerea   4½" (12cm)
Above gray. Wings blackish, feathers edged gray. *Area around eye
black.* Below white tinged yellowish on throat and breast. Tail black,
outer feathers white.

10. Rusty-browed Warbling-Finch
                    MH-T
Poospiza erythrophrys   5" (13cm)
*Head and neck mostly gray. Eye-
brow, spot below eye, throat and
breast deep rufous.* Back olive gray.
Wings blackish, feathers edged
white. Flanks buffy, center of belly
white. Tail blackish, outer feathers
tipped white.

11. Rufous-breasted Warbling-Finch
                    H-TS
Poospiza rubecula   6" (15cm)
Above gray, wings blackish edged
gray. Cheeks and chin black. *Forecrown, eyebrow and underparts
rufous.* Center of belly white. Tail
black. ♀: Lacks black on face,
eyebrow whitish. Below whitish
streaked dusky.

12. Cinnamon Warbling-Finch   **L-S**
Poospiza ornata   4½" (12cm)
Crown and rump dark gray. Back
dark brown. Wings dusky, single
bar white. Eyebrow cinnamon.
Spot below eye white. *Cheeks,
throat, breast and sides rich chestnut.* Belly rufous. Tail black, outer
feathers broadly tipped white.

1. Chestnut-breasted Mountain-Finch　H-S
Poospizopis caesar　6½" (17cm)
Above gray. Head black. Eyebrow and throat white. *Breast chestnut.* Belly white. Sides and flanks pale gray. Vent chestnut.

2. Tucuman Mountain-Finch　H-S
Compsospiza baeri　6½" (17cm)
Mostly gray. Forecrown, eyebrow, throat and streak below eye rufous. Undertail coverts rufous.

3. Cochabamba Mountain-Finch　H-TS
Compsospiza garleppi 6½" (17cm)
Above gray. Forehead, eyebrow, streak below eye and entire underparts rufous.

4. Many-colored Chaco-Finch　L-S
Saltatricula multicolor 6¼" (16cm)
Above light sandy brown, rump gray. Eyebrow white. *Forehead, lores, cheeks and sides of neck black. Throat white.* Breast pale gray. Below cinnamon, center of belly white. Tail blackish, outer feathers broadly tipped white.

5. Buff-throated Pampa-Finch　L-O
Embernagra longicauda 8" (20cm)
Rather like Great Pampa-Finch (180-1) but lores blackish and *eyebrow, spot below eye and throat buff.* Breast grayish, belly white in center.

6. Yellow-faced Siskin　L-SO
Carduelis (Spinus) yarrellii
　　　　　　　　　4" (10cm)
Like Andean Siskin (186-10) but face, throat, breast and rump much brighter yellow. ♀: Lacks black cap.

7. Red Siskin　L-SO
Carduelis (Spinus) cucullatus
　　　　　　　　　3½" (9cm)
Whole head and throat black. *Rest of body bright red except belly white.* Wings black with prominent wing patch red. Tail black. ♀: Above grayish brown. Sides of head and throat gray. Rump, wing patch and sides of breast salmon red. Otherwise white below.

8. Thick-billed Siskin　H-S
Carduelis (Spinus) crassirostris
　　　　　　　　　5" (13cm)
Like Hooded Siskin (186-8) but larger with *much heavier bill.* Band on sides of neck and nape bright yellow. *Center of belly white* (all yellow in 186-8). ♀: Like ♀ Hooded Siskin (186-9) but much heavier bill.

9. Yellow-bellied Siskin　MH-T
Carduelis (Spinus) xanthogaster
　　　　　　　　　4" (10cm)
All deep black except wings with yellow patch. Breast and belly yellow and base of tail yellow. ♀: Has grayish olive in place of black.

10. Black Siskin　H-SO
Carduelis (Spinus) atratus
　　　　　　　　　4¼" (11cm)
Black. Yellow patch on wing. Center of belly and undertail coverts yellow. Tail black with much yellow at base.

11. Yellow-rumped Siskin　H-SO
Carduelis (Spinus) uropygialis
　　　　　　　　　4" (10cm)
All deep black except wings with yellow patch. Breast, belly, base of tail and rump yellow.

12. Black-chinned Siskin　LM-TS
Carduelis (Spinus) barbatus
　　　　　　　　　4¼" (11cm)
Crown and center of throat black. Back olive yellow, lightly spotted black. Wings black with yellow patch. Rump and underparts bright yellow except center of belly white. ♀: Crown and back olive, streaked dusky. Eyebrow and underparts pale greenish yellow.

Methods and Equipment

Close-up photography of any moving object such as a bird involves two basic problems — getting enough light and sharp focus. Under tropical forest conditions it is extremely difficult, in many cases almost impossible, to solve these problems by the normal method: setting up camera and lights at some spot to which the bird will come. Many tropical forest birds spend most of their time in the treetops, up to 100 or more feet above the ground. At lower levels of the forest, reliable sunlight ("available light") is almost nonexistent. So we solve these problems by creating our own light with electronic stroboscopic flash and bringing the bird to the lights and camera, all set up in advance in an enclosure.

The bird is captured in a mist net, some 40 feet long and 10 feet high, constructed of very fine black nylon thread, which is practically invisible. After being carefully released, the bird is put in a cloth bag which gives sufficient air, yet is dark enough to keep the bird fairly quiet.

The next task is to mount the proper perch and fresh foliage in the enclosure. We try to use foliage similar to that which we have observed the birds using in the wild. If the subject's natural food is known and available, it helps to put some in the enclosure.

If quiet is maintained after the bird is put in the enclosure, it usually soon calms down and rests on the perch, if it is a properly chosen one. Often within half an hour the photography has been completed and the bird is released unharmed in its own home area.

In the accompanying sketch, the enclosure is made of fairly heavy unbleached white muslin. This provides enough light inside for focusing but keeps the birds from seeing through it. Four collapsible poles (P) along each side, with two cross braces (CB) across the middle ones, hold the enclosure up, and it becomes quite firm and rigid when the four corners are tied to convenient trees or to stakes. There is a skirt, about 12 inches wide all around, to accommodate unevenness in the ground. It is weighted down with sticks or stones to prevent the bird's escape under the enclosure.

The eight poles are constructed of 7/16-inch (outside diameter) aluminum tubing, into which a 9/32-inch round aluminum bar slides. These poles, when collapsed to their shortest length, will just fit into a 26-inch suitcase for traveling. A thumbscrew (1/4-inch × 20 thread) on the tubing can be tightened to hold the inner rod at any position, thus making the poles the right length to suit ground conditions. This is made by putting a 1/4-inch × 20 aluminum nut on the thumbscrew and peening the end threads of the thumbscrew with a hammer, so that the nut cannot come off. A 9/32-inch hole is then drilled in the tubing approximately 3/4-inch from one end. The end of the thumbscrew is inserted in this hole and the aluminum nut on the thumbscrew is welded to the tubing. The bottom end of the tubing is welded tight to keep water and dirt from getting in.

SKETCH OF ENCLOSURE
(not to scale)

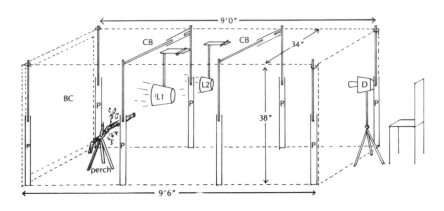

CROSS BRACE
2 needed

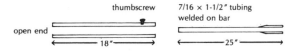

thumbscrew   7/16 × 1-1/2″ tubing
welded on bar

open end

18″   25″

POST
8 needed

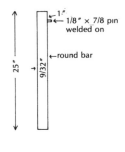

1.″
1/8″ × 7/8 pin
welded on

←round bar

25″

9/32″

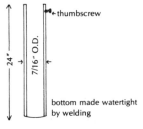

←thumbscrew

24″

7/16″ O.D.

bottom made watertight
by welding

BACKGROUND FRAME SIDE
4 needed

←round bar

24-1/2″

9/32″

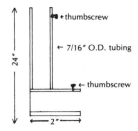

←thumbscrew

24″

← 7/16″ O.D. tubing

←thumbscrew

2″

The two cross braces are constructed of 7/16-inch aluminum tubing into which a 9/32-inch aluminum bar slides. A thumbscrew is welded to the tubing 3/4 inch from one end. The other end of the tubing is left open. A short piece of 7/16-inch aluminum tubing is welded on one end of the 9/32-inch aluminum bar. The two ends of the cross brace are slipped over the 1/8-inch pins on the poles. The cross brace is then extended until the top of the enclosure is firm and the thumbscrew is tightened.

Eight loops — one at each corner of the enclosure and two on two opposite sides — slip over the tops of the eight poles to hold the enclosure up. To prevent each loop from slipping down the pole, a 1/8-inch pin is welded on the top section of the pole about 1 inch from the end.

There is a zippered opening at one end of the enclosure through which only the lens of the camera (D) is inserted, so that all operating parts of the camera are outside the enclosure. The camera is always mounted on a tripod. There are also zippers (not shown in the sketch) in the sides, for putting in the perches and background foliage, and in the top, for inserting the lights and the background cloth.

The strobe main light (L_1) and the fill light (L_2) are suspended from the canvas top of the enclosure through zippered openings. Flashbulbs could be used, but I have found strobes more useful. The light aluminum bars holding the lights are slipped through safety pins in the top of the enclosure to keep them positioned. The two lights must be kept far enough to the sides to avoid throwing a shadow on the background cloth, but within this limitation, the angle and distance of the lights can be varied to produce a variety of pleasing results.

The background cloth (BC) is stretched over a background frame formed of the same sizes of aluminum as the poles (see sketch). The four sides of the background frame fit together to make a rectangle over which the background cloth is stretched. The corners of the background cloth are sewn to form a pocket into which the frame fits. Then the background frame is expanded to make the background cloth tight,

Author shown here using enclosure to photograph birds in the tropics. The canopy is used to keep off sun and rain.

and the four thumbscrews are tightened to hold it there. The background cloth on the background frame is inserted inside the enclosure through a wide zipper (not shown in sketch) on the top of the enclosure at the back. It helps keep the cloth clean if it is tilted inward at the top about 6 inches. To allow for this, the enclosure is made 6 inches longer at the bottom than at the top.

The background cloths have been the subject of much experimenting. In general we think a light blue color gives pleasing results, but individual preference may govern that. Many of the newer synthetic fabrics look one color in daylight but photograph a different color. The background cloth is dampened thoroughly before being put on the frame to remove all wrinkles which would show in the picture. Of course spare cloths are needed, as they get soiled quickly.

Mounting the perch and background foliage inside the enclosure has to be worked out for each setup. Sometimes the perch is stuck into the ground, sometimes it is suspended from the top of the enclosure. I have found a low tripod with a Kodapod clamp invaluable. It is important to have the perch far enough away from the background cloth so that shadows do not show on the cloth.

Selecting the proper perch for the bird is a matter which often requires much trial and error. I have frequently had a bird refuse to land on a perch, then after I have changed the perch, pose almost immediately.

After the film has been exposed, I find it important to store it in a plastic bag with one or two containers of silica gel to keep it dry. Most film manufacturers advise development soon after exposure, but I have had no trouble keeping film up to six or eight weeks after exposure, provided it is kept dry and not overheated.

I have presented the details of my technique here solely as a guide. I am sure many variations could be used which would serve equally well — perhaps better. I hope many of my readers will work out their own methods. I will be glad to help anyone in any way I can.

Photographic Locations

Abbreviations: Amaz. = Amazonas; Ant. = Antioquia; Arg. = Argentina; Bol. = Bolivar; Boy. = Boyaca; Caq. = Caqueta; Col. = Columbia; Cund. = Cundinamarca; DF = District Federal; ES = Espirito Santo; Mag. = Magdalena; MG = Mato Grosso; Par. = Paraguay; Putu. = Putumayo; RGS = Rio Grande do Sul; Sant. = Santander; Valle = Valle de Cauca; Venez. = Venezuela.

Bibliography

The following books will be found useful by students of South American birds.

Beebe, C. William, *An Ornithological Reconnaissance of Northern Venezuela.*
Blake, Emmet R., *Manual of Neotropical Birds.*
Bond, James, *Birds of the West Indies.*
Brown, Leslie, and Dean Amadon, *Eagles, Hawks and Falcons of the World.*
Clements, James F., *Birds of the World: A Check List.*
Davis, L. Irby, *A Field Guide to the Birds of Mexico and Central America.*
Delacour, Jean and Dean Amadon, *Curassows and Related Birds.*
Edwards, Ernest Preston, *A Coded List of Birds of the World.*
Eisenmann, Eugene, *The Species of Middle American Birds.*
Eisenmann, Eugene and Horace Loftin, *Field Checklist of Birds of Panama Canal Zone Area.*
Fisher, James and Roger Tory Peterson, *The World of Birds.*
ffrench, Richard P., *A Guide to the Birds of Trinidad and Tobago.*
Haffer, Jurgen, *Avian Speciation in Tropical South America.*
Haverschmidt, F., *Birds of Surinam.*
Johnson, A. W., *The Birds of Chile and Adjacent Regions.*
Meyer de Schauensee, Rodolphe, *The Birds of South America.*
_____, *The Birds of Colombia.*
_____, *The Species of Birds of South America.*
_____, and William H. Phelps, Jr., *A Guide to the Birds of Venezuela.*
Olrog, Claes C., *Las Aves Sudamericanus.*
Peterson, Roger Tory and Edward L. Chalif, *A Field Guide to Mexican Birds.*
Pettingill, Olin Sewall, *Ornithology in Laboratory and Field.*
Phelps, William H. and William H. Phelps, Jr., *Lista de las Aves de Venezuela y su Distribucion, Passeriformes.*
Ridgely, Robert S., *A Guide to the Birds of Panama.*
Robbins, Chandler S., Bertel Bruun, and Herbert S. Zim, *Birds of North America: A Guide to Field Identification.*
Short, Lester L., *A Zoogeographic Analysis of the South American Chaco Avifauna, Bull AMNH* 154(3):163–352, 1975.
Skutch, Alexander, *Studies of Tropical American Birds.*
Snyder, Dorothy E., *The Birds of Guyana.*
Thompson, A. Landsborough, *A New Dictionary of Birds.*
Wetmore, Alexander, *A Classification of Birds of the World.*
_____, *The Birds of the Republic of Panama.*

Index

Southern South America